16 $\frac{50}{}$

Feudal Society in the
Bailliage of Troyes

Feudal Society in the Bailliage of Troyes under the Counts of Champagne, 1152-1284

THEODORE
EVERGATES

THE JOHNS HOPKINS
UNIVERSITY PRESS
Baltimore and London

This book has been brought to publication with the generous assistance of the Andrew W. Mellon Foundation.

The Johns Hopkins University Press, Baltimore, Maryland 21218
The Johns Hopkins University Press Ltd., London

Library of Congress Catalog Card Number 75-11346
ISBN 0-8018-1663-7

Library of Congress Cataloging in Publication data will be found on the last printed page of this book.

To the memory of
THEODORE JOHN EVERGATES
philosopher, raconteur, humanist

CONTENTS

ILLUSTRATIONS

TABLES

ACKNOWLEDGEMENTS

For their comments at various stages of this project, I am indebted to Professors John W. Baldwin, John F. Benton, Richard Goldthwaite, and George T. Beech; the latter especially challenged me to express my thoughts more explicitly in several important areas. I also wish to thank M. Gildas Bernard, former director of the Departmental Archives of Aube, and his staff for their hospitality and assistance during my stay in Troyes; MM. Jacques Le Goff and Pierre Toubert, whose seminars in medieval social history were an impellent to my own research; Mr. Solis James, director of The Johns Hopkins University Computing Center, for guiding me into the intricacies of computer operations; and my wife for her critical reading of the early drafts of this work.

LIST OF ABBREVIATIONS

The following abbreviations are observed in the Appendix and the Notes in order to simplify the documentation. Cartularies and charter collections have been assigned letter abbreviations; other sources and secondary works appear with their short titles. The form is as follows:

For charters and cartulary materials: first the date of the document (in parentheses when it is only approximate); then the abbreviation; and finally (a) in a printed edition, the number of the document assigned by the editor, or, in lieu of that, the page number; (b) in a manuscript, the folio number, recto and verso. For example, 1218,StP,142 represents a charter dated 1218 of Saint-Pierre of Troyes, printed as number 142 in Lalore's edition.

For the Champagne surveys: the survey title, followed by the castellany register and the number of the item in the printed edition. Thus, *Rôles*,Nogent,681 represents an entry in the *Rôles des fiefs,* castellany of Nogent, numbered 681 by the editor.

Full bibliographical references are in the bibliography.

Arch.Aube	Archives du département de l'Aube: individual documents in series G (secular clergy) and H (regular clergy).
B	*Chartes de la Commanderie de Beauvoir de l'Ordre Teutonique,* in Lalore, *Collection des principaux cartulaires,* vol. III.
BF	*Cartulaire de l'abbaye de Basse-Fontaine,* in Lalore, *Collection des principaux cartulaires,* vol. III.
CB	Cartulaire de Blanche, Bibliothèque Nationale.
Ch	Lalore, *Les sires et les barons de Chacenay.*
Coutumier	Portejoie, *L'ancien coutumier de Champagne* (XIIIe siècle).
CP	*Cartulaire de l'abbaye de Chapelle-aux-Planches,* in Lalore, *Collection des principaux cartulaires,* vol. IV.
Documents I, II	Longnon, *Documents relatifs au comté de Champagne et de Brie (1172–1361).* I. *Les fiefs;* II. *Le domaine comtal.*
Etat des bois	"Etat des bois situés aux environs de Troyes," in Longnon, *Documents* II.
Extenta	"Extenta Terre," in Longnon, *Documents* I.
Feoda	*Feoda Campanie.* The original registers of 1172 (*Feoda* or *Feoda* I) were supplemented by *Feoda* II (ca. 1200), III (1200/1201), IV (1204/10), V (1210/14), VI (1222-34), and VII (after 1234). All are printed in Longnon, *Documents* I.
H	Arbois de Jubainville, "Etudes sur les documents antérieur à l'année 1285."

HD	Cartulaire de l'Hôtel-Dieu-le-Comte, Archives de l'Aube.
Histoire	Arbois de Jubainville, *Histoire des ducs et des comtes de Champagne.* Page numbers refer to the text of a charter printed here; catalogue numbers are given for all other citations.
Hommages	"Livre des hommages faits à Thibaut V," in Longnon, *Documents.* I.
L	Harmand, "Notice historique sur la Léproserie de la ville de Troyes."
Lalore	Lalore, *Collection des principaux cartulaires du diocèse de Troyes.*
LP	Liber pontificum, Bibliothèque Nationale.
M	*Cartulaire de Montiéramey,* in Lalore, *Collection des principaux cartulaires,* vol. VII.
MD	*Chartes de Montier-en-Der,* in Lalore, *Collection des principaux cartulaires,* vol. IV.
MLC	*Cartulaire de Montier-la-Celle,* in Lalore, *Collection des principaux cartulaires,* vol. VI.
Mol	Socard, "Chartes inédites extraites des cartulaires de Molême."
Mol-I, Mol-II	Laurent, *Cartulaires de l'abbaye de Molesme.* The numerals I and II refer to the cartularies in vol. II.
Mor	Lalore, "Chartes de l'abbaye de Mores."
N	Lalore, "Documents sur l'abbaye de Notre-Dame-aux-Nonnains de Troyes."
O	Cartulaire d'Oyes (Saint-Gond), Archives de l'Aube.
P	*Cartulaire de l'abbaye de Paraclet,* in Lalore, *Collection des principaux cartulaires,* vol. II.
R	Cartulaire de Larrivour (Ripatorio), Bibliothèque Nationale.
Rôles	Longnon, *Rôles des fiefs du comté de Champagne sous le règne de Thibaut le Chansonnier.*
Rôles B	"Rôles des fiefs rédigés sous la régence de Blanche d'Artois," in Longnon, *Documents I.*
Roserot	Roserot, *Dictionnaire historique de la Champagne méridionale.*
S	Cartulaire de Sellières, Bibliothèque de Troyes.
StL	*Cartulaire de l'abbaye de Saint-Loup de Troyes,* in Lalore, *Collection des principaux cartulaires,* vol. I.
StP	*Cartulaire de Saint-Pierre de Troyes,* in Lalore, *Collection des principaux cartulaires,* vol. V.
StS	Cartulaire de Saint-Etienne de Troyes, Bibliothèque Nationale.
StU	*Chartes de la collégiale de Saint-Urbain de Troyes,* in Lalore, *Collection des principaux cartulaires,* vol. V.
Th	Cartulaire de Thou, Bibliothèque Nationale.
V	Cartulaire de Vauluisant, Bibliothèque Nationale.

Feudal Society in the
Bailliage of Troyes

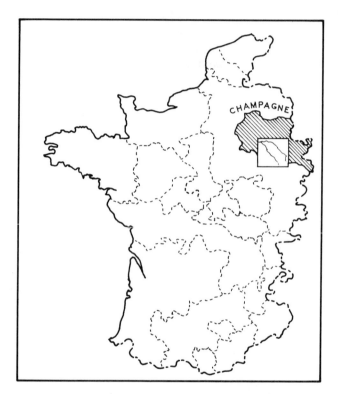

France in 1284

I
Introduction

The county of Champagne has long been considered one of the most feudalized regions in medieval France, yet there have been surprisingly few modern studies of its society in the twelfth and thirteenth centuries. The purpose of this monograph is to present a profile of that society in the area immediately surrounding the county's capital and principal town of Troyes. The *bailliage* of Troyes encompassed a fairly well-defined geographical area with a radius of thirty to fifty kilometers around Troyes and constituted about one fifth of Champagne during the century and a quarter of the county's independent political existence (1152-1284). The focus of this study is on the two essential components of feudal society, the peasantry and the aristocracy, and particularly on several aspects of social organization, such as status, community, and lineage. How was status defined? Did peasant obligations constitute "serfdom," and were they universal or were some men free? What was the significance of community franchises, and what impact did they have on social development? Did lords and knights compose a single aristocracy or two distinct social groupings? And what were the overall characteristics of fief holders and their fiefs? Answers to these and to more technical questions are of special interest here because royal influence on social institutions was minimal or nonexistent in Champagne until 1284, by which time those institutions had already crystallized into what we commonly describe as feudal society.

MEDIEVAL CHAMPAGNE AND THE
BAILLIAGE OF TROYES

The history of Champagne in the twelfth and thirteenth centuries can be seen as a process of creation, temporary dislocation, recovery, and final decline. In the twelfth century disparate local counties and lordships held by independent old families were forged into a single territorial state by their incorporation either directly into the Champagne domain or indirectly by ties of personal loyalty. The assimilation, however, was uneven and some of the personal bonds fragile, and the new principality experienced a time of troubles in the first three decades of the thirteenth century. After certain adjustments the county recovered rapidly and was restored to relative peace and prosperity until its last heiress married the king of France in 1284 and brought Champagne into the larger, royal political framework. Incorporation into the kingdom marked the symbolic end of the county and also precipitated its overall decline, as its special interests were thereafter subordinated to royal ones.

The history of independent Champagne is necessarily a reflection of the activities of its counts.[1] At the beginning of the twelfth century the counts of Blois held in addition to their hereditary lands around Blois several holdings in the eastern part of the kingdom, including the counties of Meaux and Troyes. Etienne-Henri (d.1102) ruled the family lands in Blois, while his younger brother Hugh (1097–1125) held the county of Troyes from him.* Hugh inherited the adjacent counties of Bar-sur-Aube and Vitry from his mother, but this relatively compact group of lands in no way rivaled the holdings centered around Blois. In all probability the county of Troyes and its appendages would have remained a minor territorial unit in the twelfth century if Hugh had not transferred them back to the main line in 1125, to his nephew Thibaut II (Thibaut IV of Blois, 1102-52). For the next twenty-seven years Thibaut held both the western and eastern blocks of lands. Although lack of documents precludes an accurate evaluation of his efforts, he seems to have been responsible for the development of the area around Troyes, hitherto ignored by the house of Blois. Significant development becomes apparent under his son Henry I the Liberal (1152-81), who took the eastern lands as his own and relegated the western lands of Blois, Chartres, Sancerre, and Châteaudun to his younger brothers. Henceforth, Troyes and Provins were the foci of a new territorial state, the county of Champagne, created by Henry from a large agglomeration of lands directly bordering on the royal domain.

The increase in documents in the second half of the twelfth century permits a fairly accurate assessment of Henry I. His administration resulted in conditions so peaceful and orderly that they were justly noted by contemporaries. The Champagne fairs were organized as an international institution during his reign and remained the commercial exchange center of western Europe for the next century. The two thousand barons and knights who owed him military aid made him one of the most powerful princes of his day, and his court in Troyes gained wide repute as a center of literary activity. His role in international

---

*The spelling of names is not consistent: English forms are given for well-known personages, such as Count Henry I and Philip II, king of France, whereas the French form is given for lesser persons, such as Henri of Ferreux. Both Christian names and surnames are cross-referenced in the index.

political affairs and his marriage to a gifted daughter of the king of France added to his renown. His achievements, unfortunately, were undermined by his son Henry II (1181-97), who scarcely ruled the county at all—he was a minor from 1181 to 1187 and away in the East from 1190 to 1197—and who bequeathed his successors two excruciating problems. The huge debt which he had incurred for his expedition to the East and for expenses as husband of the queen of Jerusalem had to be liquidated in the decade after his death, and, more serious for Champagne, the claim by the two daughters of his Eastern marriage to Champagne as their inheritance burdened the county with a constitutional crisis for an entire generation.

On departing for Jerusalem in 1190, Henry II had the Champagne barons swear to accept his younger brother Thibaut as count, should he himself fail to return. In 1197 King Philip II confirmed Thibaut's succession, although he was only eighteen years of age, and received his homage for lands held from the crown. Thibaut III (1197-1201) spent most of his brief reign preparing for the Fourth Crusade, of which he was a leader. His untimely death precipitated a succession crisis, which brought the county to the brink of disintegration. Countess Blanche of Navarre, widowed after two years of marriage and before the birth of her son, ruled the county under royal protection for the next twenty-one years (1201—22). The prospect of such a long regency by a foreigner was divisive in itself, but the Champenois also lost the leadership of a vigorous and widely esteemed count (there were only seven years of male rule in the forty-one years from the death of Henry I in 1181 to the accession of Thibaut IV in 1222). The difficulties were compounded when the very legitimacy of Blanche and her son was challenged by Philippe, Henry's daughter by the queen of Jerusalem, and her husband, Erard of Brienne (Ramerupt branch), younger son of one of the most powerful Champagne families. The Champagne barons had sworn to support Henry II's brother Thibaut III, but the issue of whether Thibaut's son or Henry's daughter had the better subsequent claim to the county was a new problem without theoretical solution. The barons split into two camps, and in 1215, after a decade of political maneuvering, open warfare erupted. In spite of temporary truces, an accord was not reached until Thibaut IV came of age in 1222 and the claim of Brienne's wife was bought off with 5,000 l. cash and an annual 1,200 l. rent.

Thibaut IV le Chansonnier (1222-52) further aggravated Champagne's problems after his succession by his erratic behavior. His sudden departure from the siege of Avignon in 1226 alienated the royal party, whose support had been vital for his own succession, and his subsequent flirtations with the regent Queen Blanche of Castile caused the great French barons to ally against him, adding new external complications to the old, internal ones. The nadir of these affairs was reached in 1229, when a league of French barons invaded his lands. The resulting destruction, following so soon upon that caused by the Brienne faction a decade earlier, reduced the county to chaos and financial exhaustion. The shock of 1229 forced Thibaut to reassert his leadership within Champagne, and especially over the towns which had provided his main defense and chief source of income: in 1230 and 1231 he issued communal franchises of considerable administrative autonomy to his most populous and important towns. Then in 1234 he sold his over-lordship of the counties of Blois, Sancerre, and Châteaudun to the king for a sum of 40,000 l., which he required to settle the claim of Henry II's remaining daughter, Alix. That marked the end of his misfortunes, for in the same year he succeeded his maternal grandfather as king of Navarre. The acquisition of Navarre seems to have been not only a financial windfall but also a welcome distraction from Champagne affairs, and Thibaut and his successors Thibaut V (1253–69) and Henry III (1270–74) spent considerable time in Spain. The frenetic decades of expeditions to the East ended in 1204, and after the settlement of internal and external threats by 1234, Champagne once again enjoyed a calm reminiscent of the days of Henry I. When Philip IV married the sole heiress Jeanne (1274–84), the county was peaceful, well-organized and well-governed, and prosperous.

Although southern Champagne shared the general social and eco-nomic experience of the rest of the county, there were of course unique aspects in the development of the *bailliage* of Troyes. Troyes had been the center of a county in the ninth century, although little is known about it beyond an approximate genealogy of its counts.[2] The count of Troyes probably became a vassal of the duke of Burgundy in 895/96 when the latter conquered Troyes and several neighboring areas; but when the duke failed to do homage to the king in 936, he lost the counties of Troyes, Langres, Sens, and Auxerre, that is, his entire northern holdings. It was about that time that Troyes and Meaux passed to the house of Vermandois, which held them until 1019, when the house of Blois received them.[3] Troyes was of secondary interest to the Blois line, and information about it for the eleventh century is as scarce as for the previous centuries. It is tempting to conclude from the absence of documents in the eleventh century and from the penetration by the Cistercians in the twelfth that there was little activity in the area. Only in the early twelfth century under Hugh I does the county of Troyes emerge partly from obscurity. As the third son of the count of Blois, Hugh took Troyes after the death of an older brother and held it from the eldest, Etienne-Henri. Little can be said about the internal organization of the county at that time, and there is only meager information on the relationships between Hugh and the great local lords, including several counts. It has been assumed that the principal witnesses to his charters were also his closest vassals, but merely to label a formal relationship is not to describe the actual state of affairs; most lords of the immediate vicinity were probably as independent of Hugh as he was of the Blois line from which he held the county. In 1125 Hugh left for the Holy Land and transferred the county of Troyes to his nephew Thibaut II (Thibaut IV of Blois). In spite of the family's roots in the western lands, Thibaut seems to have taken an interest in the eastern area—Bernard of Clairvaux in several instances addressed him on strictly local problems—and under Thibaut it is possible for the first time to form an idea of what the county of Troyes was composed. A charter of 1143 records that Thibaut did homage to the duke of Burgundy for the county of Troyes and certain other specified lands, and a second, undated but contemporary, charter further names all the lands which he held from the duke. A comparison of the two documents permits the deduction that the county of Troyes consisted of Troyes, Isle-Aumont, Villemaur, Chappes, Plancy, Arcis-sur-Aube, and Ramerupt, the last four being held from the count in fief (see map 1).[4] Thus, the mid-twelfth-century county of Troyes was rather small, and even then only Troyes, Isle, and Villemaur were held directly in the hand of the count of Blois.

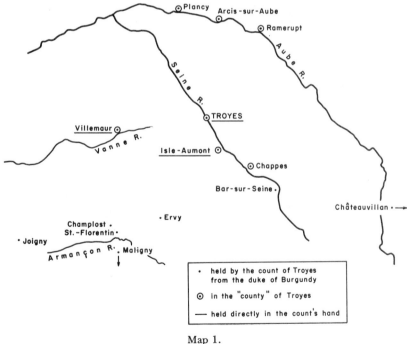

Map 1.
The County of Troyes, 1143

In 1143 the county of Troyes was just one of several counties and
other lands that had been variously amassed by the house of Blois on
either side of the royal domain, and the Blois-centered lands were still
considered the main family properties. When Count Henry I reversed
the policy by giving the western lands to his younger brothers in fief
and making Troyes and the eastern lands his own base, he adopted the
title "count of Troyes" exclusively. Within twenty years of his accession in 1152 he had created a powerful new principality composed of
twenty-six castellanies adjacent to the royal domain. Although Henry
remained "count of Troyes" and did homage for that county to the
duke of Burgundy, the county of Troyes in fact represented only a
small part of his lands and formed only three (Troyes, Isle-Aumont, and
Villemaur) of the twenty-six castellanies of his fief holders (see map 5).
In effect, the county of Troyes had ceased to exist as a separate entity
within the new and larger county of Champagne.

Castellanies remained the basic administrative units in Champagne
throughout the twelfth and thirteenth centuries. Although *baillis* appeared in the early thirteenth century, there is no information on their
functions or on the existence of *bailli*-administered districts, and the
full-scale *Rôles des fiefs* of 1252 were still organized solely by castellany. The existence of *bailliages* as distinct administrative territories
composed of several castellanies is first revealed in the *Livre des hommages* of 1265, in which the Champagne castellanies were grouped into
five *bailliages*.[5] The *bailliage* of Troyes contained ten castellanies and
covered approximately the same area as the present-day *département* of
Aube.[6] The *bailliage* was a stable administrative unit in the last years
of the county and was retained by royal officials after Champagne was
attached to the crown. Of the ten castellanies in the *bailliage* of Troyes
in 1265, eight had been in the Champagne domain since the mid-
twelfth century and formed the nucleus of the thirteenth-century
bailliage (see map 2). Troyes, Isle-Aumont, and Villemaur were from
the old county of Troyes and were held directly by the count. Five
other castellanies (Saint-Florentin, Ervy, Payns, Méry-sur-Seine, Pont-
sur-Seine) were either independent private lordships or fiefs that the
count had incorporated directly into his domain by the mid-twelfth
century. Two other private lordships (Nogent-sur-Seine and Bar-sur-
Seine) were absorbed in the early thirteenth century when their lines
failed to produce male heirs (see below, chapter V). All ten castellany
centers were on or near rivers, seven on the Seine itself. The *bailliage* of
Troyes as it appears in the thirteenth-century inventories provides a
convenient geographical framework in which specific families and communities can be examined for a study of local social conditions.
Furthermore, as an adminstrative district by which county officials
organized and recorded information about fief holders and domain

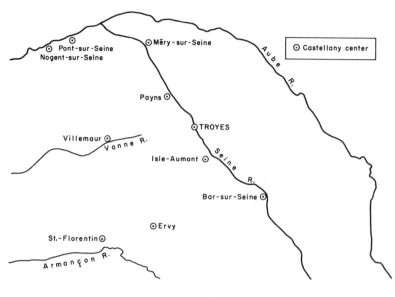

Map 2.
The *Bailliage* of Troyes, 1265

conditions, the *bailliage* also provides the structure for generalizing that quantifiable data on a level above the individual and unique castellanies.

SOURCES AND METHODS

The nature and quantity of the primary sources in the *bailliage* have of course determined the organization and scope of this enquiry. As in most studies of medieval society and economy, the ecclesiastical charters by their sheer volume provide the bulk of information on specific persons, properties, and conditions. The charters assume even greater importance here in the absence of local chronicles and narrative sources.[7] The number of extant charters, however, varies considerably by period. Before 1100 there are perhaps one hundred recorded transactions for the entire area, and these are for disparate localities, so that it is impossible to know any situation in depth or continuity. The best information before the twelfth century comes from the charters of Montier-en-Der and Molesme (late eleventh century), both on the periphery of the later *bailliage*.[8] The sudden increase in recorded acts in the twelfth century was due in part to the arrival of the monastic reformers, and especially the Cistercians: the half-century between the foundings of Clairvaux (1115) and Sellières (1168) was marked by a

Table 1
THE IMPLANTATION OF ECCLESIASTICAL
HOUSES IN THE *BAILLIAGE* OF TROYES

House	Year	Order
6th–9th centuries		
Nesle-la-Reposte	6th c.	Benedictine
St.-Loup	ca. 600	Benedictine
Montier-la-Celle	ca. 650	Benedictine
N-D-aux-Nonnains	ca. 650	Benedictine
Montier-en-Der	673	Benedictine
St-Pierre	ca. 750	(chapter)
Montiéramey	837	Benedictine
12th century		
Molesme	1075	Benedictine
St-Martin-ès-Aires	1104	Augustinian
Beaulieu	1112	Premonstratensian
Clairvaux	1115	Cistercian
Paraclet	1129	Benedictine
Vauluisant	1129	Cistercian
Larrivour	1139	Cistercian
Bassefontaine	1143	Premonstratensian
Chapelle-aux-Planches	1145	Premonstratensian
Boulancourt	1152	Cistercian
Mores	1153	Cistercian
Hôtel-Dieu-le-Comte	1157	Augustinian
St.-Etienne	1157	(chapter)
Sellières	1168	Cistercian
13th century		
Beauvois	1219	Teutonic
N-D-des-Prés	1231	Cistercian
Dominicans	1232	
Franciscans	1233	
Trinitarians	1213/60	
St.-Urbain	1262	(chapter)

Note: Only main houses are indicated.

phenomenal proliferation of these houses in the *bailliage*, the numerous granges of which dotted the entire region (see table 1 and map 3).[9] The reason for this implantation was not only the proximity to Molesme and Cîteaux but also the physical and social environment, which suited the reform ideal of the early twelfth century. We can envision the region as the reformers first saw it: a quiet, forested area, virtually devoid of men and their institutions.[10] That the implantation effectively ceased by the 1170s reflects the changing character of the region from one of relative wilderness and sparse settlement to one of increasingly populous villages and towns, a development to which the reformed houses themselves contributed.[11] In spite of initial difficulties, most of the new houses survived, and from the mid-twelfth century they, along with the older Benedictine houses, maintained careful records of their economic activities. Substantial collections of charters and cartularies

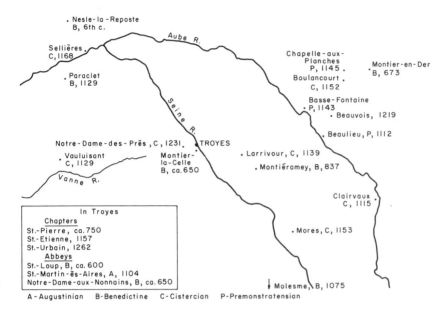

. Nesle- la -Reposte
B, 6th c.

Aube R.

Sellières,
C, 1168

. Paraclet
B, 1129

Seine R.

Notre-Dame-des-Prés ,C , 1231.

TROYES

. Vauluisant
C, 1129

Montier-
la-Celle
B, ca.650

Vanne R.

Chapelle-aux-
Planches
P, 1145 .
Boulancourt .
C, 1152

Montier-en-Der
. B, 673

Basse-Fontaine
. P, 1143
. Beauvois, 1219

. Beaulieu, P, 1112

. Larrivour, C, 1139

. Montiéramey, B, 837

Clairvaux .
C, 1115

. Mores, C, 1153

In Troyes
Chapters
St.-Pierre , ca.750
St.-Etienne, 1157
St.-Urbain, 1262
Abbeys
St.-Loup, B, ca. 600
St.-Martin-ès-Aires, A, 1104
Notre-Dame-aux-Nonnains, B, ca.650

Molesme, B, 1075

A - Augustinian   B - Benedictine   C - Cistercian   P - Premonstratensian

Map 3.
Ecclesiastical Houses in the *Bailliage* of Troyes

exist for ten abbeys in the countryside and for three chapters in Troyes itself. There are also many smaller collections for other houses, priories, and the mendicant and military orders. Altogether there are approximately six thousand extant acts, of which half have been printed, for the *bailliage* area in the twelfth and thirteenth centuries.[12]

Most valuable for the study of feudal society, but rarely available, are secular records. There are charters of course that are secular in the sense that they were issued by and for laymen alone, but very few have survived because the recipients did not possess archives. The count's scribes compiled a few cartularies in the early thirteenth century, but those were exceptional and did not represent a systematic preservation of official acts; such important acts as the grants of communes (1230–31), which created municipal autonomy and financial exemptions in the most populous Champagne towns and which had unique ramifications in social as well as urban development, were preserved only in later administrative records (see below, the *Extenta*).[13] Even a town as large and important as Troyes did not maintain records of municipal transactions until the fourteenth century.[14] The count's officials did, however, create a truly extraordinary set of secular records for Champagne: they are the administrative surveys of county domain and fief holders. They begin with the *Feoda Campanie,* a list of the names and military obligations of all fief holders of the count, drawn up originally ca. 1172 under Count Henry I and revised until ca. 1190.[15] As an inventory in which every fief holder was assigned to a castellany, occasionally arbitrarily, the *Feoda* was a powerful administrative tool for the count, and its significance was duly appreciated at the time. The document itself was kept in the count's treasury by the chapter of Saint-Etienne of Troyes, founded by Henry I in 1157 and subsequently richly endowed for its administrative service to him.[16] When Count Henry II departed for Jerusalem in 1190, he took a copy of the *Feoda* with him. In the early years of the thirteenth century, when the regent Countess Blanche of Navarre encountered political opposition and required information about the status of certain great barons, she was advised by Geoffroy of Villehardouin and Milo Breban, former Champagne officials who had become respectively marshal and butler of the Frankish Empire of Constantinople, to consult the original document (*scripta feodorum*) to learn the exact obligations of her fief holders.[17] Even later in the thirteenth century administrative surveys referred to the *antiquae scriptae* as a still legitimate authority on fief holders and their obligations.

Attempts were made to create new *Feoda* lists in the first three decades of the thirteenth century, but they were unsuccessful because of the political instability of Thibaut IV's minority and early rule, and the new lists remain incomplete.[18] In fact, the sixth and seventh *Feoda* registers (from 1222 to the mid-1230s) are simply indiscriminate lists, without reference to castellany, of men who paid homage to the count. That such attempts were made at all is indicative of the significance attached to the idea of a systematic record like the old *Feoda*. Only after a generation of peace from the mid-1230s was it possible to reestablish effective central administration and to draw up the first full-scale inventory of the count's fief holders since the original *Feoda*, the *Rôles des fiefs* of 1249–52.[19] The *Rôles* are well-organized by castellany and offer an incomparable mine of information on fief holders, their fiefs (usually valued by annual income and often described), and their rear-fief holders. The *Rôles* are unique in the type and amount of information which they contain on the entire range of fief holders in a thirteenth-century principality, and they are a rare medieval source that permits relatively simple quantitative analyses of a large fief-holding group. Two later inventories contain similar information on fief holders and their fiefs: Thibaut V's officials compiled a *Livre des hommages* (1264–65), the first survey in which castellanies were arranged by *bailliage*,[20] and Count Henry III's widow, Blanche, had a new *Rôles des fiefs* drawn up (1275).[21] These surveys, however, are not nearly as detailed as the *Rôles* of 1252 and do not yield as fruitful quantitative results.

Two other administrative records of the thirteenth century are also important for the type of information which they contain about lay society. The *Extenta terre* of 1276/78 inventories the direct rights and revenues enjoyed by the count on his own domain.[22] Organized by castellany, and occasionally by *prévôté*, it records the extent of the count's judicial authority in each locality on the domain, the exact sources and amounts of his revenues, and the specific privileges or obligations of residents in each area. The inclusion of the texts of the community franchise and commune grants is especially valuable for studying community organization and changes in the conditions of persons on the Champagne domain. The *Extenta* is actually the counterpart for the count's domain of the *Rôles des fiefs* of 1252 for his fiefs; despite the slight chronological disparity, together they present an integrated picture of lay society in mid-thirteenth-century Champagne, at the end of a century of social and economic development as a territorial state. Comparable information for reconstructing that secular society in the *bailliage* of Troyes is simply not available from the extant ecclesiastical sources alone. The last relevant administrative document of the thirteenth century is the "Etat des bois situés aux environs de Troyes" of about 1290: it furnishes the hearth sizes of many villages in the Forest of Othe (southwest of Troyes), including those of two castellany centers, that were entitled to use certain woods there.[23]

Finally, a more theoretical and cohesive image of lay society than that offered by the charters and administrative surveys is provided by the *Coutumier,* a collection of various "customs"—social and tenurial regulations prevailing in the countryside—and of twenty-nine legal decisions, mostly by the Jours of Troyes from 1270 to 1295.[24] Like similar collections in the fourteenth and fifteenth centuries, the *Coutumier* was privately collated, probably by a participant at the Jours, and for private use; but unlike the other collections, it was fully composed in its present form by about 1295 and is therefore acceptable as a source for conditions in the thirteenth century. Thus, exclusive of purely literary works, there are three basic types of sources—charters, administrative surveys, and the *Coutumier*—which furnish various and abundant information on feudal society in the *bailliage.*

Each of the three types of local sources reflects the same social and economic reality in the *bailliage,* but their images of its society are not necessarily coincidental—nor were they intended to be—because they were composed to serve particular interests at particular moments. Although charter evidence furnishes the largest volume of information for the twelfth and thirteenth centuries, the use and interpretation of that information entail several difficulties. In fact, few actual charters survive, the ultimate source usually being cartularies, which are registers of copies of charters that interested individual ecclesiastical institutions. The copies are often imperfect, for they omit witnesses and even details of transactions (such as the reasons for specific property transfers) considered irrelevant at the time of the recording but occasionally included by other parties in their own copies of the same transactions.

Moreover, charters and cartularies are primarily records of property rights and are essentially restricted to the acquisitions and favorable legal judgments of ecclesiastical institutions. The families appearing most often in those acts were the most prominent ones that also donated continually to the Church; certainly they were not representative of all fief holders. Information about the great majority of lay families that do not appear regularly in those acts is fragmentary and of limited use unless supplemented by information from other sources. So cartulary references cannot be read as a mirror reflection of secular society in general. The limitations of the other sources are the result not so much of inherent deficiencies as of modern evaluations of their significance. The twelfth-century franchises, for example, if they are interpreted as written forms of longstanding customs, give an entirely different coloring to rural conditions than if they are seen as innovative grants of privileges. Likewise, the evolution of society in the thirteenth century emerges differently if the *Coutumier* is presented as a codification of universally applicable customs rather than of conditions prevalent only in some parts of the countryside. But perhaps the major deficiency in the study of feudal societies has been the lack of close work on the administrative records of the great principalities. The Champagne surveys, at least, are central to any portrait of its feudal society because they furnish concrete inventories of domain, fiefs, and fief holders—positive descriptions by contemporary officials that are clearly preferable, when available, to the sporadic and fragmentary references to persons and properties in the charters.

The processing of the data also greatly determines how the available information finally emerges in a coherent image of feudal society. The various sources contain information of such great chronological and geographical diversity that simply to collect all available references and to fuse them into a single, comprehensive framework would result in an illusory, static presentation. The conditions depicted in the late-thirteenth-century *Coutumier* were not applicable to the franchised communities, certainly not after their privileges had been written, and conditions on the count's domain itself in 1276 were not necessarily identical in every locality to what they had been in the previous century. Likewise, the system of fiefs and rear-fiefs in the *Rôles des fiefs* of 1252 did not represent the situation of one hundred, or even fifty, years earlier. That is, the most serious procedural error would be to attempt to cast all the pieces of information from the various sources into a uniform image of feudal society for the entire period and then to rationalize the discrepancies. The discrepancies are, in fact, the residues of the extreme localism of conditions—in private lay and ecclesiastical lordships, in the count's domain, in franchised communities—and reflect the uneven and continuing development of feudal society. More subtle than the problems of information processing are the conceptual frameworks in which specific data are presented. Concepts such as "serfdom," "nobility," and "feudalism" have long traditions and accretions from later periods, and their application to medieval society has unfortunately obscured some important developments in the twelfth and thirteenth centuries. Indeed, the concepts have acquired such an independent existence that the mere presence or absence of terms such as "serf" or "noble" in the written sources is taken as proof or not of the existence of "serfdom" or "nobility." Contemporaries, of course, understood the significance of the terms for social catagories, but they did not provide convenient definitions in the documents which survive. In addition, the recent formulation that feudal society in France had developed its essential traits by the eleventh century and underwent only minor and gradual modification through the next two centuries has created an unconscious bias and a barrier against the detection and measurement of continuing social changes in the later twelfth and thirteenth centuries.

The method of this study is to present and interpret the evidence available for the *bailliage* area only. The local materials are read on their own merits, without recourse to outside information to compensate for deficiencies, and independently of conceptual schemes developed for other regions or periods. Since the value of a local study is in its specificity, as much of the *bailliage* information as possible is presented descriptively; close readings of the community franchises and the *Coutumier* in particular are important for the interpretation of rural social development. Contemporary terminology has been retained throughout in order to avoid terms such as "serf" and "noble." Neutral terms, of course, are helpful in presenting the information, so "peasantry" and "aristocracy" are occasionally used, although their meanings too are not always self-evident in the context of evolving conditions in the *bailliage*. The local data are analyzed as far as possible according to the type of source from which they originated: *pariages,* community franchises, and the *Coutumier* are considered separately from the discrete information on individual peasants, knights, and barons contained in the charters and administrative surveys. Finally, the inventories of fief holders have been analyzed quantitatively in order to provide a few numerical indices based on the entire group of fief holders in the area. The figures themselves, however, are meaningful only in terms of the specific persons and families which they represented, so an essential allied undertaking was the construction of genealogies of baronial and lesser knight families to illustrate the dimensions of the group of fief holders. Most attempts to piece together lineages beyond two generations failed, but enough of the lesser knight and unsuccessful baronial lines have been reconstructed to balance the successful baronial families, which have been best studied in the past and which too often have been taken alone as representative of the medieval aristocracy. Both the refinement of the administrative quantitative data and the construction of genealogies are time-consuming and comparatively low-yield procedures, but they furnish the only valid bases for generalizing about a medieval aristocracy.

II
The Peasantry and Rural Communities

The study of the peasantry and its community organization in medieval France is a difficult subject that has been further complicated by confusing methods of analysis and by the uncritical transmission of imprecise concepts from one study to another. The most serious impediment to the understanding of rural society in the twelfth and thirteenth centuries has been the undue concentration on "serfdom" (*servage*), a concept which was not current at that time and which, in spite of modern usage, has never been applied consistently to the medieval period. Although serfdom may prove one day a useful concept for comparing conditions in diverse societies, it is not a satisfactory vehicle by which to present the basic information on a local peasantry.

The more technical aspects of extracting and interpreting the local information also greatly influence any evaluation of a local peasantry. The legalistic and semantic methods that focus on the presence or absence of various terms (for example, *servus*) in the sources generally fail to analyze the dynamics of the situations described in the charters. Moreover, the intrinsic biases of the sources are often forgotten after their information has been extracted. All types of sources ultimately are functions of two parameters—geography and chronology—and therefore present, not complete portraits of rural society, but rather partial ones, in which particular localities and periods determined the specific information that was recorded. In the *bailliage*, for example, there are several quite different types of sources on rural conditions: private charters, *pariages*, community franchises, county administrative records, and the *Coutumier*. Charter evidence provides a large collection of concrete, though fragmentary, situations involving peasants and their lords throughout the two centuries, and the *Coutumier* presents the theoretical statements for those relationships, but only for the late thirteenth century. Conditions on the count's domain were described only by the Champagne surveys in the late thirteenth century, although the inclusion of several community franchises allows a close look at changes in specific localities from the late twelfth century. The only descriptions of the organization and control of peasants on private lordships are in the *pariages*. Thus, none of the sources contains evidence that can be extended over the *bailliage* as a whole. Each source must be analyzed independently.

Lastly, the fundamental limitations of the sources should be made clear. The sources were composed for landlords, essentially to preserve their rights and revenues; the matters dealt with most often are the classification and organization of tenants and their obligations (and occasionally exemptions). Such sources do not permit any evaluation of the material conditions of peasant life, the types and extent of possessions, or standards of living, and the occasional detailed description of persons or families cannot be woven into a general pattern. Also, demographic analysis is not possible beyond the crudest terms. The list of eighty village hearth populations at the end of the thirteenth century gives a rough sense of density, and the extrapolated figures for the size of several franchised villages and of communities on fiefs are valuable as specific illustrations; but there is simply no basis for generalizing about the distribution by size or organization of communities in the *bailliage*. Nor is it possible to estimate total population. In spite of attempts to control concepts and methods, the sources simply do not contain information on the material conditions of life. Yet the changing patterns of classification and organization of peasants by the landlords do reveal indirectly some of the dynamic elements in rural society.

THE PEASANTRY

Charters of the late eleventh and early twelfth centuries are difficult to interpret because their terms and phrases are similar to those of the Carolingian period; either the terms mask social changes or rural institutions remained unchanged during the intervening centuries.[1] About 1080, for example, the count of Brienne gave to the abbey of Molesme his hereditary (that is, alodial) rights over lands, woods, tithes, justice, and persons (*servi, ancillae*) in a certain village, the very components of a Carolingian *villa*.[2] In similar donations during the first two decades of the twelfth century, *servus* and *ancilla* seem to have been used in their ninth-century sense of tenants under the full and arbitrary disposition of their masters.[3] The paucity of charters in the *bailliage* area makes it difficult to determine whether there were other persons who might be called free at that time; from the few and scattered acts it can be concluded only that up to ca. 1120, great lords like the counts of Troyes and Brienne alienated entire domains and their resident personnel. In the first two decades of the twelfth century, however, the terminology of the charters changed: *homines* and *feminae* occurred with increasing frequency and seem to have replaced *servi* and *ancillae*, although it is not clear whether the scribes intended an absolute equation.[4] In any case, after 1120, *homines* was virtually the only term employed for the general peasant population, and there is no evidence for the existence of a concurrent group of "free" men, independent of any lord.[5] From the 1160s, and especially the 1190s, the terms *homo proprius, homo de corpore,* and *homo de capite* predominated; these, along with the unqualified *homines,* were standard throughout the thirteenth and even fourteenth centuries, becoming *home de corp* and *home de poté* in Old French.

Homines generally referred to persons who were neither knights, clerics, nor enfranchised men. In a few cases it meant all men, including non-peasants, who had a relationship with a particular lord, as in 1200 when a lord defined his *homines* as *milites, burgenses,* and *vilani,* but in the countryside the usual distinction in lay society was between knights and all the rest of the population.[6] When Blanche of Navarre came under the wardship of King Philip II in 1201, she guaranteed her actions by surrendering lordship over her *homines* and *milites* in several castellanies; and in 1255 when the lord of Rochefort gave up all his possessions in a certain village, he excepted "the fiefs of [his] knights and the justice of those fiefs, and . . . [his] *homines de corpore,* their movables, and land."[7] Another lord classified his rights as the *jus feodalis* and the *aliud jus quocumque* that he had over his *homines de corpore.*[8] Although *homines* and *homines de corpore* were interchangeable, they often indicated a slightly different perspective: the first referred to all peasants, no matter who their lords, while the second referred more narrowly to the men of a particular lord. For example, in 1255 the lord of Chacenay permitted Clairvaux to acquire land from his *homines de corpore* only with his express consent, but he permitted the abbey to acquire freely "from other men who are not my men *de corpore,*" retaining himself only the rents of any donated lands.[9]

The exact formal bond between a man and his lord was seldom explained in the charters, but men did take oaths on their initial acceptance of a lord and on occasions when disputes arose over obligations or possessions. Unfortunately, there are few clear cases of initial oath-taking. In 1216 the chapter of Saint-Etienne received a man "in fidelity and homage" and promised him the same protection that it afforded its other men, in return for which he owed 15 d. annually and swore on the Scriptures to fulfill the agreement.[10] In 1220 a man and woman "conceded" that they were *homines de capite* of Vauluisant and committed their descendants likewise to be *de corpore*; their properties and movables would go to the abbey, and they too swore to uphold the arrangement.[11] The best examples of the reception of men are in the community regulations: in 1171, for example, every newcomer to the village of Puits was required to "commit" himself to one of the two co-lords, the abbot or the count, within one year and one day; and in 1233 an oath of "fidelity" to one of the two lords of Essoyes was exacted before anyone could become a member of that "society."[12] Most of the individual cases of oaths in the charters are of course related to disputes. The man who in 1221 "acknowledged" that he was *de capite et de corpore* of an abbey and that he held lands for *terrage,* according to the custom of his village, seems to have been responding to a challenge either to his status, tenure, or rent.[13] In like manner, a man in 1225 "recognized" that he belonged to an abbey and promised to move (that is, to return) to Troyes with his family and place himself "under the power, lordship, justice, and jurisdiction" of the abbey there.[14] Other cases also suggest that peasants who had somehow evaded the control of their lords were coerced into formally recognizing their relationship and resultant obligations to those lords. [15] It appears then that oaths were required of peasants only on exceptional occasions, such as upon the initial voluntary submission to a lord, in disputes over the status of lands or persons, and on special occasions when they assumed temporary official responsibilities, especially for inquests.[16] Although rarely recorded, oath-taking by ordinary peasants was not unusual.[17]

Peasants were subjected in the broadest sense to the "jurisdiction and lordship" (*jus et dominium*) of another person.[18] The terms *jus, dominium,* and *potestas* all denoted the direct control by a lord over persons, property, or rights.[19] In some contexts *dominium* and *potestas* referred to the territorial area under a great lord's administrative control,[20] and in other cases those terms meant more narrowly the immediate domain lands of a lord, as opposed to the fiefs held from him.[21] But the full sense of the Latin as used in a variety of contexts was more abstract: "lordship" or "authority" are preferable renditions because they distinguish those terms from the associated, though not necessarily identical, right of justice.[22] Possibly the most abstract use is in the 1203 *pariage* between the abbey of Montiéramey and the lord of Ramerupt, in which they agreed to share equally everything in the village of Nogent-sur-Aube, including *terrage, taille,* justice, and tithe, and stipulated further that neither was to have "more *dominium*" than the other.[23] No matter what the exact translation in particular cases, *dominium* was the control of rights over persons, and in theory it meant that men and women were sold, alienated, or separated from their families by the arbitrary decision of their lords. In 1170 the count donated a woman, her sons, and their wives plus their house and property—for a Mass.[24] In 1176 a woman and her children were sold for 10 l.; in 1208 men and their families which were held "in alod" by a knight were sold for 80 l.; and others were sold for annual rents.[25] The men of one village even bought the count's promise not to alienate them.[26]

In the charters lordship was usually reduced to specific personal obligations and restrictions over ordinary peasants beyond the normal tenurial requirements such as rent, *corvées,* or banal restrictions. Although it is difficult to generalize about specific points because of the considerable variation from one village to another, indeed even within villages, contemporaries generally classified obligations under three headings: 1) justice, 2) *taille,* and 3) other "services" and "customs," including usually *mainmorte* and marriage restrictions. For example, in 1225 when the count transferred his rights (*juris*) over a peasant, the scribe defined them as rights of justice, *taille,* and other "exactions"; another act explicitly identifies exactions as *mainmorte* and tax on outside marriages.[27] Or, as one man stated when he confessed publicly on oath, his ancestors had always been and still were "tailleable men" and subject to the high and low justice and *mainmorte* of an abbey. [28]

Although the right of justice appears often in charters, especially when a lord claimed it over particular individuals, there is insufficient information to detail its organization or exercise at the local level. In practice, justice was simply the right to impose punishment or (usually) fine for any infraction, and it was administered by the lord's local resident official. In an immobile society a single lord would have the full claim to justice over tenants and their tenancies, but increasing physical mobility resulted in conflicts between territorial and personal justice, as peasants often came under several jurisdictions at once, for their persons and for their lands.[29] The numerous "agreements" and *pariages* from the late twelfth century testify to the efforts of lords to solve the inherent contradiction of their claims of justice in a mobile society.[30]

The antiquity of *taille* in the *bailliage* cannot be determined, but it was certainly common under that name by the mid-twelfth century. The earliest extant reference is in 1153, when the count asserted his right to collect both "*taille* and customs" in certain villages in his *potestas*; in 1158 he referred to "the exaction commonly called *taille.*"[31] Although not defined in the charters, *tallia* was always associated with the lord's authority over persons. For example, when a woman admitted on oath that she was *femina de corpore et de capite* of an abbey, she also paid her *tallia,* the symbolic recognition of that subjugation.[32] *Taille* was usually a tax in coin fixed on individuals, both men and women, and collected by the immediate lord.[33] Arbitrary *taille* was mentioned only rarely, and it seems that by the last decades of the twelfth century *taille* had become a fixed assessment, though not necessarily standardized, for most persons; in 1200, for example, Philip of Assenay collected annual *tailles* from three men of

12 s., 9 s., and 6 s., *et non amplius*.[34] The numerous intermarriage
exchange agreements between lords (see below) also indicate that *taille*
had been fixed by the late twelfth century, perhaps even as a result of
the increasing number of mixed marriages, which required exact *taille*
valuations for the accounting of exchanged persons. Since *taille* was the
major claim on a person, it was usually transferred with the person, but
lords insisted on continued payments until they were reimbursed with
persons of equal *taille* value. In 1191, for example, a woman was
required to pay 5 s. annually *pro tallia* to her original lord until he was
compensated with another woman of the same value.[35] In some cases
the *taille* of exchanged persons remained with the original lord; in
others it was shared by both the old and new lords.[36]

Occasionally *taille* was formally converted into another type of payment, the *abonamentum*. The most common form of *abonamentum*
was the privilege granted to individuals for their lifetimes, and in some
cases to their posterity, of a fixed annual payment in lieu of *taille*. One
man, for example, paid 30 s. annually (far above the original *taille*
payment) and had the choice of living with his family at Troyes or at
Montiéramey.[37] The counts of Champagne issued a number of these
commutations, copies of which were still held by the recipients during
the 1276/78 inquest on the count's domain.[38] A second type of
abonamentum was the communitywide tax on possessions, especially
for buildings and animals. The men of Vileros paid such a tax to
Molesme at the rate of 5 s. per horse, 3 s. per head of cattle, 1 d. per
sheep, and 3 s. for a house or 12 d. for men without houses; late
payment was fined at 5 s.[39] Thus, *abonamentum* was the conversion of
what had been an arbitrary personal tax into a fixed one or a tax on
possessions. Although this and other forms of *taille* commutation
would have long-range implications, the immediate consequence was
not great because only men of certain lands (that is, men under certain
lords) benefited, and even then there was little to distinguish those few
from the others who paid *taille* in name as well as in fact: both
remained under the justice and protection of a lord, paid normal rents
and other "customs," and were subjected to the same marriage and
bequeathal restrictions. One act even stressed the continuing obligations
of men with commuted *tailles*: a *pariage* provided that the agents of
two co-lords each receive "one-half of the commutations and *tailles*" of
two villages—only the formula of assessment differed, not the payment
or the relationship between men and their lords.[40] The efforts of lords
to preserve their claims to *taille* and its commuted tax, as well as the
central place of *taille* abolition in the community franchises, leave no
doubt that *taille* was the single most important right over rural inhabitants.[41]

Closely linked with *taille* was *mainmorte* (*manus mortua*). As a scribe of the count put it, the count had *"mainmorte* on those from whom he . . . [took] *taille.*"[42] Essentially, *mainmorte* was the right of a lord to take the lands and goods of his tenants who died without heirs living in the household and ready to assume immediately the deceased's responsibilities as tenant, taxpayer, and debtor.[43] For example, in 1243 a certain Josbert created a scene in court when he claimed as inheritance half the house and land of his father-in-law, but the custom was, as the Léproserie proved, that the property of a man who died "without heirs of his body living with him" (in this case a daughter) reverted to the lord.[44] As another charter expressed it, the heir had to be living with the deceased "in bread and salt."[45] *Mainmorte* was seldom mentioned in the charters; indeed, the term itself did not appear until the last decade of the twelfth century.[46] It was obviously an ordinary and uncontested concomitant of tenancy that surfaced most often in cases involving emigration, and usually within the urban environment of Troyes or the castellany towns. For example, the children of Thierry of Thuisy, a man of Notre-Dame-aux-Nonnains in Troyes, brought suit against the abbey over their inheritance (*excasure et manumortus*); although they had probably left home and were not entitled to anything, the abbey did allow them to recover their father's stall in Troyes and 15 l. cash as compensation for his personal possessions, but it retained his house, movables, and the rest of his lands.[47] In 1223 two brothers claimed the legacy of their mother, a *femina* of the same abbey; although they were probably not entitled to it and did not dispute the abbey's right of *mainmorte*, they were allowed to take possession of her real estate (*res immobiles*), valued at 10 l., for a 55 d. payment.[48] In 1238 a widower bought the right to his wife's inheritance from Saint-Loup, her lord, for 19 l.—10 l. for the land and 9 l. for the movables.[49] All these examples involve either indirect transfers of legacies or the emigration of the direct heirs, the very situations checked by *mainmorte*. In most of these cases the *mainmorte* exclusion was not strictly enforced, and emigrants could recover at least part of their parents' holdings for a payment.

Mainmorte was a more serious threat to family inheritance in urban environments, where there was a lower probability that all members of the family would remain at home, and several lords with numerous urban residents must have experienced strong pressure to abolish the claim. The chapter of Saint-Pierre lifted that burden from its men living in the suburbs of Troyes in 1194: all their possessions in buildings, tenancies, and movables could pass to their closest (not necessarily direct) heirs living in Troyes (but not necessarily in the same house) without tax.[50] In 1198 the count of Bar-sur-Seine sold an even wider privilege to his men in that town for 100 l.: men without direct heirs could bequeath property to any other of his men.[51] In the countryside, however, *mainmorte* was seldom commuted or abolished, for unlike *taille*, which was a minor tax, *mainmorte* represented ultimate control over land and acquired wealth. Even in castellany towns of private lords this claim was rarely relinquished by landlords, in spite of their accommodations for specific individuals. The general pattern was not broken until 1230-31, when the communal grants abolished inheritance restrictions in favor of other taxes in at least several Champagne castellanies and their towns.[52]

The fourth, and most widely documented, restriction on peasants involved marriage: they were prohibited from marrying persons outside their lord's control except with his permission, secured by payment of *formariage*.[53] In fact, marriages were not prevented, and lords reached bilateral agreements among themselves for the exchange of persons, property, and rights in order both to accommodate intermarriages and to balance their accounts. Occasionally the lords retained their full claims ("my right, justice, and *taille*") over their respective men and women of mixed marriages.[54] But usually the women were traded to the lords of their husbands, and the receiving lords promised in return to furnish other women for mixed marriages in the future. This meant that all rights over women, and sometimes their lands, were surrendered by one lord to another in order to prevent later conflicts over who would receive *taille* and *mainmorte*.[55] Behind the variety of arrangements was a single principle, clearly stated in many charters: lords always exchanged persons of equal value, that is, of equal *taille* assessment. When a woman was transferred, the receiving lord promised her original lord another woman "of equal value, 20 s. more or less."[56] In cases where future exchanges were still uncertain, the women continued their *taille* payments to their original lords until the latter were compensated.[57] But simpler, and more common, was the simultaneous exchange of two women, one by each lord, that assured a balance of accounts, though it often meant that a man who himself wished to marry an outsider would see his own sister exchanged in return.[58]

The most serious problem was the future children of mixed marriages, for the landlords wished to retain as many taxable persons as possible under their authority. The simultaneous exchange of two women implicitly canceled each lord's claim on his original woman's progeny, but in cases of delayed or unequal exchanges complicated situations could arise afterward. The shoemaker of Lusigny, for example, saw his family split between Saint-Loup and the lord of Chappes, each of whom took three sons; other divisions could be more complicated because there was no formula to equate sex, age, and number of children.[59] In order to avoid such difficulties and the administrative problems of dealing with the intermarriages on an individual basis, the landlords with large peasant populations developed standard exchange procedures. A few such agreements were made early in the twelfth century, but they were not widespread or standardized until the 1180s, perhaps following the count's example of 1173, when he and the newly founded chapter of Saint-Etienne allowed their men and women to intermarry freely, with their children to be divided between the two parties.[60] In the next two decades several ecclesiastical houses—all Benedictine ones near Troyes, which must have been attracting their men—concluded similar bilateral agreements: in 1180, for example, Montier-la-Celle and Notre-Dame-aux-Nonnains permitted their men and women, no matter where they resided, to intermarry freely and allowed the children to go to the father's lord.[61] There were also understandings between great lay lords and ecclesiastical houses over certain villages or areas in which their men lived together or in close proximity.[62] The number of charters dealing with intermarriages and the standard exchange procedures devised to handle the problem show that intermarriages were common and were dealt with as a matter of course by the late twelfth century; restrictions on marriage were simply defensive claims that prevented one lord from raiding the men of another through marriages.

The origin of these four basic controls over tenants—justice, *taille*, *mainmorte*, and marriage—cannot be determined with certainty, but the evidence available from the *bailliage* indicates that they were normal obligations or "customs" which fell on all persons living on the land of a lord. They were simply the adjunct of tenancy. When the tenant remained on his ancestral lands and fulfilled his numerous obligations to the landlord, these particular obligations were not isolated as a matter of concern by the lord. But when tenants and their children moved from their lands or intermarried, the traditional coincidence of tenant and tenancy was broken, and the various obligations were atomized. It is the physical mobility of persons that makes meaningful the efforts of lords to maintain claims to the specific items of *tailles*, tenancy transfers, and outside marriages, and the increasing concern by landlords with these rights in the second half of the twelfth century can be interpreted best as a reflection of increased rural migration.

There is no question about the fact of actual physical mobility of ordinary peasants at any time during the twelfth and thirteenth centuries; movement not only occurred, it was considered normal.[63] The lords of emigrants, of course, refused to acknowledge that physical separation in any way diminished the traditional rights which they continued to claim. Several intermarriage agreements explicitly included all men of their respective lords, no matter "where they move or make their residence"; and the chapter of Saint-Etienne even stipulated in an agreement of 1209 that it would retain all its "rights," especially justice, over its men who settled in a particular locality "either through marriage or any other way."[64] Since it was usually single men who departed, and since their very departure was a surrender of claim to paternal lands, the lords were most interested in asserting their other right, the *taille,* over emigrants. One son, for example, who left his widowed mother and three brothers at home in 1216 was still considered liable for an annual 3 s. tax to his lord, even though his emigration had cost him all claim to land there; his brothers paid only one-third of that tax and were entitled to inherit their father's property.[65] Another lord threatened the sons of three men who owed him *taille* that if they left "their fathers and families" they too would be liable for *taille,* but they would be exempt from it as long as they remained at home.[66] Lords could also complicate the lives of emigrants by transferring the rights over them to other lords, as one son living away from home discovered when he and his father and family were donated to an abbey.[67] The widespread nature of rural migration is best seen in the provisions of the *pariages* and the community franchises, which attracted men to specific localities (see below and in chapter III), but occasionally the influence of that mobility on ordinary, nonfranchised villages can be detected. In 1233, for example, Jean of Méry allowed his men of Dosches to use his woodlands there, with two exceptions: tenants who left the village could not use the woods in any manner during their nonresidence, and newcomers who were not under Méry's jurisdiction (that is, who had not taken an oath to him) were likewise excluded.[68] Only a significant migration of men both into and out of the village would have justified such provisions.

The considerable mobility of ordinary peasants has often been obscured by the presence of *hospites* and *albani,* who appear in the charters throughout the twelfth and thirteenth centuries. As newcomers, they were occasionally considered unreliable tenants, but they usually engaged in the same activities as the native residents: they held tenancies, for which they paid rents and performed services, they intermarried with local residents, and they shared whatever privileges the local inhabitants had been granted by their lords.[69] Although in a few instances *hospites* were promised special privileges for settling new lands, there is little consistent evidence to associate them with vacant or newly cleared lands.[70] In fact, many references in the *bailliage* are to their participation in specialized economic activities: the count referred to some *hospites* as merchants in 1177, and in 1228 Montier-la-Celle's stalls at the Provins fair were run by *hospites.*[71] An act of 1158 is particularly revealing about the origins of these men. Count Henry I granted Saint-Loup the freedom of the oven next to its church in Troyes and also freed from his justice and customs "six *hospites* and their families living on the six *manses* of the oven." The men could not be summoned by the count except through the abbot or canons, and they were completely immune from seizure by his officials, even if the men did belong to the count, because the oven and the men operating it were inviolate. However, the count still claimed *taille* from any of those men who owed it to him because, despite the oven's exemption, the count "doesn't lose [the *taille*] of my man."[72] This was an admission that some of Saint-Loup's *hospites* at its oven in Troyes had been men of the count, and he claimed their *taille,* the very payment that they had probably attempted to evade, as the sign of their relationship to him. The count granted similar privileges to the bakers of the Lépro-serie and the Hôtel-Dieu in Troyes, and in each case he included the same provision for *hospites* who were his own men.[73]

The count was one of the few lords who openly identified *hospites* with his own men, and his other acts reveal the ultimate dilemma of most landlords. On the one hand the count was careful to maintain claims over his own men who had become *hospites,* but on the other hand he encouraged the immigration of men of other lords to his franchised villages.[74] Although in some cases tenants paid their lords a tax for permission to migrate and settle on the land of another lord, [75] there must have been many more cases in which men simply left the houses of their fathers without formal adieu to the lord. The physical control of persons must have been difficult for even the great lord with a rudimentary administrative apparatus because immigrants were always welcome on the lands of other lords. In short, it was the point of view of the lord that determined whether men were his tenants or *hospites*: the *hospites* of a local lord were the men of a distant lord. The specific equation was made by Erard of Ramerupt in 1236 when he surrendered claim to a certain woman, *albam, qui erat femina mea de corpore.*[76] The essential characteristic of a *hospes* was the physical distance from his original lord, which effectively removed the lord's control; there are very few examples of emigrants being forcibly returned to their lords.[77] Simply defined, *hospites* were men, and occasionally women, who had left their natal villages and were therefore temporarily without lords.

No less obvious than the movement of men away from their lords is the reverse process, the continual reassimilation of lordless men as tenants and under social control. While some men were escaping to become temporarily "free" *hospites,* many of the latter were disappearing into the mass of *homines* as they acquired new tenancies and new lords. Often the reintegration was involuntary: in 1157, for example, the count granted Saint-Etienne as part of its foundation charter all the *homines albanos* at Troyes, Provins, and Pont-sur-Seine "if they remain completely free for one year and one day."[78] But usually newcomers had some choice in the matter: in 1171 the new men of a village had to commend themselves within one year and one day but could choose as lord either the count or the abbot of Oyes, *cui melius voluerint;* and in

1233 each *novus,* man or woman, of a village in which every resident paid either a *taille* or its commutation had to give "fidelity" to both lords before being accepted as a full member of that community.[79] In some situations there was an obvious economic advantage in choosing one lord over another: when Saint-Pierre freed all its men living in Troyes in 1194 from *mainmorte,* it extended that privilege to *albani* who placed themselves under its lordship (*dominium*), that is, who became men of the chapter; it would have been advantageous, other obligations being equal, for an enterprising immigrant at that time to accept Saint-Pierre's lordship.[80]

The count's policy was a significant factor in rural migration. In the twelfth century the count often permitted ecclesiastical houses to accept *hospites,* that is, men of other lords and, by implication, his own, although no grant is as generous as the one cited above for the new chapter of Saint-Etienne in 1157. For example, Saint-Jean-en-Chastel was allowed to accept new settlers on its property in Troyes in 1172, and in 1187 Saint-Loup was permitted—because "the times are bad"—to "receive *albani* at Troyes and to hold them just like its other *homines* there."[81] The counts generally favored internal migration and even stimulated it by their community franchises from 1175 to 1199, although they were careful to defer to the interests of local lords by prohibiting their men from entering the privileged communities. In the early thirteenth century a series of bilateral agreements opened the entire southern border of the *bailliage* (and thereby of Champagne) to the free passage (*percursus*) of men: in 1204 the countess and the duke of Burgundy opened their lands to each other's men for four years, and in 1205 she reached a similar agreement with the count of Tonnerre-Auxerre.[82] But the succession crisis became serious by 1209 and probably exacerbated the movement of persons—this time away from the count's lands instead of to them—so she closed the Champagne borders, and the king agreed not to accept Champagne men on his lands from September 1209 to Christmas 1210.[83] With the outbreak of hostilities in the *bailliage* in 1215, the southern border with Burgundy was also sealed (that is, *percursus* was suspended) for four years, and the situation probably remained unsettled until the accession of Thibaut in 1222, when relatively normal conditions should have returned.[84] Unfortunately, Thibaut's foreign policy led to complications that resulted in the 1229 invasion and the 1230-31 communal grants to his castellany towns. Only with the resolution of the major internal and external problems in the 1230s could the count return to a policy of actively attracting immigrants to his lands, and sometime between 1240 and 1276 the previous policy of at least outward deference to the interest of local lords was reversed. Henceforth, men on the count's fiefs and rear-fiefs were permitted to migrate to Troyes and become his direct men; their lords, the count's fief holders, were not allowed to challenge this invitation or to claim any rights over tenants who chose to leave.[85] Any *albus* who lived with a wife in Troyes for one year and one day without taking a lord became automatically a man of the count. And if a newcomer was involved in a dispute which came to the count's court before the residence requirement was completed, that man would also become the count's from that time because he was coming under the count's jurisdiction: the *enquêteurs* reported in the *Extenta* (1276) that many resorted to this technicality. Thus, *hospites, albani,* and *novi* were men distant from their own lords and therefore were considered to be lordless whenever they migrated; but when they accepted another lord, they exchanged their temporary physical freedom for economic opportunity and were completely reintegrated into a local community.[86]

Another avenue open to some peasants seeking escape from ordinary village life was service in the administration of a lord, whether the count, a great baron or prelate, or a simple knight. On the village level the most important official was the mayor (occasionally the *prévôt*), who generally executed his lord's directives, coordinated community life, collected the most onerous taxes, and even judged local cases.[87] As the key link between a lord and his men, the mayor was often protected by special immunity, particularly from other lords and the count's agents; he also received exemptions from certain taxes and other privileges during his term of office.[88] In some cases his office seems to have become hereditary in the twelfth century, for witness lists include sons, sons-in-law, and even "mayoresses."[89] But in spite of his privileges and his importance in day-to-day affairs, the mayor served at the will of his lord and was ultimately an ordinary tenant in any accounting: his children were exchanged like those of any other peasant, and if he sought a new lord, he had to enter formally into a new subjugation like other tenants.[90]

Nonresidential agents (*servientes*) also enjoyed privileges with their office.[91] They lived near their lord—"in our house, of our goods," according to Saint-Pierre—but exercised their duties away from his immediate protection and therefore required immunities from the count's officials.[92] These agents performed any task required by their lord but were especially involved in three areas. They collected taxes and rents: *servientes* of Montier-la-Celle, for example, collected rents of 14 l. from its stall in the Provins fair in 1187;[93] they procured goods at market, and if they represented an ecclesiastical house, they were exempted from normal commercial taxes;[94] and they acted as the local police force, a role in which they were noted for their violence: the countess had Saint-Pierre's pillory just outside Troyes torn down in 1212 because the abbey's agents had hanged several men from it.[95]

Since the count's domain was much larger than those of most lords and therefore required more specialized administration, his *servientes* were usually associated exclusively with the physical enforcement of his orders; financial matters of the county were handled by *prévôts,* specialized revenue farmers.[96] In spite of the occasional association of *servientes* with knights in the twelfth century, and in particular the inclusion of a few of them in the *Feoda* of 1172, there is no evidence to indicate that the agents succeeded in maintaining any privileges outside their office or that they ever constituted a distinct or cohesive social group.[97]

Neither office nor migration annulled the restrictions and obligations weighing on peasants. Nor did "manumission." In the *bailliage*, manumission was the transfer of rights over peasants from one lord to another, often in cases of mixed marriages; it did not grant rights to the individuals themselves and therefore cannot be considered a form of franchise. For example, when the lord of Traînel's woman married a man of Saint-Loup in 1145 and then came under the abbey's control, Traînel was forced to acknowledge that the woman was "manumitted," that is, that his rights had been formally transferred.[98] In 1161 when the count exchanged one of his women in marriage, he "manumitted" her to Saint-Loup and further "emancipated" her from his justice and customs; in 1219 a cleric of Saint-Etienne manumitted a woman, her children, and her personal possessions to the chapter "in perpetuity." [99] These and other examples demonstrate that manumission was simply the transfer of rights over persons and often also over property between lords, and in no sense did it confer privileges to the persons involved.[100]

The single mechanism that did lift obligations and restrictions from peasants was the franchise. Franchises in the sense of privileges granted to individual peasants by their lords occurred in the twelfth century, but the few references which are available for the *bailliage* are unfortunately difficult to interpret.[101] Good evidence for the lifting of personal obligations comes only from the reigns of Blanche and Thibaut, and more narrowly from 1202 to the early 1220s. Countess Blanche and later Count Thibaut "quit," "made exempt," and "freed" individuals from certain obligations, notably *taille, mainmorte,* other taxes, and often military service. In several instances such exemptions were temporary: in 1215, for example, the countess assigned one of her men to the personal service of the archdeacon of Saint-Pierre; the man's obligations were commuted to 2 s. annually, but after the archdeacon's death, he would return to the countess (and resume his previous obligations). In another case, Nicholas Wineant of Sens was freed from *taille* for ten years if he would make cloth at Troyes. [102] More common were cases in which women of the count married previously franchised townsmen or foreigners; the count's taxes on the women were then commuted. These cases differed from the transfer or commutation of *taille* on peasants who intermarried because only one lord was involved here. Furthermore, the exemptions covered all obligations except property rents and the count's justice, resulting in a full personal freedom that was unknown in the countryside. The earliest example of such a comprehensive commutation is from 1205, when the countess freed a woman from all *tallia, exactione et demanda* for 5 s. annually.[103] In the 1220s when a woman of the count married a prominent "citizen" of Troyes, the count freed them both from *taille, mainmorte,* guard duty, and military service for their lives in return for an annual 40 s.; the man, Bernard of Montcuc, became a financial agent of the count and one of the most important men of Troyes, acting as mayor of the commune from 1236 to 1239.[104] Other foreign merchants who married local women of the count were similarly exempted: Roger of Bologna "became" a man of the count when he married a *femina de corpore* of the count, but that formal submission was matched by an exemption from all *tallia, tolta et demanda* for life in return for 25 s. annually.[105]

The ultimate individual franchise was total exemption granted in return for faithful service rendered to the count's family. Blanche freed the sister and brother-in-law of her personal chaplain from "*taille, mainmorte,* fine, exaction, *corvée,* guard and military service, and escheat"; Thibaut freed the son, daughter, and all future descendants of the architect Master André from all personal taxes and miltary service and further granted each a 100 s. rent from the Troyes wine tax.[106] The succession crisis, of course, made it expedient to reward supporters of Thibaut's cause. Knights received fiefs, and great barons received "augmented" incomes and rents to their fiefs, but the lesser men, and especially the count's *servientes,* were more appropriately rewarded with tax exemptions. Gérard of Varennes, *serviens,* was released in 1222 from all taxes and received in addition a 20 l. rent from the *tonlieu* of the Ypres merchants, as well as a statement of appreciation from Thibaut for having left home and friends in order to serve the count in Troyes.[107] But such inclusive grants of exemption from all but justice were rare in the *bailliage* and were generally confined to the first decades of the thirteenth century.[108]

In sum, there were few genuine grants of franchise to individuals, and all were issued by the count. A few may have been granted in the twelfth century, but most of the extant examples come from the period of Thibaut's minority, the first two decades of the thirteenth century. As opposed to manumission and other transfers of rights over persons between lords, franchises were unilateral exemptions from personal taxes and inheritance restrictions granted to the recipients. When townsmen and merchants were involved, especially in marriage to women of the count, a substitute tax was imposed: it was more significant than the *taille* commutation often found in the countryside, since it replaced all claims and often military service as well. When loyal service was rewarded, annual revenues were added to the personal exemptions. Some men retained their charters for many years. Pierre Molventre, for example, one of the sworn men conducting the 1276/78 *Extenta* inquest of the count's domain in Pont-sur-Seine, still had his "franchise," for which he paid an annual 6 d. *de censu*.[109]   But there were few cases of individual franchise even at that date. Such grants were irrelevant after 1230-31 because the commune grants in the Champagne castellany towns covered most men of the count.[110]   Only the ecclesiastical and lesser lay lords who had never granted their men comparable privileges could still issue such exemptions after 1231, and in some cases they even borrowed the phrases of the count's grants. [111]

The obligations of *taille, mainmorte,* marriage restriction, and submission to the justice of a lord were universal and covered all tenants who did not possess written exemptions from their lords. Local administrative officials had their burdens alleviated while in office, but the basic claims on them remained. Emigration was effective in escaping a particular lord, at the expense of surrendering all claim to paternal lands, and there was probably even a hard-core group of *hospites* who never settled permanently, but most men were forced by economic necessity to acquire new tenancies and to accept new lords. Yet, inevitable as their ultimate subordination was, the very mobility of peasants was a serious threat to the landlords who strove to maintain some influence over a situation which they could not fully control. Saint-Pierre's charter of 1194 illustrates the variety of inducements available to landlords: the chapter exempted its men living in Troyes from *mainmorte* and extended the privilege also to newcomers who accepted its lordship there; but it excluded any of its men who without the chapter's permission had married women of the count, of the bishop, of Saint-Etienne, or of any other knight; and it further excluded its men who "deny us" (its lordship) and its men who had migrated to Troyes without permission in order to marry.[112]   The mobility of ordinary peasants seems to account for the way in which claims were made over them and their tenancies.

COMMUNITIES

Charter terminology of the late eleventh and early twelfth centuries, as noted above, was similar to that of the ninth: *villa* still meant "domain," a large landed estate with attached buildings and personnel under a lord's direct and unlimited control. In the first two decades of the twelfth century, however, the term was also used in a different sense: in 1117, for example, a papal act confirmed Montiéramey's churches in its *villa,* in the castle (*oppidum*) of Chappes, and in the town (*civitas*) of Troyes, terms that suggest precisely located built-up areas; another charter of that period refers to the inhabitants (*habitores*) of a *villa,* which is also closer to "village" than to "domain." [113] Certainly by the mid-twelfth century, *villa* was no longer identified with a lord's directly managed lands, which were often called *dominium,* but rather with the buildings and tenant plots at a specific locality. Henceforth, villages could be "built" and on occasion even destroyed. [114] But if *villa* became the accepted term for a population center, it did not reflect the size of the community, and it remains difficult to determine the size of particular *villae,* except in the few cases where that information can be extracted. A *villa* could be a hamlet of a few hearths, a castellany town of several hundred, or even Troyes itself, which had a population of about ten thousand. A partial remedy that permits a rough fix on village size is offered by the *Etat des bois* of ca. 1290, a list of all villages, with the number of hearths in each, that could use the count's woods near Troyes. Some eighty-four villages spread through three castellanies were recorded with their hearth numbers, and the nature of the document makes it the closest to a random sample of villages in the *bailliage* that can be expected. [115] Eighty-three percent of the villages had eighty or fewer hearths. The remaining 17 percent had one hundred or more hearths. Fully half of the villages had fewer than forty hearths each, so an average village population then would have numbered about two hundred persons. [116] If the sample is representative of the *bailliage* at the end of the thirteenth century, there was a great number of small villages, above which was a handful of small towns—the Champagne castellany centers of about two hundred hearths and about one thousand persons each— and the unique town of Troyes, which was the main urban center. [117]

The physical aspect of villages, the buildings and lands within their boundaries, were not necessarily coincidental with the communities of

Table 2
NUMBER OF HEARTHS IN SOME VILLAGES
NEAR TROYES, CA. 1290

No. of hearths	No. of villages	No. of hearths	No. of villages	No. of hearths	No. of villages
1–9	4	40–49	11	120	2
10–19	13	50	3	150–90	3
20–29	13	70–80	5	200	2
30–39	11	100	5	240	2

men whose activities in them were regulated in one way or another by their lords. Of course, many villages were under the exclusive control of a single lord, but these are the very types which seldom emerge because there are few disputes concerning their internal functioning recorded in ecclesiastical charters. Except in cases where lords issued written community franchises, villages under single lordships cannot be closely studied. Better known because of conflicts settled by written agreements are the villages shared by two lords, that is, villages which constituted multiple communities from the point of view of the lords and their tenants' obligations. The bilateral agreements between lords over the control of their respective men and rights are the best source for examining the organization and regulation of peasants in ordinary villages.

The earliest and one of the fullest descriptions of a twelfth-century village and community is given in the 1147 agreement between the abbey of Saint-Loup and the *dominus* of Charmont-sous-Barbuise. [118] The pact regulated in itemized clauses the respective claims of the abbey and the lord over persons and tenancies, and it is a rare charter in that it explains in concrete terms the control over tenure, rents, and administration in a small village (see map 4). Both parties recognized that Saint-Loup's lands were in its own domain (*in dominicatu*) and could not be tilled without its permission; but the common lands of the canons (*communes terras canonici*) could be rented by anyone (*homines*), including the lord of Charmont himself, for *terrage*. The abbey's agent (*minister*) and the lord's mayor (*major*) jointly handled any violence by tenants or petty thieves on these lands and were also empowered to reassign disputed holdings. Nonpayment or incomplete payment by anyone (*terragiator*) incurred a 2 s. fine payable to the abbot or his agent. Thus, the abbey's own lands were private and immune, but its common lands were open to all for rent and were policed jointly with the local lord. The abbey also had twenty-six house lots (*ochii*) available for a 4 s. rent and *terrage* for their associated lands; any tenant (*rusticus*) who failed to pay this rent or any other *cens* for possessions held from the abbey had to appear before its *curia* in Troyes. The lord was allowed to rent vacant lots only if no one else (that is, no other peasant) desired them. But one house lot with its inhabitant (*habitator*) was exempted from all banal regulations and justice (presumably the lord's); neither fugitives, nor thieves, nor persons guilty of false measure could be apprehended there, nor did the lord have any power (*dominium*) over it or its resident even if the latter were a newcomer (*albanus*) who had never come under the justice of Charmont. This lot was probably for the abbot's resident agent, whose immunity was necessary to keep him an effective representative of the abbey on the local level, especially in such proximity to the lord of

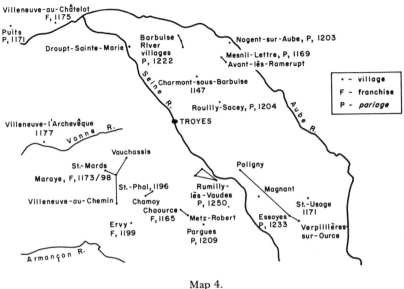

Map 4.
Villages, *Pariages*, and Franchises

Charmont. The abbey's nonresident agents from Troyes ("servientes canonicorum de pane eorum viventes") were also exempted from constraint and all legal claims by the lord, unless they were involved in theft or other openly detectable crime. The abbey's own men (*homines*) there were under the direct control of its mayor and could be summoned to appear at its court in Troyes for failure to make personal, customary, or rent payments. Whether these men lived on the abbey's direct domain or on the house lots is not clear, but they were under the lord of Charmont's justice in all other respects. Finally, intermarriage was permitted between men and women of the two parties; children and property were to be shared jointly. Newcomers (*albanus, albana femina*) were also allowed to settle and intermarry with the local residents, but the lord of Charmont had claims on them (*libertatem suam*) for their lives, though not over their children or personal possessions.

The picture of Charmont is of course incomplete because it omits the lord's own lands and men. How the settlement began is not revealed—perhaps it was originally a pious donation, since only the abbey's direct domain was fully immune from secular control—but it must have been very close to the lord's own lands and fortress, for sixteen years after the 1147 agreement the abbot's fears had materialized. Wearied because its agents "suffered and were no longer able to resist by force," Saint-Loup allowed the chapter of Saint-Etienne, which had "noble and more powerful persons," one-third of anything it could recover of

Saint-Loup's rights there. But even Saint-Etienne was not entirely successful, and the Charmont family continued its transgressions into the thirteenth century.[119] Nevertheless, the *villa* of Charmont of perhaps 100 to 125 persons emerges fairly clearly for this period. Except for the domain lands of the abbey and lay lord, tenancies and house lots were available to all persons for rent and *terrage*. Men were called variously *homo, terragiator,* and *rusticus,* all references to rural tenants without implication as to personal status. The obligations of men were mentioned only insofar as they were incurred by tenancy, and even the lord had to pay rents for lots which he occupied. Although rights of justice were carefully delineated, *taille, mainmorte,* and *formariage* were not mentioned by name.

Similar arrangements between lords in the later twelfth century were called "pacts" or "conventions." Essentially, they provided for the sharing of revenues, justice, and administration over particular villages. One of the earliest "pacts" was between the constable of Champagne, Eudes of Pougy, and the abbot of Montiéramey about 1169.[120] The two parties agreed to share the justice and *tailles* of all men in Mesnil-Lettre and Seloncourt and of the abbey's men at Avant-lès-Ramerupt; fines on the abbey's men anywhere else on the constable's lands were also to be divided. The administration of the two villages (the third was probably fully under the constable's control) was shared: the lords would select a mayor who would swear fidelity to both, but if each preferred his own mayor, then the two officials would act jointly in matters of justice and revenues and by mutual agreement (*communi consilio*) in all other decisions. The mayor(s) would be free (*liber;* "exempt from taxes") while in office. Although *tailles,* justice, and administration were shared through the mayors, all other customs, banal obligations, and tenurial revenues remained with their respective lords. Nor was there a question of commutation of any taxes or of privileges to the villagers. This joint community of two villages seems to have become fairly large and prosperous in the next century, for in 1225 the abbey purchased the other half of the *taille* and justice revenues of Mesnil-Lettre for 300 l.; if the sale price was the customary ten times the annual income, that village alone produced a 60 l. annual revenue.[121]

The agreement between the count and the abbot of Oyes is interesting because it was completed in two stages.[122] In 1171 the count gave the abbey half the village of Puits and the 100 s. annual revenue paid by twelve families; he kept the other half (and twelve other families). Henceforth, the two parties would share the justice, ban, and fines. Newcomers were required to commend themselves within one year and one day to one of the lords or be shared by both; villagers who had departed but had subsequently returned were also to be held in common by both lords. The count concluded the transaction by transferring several men to the abbey in order to balance his account of marriage exchanges, but this item was unrelated to the village sharing. Four years later another agreement regulated *tailles,* intermarriages, and the children of mixed marriages, who were divided in a unique fashion: the first born went to the father's lord, the second and third to the mother's, the fourth and fifth to the father's, and so on. A small village of only twenty-four families was bound to generate such problems under divided lordship, and the second charter corrected the oversight of the first by accommodating actual local problems. In spite of the lack of privileges to residents (women paid a 5 s. *taille;* men were taxed at will by their respective lords), the village attracted immigrants: in 1196 one local lord who had lost some men to the village attempted to recover his *formariage* and *mainmorte* over them.[123]

There were numerous bilateral agreements over persons and rights from the late twelfth century. They varied considerably in form, from brief notices in which each lord retained control over his own men while sharing nontenurial revenues to virtual treaties of complicated arrangements on the sharing of mayors, rights, and other revenues. [124] Usually the formal arrangements were not equal, since one lord already had greater rights in a particular area. For example, in the understanding between Montiéramey and the lord of Plancy over four villages on the Barbuise River,[125] all men were shared equally between the parties, but the abbot received a 4 d. rent (*pro chevagio*) from all houses in which one of his men resided, as well as one-third of all escheated movables of those who died without heirs at home and two-thirds of the tax paid for outside marriages. The lord of Plancy, however, retained what were to him the most important rights: justice, military service, plowing service, and *taille* over all men.

In one rare instance an exact parity was created between lords. In 1188 André, lord of Ramerupt, mortgaged his village of Nogent-sur-Aube, just across the river from Ramerupt, for seven years to Gautier, lord of Joigny, for 300 l. cash. Shortly thereafter André died, and at the term of the original transaction in 1195 Gautier sold the mortgage to Montiéramey for 300 l. plus 40 l. for the revenues.[126] Although the transfer itself was legitimate, there were some irregularities—crusaders had certain exemptions, and André's heir was still a minor at the time of the transfer—because in 1203 the abbey reached an agreement with André's successor, Erard, by which each would have half of the village.[127] Each party had its own lands, fields, a house with personal servants (*familia*), and up to twenty oxen and ten cows immune from the other. They had separate mayors, but the mayors had to give oaths of fidelity (*fidelitatem per juramentum*) to both and promise to act in common when taking *tailles* and fines, in exercising justice, and in holding court (*placitum*). All revenues from *terrage,* tithe, justice, and *taille* were shared equally, neither lord having more *dominium* than the other. The two mayors jointly handled all cases of theft and physical assault in the village, and if they were unable to agree on a particular disposition, the abbot and the lord would decide the case. The mayors were not given more privileges and exemptions (*libertate*) than other villagers and were explicitly subjected to *taille*, justice, and other "services and customs." Immigration was allowed to men of both parties from other villages, and newcomers were to be shared by both lords. If one of their men married and took away a woman of this village, an exchange of a woman of equal value would adjust their accounts. Finally, villagers were free to use the mill and oven of either lord. Nogent had been an ordinary village under the sole lordship of the Ramerupt family until 1188, but even the shared lordship imposed in 1203 did nothing to change the structure of the community; only the disposition of the revenues and the selection of local administrators were affected. The 40 l. annual revenue produced by this one village would have made a very respectable fief even by mid-thirteenth-century standards, and the abbey must have appreciated the solid basis of such an income, for in 1248 it purchased the other half of the village. Nogent returned to the control of a single lord, now an ecclesiastical one. [128]

In the thirteenth century a standard formula was devised whereby one party, usually an ecclesiastical institution, "associated" another lord, usually the count(ess), in authority over a particular locality. Because of the sharing principle these arrangements have come to be known as *pariages*. [129] But whether they were framed as formal partnerships or simply as settlements to disputes, they all dealt with the same problems of organization and control of peasant communities. In 1233, for example, Molesme associated the count in authority over the villages of Essoyes, Verpillières-sur-Ource, and Poligny. [130] Justice and revenues from all sources (fines, *tailles,* commuted *tailles,* escheats) and all "exactions" were shared equally. The resident *prévôt* swore to both parties and also promised to render to each one-half of the revenues, which amounted to 60 l. from those sources in 1276. [131] If the *prévôté* were sold, each party would instead receive half of the purchase price. Every newcomer (*novus*) had to swear fidelity to both lords, presumably through the *prévôt*. Although the abbey's men were allowed to immigrate and settle in these villages under the abbot's sole control, the count's men who immigrated here were to be shared by both parties. The abbey also retained its *corvées* and certain "customs" for the maintenance of its lands. Finally, the count agreed to limit his calls to military service to one day so that the men could return home the next. Molesme, like other abbeys, may have been pursuing a deliberate policy of association with the count over certain villages, for it made the same arrangements in 1250 for Rumilly-lès-Vaudes and nine other villages, one of which had two hundred hearths in 1276. [132]

The bilateral pacts in the twelfth century and the *pariages* in the thirteenth both reveal ordinary villages in the *bailliage* that for one reason or another came under joint lordship. The villagers, however, were not part of the agreements. They continued to pay their *tailles* and customary local taxes, in addition to tenurial rents, and were subjected to local bans and often to labor obligations on the domain lands of their lords. Marriage restrictions were also in force, although mixed marriages were arranged by their lords. Since the men of each lord formed a distinct community, jointly administered villages required either two mayors or one who represented both lords to their men. Village officials were delegated considerable responsibility, including judging, fining, and tax and rent collecting, all accomplished without the close supervision of the lord and for which those officials were usually rewarded with exemptions. The agreements, in short, were solely between lords for the sharing of control and revenues of peasant communities. The arrangements did not modify the internal organization of those communities, nor did they confer privileges or other "liberties" upon the inhabitants themselves.[133] With the possible exception of Charmont and a few other cases, there is no indication that it was the encroachment by laymen on ecclesiastical lands that forced the abbeys to sacrifice half their revenues to usurpers for the sake of peace.[134] In Puits it was the count who first granted half his village before joint control was arranged, and in Nogent-sur-Aube the Rame-rupt heir was fortunate in securing even half the revenues and control of the village which his father had mortgaged, for there are few examples of laymen ever repossessing property once surrendered to an ecclesiastical institution. In fact, the ecclesiastical houses were themselves probably responsible for substantial emigration by their policy of open acceptance of most men into their communities, thereby forcing lay lords to formalize procedures for the control of migrants.[135] Most of the agreements narrowed to the sharing of two basic rights: nontenurial revenues and control of the key resident official. Problems related strictly to tenancy were of course left to the respective landlords. It was the lords' claims over nontenurial obligations which were confounded by the physical mobility of peasants through emigration and marriage and which required the *pariages*.

THE *COUTUMIER*

The *Coutumier* is a late-thirteenth-century collection of statements about Champagne "customs" in current usage and of legal decisions, mostly by the Jours of Troyes in the last three decades of the century.

The collation seems to have been a private one for the convenience of rural landlords, and neither the decisions nor the customs, which are simply affirmed, were collated systematically.[136] The society of the *Coutumier* was tripartite, consisting of *noble, franc* (or *borgeois*) and *home de poest. Franc* men, however, were mentioned only insofar as they were involved in property transactions or marriages with the other two groups, and it is clear that the *Coutumier* did not intend to portray relationships among all social groups but only those between "nobles" and their tenant-subjects; that is, it recorded the basic principles by which persons and properties were controlled by the great lords in the countryside outside the Champagne (later royal) domain.[137]

Tenants were called variously *home de poest (poté), home de mainmorte,* and "man of *mainmorte* and of *taille.*"[138] They were said to be identified by three characteristics: *aages, mainmorte,* and marriage (restriction).[139] Although *aages* was not defined and in this context is unique, in other decisions it meant "coming of age," and it would be reasonable to identify it here with the obligation of paying a tax on reaching a certain age or status, in short, *taille.*[140] Moreover, since *taille* was routinely linked with *mainmorte* in other articles but was not itself discussed in the *Coutumier,* it would seem that *aages* was a way of saying "tailleable." But if *taille,* being simply a head-tax, needed little elaboration, *mainmorte,* the control over property transfers, was more complicated and required detailed regulations. A lord (*sire*) could claim *mainmorte* (or escheat)[141] of movables and real estate (*heritage*) of his tenants who died without natural heirs living at home.[142] He could appropriate land only, and not personal possessions, thereby avoiding liability for a man's debts (tenants could not use their tenancies as collateral for loans). The lord could not, however, keep escheated lands beyond one year and one day; he was required to regrant them to someone of the same "condition" as the original tenant, for he could not "hold them for himself."[143] This emphasis on the equivalence between the respective status of a tenant and his tenancy was a central principle behind many *Coutumier* articles, and it was enforced by the overlords who desired to protect the fiefs held from them from diminution of lands and personnel.[144] The overlord's permission was required for the abolition or commutation of *taille* or *mainmorte*; should the direct lord alone sell or commute either to an *abonament,* the overlord could transfer the tenant involved (that is, his lands) directly into his own domain and reimpose the former "servitude" of *taille* and *mainmorte* because the direct lord had caused a "decrease of fief."[145] An equally serious threat to the identity of land and tenant status was from the enfranchised townsmen. For example, in 1284, when two townsmen of Troyes purchased houses and lands in two villages from tailleable and mainmortable men of Erard of Arcis-sur-Aube without his permission, it was decided that the latter as overlord could reclaim the property even after the normal one year and one day limit because the consent of the overlord (*sire sovereign*) as well as that of the direct lord (*sire*) was required before the tenant could transfer property to franchised persons ("persones franchises par point de chartre").[146]

Marriages between tenants and persons of other conditions also caused difficulties in the countryside by breaking the identity in status of men and land. A decision of 1295 declared that if a nonfranchised woman married a *franc* man who died without heirs, she would enjoy the "advantage of his franchise" and remain free for her lifetime; but if she remarried, this time to an *home de poest,* who also died before her, she would then revert to her former *servitude.*[147] In practice, the franchised man probably paid his wife's *taille* as a commutation, which she was allowed to continue as long as she did not remarry someone of tailleable condition.[148] Such complications between franchised and nonfranchised persons could be readily resolved by some form of payment for commutation of claims. But there was one serious challenge which brought personal and tenurial status into a diametrical and irreconcilable opposition that could not be accommodated by a single payment: the marriage of a man without franchise to a "noble" woman. An undated decision of the Jours provided that the overlord of a woman who did marry such a man did not have to accept her low-born husband's homage for her fief, although he could if he wished. After the woman's death, her fief reverted to the overlord, and her children were disinherited; they lapsed into the "lower condition" of their father and became liable for *taille* and *mainmorte.*[149] The decision suggests, however, that the children assumed that status only if they accepted their father's property, which required a tenant of his status.[150] The fate of the children who did not assume the paternal inheritance is not clear; since they had no claim to their mother's fief, they could migrate and receive land from another lord, either in fief or in peasant tenancy, or settle in a town. But as far as their mother's overlord was concerned, the important point was that he was not compelled to accept a low-born fief holder. The assimilation of a peasant woman and a "noble" male fief holder was probably easier, since the fief of a man was not threatened by his wife's own status, and the *Coutumier* ignores the matter entirely. Thus, although intermarriage between the highest and lowest "conditions" was not prohibited outright, the practical limitations were most severe on a woman marrying below her condition, for her lands (inheritance and dowry) were denied to her children. Obviously, the ultimate justification for the separation of peasants and nobles was the two different legal systems by which their properties were controlled.

An *home de poest* was defined as *justicauble,* that is, "in the justice" of a landlord. If a tenant held properties from several lords, he could choose the justice of the lord under whom he had his main residence.[151] He had no recourse to outside courts (he could be "extradited" by his own lord and fined 60 s.). He could not appeal to his overlord except in cases of "default of law" or "bad judgment" by his direct lord; if such an appeal was sustained by the overlord, the tenant was released from the control of his direct lord, but if he lost the case, he also lost all his possessions.[152] Of course, emigration was always a solution for unbearable local conditions, but that meant sacrificing ancestral lands and other property. And ultimately, no peasant could escape his status or "condition" by emigration, for the *Coutumier* defined the custom that any stranger (*aubain*) living in a lordship for one year and one day had to become *home de poest* of that lord or become by default a man of the count.[153] In short, it was impossible to escape low-born status except by a single mechanism, the written franchise from one's landlord. As it is stated in the *Coutumier*: "It is the custom in Champagne that a man cannot have his franchise or be called free unless he has been granted a letter [of franchise] or privileges by his lord."[154]

The *Coutumier,* then, portrays a rigid, hierarchical social system based on the identity of personal status with tenurial status. In the countryside there were two mutually exclusive tenure systems, one based on fiefs held by "nobles," the other embracing all tenancies held by peasants. The overlords had ultimate authority over both fief and peasant tenancies, and they enforced the exclusion principle, which was more easily overlooked by direct lords closer to local situations, who were also probably more swayed by immediate financial returns. The inferior status of the peasant was formalized by the obligations of *taille, mainmorte,* and marriage restrictions that were imposed on all tenancies under the justice of overlords. The only accepted mechanism for the change of status and concomitant obligations was the written franchise, of which very few examples are known. The *Coutumier* confirms the evidence from charters and *pariages* that reveals the all-encompassing obligation system weighing on tenants, no matter where they migrated. Yet the *Coutumier*'s principles were not necessarily applicable on the count's domain, which represented a great collection of lands and persons in the *bailliage,* including the most populous communities and their districts. Moreover, the implicit assumption of the *Coutumier* that townsmen were franchised was possible only at the end of the thirteenth century, after community franchises had been granted to the count's townsmen.

III
Franchised Communities

Most private charters, the *pariages,* and the *Coutumier* are records of claims by landlords over property, rights, and persons; consequently they portray generally uniform and well-defined social and tenurial conditions for tenants who were not fief holders or ecclesiastics. In spite of the physical mobility of peasants, the prerequisites of land tenure resulted in the eventual submission of all tenants to the control and taxation of some landlord. Although administrative personnel and immigrants enjoyed temporary respite from tenurial and concomitant obligations, only the very few individuals who had secured written franchises from their lords were distinguished by their privileges from the general population.

Such an image of rural society is incomplete, for it omits the numerous residents of franchised communities. In their strictest form, charters of community franchises were simply confirmations of specific exemptions and privileges (such as *taille* and *mainmorte* exemptions), some of which had been granted individually on occasion by lay and ecclesiastical lords to their tenants in certain villages. But the communitywide grants had an impact on the very organization of society, for in effect they created territorial enclaves in which the sum of the privileges and exemptions conferred a new tenurial and social status on the residents. The significance of community franchises for the development of society in the *bailliage* has been underestimated, in spite of the good texts available, because of the almost exclusive attention devoted to the communal charter of Troyes (1230). The preoccupation with Troyes both as county capital and as fair town, although understandable, has resulted in a distorted perception of conditions in the surrounding *bailliage,* as well as in Troyes itself.[1] Communal features lasted only ten years in Troyes, but they continued for several hundred years in other towns which had received identical grants at the same time. Furthermore, the abstraction of Troyes and its commune from the *bailliage* context masks the fact that some rural communities had enjoyed greater "liberties" than most men in Troyes until its grant. The count granted most of the community franchises in the *bailliage,* and his communities, both rural and urban, were the most important economic and population centers of the area. His acts, therefore, were especially significant for the evolution of conditions in the *bailliage* as a whole.

THE TWELFTH CENTURY

There is no evidence of franchises having been granted to entire communities before the 1170s.[2] One of the earliest extant grants is to Chaource and its associated village of Metz-Robert in 1175 (see map 4). Chaource was a *villa* with lands and dependent personnel (*mancipii*) when Count Robert of Troyes acquired it from Charles the Bald in the ninth century; some lands there were also acquired by Montiéramey by the end of the ninth century, when it complained about violations against its men (*homines*).[3] Nothing further is known about Chaource or Metz-Robert until the 1175 "convention" by which the count freed all men living in the two villages from *taille* and all other "exaction" (*exactione*, which probably meant *formariage* and *mainmorte*).[4] Residents were exempted from *péage* and *tonlieu* on his lands, and they were free to sell their property and depart at will, that is, without tax. They were not liable for military service (*nec in exercitum nec in expeditionem*) unless the count or his personal representative appeared to lead them, and the (resident) *prévôt* of the count could exact local service (*ad submonitionem*) only to a distance from which they could return home in the evening. The *prévôt* was also responsible for justice, but a schedule of fines was established in order to prevent abuses: following the customs of Lorris, 5 s. was the fine for any offense (*forisfactum*) assessed at 60 s.; 12 d. for one assessed at 5 s.; and 4 d. for appeal (*clamor plenus*) to the *prévôt*.[5] For all these privileges the men paid 12 d. and one *mine* of oats annually.

In return for the modest residence tax, the Chaource grant effectively abolished the head tax and restrictions on marriage and property transfers, as well as the uncertainties associated with the administration of justice and military service. The community would obviously attract men from less privileged lordships, so the count protected the interests of the local landlords by prohibiting the immigration of tenants of knights in the six neighboring castellanies,[6] although not of men coming from the south (Burgundy). Immigrants could be claimed by their lords if proved to have been *de corpore* by the oaths of two knights and four villagers; this was the sole proof, and neither court decision nor duel could replace it. The check on local immigration must have been weak in practice, for a landlord was required to come to Chaource with two knights and to secure in addition the oaths of four residents. Violent confrontations were no doubt anticipated, for the count stated that the resident *prévôt* would guarantee the "liberties" of the villagers against encroachments by local knights.[7] However, the franchise neglected to protect Montiéramey's interests as it did those of lay lords, and two years later, in 1177, the abbot managed to secure the count's agreement to a new charter which isolated the abbey's own men from the influence of the privileged villages.[8] Ostensibly a joint venture in creating a *villa nova* of the two villages already enfranchised, the charter was in fact a *pariage* designed to protect the abbey's own interests without modifying the 1175 franchise to the villagers. The abbey's men were no longer allowed to settle there and share the privileges of the villages without the consent of the abbot; they were, however, exempted from all "service" to the count's *prévôt*. The abbey retained full claim to its tithes and ovens, had complete authority (*potestas*) over its domestics (*famuli et ancillae*), and affirmed the inviolability of its own lands, even for fugitives (they would be tried by the abbot's court). It also secured half of the count's revenues from justice and customs in the franchised villages, and its own *prévôt* was allowed to act jointly with the count's *prévôt* there in exercising justice.[9] The arrangement must have been profitable to the abbey because in 1209 it made a similar arrangement with the count over its village of Pargues, just six kilometers south of Chaource.[10]

Chaource retained its franchise through the thirteenth century, and a copy of the grant was appended to the 1276/78 inquest on the count's domain, the *Extenta terre*.[11] The residence tax was the same 12 d., but by then residents without draft animals were not liable for the grain payment. The residence tax was originally conceived as a standard hearth tax, but by 1276 there were a number of men without their own homes who were specifically made liable for the full tax, *pour franchise*, as were those who enjoyed the privileges of being *bourgeois* without actually residing there (*qui tient la bourgeoise dehors*). The total residence tax of 30 l. and 18 *modii* of grain accounts for about 600 men, of whom 432 (72 percent) had draft animals; the rest were probably full-time artisans and merchants, the very poor, and the nonresident members. Although essentially agrarian, this two-village community of about five hundred hearths was one of the largest of its kind in the *bailliage* by the end of the thirteenth century and also one of the most productive in revenues.[12]

A similar franchise by the count was issued to Maraye-en-Othe in 1173 and extended in 1198 to its associated villages (*villarum appendencium*) of Saint-Mards-en-Othe, Villeneuve-au-Chemin, and Vauchassis, all in the heart of the Othe Forest.[13] Villagers were exempted from *taille* and other personal taxes and from *péage* and *tonlieu* on county lands. They received a fixed schedule of fines and were free to leave the community at will. The residence tax was 12 d. and one *mine* of oats. There were no provisions for membership, which was presumably open to all, or for military service, which probably remained at the discretion of the local *prévôt*. One hundred years later the four villages numbered together over fifteen hundred persons: the central village of Maraye had

240 hearths, Villeneuve had 120, and Vauchassis 12.[14] That the franchise did in fact create new conditions which were zealously guarded by the community is shown by the unique *Extenta* entry in 1276/78 for the count's rights at Maraye: it states that the count had "nothing in his domain there, neither in lands, ovens, mills, market, *tonlieu, péage, mainmorte,* nor in any other claim except what was included in the franchise of the community," which was accordingly appended.[15] The count retained justice, of course, but the villagers had purchased all but high justice as a *prévôté* which they held in farm for 40 l. Maraye also must have had its own internal administration by that date because the count's officials had no business there except for cases of high justice. Unfortunately, there are no details on how villagers conducted their internal affairs.

The *Extenta* contains an unusually detailed description of the villagers of one of these four associated communities, Villeneuve-au-Chemin (120 hearths).[16] Four *enquêteurs* (the resident *prévôt,* two sergeants, and one villager) noted that Villeneuve shared the franchise of Saint-Mards by which each man paid 12 d., *ratione burgensie;* but the original one *mine* of oats was collected now, as in Chaource, only from those with draft animals. The villagers also held in farm from the count all nontenurial revenues, including low justice, for 170 l. The *Extenta* then lists by name sixty-five persons—half the village—who held property from the count and the amount of their rents.[17] The highest rents were paid by the Hôtel-Dieu (6 s. 4 d.) and the *prévôt's* widow (3 s. 9 d.); only ten of the sixty-five persons paid over 2 s. for rent, and the average was 12 d. The village was still essentially rural at the end of the thirteenth century (only four persons of the sixty-five were identified by economic or administrative specialization), yet the residents, no matter how poor, were considered "burgesses" and had enjoyed from 1198 privileges, including *taille* exemption, which many men of Troyes did not acquire until 1230.

Chaource and Maraye and their associated villages had existed as communities before their franchises were granted, so the charters' claims that they were "new" villages was simply a way of saying that the institutions provided by the franchises were new. An example of a village that was actually created new by its franchise (its location was "between" Pont and Perigny-la-Rose) is Villeneuve-au-Châtelot. Its "customs," meaning here the essential procedures by which the new community was to be administered, were defined by the count in 1175.[18] Most provisions are similar to those of other franchises granted to preexisting villages in that period. Each resident paid the 12 d. and one *mine* of oats *pro hostitia,* as well as 4 d. rent (*de censu*) for each *arpent* of land that he cleared. Residents were free to sell and dispose of property and were exempted from *péage* and *tonlieu* on the count's lands. They were not liable for military service unless the count appeared in person. The newness of Villeneuve-au-Châtelot is particularly revealed by the clauses which controlled violence: since there was no resident *prévôt*—the nearest one with responsibility for this village resided at Pont—there were two long regulations concerning duels and violence on market days.[19] And a completely novel feature was the creation of an internal administration: six *scabini* were to deal with community affairs and were entitled to sit on the *prévôt*'s plea. The manner of selecting these officials was not stated, but by 1276 they had been replaced by a single *prévôt* elected by the community; he received the oaths of new members and in return gave his own, for "by his oath he was to be trusted."[20] This village was created to attract immigrants to clear the forest, and therefore an especially strong guarantee for newcomers was included: neither knights nor any other person could take a villager away under the guise of prior obligations or contracts, unless the man involved was proved to be *homo de corpore* of the claimant and to have been held in "ancient and tailleable commendation."[21] Villeneuve is the only example in extant documents of the creation of a physically new village with the issuance of a franchise charter; all other franchises were to preexisting villages. In 1276 its "customs" of 1175 were called a "franchise" by county officials.[22]

The community franchises were granted by Count Henry I in the 1170s, the same years that saw the appearance of the first inventory of the count's fief holders, the *Feoda Campanie*, and the last decade of his rule. His successor Henry II never attended closely to Champagne affairs, and only in the brief reign of Thibaut III (1197–1201) did the count's interest return to community franchises and to administration in general (new registers of the *Feoda* were also planned). In the *bailliage* Thibaut extended the Maraye franchise to its associated villages in 1198, and in 1199 he granted a franchise to the castellany town of Ervy. This grant is unique in that it is an abbreviated form of the customs of Lorris, the only such example in the *bailliage*. Moreover, it was for a county castellany center, the only one to receive a franchise in any form before the communal charters of 1230. A possible explanation for this anomaly is that the counts held only half of the town and castellany of Ervy until the late 1190s; the other half was held by the lords of Ervy. It would seem that Thibaut III, the first count to hold the entire town and castellany, reissued a charter granted originally by the Ervy lords to their own men and extended it now to all residents.[23] In any case, the franchise of 1199 applied to all men of the count living within the castellany of Ervy at that time and to all newcomers (*albani*) who lived in the township of Ervy.[24] They paid a residence tax of 6 d. for a house and one *arpent* of land, and those who tilled lands within the town limits with their own plows paid an additional one *mine* of grain, but never more. They enjoyed the usual exemption from *tonlieu,* regulation of fines, protection at market, and freedom to sell property and depart at will, but here the count retained *mainmorte* on those who died without heirs. A man's oath carried great weight in legal matters: if he were accused and had no (favorable) witnesses, he could clear himself by his own oath (*per solam manum se deculpabit*), and he could not be held pending trial if he promised to appear for judgment. The count, of course, still had ultimate authority over the community through his *prévôt* and still required military service whenever he deemed necessary. In 1276 the *Extenta* reported that the franchised men there paid a 2 s. residence tax (up from the original 6 d.) and that those who farmed with animals also paid in grain.[25] The community comprised 155 members, although the actual town population was probably larger, as there were men of ecclesiastical houses who did not enjoy the franchise. Nevertheless, 77 (50 percent) of the 155 still farmed with their own animals, and Ervy retained the rural aspect of the communities which received comparable franchises in the late twelfth century. In fact, Ervy owed its importance to being a frontier toll station for the Champagne fairs: in 1276 its *péage* of 300 l. was the largest of its kind in the *bailliage.*

Extant texts of twelfth-century franchises exist for only a handful of communities in the *bailliage.* The grants, all from the count, were similar: *taille* was abolished, and residents could freely sell their property and leave the communities; tolls on their goods for personal consumption were lifted on county lands; judicial fines were standardized; and newcomers were openly accepted. In short, arbitrary personal claims were replaced by a small residence tax, and blatant local administrative abuses were checked. The count, however, was still the lord and retained ultimate authority, especially in justice and military service, through his resident *prévôt.* All franchised communities were on the Champagne domain, in forested areas yet to be cleared; chronologically they followed the last major Cistercian foundation in the *bailliage* (Sellières, 1168). That franchises were not granted earlier was probably due to the lack of a definite policy to control demographic and economic development; that they were not granted under Henry II and not for a full generation after 1199 was due to neglect of home affairs by Henry and to the troubled political situation during Thibaut IV's minority.[26]

Both the community franchises and the *pariages* were in effect responses by landlords to the increased physical mobility of tenants through migration and intermarriage, and both, despite their different forms and purposes, contributed to the same community development. By creating uniform obligations for all local inhabitants, no matter who their lords, they reinforced community organization based on residence instead of personal relationship. Whereas the *pariages* merely accommodated physical mobility by adjusting the various landlords' claims over persons, property, and revenues, the franchises represented a deliberate policy to exploit the great movement of persons already under way by attracting them to specific localities with favorable privileges. Also, the count's franchises, unlike the *pariages* and other agreements between lords, were innovative acts that created new "customs" sanctioned by his authority, and they conferred actual privileges on their recipients. Once granted, however, the franchises became fixed customs, and when inserted into the *Extenta* one hundred years later, they remained as valid as when originally issued. Yet in 1200, only a small minority of all *bailliage* inhabitants, whether on the count's domain or on private lordships, had been granted such privileges.

THE COMMUNES OF 1230-31

The three decades of political instability and violence that marked the minority and early rule of Thibaut IV formed the background to the communal charters of 1230-31. The terms of the 1190 agreement among the Champagne barons provided for the succession of Thibaut III when his brother Henry II died in Jerusalem in 1197, but Thibaut's own untimely death at the age of twenty-one in 1201 produced an unanticipated situation and created the succession crisis which engulfed all Champagne for a generation. Difficulties must have developed at the start of Blanche's regency, although there are few details of exactly what was happening in that first decade. Her query to Geoffroy of Villehardouin and Milo Breban (ca. 1205) concerning specifically the status of the counts of Blois and Sancerre indicates that trouble was developing among even the closest relatives.[27] Although Blanche was under the guardianship of King Philip, in 1209 she had to purchase for 15,000 l. a guarantee that no legal challenge to her son's claim would be considered before he had reached twenty-one years of age.[28] There must have been considerable behind-the-scenes maneuvering throughout the period, but a full-scale crisis was averted until 1213, when the cardinal legate and several Champagne barons declared openly for young Thibaut. In 1214 the king, the archbishops of Reims and Sens, the bishops of Langres, Châlons, and Autun, the duke of Burgundy, and the count of Nevers all accepted Thibaut's homage for Champagne lands held from them; other lords followed suit shortly thereafter, confirming in fact Thibaut's control of Champagne lands and hence his succession.[29] Hostilities erupted in 1215, but the Brienne (Ramerupt) forces were temporarily checked by two important assemblies. In

Lateran IV the pope elicited the support of the powerful Champagne prelates, who thereafter maintained a veritable barrage of condemnations, excommunications, and interdicts until Thibaut's opponents had finally ceased hostilities.[30] In 1216 the king called the French barons to an assembly at Meaux, where it was decided that Thibaut could not be dispossessed of lands for which he had given homage.[31] In spite of the official sanctions, violence continued until a truce was arranged in 1218, and in 1219 several of the Brienne faction took an honorable exit from a hopeless situation by departing for the East. Insecurity in the *bailliage* continued, for as late as 1220 a *prévôt* of the countess of Joigny refused to enter Thibaut's lands without a written safeguard. [32] Only in 1222, when Thibaut came of age, was the conflict dissipated, and Brienne and his wife gave up their claims in return for a large rent in the same year.[33] But young Thibaut's problems did not end, for he soon complicated Champagne's politics with his escapades involving the regent queen of France and his cavalier treatment of the other French barons. When the latter finally organized a league and attacked him in 1229, he was virtually isolated, and the entire southern part of the *bailliage* was easily ravaged by the invaders.[34] Aubri of Trois-Fontaines reported that the count of Bar-le-Duc alone burned seven hundred villages and that Thibaut burned his own villages in order to deny them to the enemy.[35] It was indeed a strange predicament for a count of Champagne—one of the most powerful princes in the late twelfth century—to be without allies and incapable of defending his own lands.

The *bailliage* of Troyes was the geographical focus for both the internal conflicts in the second decade and the external ones in the third. The county of Brienne bordered on the eastern edge of the *bailliage,* and the Brienne challengers had their strongest support in southern Champagne. Moreover, the invaders of 1229 caused their greatest destruction in the same region, especially in the urban areas on the count's domain. Shortly after the French armies departed in the summer of 1230, Thibaut issued communal franchises to some of his towns as reward for loyal services rendered (Saint-Florentin and Bar-sur-Seine, at least, had been severely damaged) and to redress what must have been excessive wartime taxation. The extant charters issued to four of the ten castellany centers in the *bailliage* in the fall of 1230 and the spring of 1231 are virtually identical. Those for Troyes (September 1230) and Saint-Florentin (May 1231) applied to the count's men living within those townships (*finage*), while those for Villemaur and Bar-sur-Seine (both June 1231) included men in both the towns and their surrounding castellanies. The charter of Troyes was the prototype, and all four grants cover the same points in identical phrasing. Only the values of the *prévôté* "farms" and a few uniquely local points are different.[36]

The count "franchised" all his men and women living in the four towns and in two of their castellanies, and he prohibited men on his other domainal lands from immigrating to share the privileges without his express consent. He also denied entrance without his permission (as overlord) to men on Champagne fiefs and on lands under his guard; men who did immigrate, claiming to have his permission when in fact they did not, were granted fifteen days safe-conduct in which to leave. All other men were allowed to join the franchised communities; and if they decided not to stay, they too had fifteen days in which to depart under the count's safe-conduct.

The franchises of 1230-31 in their narrowest sense abolished *taille* and personal taxes (specified as *mainmorte* in the Saint-Florentin text) over the count's men in these areas. In return, the men paid a property tax at the rate of 2 d. per pound value of real estate (*heritage*) and 6 d. per pound value of movables, excluding clothes and household furniture, but including gold and silver utensils, especially wine cups. In effect, arbitrary *taille* and inheritance restrictions were converted into a standard-rate tax on wealth. This provision was the one innovation of 1230-31 that was never modified in any town thereafter. The tax was collected by the mayor and the twelve *jurée* (local townsmen chosen each year by the count) on the basis of self-assessments by each member of the community on oath. Anyone accused of false declaration could clear himself by another oath, which the tax collectors could believe "according to their good conscience." Anyone who paid a straight 20 l. tax was exempted from "oath and assessment of that year."

The franchises also covered several specific areas of past conflicts and abuses. The count guaranteed unrestricted commercial transactions, including the buying and selling of land, a source of possible contention with rural landlords. He promised assistance to any townsman arrested for any reason, and he would reimburse in full anyone seized by his own creditors. Several clauses concerned wartime conditions, still fresh in the minds of most townsmen (the count's army had assembled in Troyes in 1229 to meet the attack of the French barons). Although the count retained his right to military service (*ost et chevauchée*), he promised not to abuse it; he would not require service except when necessary (*fors que par mon besoin*). Men who paid a tax of 20 l. or more were expected to keep a crossbow and fifty arrows at home. Those over sixty years of age were exempted from service but were encouraged to send a substitute if they could afford one. If a call-up occurred during fair time, the merchants and moneychangers essential to the conduct of the fairs were required to send replacements. The count also promised not to use military requisitioning as an occasion to despoil his debtors: all requisitions for horses and wagons were to be arranged by the mayor, who would pay in coin from the count's own rents.

Such extensive exemptions from personal taxes and regulations of local abuses were, of course, sufficiently important privileges to have embodied in a charter from the count. But the grants of 1230–31 went further by providing internal self-administration for the townsmen, under the count's ultimate authority. The count or his representative (the "receiver" later in the century[37]) each year would select thirteen men of each community who would have fifteen days in which to elect one of themselves as mayor; or, if they could not agree, the count himself would choose the mayor. The twelve men and the mayor would then "swear on the Scriptures that they will preserve my [the count's] right and that of the community of [in this case] Troyes and [that] they will govern the town [vile] and the affairs of the town in good faith."[38] The thirteen were known collectively as the jurée, the sworn.

How the jurée "governed" the town and its "affairs" was not fully explained, but two functions in particular were stressed. One major duty was tax collecting. On the Feast of Saint Andrew (November 30) the jurée collected the wealth tax of 6 d. and 2 d. on the self-assessed value of all members of the community. Anyone suspected by three of the collectors of not declaring his full worth could clear himself by oath, but in no case was there to be a fine (for false declaration). The second basic function of the jurée was the judging of civil and minor criminal cases involving townsmen. Each community held in farm the "prévôté and justice" (that is, minor justice) of its town and of the lands and vineyards within the township. This meant that the jurée judged and then kept the fines levied in all cases involving members of the community (li borgois), temporary residents, and strangers. The count received 20 s. of the fixed 60 s. fine for false measure, anything over 20 s. imposed on a stranger (estrenge), and the entire fine on the victor of a duel; and in all cases the jurée was to set fines according to the local custom. The count reserved to himself only high justice—over murder, rape, and larceny, no matter where they were committed—and the "justice and guard" of "my churches, my knights, my fief holders, and my Jews." Disputes involving any of these would be heard in his own court, and the fines would also be his, though again the fines would be determined by the respective jurées in accordance with local custom. Townsmen were also promised that in cases involving their properties, judgment would be rendered within their own towns; cases would not be transferred outside unless the count himself were personally involved, but even then judgment would be in accordance with local usage.

In short, the count granted his men considerable independence in local affairs through the mayor and the jurée. The significance of the *jurée* as an administrative institution is, not that it was a collection of specific privileges or revenues, but rather that it was an open-ended form of municipal self-government in all matters not explicitly reserved to the count. The *jurée* was the constitutive element of the communes (both *comune* and *communeté* were used in the texts) and distinguished these franchises and their communities from all others.[39] The mayor and the *jurée*, being responsible both to their fellow townsmen and to the count, were granted sufficient authority to carry out their duties. Their judgment in legal cases was not to be questioned, and in the event of a bad decision (*jugement que ne fust soffisanz*) the matter was merely to be brought to the attention of the count; under no circumstances were the members to be fined. The *jurée* was completely responsible for tax collecting, although the count could send an overseer during the actual collection of the wealth tax. They also collected the *prévôté* revenues, mostly the fines that they themselves imposed in court judgments, which they held in farm from the count for a fixed annual sum. Previously, a *prévôt* of the count farmed these revenues, but since he kept the very fines that he imposed, there were many abuses in spite of the strict guidelines laid down in 1201 for all Champagne *prévôts*.[40] In effect, the *prévôté* was purchased by each community as a farm to be administered by its own officials, the *jurée*.

As a corporate person the *jurée* never died, and unfinished business and debts at the end of one term were passed on to the incoming thirteen men. This proved the undoing of the commune of Troyes, which accumulated so many debts in the 1230s without any mechanism of liquidation that it failed as a viable financial organization in 1240. When the count reissued the charter to Troyes in 1242, he did not mention the *jurée*, the *comune*, or the judgments and fines (that is, the *prévôté*), although all other personal and property privileges of the original 1230 grant remained intact.[41] Only the institution of the *jurée*—the commune—was eliminated. Henceforth, the wealth tax would be collected by twelve "men," in lieu of the *jurée*, on oath and under supervision of a sergeant of the count. With the loss of its *jurée*, Troyes also lost all right of self-administration, including justice and its concomitant *prévôté* revenues; in the *Extenta* of 1276/78 its *prévôté* was held in farm by a private person directly from the count. The three other communities which did retain their communes continued to hold their own *prévôtés* in farm, administered by their *jurées*, as provided in the original franchises.[42]

In its second sense, *jurée* was a technical term that referred to the specific method of tax assessment and collection prescribed in the original franchises of 1230-31, that is, the 2 d. and 6 d. rate collected on the sworn self-assessment of each man's worth. The *Extenta* states that "the count has *jurée* from his men" (*habet ibi dominus juream in hominibus suis*). The count's men of Troyes, although they had lost their commune in 1240, retained this method of taxation. The *Extenta* listed the *jurée* revenue from Troyes in the same manner as it did those of the communities which still had communes: the *jurée* as a method of taxation survived long after the *jurée* as an institution of thirteen municipal officials had failed. The *Extenta*, it will be recalled, was an account of the count's rights and revenues on his domain; where communities had charters of franchise or other exemptions, those were noted, and copies of the grants were included in the inquest. Saint-Florentin, Villemaur, and Bar-sur-Seine still had viable communes at that time, so texts of their franchises were appended to the *Extenta*. The twelfth-century franchises for rural communities were also copied. But the original franchise for Troyes was neither copied nor cited, as it was no longer operative; and if the *Extenta* copies were the sole sources for studying the communal franchises, it would have to be concluded that Troyes had never received one. Troyes was listed only for the *jurée* tax established by the original grant. Curiously, the *Extenta* also lists *jurée* revenues for five other castellany centers—Isle, Méry, Payns, Nogent, and Pont—none of which possesses an extant franchise. It is possible, therefore, that other towns mentioned in the *Extenta* with *jurée* values but without appended franchises had, like Troyes, received communal charters in 1230–31 and then had lost the *jurée* of self-administration, retaining only the *jurée* of tax assessment.

Ervy, of course, did not have a *jurée* value in the *Extenta* because its franchise of 1199, a variation of the Lorris customs, was still effective. A 2 s. residence tax was collected instead of a *jurée* assessment, and its small *prévôté* revenue was farmed by a private *prévôt* directly from the count. As was generally the case, once a community received a franchise of whatever form and extent, that custom became fixed and was not altered when more liberal privileges were extended to other communities. Ervy was the only county castellany town (and castellany) that received communitywide privileges before 1230, and it did not benefit from additional privileges in 1230-31. Isle-Aumont was also a special case. It had a castle from the early twelfth century, was a Champagne castellany from 1143 at least, and had mayors of its own in the twelfth century, but it was associated with Troyes in a single Troyes-Isle register in the *Feoda* of 1172 and in county registers into the thirteenth century. The *Extenta* states only that the *jurée* was collected "as in Troyes." In view of the long administrative association with Troyes, it would have been surprising if Isle did not receive a franchise at the same time as Troyes, or at least share the grant to Troyes. In fact, there is one reference to a commune at Isle: a certain Bochard who had been mayor in ca. 1222 was called mayor of the commune of Isle in 1235.[43]

There is also a single such reference for Méry: in the *Rôles des fiefs* of 1252 Pierre of Droupt-Sainte-Marie, *major communie de Meriaco,* held a rear-fief that the sergeants of Méry were ordered to seize because he failed to do homage for it.[44] As Troyes was associated with Isle, so was Méry with Payns. The *Extenta* of Payns begins with the statement that "Payns is in the *prévôté* of Méry" and that its *jurée* was collected with that of Méry. Payns had been an important castellany center in 1172, but by 1275, it had declined to such an extent that there were only two knights listed in its castellany; in effect, Payns had ceased to exist as a castellany, so it was linked administratively with Méry. There is no specific reference to a commune there, but the *Extenta* reports that the *jurée* of Payns applied to the count's men of that castellany, except those living in Le Pavillon, a *liber locus* of eight tenements with its own tax system. The situation was analogous to that of Ervy, in that a community which already had a franchise did not receive the *jurée* later.[45] Thus, Payns must have secured its *jurée* (and franchise) after that small community had received its customs, and Payns probably held the same type of privileges as Méry, with which its taxes were collected.

There is no evidence for a franchise at Nogent, which was a private lordship until the 1190s and which entered the Champagne domain as a castellany center in 1199/1200. Nogent was held ultimately from the abbot of Saint-Denis, to whom Thibaut IV did homage in 1226.[46] The *jurée* for Nogent in the *Extenta* was the largest in the *bailliage* except for Troyes, and its huge *péage* revenue was farmed by a *prévôt.* It is tempting to argue by analogy with Bar-sur-Seine, which clearly did receive a franchise, that Nogent received one at the same time: both castellanies entered the count's domain at about the same date, both were compact territories on either end of the Seine approach to Troyes, and both had *jurée* revenues in 1276/78, although only one has an extant franchise. Information for Pont is even less satisfactory. It entered the domain by the mid-twelfth century, had a county *prévôt* in 1153, and was a castellany center in 1172.[47] Its *jurée* value in the *Extenta* was the smallest in the *bailliage,* so small that it was included as just another revenue with the *prévôté* farm held from the count; in all other *Extenta* registers, the *jurée* revenues were carefully distinguished from the general *prévôté* farms.

In sum, in 1276/78 nine of the ten castellany towns in the *bailliage* paid a *jurée* tax; the tenth, Ervy, still paid the residence tax established by its 1199 franchise. Of the nine towns, three (Saint-Florentin, Bar-sur-Seine, Villemaur) retained their communes created by the franchises of 1230-31, and one (Troyes) had lost its commune through debt in 1240. Two other towns with *jurée* revenues in the *Extenta* had mayors of communes in 1235 (Isle) and 1252 (Méry), and another (Payns) probably shared the privileges of the latter. Only two towns (Nogent and Pont) with *jurée* taxes in 1276/78 lack evidence of communes and of the manner by which their *jurée* tax systems were established. Thus, seven of the nine towns can be definitely associated with the communal franchises of 1230-31.

In the second and third decades of the thirteenth century, the *bailliage* of Troyes was the locus of serious internal and external challenges that undermined the very cohesion of the county of Champagne as it was constituted from the mid-twelfth century. There is evidence for destruction of at least two castellany towns, but conditions were general, especially after the invasion of 1229. The charter of Troyes of September 1230 was a carefully constructed document, and the fact that it was reissued without modification eight and nine months later to at least three other castellany towns in the *bailliage* proves that it was a well-designed solution to a general problem.[48] The solution consisted of granting personal and property liberties and a considerable measure of local self-government to the count's men in his castellany towns, the most important economic, population, and administrative centers in the *bailliage*. It appears that all the castellany centers, with the exception of Ervy, which already possessed a franchise, received identical charters in 1230-31 and that all but three of them lost the privilege of self-administration before 1276/78, although they retained the new tax system created by the grants. The case of Troyes is the easiest to follow because it was the largest and the most important town of the *bailliage,* and its failure in self-administration is most observable.[49] That five other communal failures in far smaller towns have left no records of their demise is not surprising; charter copies and confirmations, and even county surveys, recorded acquisitions and privileges gained and guarded, not failures or deprivations.

In 1230-31 when the communal franchises were issued, a Cistercian monk, Aubri, was composing a "critical" universal history in the tranquillity of the forest and abbey of Trois-Fontaines, to the northeast of the *bailliage* but within "listening" distance. His critical appraisal of information, based on a skepticism of dates, traditions, and events, was unique among universal chroniclers, probably the result of his access to a large number of manuscripts. Aubri dropped his "sources" from about 1220 and supplied the bulk of the subsequent information (to 1241, when the chronicle ends abruptly) from his own general knowledge. In the absence of a local Troyen chronicle, his terse and pointed testimony is particularly valuable as a contemporary witness. Under the year 1231 he made a cryptic remark whose import should now be obvious: "The count of Champagne created communes of townsmen and peasants, whom he trusted more than his knights."[50] The remark was not idle. In less than one year the count had franchised his men in all his castellany towns, and probably in most of the surrounding castellanies,[51] from the traditional tenurial concomitants of *taille* and inheritance and marriage restrictions. The new tax system and municipal self-administration separated those residents from all other rural and urban tenants under private lords and still subject to the old obligations and restrictions. With a few strokes of the pen, the count had effectively created a new social category under his authority.

CONCLUSION: COMMUNITIES AND LIBERTIES

The interpretation of social conditions in the *bailliage* depends finally on an evaluation of the chronology and uniformity of those conditions. It is clear that at least from ca. 1120 there existed a single peasant population, the *homines* or *homines de corpore*. Irrespective of the multiplicity of specific obligations and their various local names, all tenants were subjected to essentially similar tenurial and residential taxes, rents, services, and customary restrictions.[52] Since most charters of the early twelfth century reveal no concern with peasants except as components of great estates, the deduction is that the peasant population remained stable and caused little worry to the landlords. Of course, the relatively few charters in this period cannot sustain close comparison with the numerous acts later in the century, but available evidence seems to indicate little peasant mobility at that time. But from the mid-twelfth century there is abundant evidence of peasant migration, and the multiple responses by landlords from the 1170s suggest that peasant movement was increasingly disrupting the traditional claims of landlords over tenants. The numerous references to *hospites* also point to considerable peasant mobility. One can only speculate on the reasons for the increased peasant migration. The breakup of the old domainal organization may have been a factor—the directly controlled estates of the early twelfth century seem to differ substantially from the self-administered villages under mayors later in the century and thereafter—but the causation could well have been opposite: peasant migration itself may have contributed to the disintegration of the old domain. Population increase is always a possible factor, but it simply cannot be measured in this period. Perhaps the single most demonstrable factor was the creation of the new territorial state of Champagne and its guarantee of safe passage over long distances, for it facilitated rural migration and opened a viable alternative to local conditions, whether a harsh landlord or overcrowding at home. In any event, once young

men left their families to settle and marry in distant lordships, they set
in motion a process that required landlords to readjust their claims on
persons. For reasons that are still unclear, peasant migration increased
greatly in the twelfth century; that it did and that it became a normal
aspect of rural life is certain.

As the physical mobility of persons into distant villages by migration
and through marriage increased in the second half of the twelfth
century, landlords were forced to be specific in their claims over
tenants, which for the first time were classified as basically four: (1)
mainmorte, the ultimate control by a landlord over his tenancies; (2)
taille, the head tax on all tenants, formerly arbitrary in amount and
occasion, now usually a fixed annual payment; (3) *formariage,* the tax
on marriages to persons outside the lord's control; and (4) justice, the
right to judge and discipline all residents. Except in the very few
instances of individual or temporary occupational exemption, those
claims were universal and the normal adjunct of peasant tenancy, and
the landlords clung to them against the insecurities engendered by
tenant emigration. The *hospites* were a transitory group that enjoyed a
temporary respite from their obligations and virtually complete "freedom," but ultimately most of them were forced to return to a landlord
for tenure with all its obligations. There is no evidence from the
bailliage that any other restrictions, such as prohibitions from clerical
status, or obligations, such as *corvée,* were ever considered essential to
tenant status.[53] Nor, of course, did uniformity in tenurial and residential obligations obscure differentiations by wealth or occupation.

The 1170s emerge as an important decade for peasant development.
Landlords agreed to standardized, written exchange procedures for the
intermarriages of their tenants, and in more comprehensive agreements
they began to resort to the joint administration of villages in which
tenants of two lords had become considerably mixed. Both arrangements were between landlords, responses to a situation already out of
their full control. At the same time, the count of Champagne developed
a policy of taking advantage of the floating population by enticing
migrants to his forested lands by means of exemptions and privileges.
Despite previous agreements on intermarriage and the control of villages, the coincidence of written agreements on these problems in the
1170s indicates that there was indeed an increasing peasant mobility
and that it was creating serious disruptions to landlords' claims over their
tenants. In fact, peasants moved and married almost at will, leaving to
their landlords the adjustment of the various tax claims. The latter
often came into conflict, as they sought at once to regain control over
their own emigrants and to assert control over immigrants. The flow of
tenants from one tenancy and landlord to another was continuous and
normal. The charters in which violence seems to have been done to

tenants by transfer, donation, or sale (see chapter II) were actually methods of adjusting landlord claims to revenues from tenants. The *pariages* performed the same function on the village level.

There is no evidence that lay or ecclesiastical lords imitated Henry I and Thibaut III in the creation of franchised communities. By 1200 only a few such communities existed, all on the count's domain. They enjoyed exemptions from the head tax and often from control of property transfer, as well as economic privileges, such as exemption from *péage* on the entire county domain. Various lords did, of course, sporadically offer a specific exemption to an individual or community, but without consistency. Against this background, the communes of 1230-31 were a violent innovation. A single grant to Troyes would have been significant in itself, although not upsetting; grants to seven and perhaps nine castellany centers constituted a major transformation in the *bailliage,* as Aubri of Trois-Fontaines realized. Indeed, the impact of the communal grants was so great that several landlords felt compelled to copy the count's charters in grants to their own men.[54] In general, however, the lesser lords retained most of their traditional claims over tenants, so that the effect of the commune grants was to create a different set of conditions on much of the Champagne domain (at least four entire castellanies shared the privileges of their main towns); by the end of the thirteenth century there existed a sharp divide between conditions on the county (then royal) domain and those on private lordships.[55] The dichotomy was especially important in terms of the concentration of population and economic activity. The count's castellany towns of 200–240 hearths, such as Villemaur, Ervy, and Bar-sur-Seine, were among the largest population centers in the *bailliage,* four to five times larger than most villages (see table 2). These small towns functioned as administrative and commercial centers intermediate between the agrarian villages and the truly urban center of Troyes, which with its population of about ten thousand dominated the entire region.[56] The communal grants created a new status for the count's townsmen and distinguished them from all other Champagne residents. Although they were still men of the count, they were essentially identified in the *Extenta terre* of 1276/78 as being under the count's justice; their other obligations had been reduced to a single tax on their wealth, the *jurée.*[57] The *Extenta* also reported that many immigrants who had not yet fulfilled their residence requirements became involved in legal proceedings in order to come under the count's justice and thereby qualify as his men.

Residents of franchised communities were distinguished mainly by their exemption from *taille*: in rural communities a hearth tax replaced it; in the communes the *jurée* was its substitute. *Taille* appears to have been the single most important burden on rural tenants, even in the late twelfth century when it was abolished by the community franchises. If the village of Villeneuve-au-Chemin was typical in 1276/78, property rents were generally below 2 s. annually and averaged about 12 d. A 5 s. *taille,* which seems to have been standard in intermarriage exchange agreements, was relatively high, and its commutation to a 12 d. hearth tax was a significant reduction.[58] The *jurée* paid by townsmen was undoubtly higher, but then the stigma of *taille* itself was removed. It is not clear whether the franchised communities were also exempted from *corvées,* which were included among the "customs" from the eleventh century.[59] *Corvées* seem to have been normal requirements for tenants throughout the twelfth and thirteenth centuries and appear in descriptions of Champagne fiefs and in grants to ecclesiastical institutions. [60] The *pariages* also specify that *corvées* and plowing duty were ordinary requirements of residents and were therefore items to be regulated in jointly administered communities.[61] There is only one example of an individual being exempted in a personal franchise from the *corvée,* another demonstration that franchises did not include exemptions from ordinary tenurial obligations.[62] The matter is entirely ignored in the community franchises, but it would seem that labor obligations were included in the exemptions from "exactions," for the *Extenta* lists *corvées* in only a few small and scattered communities on the count's domain. It appears that franchised villages and towns did not ordinarily perform *corvées,* although they may have for other property that carried such an obligation.

Both franchised and nonfranchised persons were still liable for military service and banal obligations. Several of the twelfth-century franchises required that the count or his personal representative appear in person to lead the men, obviously a guarantee against abuse by local officials; the commune charters include Thibaut's promise to call up men only when necessary, but the right of the count to exact military service was never questioned and never commuted on the community level. Only the most generous of the few individual franchises to loyal agents ever allowed an exemption from military service. Likewise, banal monopolies continued for the franchised. In the *bailliage* the ban appeared in its strictest form as the requirement that local residents grind their grain at a specific mill, bake at one oven, and, occasionally, even purchase their wine from a certain seller during a prescribed period.[63] The twelfth-century franchises make no mention of banal obligations, and the 1203 *pariage* over Nogent-sur-Aube appears unique in formally allowing residents to use freely the mills and ovens of either lord of the place. The commune grants insisted that the count's men still use his ovens and mills in their respective towns; only in the event that those facilities were inadequate could they go elsewhere, and then only under the direction of the mayor of the commune.[64] The ban was solely an economic exaction, without link to franchise status.

Ultimately, the conditions of tenants reflected the will or policy of their landlords, tempered by necessity. Entire villages under a single lord were most likely to receive either a full franchise or economic privileges, especially if their lord were the count. Some of the count's villages, of course, were never granted privileges.[65] Villages under joint or multiple lordship were not likely to receive such benefits: the *pariages* provided only for joint control of administration and a strict accountability of nontenurial revenues. Villages that were even more fragmented, especially among family members, and lacked common administration were the least likely of all to receive privileges, much less franchises.[66] It was not the village that determined a tenant's status but rather the community, the local residents of a specific lord. Only the count's men of Troyes and of the other castellany towns, not those of the local ecclesiastical institutions, were members of the communes. Personal and property "liberties," as well as economic privileges, were granted to members of particular communities, that is, the men of certain lords, and those who had failed to secure membership in such communities by the mid-thirteenth century were condemned to an inferior status. The *Coutumier,* written by and for the landlords, recognized the threat to the countryside posed by *franc* men, who were invariably identified as townsmen and unconsciously considered men of the count. It attempted to maintain the identity of tenant and tenancy status so that the townsmen, some of whom were probably essentially peasants but who enjoyed the franchise, could neither inherit nor purchase peasant tenancies unless they assumed the concomitant peasant obligations. The same option was open to the children of mixed aristocratic-peasant marriages. By the mid-thirteenth century the *homines de corpore* were no longer all rural tenants but in the main tenants under private justice who were still subjected to *taille, mainmorte,* and marriage tax. Whether they can be called "serfs" is a matter of interpretation. That term was not current in the *bailliage* at the time and was used only twice in the *Coutumier,* both cases being court decisions in which the language may have been influenced by foreign royal officials or by inference from translations of Roman law.[67] In any event, all the sources agree that those who had "liberties" at the end of the thirteenth century were either fief holders or members of communities that had received formal grants of franchises, most of which were from the count and on his domain.

IV
The Fief Holders
A QUANTITATIVE ANALYSIS

Although charter evidence furnishes most of the details on medieval aristocratic families, it does not provide an accurate profile of the entire aristocracy, nor does it reveal how representative the few well-documented families were of all fief holders. Accordingly, it is difficult to generalize about any local aristocracy on the basis of charters alone.[1] The Champagne county surveys offer a solution to the dilemma, for they furnish information on virtually all fief holders of the count, including those who appear rarely or not at all in the extant ecclesiastical acts, in the years 1172, 1252, 1265, and 1275.[2] These administrative records constitute a series in the statistical sense of being, theoretically at least, inclusive censes of the count's fief holders in a standardized reporting system and within the context of administrative areas defined by contemporary officials. The survey data on the fief holders, their sex, status, military obligations, fiefs, and fief incomes, can be analyzed quantitatively without the serious methodological problems encountered by attempts to quantify charter information.

The following analyses are quantitative rather than statistical, in that they present frequencies of occurrences, accumulations of quantities, and relative percentages, but do not include the more sophisticated statistical techniques that are now routine in other social sciences. For medieval society especially, where it is seldom possible to obtain any standardized quantifiable data, a primary goal is to establish accurate frequency tables whenever such data are available. The processing of the Champagne registers greatly determines the resultant figures, and since each survey is unique, each is examined separately here. The data in their original form in all the surveys were organized by castellany, and so the castellany has been retained as the basic unit of the tables. The castellany is the crucial divide at which individuals and families lose their absolute uniqueness and become classifiable types, and the ten castellanies of the *bailliage* of Troyes provide an administratively-defined grouping large enough for significant quantitative operations. Thus the level of generalization is the *bailliage*, for the purpose of this quantitative undertaking is to present a valid technique for generalizing above the level of individual lordship and castellany, and ultimately of *bailliage* and province. Since preliminary sampling showed that the results obtained for these castellanies are remarkably close to those obtained for the entire county of Champagne, the percentages are carried to the first decimal, even when a small population occasionally would not seem to justify, and indeed might be construed to distort, such precision. Actually, the *bailliage* of Troyes has been favored by the best ratio of preserved registers in Champagne, and its registers also generally possess the most complete information for each category of data. It may well turn out that the aristocracy of this *bailliage* can be measured more precisely than any other local aristocracy in France from the mid-twelfth century through the thirteenth century.[3]

THE *FEODA CAMPANIE,* 1172

The *Feoda* is a list of about 1,900 direct knights and lords in the twenty-six castellanies of the count of Champagne in 1172.[4] The registers are organized by castellany, and all but one record the liegeance and castle guard owed by each man. A few registers contain additional information, such as the composition or location of a fief, but it is too sporadic for systematic evaluation. A typical *Feoda* entry is: "N(name), liege and Y(amount) guard." Important local lords appear simply as *"Dominus* of X(place)"* and are usually grouped at the head of the registers.

The concept of castellany was loose in 1172 and did not yet represent the fixed geographical area which it was to become by the mid-thirteenth century. Some knights with fiefs close to Troyes were listed in the castellanies of Rosnay, Bar-sur-Aube, or Laferté-sur-Aube, which belonged to the thirteenth-century *bailliage* of Chaumont; and others were listed in two or more castellanies, probably due to scribal efforts to thoroughly canvass all fief holders of the count. Eight castellanies in 1172 would form the nucleus of the thirteenth-century *bailliage* of Troyes (see chap. I and maps 2 and 5). Troyes, Isle, and Villemaur were the only parts of the old county of Troyes that were still retained directly in the count's hand in 1172. Ervy, Payns, and probably Méry had been incorporated into his domain by the early 1140s, as had Saint-Florentin and Pont, both of which seem to have been taken from the lord of Traînel. The eight castellanies of 1172 represented the directly-administered domain of the count and his fiefs clustered around their respective castellany towns. The great private lordships in the area, although not formally within the count's castellanies, were attached to his castellanies for administrative purposes.

Table 3 shows the numerical breakdown of the *Feoda* by castellany

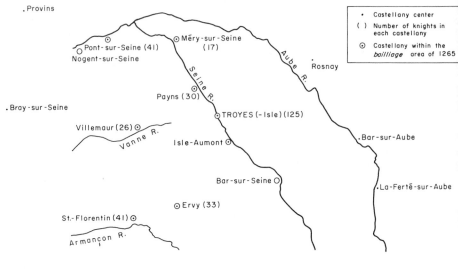

Map 5.
Champagne Castellanies, 1172

register. Troyes and Isle comprised a single register, although castle guard was assigned to one or the other castle. The column entitled "raw" gives the total itemized entries in the edited *Feoda*. While most entries are for individuals, a few are "multiple," in which a man's *filii* or *heredes* are mentioned. The raw and multiple entries together (with the unexplained exception of Ervy) are very close to the grand total (*summa militum*) calculated by the scribes themselves at the end of the entire *Feoda*; obviously they were counting actual persons, not entries, and their arithmetic was not as faulty as the editor supposed.[5] Unfortunately, the scribes did not cross-reference the castellany registers once collected at Troyes, and they failed to cancel from the *Feoda* summation the "duplications," entries of persons listed in two or more castellanies. Most duplications are accounted for in the immediate *bailliage* area, although a few are from other areas of the county. All persons clearly identifiable in duplication entries have been assigned here to the castellany in which information about them is most precise, as, for example, a reference to liegeance or a specific term of castle guard.[6] The "refined" number of persons is obtained by adding the multiple entries to and subtracting the duplications from the raw figures. After all adjustments, the eight-castellany area contains 313 individuals, a decrease of 10.3 percent from the raw figures, who account for 16.6 percent of the count's fief holders in Champagne. The 313 fief holders ranged from a handful of important local lords (*domini*), who probably did not consider their properties and castles to be in any Champagne castellany, to poor knights, some of whom did

Table 3
FIEF HOLDERS OF THE COUNT, 1172

Castellany	Raw[a]	Multiple[b]	Duplication[c] Bailliage	County	Refined[d]	Summa Militum[e]
Troyes-Isle	128	6	6	3	125	135
St.-Florentin	39	4	1	1	41	42
Ervy	35	—	1	1	33	40[f]
Villemaur	25	2	1	—	26	27
Pont-sur-Seine	42	—	—	1	41	42
Méry-sur-Seine	21	—	2	2	17	21
Payns	43	—	10	3	30	42
Total	333	+12	−21	−11	313	349

[a]Total itemized entries in the edited *Feoda.*
[b]Additional persons in the raw entries.
[c]Duplicate entries for the same person.
[d]Sum of the raw and multiple numbers minus the duplications.
[e]Grand total calculated by the scribes of the *Feoda.*
[f]The total furnished at the end of the Ervy register is 40, but the consolidated *summa militum* at the end of the entire *Feoda* is 39 (see also note 5).

not even hold land. With the exception of the *domini* and a few others (five viscounts, one mayor, two townsmen, one cleric, and six *homines*), the fief holders were not identified by status and were probably all knights, as they were so identified collectively in the *summa militum* and individually in contemporary charters.[7] There were only six women (1.9 percent) listed in the *bailliage*, half of the twelve in all Champagne.

All persons in the *Feoda* owed the count military service in time of war, but not all were required to perform annual guard duty in his castles. Table 4-A presents the terms of regular "reserve" duty owed in each castellany, and figures 1-A and 1-B give the total percentages.[8] Of the 313 fief holders, 129 (41.2 percent, or 45.6 percent if the Payns register, which omits all reference to guard, is excluded) owed some regular castle guard.[9] Of the 129 who owed service, 39.5 percent were listed for unspecified guard (*garda, custodia, estagium*), which seems to have covered tours of duty of one month or less.[10] The most common fixed terms were for 7–8 weeks (24.8 percent), 9–12 weeks (15.5 percent), and 5–6 weeks (10.1 percent). Only seven persons (5.5 percent) owed from six months to all-year service. Since all entries in the *Feoda* are positive attributions, the absence of notation for guard would indicate that such duty was not required, at least not in the count's castles. The majority of knights (58.8 percent, or 54.4 percent if Payns is again excluded for failing to mention guard) lacked such references and apparently did not owe annual duty in his castles, being liable only in the event of outright hostilities.[11]

The distribution of the burden of castle guard is more clearly shown

Table 4
CASTLE GUARD, 1172

A. *Terms of service*

Castellany	Tours of duty (weeks)								Total service	(percent)	Blank	Total Knights
	"Guard"	4	5–6	7–8	9–12	13–24	25–36	37–52				
Troyes-Isle	34	—	7	4	4	—	—	2	51	(40.8)	74	125
St.-Florentin	2	—	—	8	4	—	—	—	14	(34.1)	27	41
Ervy	9	—	—	—	3	1	1	3	17	(51.5)	16	33
Villemaur	4	—	2	2	2	1	—	—	10	(38.5)	16	26
Pont-sur-Seine	2	2	2	15	5	3	—	1	30	(73.2)	11	41
Méry-sur-Seine	—	—	2	3	2	—	—	—	7	(41.2)	10	17
Payns	—	—	—	—	—	—	—	—	—	—	30	30
Total	51	2	13	32	20	4	1	6	129		184	313
Percentage	(16.3)	(0.6)	(4.2)	(10.2)	(6.4)	(1.3)	(0.3)	(1.9)	(41.2)		(58.8)	(100.0)
Percentage of total service	(39.5)	(1.5)	(10.1)	(24.8)	(15.5)	(3.1)	(0.8)	(4.7)	(100.0)			
Total excluding Payns register[a]									(45.6)		154	283
Percentage											(54.4)	(100.0)

B. Accumulated duty-time

Castellany	Duty time (weeks)							Total weeks	(percent)	"Guard"	Theoretical[b]	
	4	5–6	7–8	9–12	13–24	25–36	37–52				Total	(percent)
Troyes-Isle	—	42	32	48	—	—	96	218	(22.3)	136	354	(29.9)
St.-Florentin	—	—	64	48	—	—	—	112	(11.5)	8	120	(10.2)
Ervy	—	—	—	36	24	36	144	240	(24.5)	36	276	(23.4)
Villemaur	—	12	16	24	—	—	—	52	(5.3)	16	68	(5.8)
Pont-sur-Seine	8	12	120	60	56	—	40	296	(30.3)	8	312	(25.7)
Méry-sur-Seine	—	12	24	24	—	—	—	60	(6.1)	—	68	(5.1)
Total	8	78	256	240	80	36	280	978	(100.0)	204	1182	(100.0)
Percentage	(0.8)	(8.0)	(26.2)	(24.5)	(8.2)	(3.7)	(28.6)	(100.0)				
Percentage of theoretical total		(6.6)	(21.7)	(20.3)	(6.8)	(3.0)	(23.7)			(17.2)		(100.0)

Note: Categories of service are inclusive and follow the *Feoda:* there are no cases of service over one month and less than five weeks.
[a]See note 11.
[b]See note 12.

when the terms of duty are accumulated (table 4-B). The theoretical total of duty-time rendered in the count's castles is obtained by accumulating the specified terms of service and adding unspecified "guard" as if it were four weeks duty (there are only two instances of guard being fixed at four weeks and none at less than four weeks).[12] Of all 313 knights, the 31.3 percent who rendered "guard" or up to eight weeks service provided 46.2 percent of the total duty-time; the remaining 53.8 percent of duty-time was performed by knights giving from nine weeks to all-year service, but they comprised only 9.9 percent of all the fief holders. The rest of the knights (58.8 percent) did not perform any regular castle guard. Thus, more than half of those who held fiefs from the count furnished him no regular castle guard. Most of the duty-time was provided by 10 percent of his fief holders.

The predominant concern of the *Feoda* with both castle guard and liege homage naturally raises the question of their correlation. Of the 283 persons (excluding the 30 in the Payns register for whom neither guard nor liegeance is indicated), there are 149 (52.6 percent) references to liegeance—47 percent for liegeance to the count and 5.6 percent for liegeance to another (usually named) lord (table 5-A). Liegeance varied by castellany, from a high ratio in Troyes-Isle, Méry, and Ervy (53–60 percent) to a low ratio in Saint-Florentin (26 percent), but it is difficult to draw conclusions from such a narrow data base as to why the percentage of liegemen varied.[13] When the figures

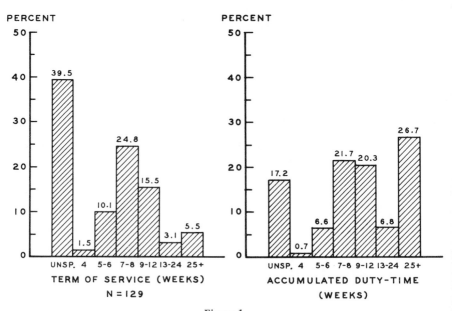

Figure 1
Castle Guard, 1172

are taken together, however, there is an important correlation between liegeance and military service: 58.6 percent of the liegemen owed some castle guard, compared with the 45.6 percent of all the knights who did. There is even greater discrepancy in duty-time (table 5-B): liege-men performed a disproportionate share of duty-time for tours of over three months (70–100 percent) and for unspecified guard, which was probably up to one month (77.4 percent). That is, the liegemen of the count who also performed castle guard constituted 27.5 percent of his knights, yet they furnished 64.1 percent of the total duty-time in his castles.[14] Liegemen filled most of the duty-slots, with the exception of two month tours of duty, and provided the mainstay of castle guard. This direct correlation between liegeance and castle guard confirms the report in ca. 1205 of two former officials who linked liegeance and castle guard when referring to the count's knights.[15] Nevertheless, over half of the Champagne fief holders in 1172 were neither liege to the count nor obligated for regular service in his castles, according to his own official records.

In the two decades following 1172 the county scribes attempted to keep the *Feoda* current by correcting the original entries whenever fiefs were transferred. Old entries were crossed out and new ones entered beside them, such as "his son," "his wife," and "he still lives." It is, of course, impossible to determine whether all transfers were in fact noted, although each register has at least one emendation. The Troyes-Isle register had fifty (40 percent) of its original 125 entries modified by ca. 1190, the highest and no doubt the most accurate ratio of change, as it would have been easier to enter changes in records kept at Troyes for its immediate castellany than for outlying ones. The Troyes-Isle transfers were: twenty-one (42 percent) to sons and twelve (24 percent) to widows of original holders, and four (8 percent) to probable but not direct heirs; three (6 percent) fiefs reverted to the count, and eight (16 percent) were reassigned by him to persons not related to the original holder, while one fief was granted to an abbey, and another was still held by its original possessor. In short, thirty-four (68 percent) fiefs were retained by and sixteen (32 percent) were transferred from the original holder's immediate family. If the revised entries are assumed to include all actual transfers of fiefs from 1172 to ca. 1190, then sixteen (12.5 percent) of the original 125 fiefs in this register had escaped the control of their original holders in this twenty-year period. Notations in other registers confirm the loss of fiefs by mortgage, sale, alienation, and natural disaster, in addition to reassignment by the count. [16] Although the strong family control over fiefs is obvious and is usually taken as an achievement of the late twelfth century, it should be noted that a 12.5 percent overall loss of fiefs from original holders' families in a relatively peaceful generation does represent a normal instability in

Table 5
LIEGEMEN OF THE COUNT, 1172

A. Castle guard of liegemen

Castellany	"Guard"	Tours of duty (weeks)						Total service	Blank	Total liege	(percent)	Secondary liegeance	Total Knights
		5–6	7–8	9–12	13–24	25–36	37–52						
Troyes-Isle	30	4	2	3	–	–	2	41	27	68	(54.4)	2	125
St.-Florentin	2	–	1	–	1	1	–	3	8	11	(26.8)	4	41
Ervy	5	–	–	3	1	1	3	13	7	20	(60.6)	6	33
Villemaur	3	1	1	1	–	–	–	6	4	10	(38.5)	3	26
Pont-sur-Seine	1	1	4	4	2	–	–	12	3	15	(36.6)	–	41
Méry-sur-Seine	–	1	–	3	–	–	–	3	6	9	(52.9)	1	17
Total	41	7	8	13	3	1	5	78	55	133		16	283
Percentage of liegemen								(58.6)	(41.4)	(100.0)			
Percentage of guard by liegemen										(47.0)		(5.6)	(100.0)

B. Accumulated duty-time by liegemen

	"Guard" or 4	Tours of duty (weeks)						Total
		5–6	7–8	9–12	13–24	25–36	37–52	
Total duty-time[a]	212	78	256	240	80	36	280	1182
Duty-time by liegemen	164	42	64	156	56	36	240	758
Percentage of duty-time by liegemen	(77.4)	(53.8)	(25.0)	(65.0)	(70.0)	(100.0)	(85.7)	(64.1)

[a] See table 4-B.

fief tenure; a period of insecurity and high mortality could have transformed this normal attrition into an important mechanism of change.

THE *RÔLES DES FIEFS*, 1252

The *Feoda* was recognized as an important document in its time and was consulted by county officials as ultimate authority whenever oral testimony was in doubt.[17] Indeed, the idea of a *Feoda* had taken such firm root that there were several attempts to compose entirely new sets of registers under Henry II and during Blanche's regency. But these attempts miscarried, and *Feoda* II, of 1200/1201, through *Feoda* V, of 1210/14, survive only as fragmentary registers of limited use in their present state, save for important clues on the development of liegeance (see below).[18] These registers are concrete evidence of the administrative chaos of Blanche's regency and the seriousness of the Brienne challenge, which prevented further attempts to draw up similar registers until Thibaut IV was actually of age and in full possession of the county. Thibaut's first surveys, however, do not equal the original *Feoda* of 1172: *Feoda* VI, of 1222–34, and *Feoda* VII, of after 1234, are simply haphazard collections of homages rendered to him in the form of "N(name) does liege homage for X(fief) in castellany C." Obviously, Thibaut's priority of business on coming of age was to secure the homages of his fief holders, and the spirit of the two surveys, even in their fragmentary state, is different from that of the original *Feoda* and its continuations to ca. 1214. Thibaut's surveys are not properly administrative at all in the sense of being systematic collections of information but are rather testimonial, in that they record the fact of homages rendered.[19] Only after conditions had stabilized in the county was it possible to resume careful administrative functions, and in the 1240s an ambitious and entirely novel attempt was made to record data on Champagne fiefs and their holders in a more systematic and complete manner than ever before.[20]

The *Rôles des fiefs* are composed of test surveys conducted in several castellanies (including Nogent and Pont in the *bailliage*) in 1249 and the main body of registers compiled by touring *enquêteurs* for the entire county in 1252.[21] The *Rôles* were the first systematic survey of Champagne fief holders since the original *Feoda* and the fullest of all such inquests, with descriptions of many holdings in detail as to composition, location, expected annual revenue, assigned castle guard, and names of rear-fief holders and their holdings. Also noted was any

other information that identified a fief, such as the name and relationship of the present to the previous holder and the method of fief
transfer. All in all, it is the most complete dossier available for a
mid-thirteenth-century aristocracy, and it offers an exceptional opportunity for quantification because it was intended to be an all-inclusive
survey of vital statistics of Champagne fief holders. Registers are extant
for only 62 percent of the county, but nine of the ten castellany
registers survive from the *bailliage* of Troyes.

Several simple but important refinements must be made on the *Rôles*
data before they can be subjected to quantitative analysis. The registers
were kept separately by castellany, and often emendations were made
at the end of registers to supplement or modify previous entries, as in
the case of fief transfers effected during the course of the inquest. Most
such situations are obvious and can be readily adjusted. Henri of
Ferreux, for instance, is listed for a fief worth twenty *libratae terre* [22]
in Nogent, but at the end of the register his widow Margaret is listed for
all his possessions, as is their son Jean; Jean's wife has a separate entry
for her dowry and inheritance in the same village.[23] Only two entries,
those of Henri and of his daughter-in-law, are counted here; the additional listings are considered duplications. A more complicated situation arises when a person appears in two or more registers, occasionally
for the same, but usually for different properties. For such multiple
listings the procedure here has been to assign every person to the
castellany in which he had his "main-holding" from the count, a
solution which is technically acceptable because only eight of all the
bailliage entries are for persons with main-holdings outside the *bailliage*.
The criterion for main-holding is the highest fief revenue, if given, or
the greatest amount of castle guard, or, in lieu of both, the most exact
statement on fief composition. For example, Gérard of Saint-Benoît is
listed in Nogent for a 30 *l.t.* fief at Chappelle-Geoffroy, for which he
owed a full year's guard. He is also listed for an 8 *l.t. terrage* from his
wife's inheritance at Pont, but obviously his main-holding was at
Nogent.[24] Slightly more difficult is the case of Etienne of Saint-Loup:
listed in Pont for a 15 *l.t.* income, he is also listed in Nogent for the
same amount, which is described as lands, woods, and rents, and he
owed two months castle guard; his four rear-fief holders and their
properties (worth 22 *l.t.* annually) are also listed. A third entry is for
his wife's rent in Sezanne. The full description of his property, military
obligation, and rear holders in the Nogent entry indicates that Nogent
was his main-holding area; this is confirmed by an earlier survey which
lists him for property and guard at Nogent but also for some property
at Pont.[25] The assignment here to a main-holding castellany applies
only to persons (not fiefs) and only to multiple fief holders; it is used
to prevent duplications of main holders and is in large part a formality,

since most of the following analyses are at the *bailliage* level. Duplicate property listings are canceled automatically under the appropriate holder.

The *Rôles* contain 337 entries for the nine extant castellany registers (that of Villemaur is missing). After the duplicate and multiple listings have been adjusted, there remain 279 persons with main-holdings, a diminution of 14.3 percent from the total raw entries. Of the 279, 213 (76.3 percent) are men and 66 (23.7 percent) women; this contrasts with the virtual absence of women from the *Feoda* of 1172. Some of the women were temporary holders, for husbands then in the East or as guardians for sons, but others were holders in their own right for inheritances and dowries. Although the old aristocratic families had always passed property through both male and female lines, the possession of ordinary knights' fiefs by women was new and seems to have become common only after the *Feoda* of 1172. Throughout the thirteenth century about one-fifth of the fief holders at any time were women.

The *Rôles* also reveal important changes in the types of social status represented by the count's fief holders (see table 6 and figure 2). Whereas almost all persons in the *Feoda* of 1172 were knights, only 104 (37.3 percent) of those in the *Rôles* were *domini* (or in a few cases *milites*).[26] Forty-five (16.1 percent) others were nonknighted *armigeri*. Another fifty-seven (20.4 percent) men were listed without status; while some of these may have been ecclesiastics, rich peasants, or townsmen (like Pierre of Droupt, mayor of the commune of Méry [see chapter III]), most were probably knights, like Pierre of Floregny, who held a 30 *l.t.* revenue and is identified both in an earlier survey and in a charter of 1263 as a knight.[27] Altogether, eleven men can be positively identified from other sources (mostly charters) as to status, so the total of unknown men and women is reduced to fifty-four (19.4 percent) for the entire population of 279 direct holders. The omission of status in the *Rôles* is probably due to scribal negligence, for there is no evidence of a systematic bias that would define a special status-less group; therefore, the relative distribution of known status may be taken as representative of the entire fief-holding group. The breakdown of known status (225 persons of the 279) is: 50.2 percent *domini*, 20.4 percent *armigeri*, 22.4 percent *dominae*, 4.7 percent unmarried *domicellae*, and 3.3 percent miscellaneous (four viscounts, one *serviens*, and two ecclesiastics).[28]

The *Rôles* are essentially an account of property, and entries are organized according to fiefs, with all information on property composition and value, military obligation, and method of acquisition clearly ascribed to individual fief or rear-fief. Of the 279 direct holders, 208 (74.6 percent) held a single fief from the count, while 58 (20.8 percent)

Table 6
FIEF HOLDERS, 1252

Castellany	Raw	Refined	Dominus[a]	Armiger	Domina	Domicella	Other	Blank Men	Blank Women
Troyes	62	47	24 [27]	6	10	—	—	7 [4]	—
Isle	55	48	13 [16]	8	10	4	1 [2]	12 [8]	—
St.-Florentin	33	23	6 [7]	3	4	—	3	7 [6]	1
Ervy	56	45	19	7	4	2	1	11	—
Pont-sur-Seine[b]	34	32	7	9 [10]	8	1	1	6 [5]	1
Méry-sur-Seine	22	16	6	1	4	—	—	2	3
Payns	9	8	4	1	2	—	—	1	—
Nogent-sur-Seine	28	25	10 [11]	6	4	1	—	3 [2]	1
Bar-sur-Seine	38	35	15 [16]	4	2	2	1	8 [7]	3
Total	337	279	104 [113]	45 [46]	48	10	7 [8]	57 [46]	8
Percentage of Total		(100.0)	(37.3) [40.5]	(16.1) [16.5]	(17.2)	(3.6)	(2.5) [2.9]	(20.4) [16.5]	(2.9)
Percentage of total, blanks excluded		—	(48.6) [50.2]	(21.0) [20.4]	(22.4)	(4.7)	(3.3) [3.3]	—	—

Note: Numbers and percentages in brackets represent adjusted figures for persons who appear without status in the *Rôles* but who are identified in the charters or the surveys of the 1220s or of 1265.

a See note 26.

b The editor notes that the manuscript is mutilated and that it probably contained additional entries.

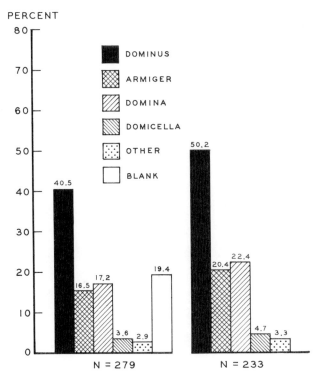

Figure 2
Fief Holders, 1252

held two fiefs, and 13 (4.7 percent) held three or more (see table 7-A and figure 3-A). The *domini* had the highest proportion of multiple fiefs, yet the great majority of *domini* had single holdings. The predominance of single fiefs in 1252 confirms that the rare mention of multiple holdings in the *Feoda* of 1172 indeed meant that most knights at that time held only single fiefs from the count. Also, more than half (56.6 percent) of the direct holders in 1252 did not have any rear-fief holders at all, being responsible solely for their immediate fiefs (see table 7-B and figure 3-B).[29] Thus, most direct fief holders had only one fief and no rear-fief holders.

Most fiefs were valued in *libratae terre* (*livres de terre*), units of assessment of the estimated annual yield of a fief from all sources of revenue, including land, rents, tolls, fines, banal monopolies, and justice. This form of assessment first appeared at the beginning of the thirteenth century, although the *Feoda* of 1172 had listed fiefs composed of a variety of revenues, both in cash and in kind, indiscriminately with landed fiefs.[30] By the mid-thirteenth century the *librata terre* was the standard unit of fief assessment, and in the *Rôles* fief

Table 7
FIEFS AND REAR-FIEF HOLDERS
OF DIRECT HOLDERS, 1252

A. *Fiefs per direct holder*

Castellany	Total	1	(percent)	2	3+
Troyes	47	32	(68.1)	14	1
Isle-Aumont	48	40	(83.3)	7	1
St.-Florentin	23	15	(65.2)	6	2
Ervy	45	30	(66.7)	11	4
Pont-sur-Seine	32	26	(81.2)	6	–
Méry-sur-Seine	16	11	(68.8)	3	2
Payns	8	6	(75.0)	–	2
Nogent-sur-Seine	25	18	(72.0)	7	–
Bar-sur-Seine	35	30	(85.7)	4	1
Total	279	208		58	13
Percentage of total	(100.0)	(74.6)		(20.8)	(4.7)
Status of holder					
Dominus	113	75	(66.4)	30	8
Armiger	46	33	(71.7)	11	2
Domina	48	40	(83.3)	7	1
Domicella	10	9	(90.0)	1	–
Other	8	6	(75.0)	1	1
Blank	54	45	(83.3)	8	1

B. *Rear-fief holders per direct holder*

Castellany	Total	1	2	3–4	5–9	10+	None
Troyes	47	5	4	3	3	4	28
Isle-Aumont	48	12	6	3	2	1	24
St.-Florentin	23	2	–	1	5	1	14
Ervy	45	5	5	4	2	1	28
Pont-sur-Seine	32	5	8	1	1	2	15
Méry-sur-Seine	16	3	2	3	–	–	8
Payns	8	1	1	2	1	–	3
Nogent-sur-Seine	25	6	2	2	–	1	14
Bar-sur-Seine	35	6	2	2	–	1	24
Total	279	45	30	21	13	12	158[a]
Percentage of total	(100.0)	(16.1)	(10.8)	(7.5)	(4.7)	(4.4)	(56.6)
Status of holder							
Dominus	113	17	9	15	7	6	59
Armiger	46	9	11	1	–	2	22
Domina	48	9	5	2	1	2	29
Domicella	10	3	–	–	–	–	7
Other	8	3	1	–	–	1	3
Blank	54	4	4	3	4	1	38

[a]See note 29.

values are usually expressed in five- or ten-pound units, with greater precision at the lower levels (for example, 2 *l.t.* or 4 *l.t.*) and less at the higher. The values for fief incomes furnished by the *Rôles* are for actual incomes enjoyed by the direct holders and do not include the values of rear-fiefs held from them.[31] A typical *Rôles* entry is: "*Dominus* Guillaume Rex, under oath [reported that he] holds at Courbeton a house, lands, men, justice, *cens*: about 15 *libratae terre*. He owes three weeks guard."[32]

Although the *Rôles* list only fiefs held directly or indirectly from the count—and it is impossible to determine what other properties were held either in alod or in fief from other great lords or ecclesiastical houses—there are several reasons for supposing that the *Rôles* entries usually represented at least the greater part, if not the entirety, of personal holdings. In several cases fiefs of the count which existed in 1172 or in the early thirteenth century and which disappeared from the *Rôles* altogether can be shown by charter evidence to have been alienated to ecclesiastical houses (see chapter V). Also, the great range of fief values and especially the inclusion of valuable fiefs of over 100

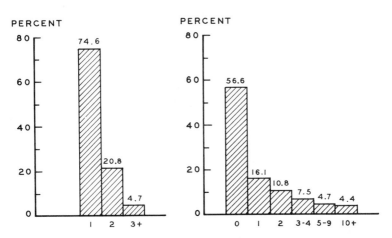

Figure 3
Fiefs (*left*) and Rear-Fief Holders (*right*)
per Direct Fief Holder, 1252

l.t. with castles and fortifications indicates that entire holdings were represented in the valuations, irrespective of whether or not the valuations themselves were exact.[33] Finally, there are cases in which families divided their inheritances and subsequently appeared in the surveys for their respective shares, proving that the original unitary fiefs were the entire family properties.

There are three general ways of tabulating fief incomes: by taking the

Table 8
ANNUAL FIEF INCOMES, 1252

A. Frequencies

Value	Individual Fiefs	Sole or First Fiefs						
		Dominus	Armiger	Domina	Domicella	Other	Blank	Total
200+	5	1	—	2	—	—	—	3
160	2	—	—	1	—	1	—	2
140	2	1	—	—	—	—	1	2
120	4	1	1	1	—	—	—	3
100	4	2	—	—	—	—	1	3
90	1	—	—	—	—	—	—	—
80	1	1	—	—	—	—	—	1
70	1	—	—	—	—	—	—	—
60	6	2	2	—	—	1	1	6
50	5	3	—	—	—	—	—	3
40	16	8	2	1	1	—	1	13
30	23	12	4	—	1	—	1	18
20	34	13	3	4	1	1	2	24
10	51	15	7	8	3	2	10	45
1	84	14	13	13	3	1	11	55
Subtotal	239	73	32	30	9	6	28	178
Nonvalued	193	40	14	18	1	2	26	101
Total	432	113(40.5)	46(16.5)	48(17.2)	10(3.6)	8(2.9)	54(19.4)	279(100.0)

Note: 10 = 10–19 *l.t.*

B. Accumulations

Value	Individual Fiefs	Sole or First Fiefs						
		Dominus	Armiger	Domina	Domicella	Other	Blank	Total
200+	1,040	240	—	400	—	—	—	640
160	320	—	—	160	—	160	—	320
140	280	140	—	—	—	—	140	280
120	480	120	120	120	—	—	—	360
100	400	200	—	—	—	—	100	300
90	90	—	—	—	—	—	—	—
80	80	80	—	—	—	—	—	80
70	70	—	—	—	—	—	—	—
60	368	120	120	—	—	68	60	368
50	250	150	—	—	—	—	—	150
40	645	285	80	40	40	—	80	525
30	690	330	120	30	—	—	60	540
20	710	255	65	85	20	—	80	505
10	622	169	83	99	35	25	139	550
1	355	48	46	45	14	1	60	214
Total	6,400	2,137	634	949	139	254	719	4,832
Percentage		(44.2)	(13.1)	(19.6)	(2.9)	(5.2)	(14.9)	(100.0)

Note: 10 = 10–19 *l.t.*

total income of all fiefs for each fief holder, by taking all individual fiefs separately, and by taking the sole or first fief (usually the most valuable) listed. Total fief incomes are of limited use in several respects because they do not accurately represent total personal income. Rear-fiefs often contributed to total incomes and in some cases were the most important part of combined incomes: Pierre(la Biarde) of Ville-sur-Arce, for example, was a *dominus* with 18 *l.t.* held directly from the count, but his three rear-fiefs of 5, 10, and 60 *l.t.* made his income 93 *l.t.*, not 18 *l.t.*[34] Conversely, there are cases in which a direct holder subinfeudated his entire fief, retaining "nothing in his hand."[35] Furthermore, the infinite variety of combinations of fiefs and the frequency of transfers due to untimely death, personal ingenuity, and plain luck makes it difficult to arrive at useful figures on total incomes per se. Finally, 74.6 percent of the direct holders held only single fief incomes (see figure 3-A). It is more useful to analyze individual fiefs and then to examine their precise combinations in specific family histories.

There were 432 distinct fiefs held directly from the count, 239 (55.3 percent) of which were valued in *libratae terre*, ranging from 1 to over 200 *l.t.* Both the frequencies of occurrences and the accumulated incomes of the fiefs are here tabulated in ten-pound categories (table 8, and figure 4). For example, there were fifty-one fiefs valued from 10 to 19 *l.t.*, and their accumulated incomes amounted to 622 *l.t.* Since there is no adequate index of standard of living, it is difficult to translate annual fief incomes into equivalent levels or styles of living; but in order to provide an indicator of the relative distribution of revenues among fief holders, the number of fiefs in each category is compared with their respective accumulated incomes. Thus, the median value of individual fiefs of just under 20 *l.t.* is deceptive, for a comparison of the distribution of fiefs and their accumulated incomes reveals a substantially skewed curve. Of all valued fiefs, 70.7 percent were worth less than 30 *l.t.* annually, and yet they made up only 26.3 percent of the total accumulated incomes of all fiefs. In contrast, the seventeen fiefs valued at 100 *l.t.* or more represented only 7.2 percent of the fiefs but constituted 39.3 percent of the accumulated income (table 9).

The distribution of fief incomes varies, of course, by castellany and by the status of the holder. The registers of Isle and Saint-Florentin, both of which have exceptionally high response ratios on fief values, show the contrast by castellany. Isle was a large castellany of sixty-seven individual fiefs, of which 64.2 percent were valued (compared with the 55.3 percent for the *bailliage* as a whole). Fully 95.1 percent of its forty-three valued fiefs were worth under 30 *l.t.*, and it did not have any fief worth 50 *l.t.* or more. Isle had generally modest fiefs: although they accounted for 15.5 percent of *bailliage* fiefs, they pro-

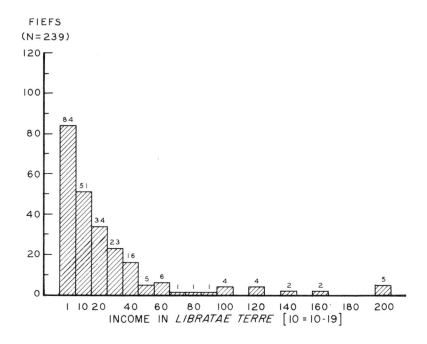

FIEFS
(N=239)

INCOME IN *LIBRATAE TERRE* [10 = 10-19]

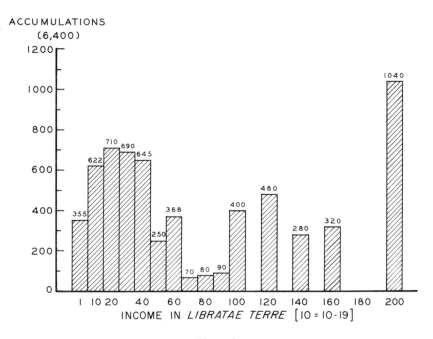

ACCUMULATIONS
(6,400)

INCOME IN *LIBRATAE TERRE* [10 = 10-19]

Figure 4
Fief Incomes, 1252

vided only 8.6 percent of the accumulated *bailliage* incomes. By contrast, Saint-Florentin with thirty-six individual fiefs had twenty-four valued (72.2 percent, the highest response ratio). Its fiefs were more valuable than those of Isle and ranged up to 200 *l.t.*: it had 8.3 percent of the *bailliage* fiefs but accounted for 14.5 percent of the accumulated incomes. And yet, even in Saint-Florentin the majority of fiefs (69.2 percent) were worth less than 30 *l.t.* Thus, in spite of differing response ratios on fief valuations by castellany register, the general *bailliage* distribution of fief incomes is consistent.

The values of individual fiefs by themselves do not reveal whether fief incomes varied according to the status of their holders. The most efficient way in which to link fiefs and their holders is to use the value of sole fiefs for the 74.6 percent of the holders who held only one fief and the value of the first (usually the most valuable) fief listed for the remaining 25.4 percent who had multiple fiefs (table 8).[36] In this manner fiefs and persons are cross-tabulated; and although the data base is reduced from 239 valued fiefs to 178 valued sole or first fiefs, the proportion of valued fiefs increases from 55.3 percent to 63.8 percent, thus improving the reliability of the available valuations.[37] In fact, all calculations of frequencies and accumulated incomes are virtually identical for both the individual fiefs alone and for the sole or first fiefs because the additional fiefs had the same distributions of values as the first or sole fiefs (table 9). The *domini, dominae,* and miscellaneous group (which included several viscounts) had the more valuable fiefs, while the *armigeri, domicellae,* and those without title had the less valuable ones. The average fief of a *dominus* was worth 29.2 *l.t.*, compared with the average fief of an *armiger* of 19.8 *l.t.*; but the respective medians of 25 *l.t.* and 10 *l.t.* are more indicative of the discrepancy in incomes for most persons in the two groups. The *domini*

Table 9

DISTRIBUTION OF FIEF INCOMES AND ACCUMULATED INCOMES, 1252

Income (*l.t.*)	Total incomes[a] Percentage of fiefs	Individual fiefs[b]		Sole/first fiefs[c]	
		Percentage of fiefs	Percentage of accumulated incomes	Percentage of fiefs	Percentage of accumulated incomes
1–19	51.6	56.4	13.3	56.1	15.8
20–49	32.0	30.5	31.9	30.9	32.5
50+	16.3	13.1	52.8	13.0	51.7
Under 30	62.7	70.7	26.3	69.6	26.3
100+	10.8	7.2	39.3	7.3	39.2
Average	36.4 *l.t.*	22.1 *l.t.*		27.1 *l.t.*	

[a]184 (65.9 %) of total incomes are valued.
[b]239 (55.3 %) of individual fiefs are valued.
[c]178 (63.8 %) of sole or first fiefs are valued.

had proportionately fewer fiefs in the 1–19 *l.t.* range and an increasingly larger share of fiefs worth over 20 *l.t.* Compared with the overall distribution of sole/first fiefs valued under 30 *l.t.* (69.6 percent), the *domini* had only 57.5 percent in that range, whereas the *armigeri* had 71.1 percent, the *dominae* 83.3 percent, and the nontitled 82.1 percent.

Notwithstanding the evident discrepancies by castellany and status, the most significant discrepancy was between the minority of fief holders, of whatever status, who held the most valuable fiefs and the rest of the fief holders, who held modest and even low-valued fiefs. This is clearly illustrated when the number of valued fiefs is plotted against their accumulated incomes (table 9, figure 5). Over half (56.4 percent) of the 239 fiefs were worth less than 20 *l.t.* annually and together constituted only 13.3 percent of the total accumulated fief incomes, whereas the great fiefs which ranged from 50 *l.t.* to over 200 *l.t.* represented only 13.1 percent of the fiefs but absorbed half (52.8

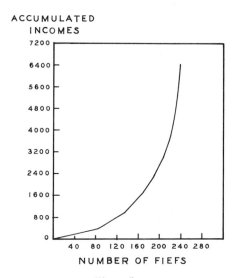

Figure 5
Distribution of Fief Incomes and
Accumulated Incomes, 1252

percent) of the available fief income. An intermediate group of fiefs ranging from 20 *l.t.* to just under 50 *l.t.* (30.5 percent) was an imprecisely bounded layer between the few valuable and the many lesser fiefs, and it consumed the remaining 31.9 percent of accumulated incomes.

It would be of great interest to establish quantitative correlations between the various income levels and the respective compositions of the fiefs. Unfortunately, the *bailliage* sample is too small for the wide range of possible combinations of fief components to reveal significant patterns. Moreover, many of the most valuable fiefs, especially those over 50 *l.t.,* understandably are not described in their numerous parts. Also, the nonvalued fiefs have proportionately fewer specifications, perhaps in this instance the result of scribal ignorance. So the following figures are indicative only of the general degree to which various components were present on the 279 sole or first fiefs. Most properties were obviously landed, but only half (48 percent) specifically had arable; and fewer contained fields or pastures (22 percent) or woods (24 percent). Almost one-third (29 percent) had *cens* revenues, and one-third (29.4 percent) had resident tenants (*homines*) or immigrants (*albani*). Ovens appeared on 14 percent of the fiefs, and mills or both mills and ovens on another 6 percent. In none of these components is there a strong correlation with the level of fief income or status of the holder. However, as might be expected, the important financial rights of *péage, tonlieu,* tolls, or market revenues were noted for only 11 percent of the fiefs; and some of these references may well have been to shares, say of *péage,* and not to the entire right. More surprising, rights of justice were found on 23.7 percent of the 279 fiefs (17.6 percent of all 432 individual fiefs) and were directly linked to fief income. Only 12.9 percent of the nonvalued and 15.3 percent of the 1–9 *l.t.* fiefs had any rights of justice (expressed simply as "justice"), whereas over 30 percent of the 10–30 *l.t.* fiefs had some justice. Justice was probably universal on fiefs valued over 50 *l.t.,* where the failure to mention it was probably due to the avoidance of redundancy. The 120 *l.t.* fief of Isabel of Dannemoine, for example, is listed as the "entire village," but in 1273 when the fief was sold to the count, justice constituted one-third of the total revenue.[38] In other cases it can be shown that the justice of a fief had actually been assigned out and was no longer part of a holding.[39]

All these percentages would be slightly higher, if the largest and most valuable fiefs are assumed to have contained all the various components, but the general magnitudes would still hold true, especially in the case of justice and commercial rights. It would be difficult to make a case for deliberate omission of any of the important components, for these were fiefs held from the count and inventoried by official *enquê-teurs,* who took testimony on oath; it is unlikely that they would have omitted, virtually at will, such important information on fiefs.[40] Even this partial and approximate analysis of fief composition weighs against the stereotyped fief consisting of tracts of arable, resident tenants, and banal and other rights. Champagne fiefs often consisted only of parts of mills, fields and vines, or simply grain, *terrage,* or customary rents. It seems, from the individual cases as well as from the quantitative results, that only the more valuable fiefs fit the image of complete estates with arable, pastures, fields, woods, men, banal rights, and justice.[41]

A direct correlation can also be established between the level of fief income and the possession of a castle or fortification. The four valued fiefs with castles each yielded from 100 to 120 *l.t.* annually, ranking among the 7.3 percent of all fiefs worth 100 *l.t.* or more. Fortified houses (*domus fortes*) appeared on fiefs ranging from 5 to 100 *l.t.*, but seven of the ten so valued were worth 30 *l.t.* or more, ranking in the minority (23.1 percent) of fiefs worth 30–99 *l.t.* (see also below). Simple houses (*domus*) were recorded on 27.5 percent of the fiefs, most of which were valued under 40 *l.t.* The remaining 60 percent of sole/first fiefs (70 percent of all individual fiefs) did not have any dwelling mentioned. The absence of dwellings on so many fiefs cannot be explained by scribal neglect, since buildings were as much accountable as other items on the count's fiefs. It is of course possible that houses were located on other private fiefs or alods and that some fief holders lived in rented dwellings in villages or towns. Also, some knights lived together with relatives (for example, two brothers, knights of Bouy-Luxembourg, shared a house). But the most general explanation lies in the meaning of *domus*: in early-thirteenth-century references it was juxtaposed with castle and may have meant a fortification of some sort,[42] but by mid-century it was clearly not a fortification, although it probably retained the connotation of a particularly heavy or permanent type of structure, as opposed to most peasant dwellings. In the *Rôles* the absence of *domus* on fiefs probably indicates that most fief holders of lower incomes lived in more modest houses, not so distinct from peasant homes, which were always referred to in other sources as hearths, not as houses.[43]

The *Rôles* furnish fuller information on the castle guard assigned to each fief, although in practice multiple fief holders usually owed service for only one of their fiefs. There is information on guard for 192 (68.8 percent) of the 279 fief holders (table 10, figures 6-A and 6-B). More precise than the original *Feoda*, which records only the fact that guard was owed, the *Rôles* also include notations for those who explicitly did not owe guard (*non debet gardam*), as well as for those who gave uncertain responses ("he doesn't know about guard") and those who were required to report later. In all, ninety-four (33.6 percent) fief holders owed some guard, compared to 45.4 percent in 1172. Another third (28.0 percent) explicitly did not owe service, and 7.2 percent were unsure about their obligation or were to answer later. The remaining third (31.2 percent) failed to mention guard, and their fiefs probably did not owe any. There is no significant correlation between the length of service and the status of the holder.[44] Nor is there any link between length of service and the value of the fief in 1252.[45]

Table 10
CASTLE GUARD, 1252

Castellany	Total	"Guard"	Tour of Duty (weeks)						Total Service	None	Unknown	Blank
			to 4	5–6	7–8	9–12	13–24	25–52				
Troyes	47	—	—	—	—	2	—	1	3	14	6	24
Isle	48	4	5	12	—	1	—	1	23	11	3	11
St.-Florentin	23	—	1	—	1	1	—	—	3	11	1	8
Ervy	45	3	8	—	—	3	1	1	16	17	1	11
Pont-sur-Seine	32	2	3	3	9	—	1	—	18	6	—	8
Méry-sur-Seine	16	—	2	3	—	—	—	—	5	3	3	5
Payns	8	—	1	1	—	—	—	—	2	4	1	1
Nogent-sur-Seine	25	—	1	—	7	2	1	—	13	5	1	6
Bar-sur-Seine	35	4	6	—	—	1	—	2	11	7	4	13
Total	279	13	27	19	17	10	3	5	94	78	20	87
Percentage of service		(13.8)	(28.7)	(20.2)	(18.1)	(10.6)	(3.2)	(5.3)	(100.0)			
Percentage of total	(100.0)								(33.6)	(28.0)	(7.2)	(31.2)

Status of holders

	Total	"Guard"	to 4	5–6	7–8	9–12	13–24	25–52	Total Service	None	Unknown	Blank
Dominus	113	5	10	5	5	5	1	2	33 (29.1)	35 (31.0)	14	36 (31.9)
Armiger	46	1	6	2	4	1	1	2	17 (37.0)	11 (23.0)	4	14 (30.4)
Domina	48	2	7	7	2	—	—	—	19 (39.6)	16 (33.3)	2	11 (22.9)
Domicella	10	1	1	1	2	—	—	—	5 (50.0)	3 (30.0)	—	2 (20.0)
Other	8	—	—	1	2	2	—	—	5 (62.5)	1 (12.5)	—	2 (25.0)
Blank	54	4	3	3	2	2	—	1	15 (27.8)	12 (22.2)	5	22 (40.7)

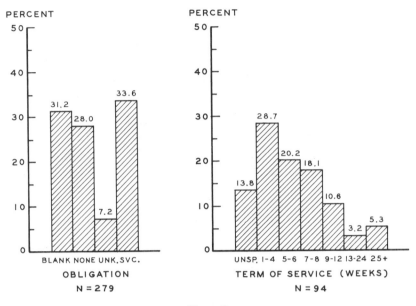

Figure 6
Castle Guard, 1252

None of the *domini* in the *bailliage* area in the *Feoda* of 1172 owed
guard, nor did their descendants in the *Rôles*. The only two castle
holders in 1252 who did owe service were continuing obligations
incurred by their non-*domini* ancestors in the twelfth century.[46] Traditionally, the county defenses were anchored on the count's castles
controlling river routes, and the heaviest castle guard in the twelfth and
early thirteenth centuries was assigned in the castles on the Seine
approach to Troyes. A dozen or so inland castles held privately by great
lords gave depth to the river-based castles of the count and were
renderable to the count whenever he needed them. But the count's
general defensive posture in the *bailliage* shifted in the first two decades
of the thirteenth century with his acquisition of two private lordships
(Nogent and Bar-sur-Seine) on the Seine, which became the new Seine
outposts (from Troyes), and with the spread of fortified houses (*domus
fortes*) between the Seine and the Armançon. The fortified houses,
running from Bar-sur-Seine through the Forest of Chaource to Saint-
Florentin, secured the southern frontier with Burgundy, hitherto ex-
posed except for a few strong points (map 7).[47] The exact military role
of these new fortifications is not clear, but their spread was undoubtedly tied to the succession crisis and to the support of the lesser
families for Thibaut IV against some of the old aristocracy of the
castles. In any case, the holders of fortified houses, like those of castles,
were generally exempt from service in the count's castles; only six

holders of such fortifications owed guard, and all were continuing the obligations of their ancestors. For example, the lords of Saint-Phal in 1252 still owed the all-year service at Isle that their ancestors had owed in 1172, but sometime before 1265 they transferred that duty, by what they claimed was a customary option, to their own fortification at Saint-Phal.[48] Although the count's castles with the longest tours of duty in 1172 also had the heaviest obligations in 1252, the spread of fortified houses seems to have been linked to the general decrease in service rendered at his castles and to the decline in overall importance of those few strongpoints.

Finally, at the end of each *Rôles* entry the *enquêteurs* recorded the names and possessions of the rear-fief holders. Actually, 56.6 percent of the 279 direct holders had no rear-fief holders. And 46 (16.5 percent) direct holders accounted for 325 (75.6 percent) rear holders (figure 3-B, table 11).[49] The system of fiefs and rear-fiefs was sharply dichotomous, with a few direct holders controlling most of the rear-fiefs. Only 12 percent of the rear holders were also direct holders (see below). Most of the references to relationships between rear holder and overlord were to brothers, sisters, and in-laws (78.1 percent, or fifty of the sixty-four such references), with very few cases to parents, children, and other relatives; but those explicit references were offered for only 10 percent of all rear-fief holders, so it appears that the fief and rear-fief systems were on the whole mutually exclusive.

Table 11
THE FIEF AND REAR-FIEF SYSTEM

	Fief Holders	
no rear-fief holders	*with rear-fief holders*	
56.6%	43.4%	N = 279
	26.9% 16.5%	
	↓ ↓	
	Percentage of	
	rear-fief holders	
	24.4% 75.6%	N = 430

In all, there were 430 rear-fief holders (table 12, figure 7), of whom 78.1 percent were male and 21.9 percent female, virtually the same ratio as for the direct holders (76.3 percent and 23.7 percent, respectively). It is difficult, however, to present an accurate breakdown of social status because half (50.2 percent) of the rear-fief holders were not identified by status. If the nonascription of status is assumed to be random and not itself indicative of a particular status, then the breakdown of known status can be used: 70.1 percent *domini,* 4.2 percent *armigeri,* 19.2 percent *dominae,* 0.5 percent *domicellae,* and 6.1 percent others. Compared to the respective ratios of direct fief holders, there were proportionately more *domini* and fewer *armigeri* among

Table 12
REAR-FIEF HOLDERS, 1252

Castellany	Total	Dominus	Armiger	Domina	Domi- cella	Other	Blank Men	Blank Women
Troyes	161	75	1	15	—	2	52	16
Isle	56	9	—	4	1	4	24	14
St.-Florentin	41	11	—	4	—	—	21	5
Ervy	59	17	3	5	—	3	29	2
Pont-sur-Seine[a]	48	18	1	10	—	1	15	3
Méry-sur-Seine	15	4	—	1	—	2	6	2
Payns	7	1	—	2	—	—	2	2
Nogent-sur-Seine	24	4	4	—	—	—	11	5
Bar-sur-Seine	19	11	—	—	—	1	6	1
Total	430	150	9	41	1	13	166	50
Percentage of total	(100.0)	(34.9)	(2.1)	(9.5)	(0.2)	(3.0)	(50.2)	
Percentage of total, blanks excluded	(100.0)	(70.1)	(4.2)	(19.2)	(0.5)	(6.1)		

[a]The editor notes that the manuscript is mutilated and that it probably contained additional entries.

rear-fief holders. But while omission of status may be more significant for the rear-fief holders, it is correspondingly more difficult to check with charter evidence because the rear-fief holders are seldom mentioned in the charters.

Almost all rear-fief holders (91.7 percent) had a single rear-fief, and of the 430 sole or first rear-fiefs, 203 (47.2 percent) were valued in *libratae terre* (tables 13-A, 13-B, 14, and figures 8 and 9).[50] Generally, rear-fiefs were less valuable than the direct fiefs. The preponderance of rear-fiefs (81.3 percent) was worth less than 30 *l.t.*, and the median rear-fief was worth about 10 *l.t.*, that is, about 10 *l.t.* less than the median direct fief. As with direct fiefs, the more valuable rear-fiefs were held by *domini*. But there is another important factor here: 52 (12 percent) of the rear-fief holders were direct fief holders, and these men held the more valuable rear-fiefs that controlled 20 percent of the accumulated rear-fief income. Their rear-fiefs averaged 27.8 *l.t.*, far above the overall rear-fief average of 16 *l.t.* and actually on a par with the average direct fiefs (27 *l.t.*).[51] For these men, to hold in rear-fief was simply an arrangement for controlling income which for some reason could not be held directly from the count. This subgroup was distinct from ordinary rear-fief holders whose only income was a single rear-fief, which in most cases consisted of fragmentary revenues, often grain or minor rents. Only a handful of all rear-fiefs had justice, tax, or banal revenues.

In spite of some variation by castellany, an exceptionally precise and

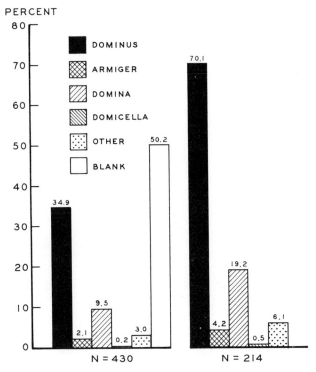

Figure 7
Rear-Fief Holders, 1252

coherent image emerges of fief holders and their fiefs in the mid-thirteenth-century *bailliage,* and the figures as a whole agree to within a few percentage points with those for the entire county of Champagne.[52] Half of all fief holders were *domini,* and one-fifth each were nonknighted *armigeri* and *dominae.* Although the breakdown by status was about the same for rear-fief holders, there was a sharp difference in their respective holdings and incomes: the median fief was just under 20 *l.t.,* the median rear-fief only about 10 *l.t.* The low value of rear-fiefs may have been one factor in their eventual disappearance from the count's inventories altogether (see below). Moreover, the tenure system itself was formally two-tiered: 75.6 percent of the rear-fief holders were controlled by only 16.5 percent of the direct fief holders. The rear-fief system was independent of and subordinate to, rather than integral with, the direct fief system, and the families moved within their respective tenure systems.

Within the direct fief system, the twelfth-century dichotomy in titles was reflected in the incomes and composition of the mid-thirteenth-century fiefs. Although half of the fiefs were worth up to 20 *l.t.,*

THE FIEF HOLDERS

Table 13
ANNUAL REAR-FIEF INCOMES, 1252

A. *Frequencies*

Value	Individual Rear-Fiefs	Dominus	Armiger	Domina	Domi-cella	Other	Blank	Total
200+	1	1	–	–	–	–	–	1
120	2	1	–	1	–	–	–	2
80	1	–	–	–	–	–	–	–
70	2	2	–	–	–	–	–	2
60	6	6	–	–	–	–	–	6
50	4	2	–	–	–	–	2	4
40	9	3	1	1	–	–	4	9
30	16	7	1	1	–	–	7	16
20	23	11	–	–	–	–	11	22
10	42	17	1	–	–	–	20	38
1	113	30	2	10	1	6	54	103
Subtotal	219	80(39.4)	5	13	1	6	92	203
Nonvalued	250	70	4	28	–	7	118	227
Total	469	150(34.9)	9(2.1)	41(9.5)	1(0.2)	13(3.0)	210(50.2)	430(100.●

Sole or First Rear-Fiefs (spanning the Dominus–Total columns)

Note: 10 = 10–19 *l.t.*

B. *Accumulations*

Value	Individual Rear-Fiefs	Dominus	Armiger	Domina	Domicella	Other	Blank	Total
200+	200	200	–	–	–	–	–	200
120	240	120	–	120	–	–	–	240
80	80	–	–	–	–	–	–	–
70	140	140	–	–	–	–	–	140
60	360	360	–	–	–	–	–	360
50	200	100	–	–	–	–	100	200
40	365	125	40	40	–	–	160	365
30	483	210	30	30	–	–	213	483
20	507	247	–	–	–	–	240	487
10	518	221	10	–	–	–	242	473
1	453	115	7	43	3	21	228	417
Total	3,546	1,838	87	233	3	21	993	3,365
Percentage		(54.6)	(2.6)	(6.9)	(0.1)	(0.6)	(35.1)	(100.0)

Sole or First Rear-Fiefs (spanning the Dominus–Total columns)

Note: 10 = 10–19 *l.t.*

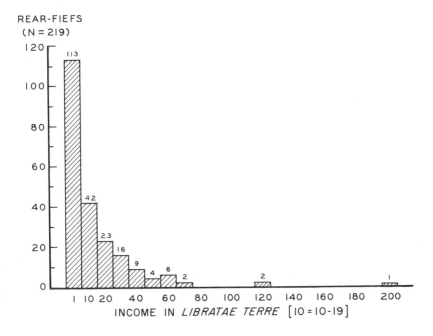

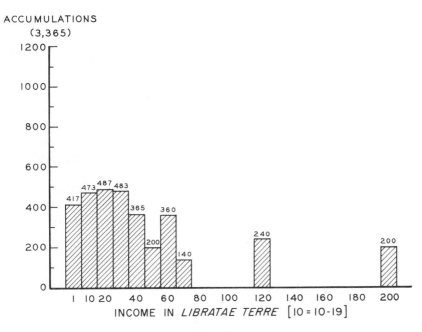

Figure 8
Rear-Fief Incomes, 1252

altogether they furnished their holders with less than one-third of the total income available to the minority of fief holders who had fiefs worth 50 *l.t.* or more. The wealthy families were the only ones with full estates including justice and lucrative commercial rights, and they supported most of the rear-fief holders (the lord of Chappes, for example, had forty-three rear-fief holders). Yet in the early thirteenth century an intermediate group of fief holders emerged: they held the newly constructed fortified houses, supported several rear-fief holders,

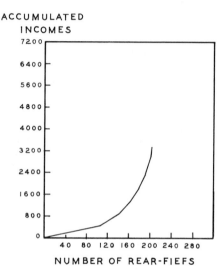

ACCUMULATED
INCOMES

NUMBER OF REAR-FIEFS

Figure 9
Distribution of Rear-Fief Incomes
and Accumulated Incomes, 1252

Table 14
DISTRIBUTION OF REAR-FIEF
INCOMES AND ACCUMULATED
INCOMES, 1252

Income (in *l.t.*)	Percentage of rear-fiefs (N = 203)	Percentage of accumulated incomes
1–19	69.5	26.4
20–49	23.1	39.5
50+	7.4	34.1

and had incomes ranging from 30 to 50 *l.t.*, or multiples thereof, since they often held several properties. Thus, the two-level, lord-knight fief system of the twelfth century evolved into four distinct levels of fiefs and rear-fiefs by 1252: the rear-fief holders (10 *l.t.* median, usually of fragmentary revenues), the lesser fief holders (20 *l.t.* median, with some consolidated properties but no rights), the new intermediary group (30–50 *l.t.*, with fortified houses, a few rear-fief holders), and the wealthy old families (over 50 *l.t.*, with castles, great estates with full rights, and numerous rear-fief holders). The four groups together composed the aristocracy by virtue of status and tenure, but only the two latter groups—the holders of castles and of fortified houses, who together comprised 22.5 percent of all fief and rear-fief holders and absorbed 61 percent of the accumulated fief and rear-fief incomes—possessed the physical symbols of superior standing, as well as rights of justice and taxes on trade, and men holding rear-fiefs from them.[53]

TRENDS, 1172–1275

There were two final surveys of fief holders and their fiefs before the county fell under royal influence in 1284. A *Livre des hommages* was compiled by 1265, and a new *Rôles des fiefs* was drawn up in 1274-75. The surveys contain generally similar entries, although they are far less detailed than the *Rôles* of 1252 with respect to fiefs, incomes, and military service and therefore are not subject to comparable quantitative analysis. But the new surveys do contain important data which corroborate the information in the earlier *Rôles* and which furnish points of reference for the longer trends from 1172, just after Henry the Liberal organized the county, to 1275, only a decade before the county was tied officially and irrevocably to the royal house.

Taken together, the four surveys of 1172, 1252, 1265, and 1275 show a striking overall decrease in the number of direct fief holders of the count (table 15). The numerical decline can be measured in several ways. First, if only the original eight-castellany area of 1172 is considered, and if Méry is assigned in 1275 what appears to have been its stable number of 17, then the decrease from 1172 to 1275 for the fixed eight-castellany area was 43.1 percent. Second, if the mid-thirteenth-century, ten-castellany area is imposed on 1172, with the earliest figures for the "new" castellanies of Nogent (eleven in 1200) and Bar-sur-Seine (thirty-five in 1252) projected back to 1172, and if Méry is again assigned seventeen in 1275, then the decrease was 41.6 percent. Both methods are based on fairly fixed geographical areas and express the actual numerical decrease in most castellanies. A third method is to consider the historical development of the *bailliage* from eight to ten castellanies: if the eight-castellany area of 1172 is compared with the ten-castellany area of 1275, again with Méry's figure being supplied, the decrease for the *bailliage* which was larger by two castellanies was 32.9 percent.[54] However, two distortions, geographical and chronological, are inherent in these calculations. Three castellanies (Ervy, Méry, and Villemaur) remained relatively stable, whereas four (Troyes, Isle, Pont, and Bar-sur-Seine) lost about half their number, and two others declined even more sharply (Saint-Florentin by 75 percent and Payns almost entirely). Moreover, within the original eight-castellany area the decrease of direct fief holders in the eighty years from 1172 to 1252 was only 20.4 percent, compared with the 28.9 percent for the next twenty-three years, 1252-75, and compared to the 43.1 percent for the entire period 1172–1275. The sharp decline from the mid-thirteenth century might suggest that the later surveys are incomplete, were it not for the fact that three of the original castellanies remained remarkably

Table 15
FIEF HOLDERS, 1172–1275

Castellany	Feoda, 1172	Rôles, 1252	Hommages, 1265	Rôles B, 1275
Troyes	125 b	47	45	32 a
Isle-Aumont	– b	48	41	36
St.-Florentin	41	23	18	10
Ervy	33	45	[45]	34
Villemaur	26	[30]	30	25
Pont-sur-Seine	41	32	26	22
Méry-sur-Seine	17	16	17	[17]
Payns	30	8	2	2
Nogent-sur-Seine	[11]	25	18	13
Bar-sur-Seine	[35]	35	33	19
Total	313	279	230	193
Probable total	[359]	[309]	[275]	[210]

Status of holder [c]

Dominus		104 (48.6)	84 (56.7)	56 (44.8)
Armiger		45 (21.0)	12 (8.1)	31 (24.8)
Domina		48 (22.4)	31 (20.9)	28 (22.4)
Domicella		10 (4.7)	7 (4.0)	9 (7.2)
Other		7 (3.3)	14 (9.4)	1 (0.8)
Blank		65 [23.3] d	82 [35.7] d	68 [35.2] d

Sex

Men	297 (98.1)	213 (76.3)	185 (80.4)	153 (79.3)
Women	6 (1.9)	66 (23.7)	45 (19.6)	40 (20.7)

Note: Brackets in the upper part of the table indicate numbers that have been assigned to compensate for missing registers, as explained in the text.
[a] The beginning of the Troyes register is damaged; the figure should be slightly higher.
[b] There was a single Troyes-Isle register in 1172 (see table 3); the figure given here for Troyes applies to both areas.
[c] Percentages for specific status groups are based on known status only, except as in note d. See also note 56.
[d] Percentages for non-attributed status are based on the total number of persons.

stable during the entire hundred years and through four surveys.[55] It seems reasonable to conclude that the decline in actual fief holders was in the range of from 20.4 percent to 43.1 percent and that the most accurate figure is about 40 percent.[56] The disappearance of direct holders cannot be explained by subinfeudation, for the number of rear-fief holders decreased even more drastically.

In spite of the overall decrease in numbers, the ratios of men and women and of each status group remained the same throughout the thirteenth century. In 1252, 23.7 percent of the fief holders were women, and in 1265 and 1275 they were respectively 19.6 percent and 20.7 percent; women held about one-fifth of the count's fiefs at any time, either in their own right as inheritance or in dowry, wardship, or escheat. The status categories also remained stable, although the terms changed: the 1326 copy of the 1275 *Rôles des fiefs* translated *dominus* as *monsieur, domina* as *dame, armiger* as *escuier,* and *domicella* as *damoiselle.*[57] On the whole the variations in status are not substantial, except for the nontitled persons, who increased from 23.3 percent in 1252 to 35 percent in 1265 and 1275; but this cannot be explained on a purely quantitative basis.[58] The *domini* remained at about half the fief-holding population, and the *armigeri* and *dominae* each at about one-fifth; the remaining tenth were *domicellae* and miscellaneous. The relative stability in distribution of status groups in the second half of the thirteenth century is important because it indicates that the earlier normal progression of boys from *armiger* to *miles/dominus* and of girls from *domicella* to *domina* was no longer necessarily operative. Some *armigeri* retained that status for their entire lives, as did some *domicellae* even after marriage. The sharp twelfth-century division between *domini* and *milites* was upset by the turn of the thirteenth century, and a new equilibrium was reached by the mid-thirteenth century, when the fief holders were comprised of four clearly-defined status groups.

The surveys of 1265 and 1275 also confirm certain long-term developments, particularly the imposition of liegeance and the decline of castle guard. In 1172 only 47.0 percent of all fief holders were liege to the count, while 5.7 percent owed primary liegeance to another lord; 47.3 percent provided no information on that point (table 16). *Feoda* II and III, of 1200/1201, although fragmentary, show that the percentage of liegemen had risen slightly to 56.6 percent. But *Feoda* IV and V, of 1204/10, make apparent a sharp increase in liegemen to 78.4 percent and a comparable decrease in blank entries and in liegemen of other lords.[59] The increase in liegeance in the first decade of the thirteenth century can be linked directly to the developing succession crisis, when there began a determined effort to procure liege homage from all the count's fief holders. For example, Jean of Thil was liege to the count of Brienne, but in 1210/14 he promised that his heirs would be *totius ligius* to the count of Champagne in the future.[60] The lords of Ramerupt, the collateral line of the Brienne family, were not listed in the *Feoda* of 1172 or of 1200 because they held their properties directly from Brienne; but by 1210/14 Erard of Ramerupt was listed in *Feoda* V as liege to the count of Champagne.[61] The fragmentary registers of 1222–43 confirm the higher percentage of liegemen at about 80 percent of the fief holders. Although the *Rôles* of 1252 and 1275 do not record liegeance—they were registers of fiefs—the *Livre des hommages* of 1265 does: 73 percent of the fief holders were liege to the count. The purely quantitative conclusion can be illustrated by the many cases of liegeance being imposed upon fief holders or purchased from them by the count in return for an increase ("augmentation") in their fief revenues.

The decline in castle guard was also dramatic: only twenty-four men (10.5 percent) in 1265 rendered any guard at all. The percentage was

Table 16

LIEGEANCE, 1172–1265

	Feoda I 1172	Feoda II/III 1200/1201	Feoda IV/V 1204/14	Feoda $VI^{a,b}$ 1229	Feoda VI^b 1222–43	Feoda VIII^b 1234–40	Hommages 1265
Liege	133 (47.0)	72 (56.2)	73 (78.4)	136 (69.4)	330 (79.4)	104 (80.6)	168 (73.0)
Not liege	16 (5.7)	20 (15.6)	4 (4.3)	29 (15.7)	76 (17.7)	15 (11.6)	18 (7.8)
Blank	134 (47.3)	36 (28.2)	16 (17.3)	19 (14.9)	22 (2.9)	10 (7.8)	44 (19.2)
Total	283	128	93	184	428	129	230

[a]Knights in the countess's dowry.
[b]Figures calculated from fragmentary registers for the entire county.

down from 33.6 percent in 1252 and 45.4 percent in 1172. The *Rôles* of 1275 fail to mention guard altogether, an indication that for practical purposes fief tenure had been divorced from military service. One of the primary reasons for keeping fiefs distinct in the twelfth and thirteenth centuries was to keep intact the assigned castle guard, which theoretically could not be diminished if the original fief were divided. With the decline in importance of castle guard, the requirement of keeping properties separate was eliminated, and single fief holdings increased from 74.6 percent in 1252 to 92.7 percent in 1275. That is, the fact of fief tenure was by then sufficient to encompass all fief holdings, and individual properties and their lines of transmission were no longer as crucial as they had been in 1252.

The *Rôles* of 1275 are far less specific about fief components than those of 1252, but several important contrasts can be obtained. In 1275, 37.3 percent of the fiefs had resident tenants, and 33.7 percent had justice, compared with 29.4 percent and 23.7 percent, respectively, in 1252. This increase in tenants and justice by about 10 percent coincides with the decline in the number of fief holders by about 32 percent (from 309 to 210; see table 15). The less important fiefs seem to have been omitted from the survey of 1275, hence the increased ratio of tenants and justice on the remaining fiefs. Furthermore, there was a sharp drop in the number of rear-fief holders (from 430 to 88) and in the percentage of direct holders who had rear-fief holders: only 21.2 percent of the fief holders in 1275 had rear-fief holders, compared with 43.5 percent in 1252. In short, it seems that the lesser fiefs and rear-fiefs of 1252 had either disappeared or were no longer accorded their former status by county officials.

The essential changes in the fief holders as a group in the century from 1172 to 1275 were in organization and size. In the twelfth century the *domini* were only a handful of men from very old families;

by the mid-thirteenth century about half of the fief- and rear-fief holders were called *domini*. Also, women, who do not seem to have been accountable for ordinary fiefs in the twelfth century, by the mid-thirteenth century consistently represented about 20 percent of the count's fief holders. The new status differentiations did not conceal the continuing social preeminence and financial importance of the old families, which did not, however, recover their political influence (see chapter V). The decrease in the number of fief-holding families was another major development. A decrease of at least 20 percent, and more probably about 40 percent, for a group of less than three hundred families was a serious event in a period when other sectors of the population were continually increasing. The decrease can probably be explained by the outright disappearance of some fiefs and their possessors (see chapter V) and also by the loss of fief status for numerous small holdings of grain and rents. Thus, only the more important fiefs retained their status, and a whole layer of rear-fiefs practically disappeared as far as the official inventories were concerned. The result was that the fief-holding aristocracy became a smaller, more uniform, and more cohesive group vis-à-vis the general population.

V
The Aristocracy
COUNTS, LORDS, AND KNIGHTS

The interpretation of a local aristocracy and its development depends considerably on the methodological resolution of two fundamental problems: the lack of contemporary definitions of aristocratic status and the inadequacy of genealogical evidence for aristocratic families. Since charter references usually furnish the basic information for family trees, good genealogies can be constructed only for the families that appear frequently in the ecclesiastical cartularies because of their continuing generosity to local monasteries, that is, the most powerful and wealthiest families. Genealogies for the lesser fief-holding families contain many lacunae which simply cannot be filled from charter references alone, so their histories remain fragmentary at best. Fortunately for the study of the Champagne aristocracy, the administrative surveys of the counts inventoried all fief holders, both the great and the ordinary, their titles, possessions, and often other information about their families. The integration of this survey data on particular persons and properties with the information supplied by the local charters substantially increases the number of fief-holding families that can be examined in some detail. The Champagne registers have already yielded quantitative parameters for the fief-holding population in general (chapter IV), in which the characteristics of the entire group serve as standards of comparison for individual families. The overall quantitative results are a corrective to the concentration on the best-documented, hence usually unrepresentative, families because they permit a rough assessment of the representativeness of particular families, their possessions, and histories. Thus, the administrative registers present the quantitative framework for evaluating individual families and supplement the charter evidence with valuable information on genealogies and actual fiefs.

The second major problem is terminology: How is the aristocracy to be defined? Exclusive reliance on charter terms is not satisfactory for the *bailliage* because references to castle-holding and to titles of nobility—the two traditional criteria of aristocratic status—for particular families are quite fortuitous in the extant charters. Most castles in the *bailliage*, for example, are first mentioned in the early twelfth century, yet several of the most prominent local families whose activities and influence leave no doubt that they possessed castles are not associated with castles in any of the extant early charters. Furthermore, if castle-holding were the sole criterion of aristocratic status, many of the castellan families whose territories were absorbed into the count's domain before the mid-twelfth century—before charters were abundant—and who were not identified in earlier charters as castle holders would have to be excluded from the aristocracy altogether. In like manner, references to certain titles, such as *nobilis* (or *illuster*) *vir*, are insufficient because ecclesiastical scribes applied the terms sporadically, often omitting them when their use would have been legitimate; as a result, the extant charters do not necessarily qualify as "noble" all persons who merited that title in the twelfth century (the term *castellanus* was not current here, although it was common in northern Champagne). Also, the chronology of title usage must be carefully controlled because the meanings of the terms changed as society itself evolved: titles did not carry the same connotation in 1250 as they did in 1100 or 1150. In short, the reliance on any single criterion, be it title or possession, based on charter references alone is unsound method until that element can be interpreted within the context of the relevant family histories. Again, the Champagne inventories act to check and complement the charter evidence: they furnish an administrative, secular, and systematic classification of all fief holders, independent of charter terminology. Significantly, the surveys do not refer to "noble" or "castellan" in any of their forms. They employ rather *comes*, *dominus*, and *miles*, and these are the categories in which the *bailliage* families are classified here.

Each of the titles had a distinctive history, tied to the development of the respective families. The *comes* title had a relatively simple evolution. In addition to the count of Troyes, there were three other counts in the *bailliage* area in the eleventh century. Only their families—and more narrowly, only one member of each house—carried the title in both the private charters and the official Champagne inventories. No new families ever adopted the *comes* title, and only one of the three families survived through the thirteenth century, to outlast even the count of Troyes. The *dominus* title had a more complicated evolution. In the eleventh and early twelfth centuries the ecclesiastical scribes often referred to men of considerable local importance without affixing any title to their names. But from about 1120/30 the charters routinely employed *dominus* as the exclusive title of a small group of families. The men were called simply *domini*, never *milites*. This distinction for a minority of the twelfth-century families is corroborated by the *Feoda* of 1172, in which the same men were identified by the count's scribes as *domini* and thereby distinguished from all other fief holders.[1] The restrictive use of the title lasted through the reign of Henry I (d. 1181).

Thereafter, the *dominus* title was gradually attached to men who were unrelated to the *domini* families and who until then had been designated *milites*. By the early thirteenth century the new style had permeated the charters; although the descendants of *domini* families were still entitled *domini*, the descendants of twelfth-century knight families were qualified variously *domini* or *milites*. There is no evident explanation for the change in title attribution, and it is especially difficult to interpret because the official administrative documents did not adopt the new practice until the *Rôles des fiefs* of 1249-52, in which the descendants of the twelfth-century *domini* and *milites* families were listed together indiscriminately as *domini*.[2] It would appear that the term was debased in the first half of the thirteenth century as the small group of twelfth-century lords was penetrated by ordinary knights and that the two groups fused into a single social group by the mid-thirteenth century.

Table 17 is an attempt to test the fusion hypothesis by isolating the leading families. Since contemporary sources did not explicitly define an "aristocracy" or isolate the families of which it was composed, several indirect criteria are employed to produce that definition. Columns I and II list the families whose members were qualified as *comes* or *dominus* in the extant charters of 1075–1125 (ending with the transfer of the county of Troyes to the main Blois line) and 1126–72 (ending with the composition of the *Feoda*). A few families appeared early without their appropriate titles—both the Chappes and the Chacenay, for example, appeared from the late eleventh century but were not styled *domini* until 1137/38—although the histories of those families suggest that the late occurrence of such references is not related to the development of the families (that is, they did not "rise" to that level) but is rather a reflection of extreme localism and the varied accomplishments and styles of the monastic scribes.[3] The *Feoda Campanie* (1172) and its continuations into the early thirteenth century are important counterpoints to the charter evidence because the count's scribes worked from the perspective of a great secular prince and were not under pressure to defer to personal sensibilities when assigning titles in the official administrative records. Column III lists all persons designated *comes* or *dominus* in the *Feoda* who belonged in the castellanies of the later *bailliage* of Troyes or in the castellanies of Rosnay and Bar-sur-Aube, if their descendants were listed in the thirteenth-century *bailliage* of Troyes. Although a few of these old families were without title in the first *Feoda*, they did appear with title in the special register of "great fiefs" in *Feoda* II of ca. 1200 (column IV).[4] Columns I through IV demonstrate that both the ecclesiastical charters and the Champagne registers agree in defining a precise group of about a dozen count and lord families who were distinguished by title from the

Table 17
THE OLD ARISTOCRACY

	I 1075–1125 charters	II 1126–72 charters	III 1172 *Feoda* I	IV ca. 1200 *Feoda* II	V 1212 "barons"	VI 1214 "banners"	VII 1224 "barons"	VIII 1304 "castellans"	IX 1314 "nobles"
Counts									
	Bar-sur-Seine	Bar-sur-Seine	Bar-sur-Seine	Bar-sur-Seine	Bar-sur-Seine, M. IV [minor]				
	Brienne	Brienne	Brienne	Brienne		Brienne		Brienne	
	Ramerupt								
Lords									
	Chacenay[b]	Arcis	Arcis[b]	Arcis	Ramerupt,[a] Er. I	Ramerupt,[a] Er. I	Ramerupt,[a] Er. I		
	Chappes[b]	Chacenay	Chacenay	Chacenay	Arcis, Jean II	Arcis, Jean II	Arcis, Guy	Arcis	
	Plancy[b]	Chappes	Chappes[b]	Chappes	Chacenay, Er. II	Chacenay, Er. II	Durnay,[a] Jac.		
		Plancy[b]	Plancy[b]	Plancy	Chappes, Cl. V	Chappes, Cl. V	Chappes, Cl. V	Chappes	Chappes
						Plancy, Ph. I	Plancy, Ph. & Guy	Plancy	Plancy, Ph.
						Jully,[a] Guy		Jully	Jully, Jean
	Dampierre	Ervy	Dampierre	Dampierre	Dampierre, Guy II			Dampierre	Dampierre, Gm. IV
	Méry	Dampierre							
	Payns	Nogent	Nogent						
	Pont								
	Pougy	Pougy	Pougy	Pougy	Pougy, Guy [minor]	Pougy, Milo I	Pougy, Man. II	Pougy	Pougy, Gm.
	Traînel	Traînel	Traînel	Traînel		Traînel		Traînel, Hen. II	Traînel, Hen. II
		Marigny[b]	Marigny[b]	Marigny	Marigny,[a] Gar. III	Marigny,[a] Gar. III	Marigny,[a] Gar. IV	Marigny [Thil]	Marigny, Gm.
								Traînel [Estemay]	Traînel, Dreux III
	Villemaur[b]	Villemaur[b]	Villemaur[b]	Villemaur[b]					
	Vendeuvre	Vendeuvre	Vendeuvre	Vendeuvre					
Others[c]									
	Charmont	Charmont	Charmont[b]	Romilly					
				St-Phal				St-Phal, Etienne	St-Phal, Etienne
					St-Maurice, Hugh			Cléry, Hugh	Cléry, Hugh

Sources: Columns I and II: charter references, some of which are given in the Appendix. Columns III and IV: respective *Feoda* lists. Column V: Jean Longnon, *Recherches sur la vie de Geoffroy de Villehardouin* (Paris, 1939), p. 102; also in A. Teulet, ed., *Layettes du Trésor des Chartes* (Paris, 1863), vol. I, no. 1031. Column VI: *Documents I*, pp. 437–38. Column VII: *Coutumier*, p. 144. Column VIII: *Documents I*, pp. 440–41 (there are two lists—one of 1302 and one of 1304—which agree, except that Pougy and Chappes appear only in the former). Column IX: *Documents II*, pp. 515–16.

[a] Surname of the main family is cited in the document.
[b] Name appears without title.
[c] See chap. V, n. 35.
[d] Collateral line

larger group of knights in the twelfth century.[5] Members of these families appear regularly in charters from the early twelfth century, and they are the only families in the *bailliage* with traceable genealogies throughout the century. The best-documented knight families, in contrast, yield linear filiations only from the late twelfth century.

Since the term *dominus* became common coin in charters of the thirteenth century and was applied by the count's *enquêteurs* in the *Rôles* of 1252 to many men who lacked *domini* ancestors, different criteria are required in order to determine whether the old families of counts and lords continued in fact to maintain their exclusiveness after they had lost the monopoly of their titles. One method is to test their continued preeminence in the actual affairs of the *bailliage* by obtaining "slices" of key local families who attended important assemblies and military convocations on specific dates. Column V lists those of the *bailliage* who in 1212 attended Blanche of Navarre's council of "barons and vassals," which formulated succession procedures for great estates lacking male heirs.[6] The central decision was that the eldest daughter would inherit integrally a single castle or fortified house and that the remaining daughters each would receive lands and rights with a total annual revenue about equal to that of the eldest. If there were more than one fortification, the daughters would select their preference by age-rank. Since this regulation applied to all "castellans and vassals who have castles or fortified houses," the approval of the greatest Champagne families was a *sine qua non* for its implementation. In 1224 Thibaut IV called another council of "barons and castellans" to resolve the related question of male succession to castles and fortified houses (column VII).[7] The regulation paralleled the one adopted for females in 1212: the eldest son took his preference if there were more than one fortification, and younger sons chose in turn from the rest of the property. Again the principle of undivided fortifications was imposed, but revenues, of whatever source save the justice within the fortification, were to be shared equally among all sons. As in 1212, formal consent by all leading Champagne families was a prerequisite to making the arrangement work. A third list for the early thirteenth century is of the "knights bearing banners" who were summoned to military service, probably for the battle of Bouvines (column VI).[8] Columns V through VII effectively filter the great local families from the numerous *domini* in the charters of the early thirteenth century.

Unfortunately, none of the thirteenth-century surveys of fief holders distinguished on the basis of title alone between the great and the modest families. The *Livre des hommages* (1265) introduced the double title "*dominus* N(name), *dominus* of X(place)," which was translated in the fourteenth-century French copy as "*monsieur* N, *sire* of X." The *Rôles des fiefs* of 1275 qualified some men simply as "*sire* of X." But those titles were not affixed in any systematic manner, and it is impossible to make a case for precise usage, even though the distinction may have represented an attempt to preserve some sense of social differentiation.[9] The series of lists in table 17 are conveniently terminated by two documents of the early fourteenth century. Column VIII lists the men designated "castellans" of Troyes in the military convocation of 1304; nine of the seventeen are within the limits of the *bailliage* as defined in 1265.[10] More important as an end point is the petition of 1314 to the king in which the petitioners acted in the name of "the nobles and commons of Champagne" (column IX). They declared that they were "much grieved" by the taxes levied on them and that they could no longer suffer "in good conscience" to pay the amounts assessed because their "honors, franchises, and liberties" were threatened. They decided, therefore, that twelve among them would determine their respective assessments.[11]

The lists in table 17 of important families in the twelfth, early thirteenth, and early fourteenth centuries are assembled from various sources which were themselves determined by different criteria: ecclesiastical and county records, important assembly and military convocation attendance lists, and a royal petition. The same families which possessed the exclusive *dominus* qualification in the twelfth-century charters and the *Feoda* of 1172 were called the "great fief" holders in the *Feoda* of ca. 1200; they attended the baronial councils on inheritance procedures in 1212 and 1224; they were knights banneret in 1214; and they protested as a self-appointed group against royal taxation in 1314. Given the vagaries of individual lives and circumstances that might determine a man's presence or absence on each list, the coincidence of specific families on the lists through the two centuries is remarkable. It suggests that in spite of the arrogation of the *dominus* title by the knights in the thirteenth century, the old families managed to preserve their group identity.[12] They were the leading families of the area before the count of Champagne effectively organized it as part of a great territorial state in the mid-twelfth century, and although they cooperated under his leadership for over a century, they continued to identify themselves as spokesmen for the countryside, and were probably deferred to as such, after the county had been attached to the royal organization. The single factor which established and secured their ascendancy seems to have been that of blood.

THE OLD ARISTOCRACY

Table 17 identifies what may be called the old aristocracy, the elite of counts and lords whose families can be traced continuously from at least the second half of the eleventh century. Although the *domini* did not carry the prestige of the *comites,* they were more important on the *bailliage* level because they provided the bulk of the local aristocracy. At one time or another members of these families served the count of Champagne in high office, attended him at important assemblies, and provided leadership for his military expeditions; their younger members filled ecclesiastical posts in neighboring sees, abbeys, and chapters. In spite of radical changes in both the political and social environments from the mid-twelfth century, this aristocracy appears to have maintained at least an informal cohesion and sense of group identity through the next century.[13] Yet, the formal appearance of group stability is belied by the individual family histories, which reveal a considerable variety of conditions and fates, and central to any evaluation of a medieval aristocracy is the measure of family survivability within the overall group continuity. In order to simplify the presentation here, the great fief-holding families are classified according to the three general processes that characterized their lineage development: a few continued as unitary houses throughout the twelfth and thirteenth centuries, others segmented from the great families into collateral lines, and many disappeared outright as families and lordships (map 6).[14]

Of the three local count families in this area in the tenth century, only one, the Briennes, survived through the thirteenth century. They were the most powerful of the three and continued the longest; only once in over three hundred years did they fail to produce a direct male heir, and then an uncle easily continued the line. Through marriage they acquired two neighboring counties (Bar-sur-Seine and Ramerupt), which they passed on to younger sons. What especially marked the Briennes from the local families was their success in the East. From the late twelfth century they developed a worldwide reputation in both Constantinople and the duchy of Athens, and they contracted marriage alliances which lifted them above the *bailliage* level onto the European scene; in fact, after Gautier IV (1221-46) the family was mainly involved in activities outside Champagne. Perhaps the unfortunate experience of their Ramerupt cousin's challenge to Thibaut IV forced a certain prudence in local affairs, or it may have been simply that Brienne's proximity to Troyes and its counts permitted little maneuvering within Champagne. In any event, by the thirteenth century when their local activities had been effectively restricted by the greater power of the count of Champagne, their standing had been enhanced by their Eastern exploits, and they continued to be regarded among the very highest of Champagne families. Another family to reach European prominence was that of the lords of Dampierre (Aube). They first appeared in the mid-eleventh century and soon produced several prominent church officials, including a bishop of Troyes, and held the

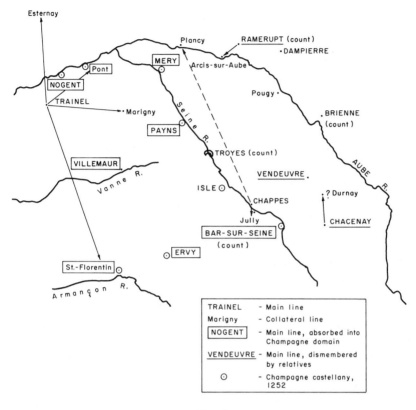

Map 6.
Counts and Lords of the *Bailliage*

constableship of Champagne, which was probably the vehicle for their
subsequent marriages to the Bourbons and the counts of Flanders (a
Dampierre became the third wife of Thibaut IV). These distinguished
matches meant that Dampierre, with its attached lordships of Saint-
Dizier and Saint-Just and part of the viscounty of Troyes, was assigned
to younger sons when the elder brothers moved on to better holdings.
The Dampierre properties seem to have remained undiminished and
guaranteed an important local role for the younger line which retained
them, but Dampierre had, in effect, become a collateral family.

    Perhaps the most important local lords below the counts in the
twelfth century were the Traînels. From an early date they held a large
block of lands between Troyes and Sens, bounded by the Seine and the
Armançon, that included Pont-sur-Seine and Saint-Florentin, both of
which were absorbed into the Champagne domain as castellany centers
before 1172.[15] Many other properties were lost as dowries to daughters
and lordships to younger sons, although the main family did preserve

extensive holdings. Only Anselm II (d. 1185), butler of Champagne and confidant of Count Henry I, held high office, but the Traînels retained their place among the very exclusive local families into the fourteenth century. Two other great families, the Chappes and Plancy, also appeared in the last quarter of the eleventh century and were probably closely related, since the Plancy always held their castle directly from the Chappes. The Chappes appear more often in the charters, probably because of their greater resources, but both families were regarded as great lords throughout the twelfth and thirteenth centuries. The main Chappes line managed to survive the Crusades and retain its immediate properties intact, a strip of land on the right bank of the Seine between the Champagne castellany of Isle and the county of Bar-sur-Seine. A Chappes was chancellor of Champagne (Guy, 1191–1203) at the same time that a Plancy was bishop of Troyes (Haice, 1191-93), but neither family held other high offices.

The counts of Brienne and the *domini* families of Dampierre, Traînel, Chappes, and Plancy are the only ones which appeared firmly established by 1100 and which also had direct descendants who retained their social standing for the next two hundred years. They were the "great fief" holders in ca. 1200, they attended the baronial councils in the early thirteenth century, and they appeared among the small group of "nobles" in 1314. But these old lines accounted for only half of the aristocracy in the *bailliage* at any given time. The remaining social space was filled by collateral, or segmentary, lines. Although it is impossible to trace all the sons of great families and their minor lordships, especially when names were changed, the development of important collateral lines clearly emerges as a central phenomenon of aristocratic development. The significance of segmentation is that it was the process by which new, semi-autonomous political and social units were created with standings similar to those from which they originated.[16]

The counts of Ramerupt-Arcis provide one of the most interesting examples of segmentation in the *bailliage*. They had united (or re-united) the two neighboring properties by the time of their first appearance in ca. 970, but in the early twelfth century the lands were split between two heiresses: Ramerupt went with one to her Brienne husband, and Arcis-sur-Aube went with the other to become an independent lordship. The Arcis lords were represented in all the major assemblies and all lists of great families to the fourteenth century, but they appeared in very few ecclesiastical documents and seem to have played a rather unobtrusive role in *bailliage* affairs. Ramerupt, on the other hand, exercised an inordinate influence in the *bailliage*. The main Brienne line kept the Ramerupt property for two generations—Gautier II was "count of Ramerupt and Brienne" in 1136—before passing it to a younger son in the late twelfth century. The new Ramerupts, however, emerged as *domini*, like their Arcis cousins, and held their lands in rear-fief from the count of Brienne. It was Erard I of Ramerupt (styled "of Brienne") who married Philippe, daughter of Henry II of Champagne and the queen of Jerusalem, and claimed Champagne on her behalf. The liquidation of the claim in 1221 cost Thibaut IV 5,000 l. and an annual 1,200 l. rent, but Ramerupt as a lordship came to an abrupt end shortly after the death of Erard I (see below).

Ramerupt and Arcis may have been based on properties which had originally been distinct, but most other segmentary lines were carved out of the very properties of the main lines, as in the cases of Jully, Marigny, and Esternay. The Jully-sur-Sarce line segmented in the late twelfth century from Chappes. Guy, called variously "of Chappes" and "of Jully," held his inheritance in rear-fief from his brother Clarembaud IV of Chappes but was accepted among the barons in the council of 1212. Since Guy left only two daughters, his son-in-law Guy of Sailly (a Joinville segment) adopted the Jully title as his own in 1221 and made Jully and its fortress his main holding; Sailly's descendant appeared as lord of Jully in 1314. But it was the lords of Traînel who were most successful, as might be expected, in projecting two of their collateral lines, Marigny-le-Châtel and Esternay, into the small elite of late-thirteenth-century families. The Marigny were very successful in terms of offices and marriages: the founder, Garnier II, was marshal of Nevers, his brothers Anselm and Milo were butler of Champagne and abbot of Saint-Manin of Auxerre, and his descendants included a constable of Champagne and a bishop-elect of Verdun. The Marigny line appears with its Traînel cousins in all the crucial indices of great families, but like Guy of Jully, Garnier V of Marigny (d. 1267) left only two daughters, one of whom took the entire Marigny estate to Guillaume of Thil (probably descendant of the viscounts of Bar-sur-Aube), who assumed the Marigny title by 1304. The Esternays were in the strictest sense a collateral line of the Marigny, but they appeared with the Traînel name in the early fourteenth century among the older families.

Finally, there is one example of a family which managed to reach the highest levels and which was clearly a collateral branch, although it cannot be linked with certainty by available evidence to any particular old family. The Pougys emerged suddenly in the middle of the twelfth century and within a hundred years had achieved an impressive record with regard to marriages and offices. Eudes I was constable of Champagne, and his brother became bishop of Troyes. Eudes' descendants were a bishop of Nevers, an archdeacon of Beauvais, and an abbess of Notre-Dame-aux-Nonnains, and others married into the highest of local families. Yet the origin of the Pougy family is not known, nor is there evidence of it before the mid-twelfth century. The Pougys, however, were the exception. Many other younger sons of great families did not found collateral lines and were probably similar rather to the Durnays, a well-placed mid-twelfth-century segment of the Chacenay family. The Durnays made excellent marriages and through their wives even picked up remnants of both the county of Bar-sur-Seine and the lordship of Vendeuvre; but they did not appear with the older families in any of the critical lists (table 17), except in the council of barons in 1224, when Jacques seems to have substituted for his Chacenay cousin (who was probably still at odds with Thibaut IV for his opposition during the succession crisis). The Durnays apparently made a deliberate attempt to reconstitute the Vendeuvre estate by purchasing at least two shares in addition to their dowry acquisition, but they failed and so remained indistinguishable from the numerous lesser lords in the thirteenth-century *bailliage*. There were probably many collateral lines like the Durnays who possessed the requisite background but who failed to be considered among the highest families. On the other hand, there is no evidence for the rise of new lines, except for the remote possibility of the Pougys. In sum, among the great collateral lines, the Arcis were probably originally a segment of the Ramerupt counts, and Ramerupt itself became a segment of the Briennes; Chappes produced Plancy, and Traînel produced Marigny and Esternay. All segments but the last one were founded in the twelfth century, and only the very few old aristocratic families lifted any new lines up to their own level of prominence in the period.

No less significant than segmentation is the complete disappearance of great families and their lordships. Well-documented cases of extinguished lines whose lands were incorporated into the Champagne domain are available from the late twelfth century. One of the clearest examples is that of Nogent-sur-Seine. Milo I of Nogent appeared as a *vir illuster* (1127) and *dominus* (1146) with knights holding in fief from him. His son-in-law took the title "lord of Nogent" (1161), and it was probably the latter's son who appeared in the *Feoda* (1172) as one of the *domini* of the area, along with the Traînels and Chappes. Both Milo II and his brother died by 1186; their mother was *domina* of Nogent until ca. 1190, when she was called the "former lady" of Nogent. Nogent entered the count's domain shortly thereafter, and in 1199 Thibaut III assigned it as part of his wife's dowry. When Nogent was inventoried as a Champagne castellany with ten knights in 1200, a notation in *Feoda* II stated that this was the first time that the knights were entered on the count's rolls. In fact, Nogent was ultimately a fief of the abbot of Saint-Denis, and its status must have hung in abeyance during the next few uncertain decades, for only in 1226 did Thibaut IV do homage for the castle and lands of Nogent and pay 2,000 l. in order to recover the cross and altar which the abbot held as security.

At about the same time, Thibaut incorporated another stronghold on the Seine, the county of Bar-sur-Seine, which guarded the strategic southern approach from Burgundy. The counts of Bar-sur-Seine belonged to one of the oldest and most distinguished local families, producing two bishops of Langres, an abbot of Cîteaux, and a Grand Master of the Temple and arranging marriage alliances at the highest level. This apparently vigorous line ended suddenly when Milo IV and his two childless sons died in the East in 1218-19, leaving only Milo's widow and a daughter. Thibaut IV seized the opportunity and within a few years had purchased the major part of the county; in 1227 he reissued the *mainmorte* exemption of 1198 to the townsmen of Bar-sur-Seine, and in 1231 he granted them a franchise. In the *Rôles* (1252) the former county of Bar-sur-Seine was a Champagne castellany with thirty five fief holders. Both Bar-sur-Seine and Nogent are observable cases in which the lack of direct male heirs of a substantial lordship provided the count of Champagne the opening by which to acquire and absorb an entire castellany or county directly into his domain.

There were also families which failed earlier in the twelfth century but which have been rarely studied because of the paucity of evidence. Their position among the old aristocratic families must be inferred mainly from indirect evidence, but their presence among the aristocracy of the time would modify any interpretation of both the evolution of the local families and the formation of the county of Champagne. Pont-sur-Seine, for example, long held by the lords of Traînel, seems to have emerged as a line of independent lords in the early twelfth century, although their precise relationships cannot be reconstructed. Yet Pont had entered the Champagne domain by mid-century and was thereafter a county castellany. It cannot be determined how the Traînels lost Pont, but as late as 1208-9 their descendants were liquidating what were probably their vestigial possessions in that area, including the *péage* of Pont, which they sold to Countess Blanche. Similarly, Payns had a *dominus* in ca. 1113—Hugh, founder of the Templars in 1118. But Payns had a viscount in 1140, indicating that it was already in the Champagne domain, and in 1172 it was a county castellany. In 1236 a certain Etienne, *armiger*, of Payns sold two-thirds of the tithe of Payns, which he held "in pure and free alod" for 42 l. In both Pont and Payns the castles and main castellany lands were somehow lost by the original holders; their thirteenth-century descendants retained only a few minor revenues in what had been sizable family lordships, large enough to constitute Champagne castellanies. A third Champagne castellany of 1172 that had been acquired from private hands was Villemaur. Manasses of Villemaur was probably lord of the place in 1122 because his sons Eudes (*vir nobilis*, 1127) and Dreux (who seems to have founded a collateral line) both had the *dominus* title in 1158. But Villemaur was in the Champagne domain in 1143, and the Villemaur register of the *Feoda* (1172) was headed by "Manasses," whose widow later married the marshal of Champagne, Milo Breban (of Provins, d. 1194/97). The Villemaur family is not heard of in the thirteenth century. Pont, Payns, and Villemaur were like Ervy and perhaps Méry (which had *domini* in 1160/70 and 1097/1104, respectively), in that they had been secured by the count of Champagne from their original possessors in the course of the twelfth century. Their families certainly were of the aristocracy at that time and would have been counted among the important local families in the early thirteenth century, had they survived as independent lordships.

In the thirteenth century three other great families expired, all with unusually good documentation on their dismemberment. The Vendeuvre-sur-Barse appeared first in 1075 and were qualified *domini* in 1121 when two brothers mortgaged their castle to Count Hugh of Troyes; apparently they recovered it, for their descendants were co-lords of the place. At the end of the twelfth century, however, both lines failed to produce male heirs; three daughters of one branch and one of the other took their share of Vendeuvre to their husbands, and younger sons received successively smaller fragments, until in 1265 a great-grandson held one-eighth of the original property. The Durnay family attempted to reconstitute the estate: Gérard purchased at least one share in addition to his wife's portion in 1244, and his son added another in 1268, but Vendeuvre was never entirely put together and never regained its former eminence as a great fief. The dismemberment of Vendeuvre came before the baronial council of 1212 and was an excellent example of the problem addressed by the barons—it may even have prompted the council's sitting. The barons prohibited the division of castles among female heiresses: by 1252 Vendeuvre was shared by persons so distantly related as to be virtual strangers, and as a military structure it was obviously less effective than it would have been under a single head. However, Vendeuvre was divided according to the council's provision for the equal sharing of revenues by all heirs: all the Vendeuvre descendants were assured of modest revenues, although none could approach the income and prestige attained by Vendeuvre as a unitary lordship in the twelfth century.

Two other great families died out in the mid-thirteenth century. The lords of Ramerupt survived only a few generations after they had segmented from the Briennes (see above). Erard I left two sons, both of whom died in the East in 1249-50; his remaining four daughters (one other had died young, and one was an abbess) divided Ramerupt, and in the *Rôles* of 1252 each son-in-law was listed for one-quarter of the estate. One of them, Henri VI, count of Grandpré, acquired at least one other quarter and subsequently carried the title of lord of Ramerupt,

but to a count of Grandpré, Ramerupt was simply a source of additional revenues. For all practical purposes the house of Ramerupt,
originally a county, then a lordship, ceased to exist in the *bailliage*. The
Chacenays were the last great family to disappear in the thirteenth
century. They were mentioned from 1076 among the *viri illustri* and
were called *domini* from 1138. They held fiefs from several great lords,
including the duke of Burgundy, and their castle from the bishop of
Langres; they produced an abbot of Clairvaux, made substantial marriage alliances, and segmented the Durnays. Erard II of Chacenay (d.
1236) was one of the staunchest supporters of Erard of Brienne
(Ramerupt) and came under numerous ecclesiastical condemnations,
ranging up to excommunication. Perhaps also because of his compro-
mised position, he was absent from the council of 1224, being replaced
by his cousin Jacques (of Chacenay), lord of Durnay. By 1250 Erard's
two sons had died in the East and the Chacenay estate was divided
among the children of his two daughters, similar to the way in which
Vendeuvre was divided. Wrangling over the division lasted several
decades, but by 1273, or at the latest 1286, Chacenay ceased to exist as
a unitary lordship.

Disintegration of the great families of counts and lords seems to have
occurred regularly throughout the twelfth and thirteenth centuries. It is
impossible to determine the reasons for the early-twelfth-century de-
mises (Pont, Payns, Villemaur, and perhaps Ervy and Méry), but those
of the late twelfth century (Nogent and Vendeuvre) were clearly
instances of the lack of male heirs, and all three cases of the mid-
thirteenth century (Bar-sur-Seine, Ramerupt, and Chacenay) involved
the death of all direct male heirs in the East. Of the lordships incorporated by the counts of Champagne directly into their domain, four
(Pont, Nogent, Bar-sur-Seine, and perhaps Méry) were on the Seine, and
one (Villemaur) was on the river Vanne, an important route from
Troyes to Sens.

In sum, the local aristocracy in the early twelfth century was com-
posed of about a dozen families: three lines of counts (Brienne, Bar-sur-
Seine, and Ramerupt) and the rest *domini* (Traînel, Dampierre, Plancy,
Chappes, Payns, Villemaur, Nogent, Vendeuvre, and perhaps Ervy and
Méry). By the end of the century three segmentary lines (Arcis, Pougy,
and Marigny) took their places among the "great fief" holders of
Champagne, and soon two other collateral lines (Ramerupt lords and
Jully) were accepted into their ranks. In all, these five segmentary lines
just maintained the overall size of the old aristocracy because during
the twelfth century at least four old families died out (Payns, Villemaur, Pont, Nogent, and perhaps Ervy and Méry), and their lands and
castles became Champagne castellanies. In the thirteenth century three
other main lines (Bar-sur-Seine, Vendeuvre, and Chacenay) and one

segmentary one (Ramerupt lords) died out; only one of these (Bar-sur-
Seine) was absorbed by the count of Champagne, the others being
divided among heiresses and collateral relatives. Two collateral lines
(Jully and Marigny) survived only because their titles and properties
were assumed by the husbands of their sole heiresses and were accepted
among the elite as continuators of the original lines. As a result of the
various family histories, the total size of the restrictive group of great
families was about the same at the beginning of the fourteenth as at the
beginning of the twelfth century. But the composition had changed
drastically: half of the original lines had died out, and their properties
were lost to baronial control either through integral transfer to the
Champagne domain or by fragmentation among indirect heirs. It was
the segmentary lines that not only provided suitable marriage partners
on the local level but also gave a sense of number to the handful of
families caught in the web of untimely births and deaths, inheritance
requirements, and the expanding power of the count of Champagne.

It is necessary to define the old aristocracy of the *bailliage* in terms of
the construct of table 17 because the extant charters do not encompass
all the families with similar attributes at any one date and because the
charter terminology cannot be interpreted apart from the actual families to which it referred. Once the aristocratic families have been
isolated, the charters yield important information that in conjunction
with the county administrative records permits further precision in the
definition of this social group. One of the most interesting phenomena
is the depth of the lineages that can be constructed. The counts
(Troyes, Bar-sur-Seine, Brienne, and Ramerupt) appeared in the earliest
charters, from the mid-ninth century to the mid-tenth century, and
their genealogies can be traced continuously from their first appearances through the thirteenth century. In contrast, the *domini* can be
traced only from the second half of the eleventh century, although
many of them were not entitled *domini* until 1120/30. In spite of the
one-hundred-year differential between their observable appearances, the
counts and lords together formed a single group of established and
leading local families in the twelfth century. They dominated secular
and ecclesiastical offices, they intermarried, and they generally maintained a distance from their knights. In contrast, the knights have
traceable genealogies from the mid-twelfth century at the earliest and
generally from the 1170s, a full century after the *domini*. The charters
of course were mainly records of property acquisitions by ecclesiastical
houses, so the respective appearances of counts, lords, and knights in
such documents mirror the corresponding increase in economic resources successively available to each group.[17]

Although the *bailliage* references are insufficient to establish the
point conclusively, the counts and lords of the twelfth century were
also probably understood to constitute the "nobles." *Nobilis vir* was

used infrequently in the charters, and not all the important families are represented with that qualification in the extant acts, although it would seem that the scribes used it deliberately when referring to men such as the lords of Traînel and Chappes.[18] Better documented for the *bailliage* because of the surveys is the possession by the old families of castles and surrounding castellanies, which survived intact within the Champagne castellany system and provided fiefs for their knights. Vendeuvre had a castle in 1113, was a "castle and honor" in 1120, and was called a "castellany" in the *Rôles* of 1252; it also had at least thirty two rear-fief holders. Chappes had an *oppidum* in 1117, was termed a "castellany" by the count in 1175, and had forty three rear-fief holders in 1252. Nogent lacks comparable references for the twelfth century, but the lord of Nogent had a number of knights holding from him in 1146, and when Nogent entered the Champagne domain in 1200, there were ten knights in that castellany. Bar-sur-Seine of course was not called a castellany while it remained an independent county, but it possessed a castle in 1103, and it had thirty five fief holders as a Champagne castellany in 1252. The knights within districts such as Nogent and Bar-sur-Seine, which became direct Champagne domain, became themselves direct fief holders of Champagne in the thirteenth century, whereas those who held from families like Vendeuvre and Chappes, for instance, who survived into the thirteenth century but who became liegemen of the count, were counted as rear-fief holders in the Champagne system. In 1252 only 9.1 percent of all direct fief holders had five or more rear-fief holders, so the number of rear-fief holders, as well as the possession of a castle and castellany district, was clearly associated with the small group of old families.[19]

It is difficult to compare the values of castellany-fiefs with those of lesser fiefs because the great holdings generally were not valued in the *Rôles*. The lady of Traînel, for example, sent exceptionally clear descriptions with values of the thirteen rear-fiefs held from her that yielded together 360 *l.t.*, but she failed to report her own income. Only one great fief, that of Arcis, can be valued with reasonable accuracy. In 1218 the lord of Arcis went pledge for Countess Blanche for 200 l., which was about a year's income from his estate, for the revenue of the *"péage* and *prévôté"* of Arcis was worth precisely that amount in 1222. Arcis probably produced the same amount in 1273 because a dowry of 200 l. (again the annual income) was promised to one of the daughters. The *Rôles* of 1252 call Arcis a "castle and castellany" consisting of several villages. The lord of Arcis had in addition a fief of 35 *l.t.* assigned by the countess in 1218 on the fairs of Troyes, although only 22 *l.t.* of that income still went directly to the family in 1252. There were twenty three rear-fiefs in this "castellany" in 1252, but they were not valued.[20] Arcis was in the over-100 *l.t.* category, that is, among the 7.3 percent of most valuable Champagne fiefs, but it was probably not one of the wealthiest estates; the counties of Brienne and Bar-sur-Seine and the lordships of Traînel, Ramerupt, and Vendeuvre appear to have been even greater castellany-fiefs with larger total revenues. Jacques of Durnay, for example, paid a 300 l. relief for his wife's share of Bar-sur-Seine in 1219; if that was about equal to an annual revenue for that share, then the entire fief must have produced a larger income. Vendeuvre was probably worth even more, about 400 *l.t.*, and had thirty two rear-fiefs worth another 400 *l.t.*[21] The comparative range of these annual incomes is also reflected in the size of the dowries. Milo I of Pougy gave his sister half of the village of Mesnil-Lettre (justice, *taille,* woods, *corvée*) and one-third of its safeguard as dowry; her husband sold it all for 300 l. in 1222.[22] In 1234 the daughter of Erard I of Ramerupt received 140 l. annually for her dowry; in 1259 the dowry of a Chappes daughter, part of the viscounty of Troyes, was sold by her husband for a 211 l. rent. Such incomes were clearly out of the range of ordinary knights, most of whom had under 30 *l.t.* or even 20 *l.t.* as total annual incomes.

The old families were essentially endogamous, and only from the mid-thirteenth century can intermarriages with lesser families be documented. Two Brosse brothers, for instance, married Chappes sisters, who were not, however, of the main line.[23] Some daughters were sent into local abbeys, and a few became abbesses. Younger sons appeared in all the local abbeys and chapters and were especially active in Clairvaux, Cîteaux, Langres, Nevers, Châlons, and Laon, as well as Troyes and its major collegials of Saint-Pierre and Saint-Etienne. Some younger sons changed their names and headed minor lordships, but there was a general reluctance of the major collateral lines to alter their old family names.[24] The old families also rarely adopted the *armiger/domicellus/ escuier* title in the thirteenth century when they no longer monopolized their former titles. About 16 percent of the fief holders were non-knighted by the mid-thirteenth century, many for their entire lives, but few members of the old families ever retained that status for long. They did hold it when they were obviously minors, but they quickly shed it for the *dominus* status on coming of age: both a Chappes and a Pougy, for instance, were *domicelli* in 1240/41, but they were both *domini* by 1252.

Thus, given the genealogies of the old families, it is possible to identify several consistent characteristics of the aristocracy. They had the earliest traceable genealogies, from at least the eleventh century. They were termed counts and lords, and occasionally nobles, in the twelfth century. They held castles from at least the early twelfth century and had relatively large numbers of knights who held fiefs from them. They were called the "great fief" holders by the count's scribes, and they attended the baronial councils on inheritance procedures in 1212 and 1224. They had the most lucrative estates in the mid-thirteenth century and absorbed a disproportionate share of the total available fief income. Finally, they were the families to rise against royal taxation in 1314. The old families would seem to have maintained their dominance throughout the twelfth and thirteenth centuries. Yet their relative position among all fief holders had changed considerably. In the mid-twelfth century they were still independent of the count of Troyes, with whom they maintained essentially political alliances with military and consultative responsibilities. The *Feoda* of 1172 for the first time placed them within a larger and more formal system. Although they continued to hold their "castellanies," those had been arbitrarily subordinated to the Champagne castellany system. Of course, the old families were never obligated for guard duty in the count's castles, but their own castles were nevertheless made renderable to the count whenever he needed them. Moreover, a second step in subjugation came in the early thirteenth century when the count of Champagne finally imposed liegeance on the segmentary lines which until then had been simply rear-fiefs of the main families. Marigny in ca. 1200, Ramerupt and Pougy in 1204/10, Jully in 1206, Dampierre in 1218, and Esternay in 1222/43 became liege to the count.[25] Traînel, Chappes, and Chacenay had been liege since 1172. Nogent and Bar-sur-Seine had been absorbed into the count's domain, and Vendeuvre had been dismembered. Plancy was made specifically accountable to the lord of Chappes. Only Arcis and Brienne were not recorded as being liege to the count in an extant register of the early thirteenth century.

From the composition of the *Feoda* in 1172 to the succession of Thibaut IV in 1222 the old aristocracy was transformed from substantially independent castellans with only political and military ties to the count of Troyes into great estate holders within the Champagne fief system. They remained the wealthiest fief holders, and they controlled the internal administration of their castellanies, but they lost their military significance and freedom of action, especially after the succession crisis. An entirely new political and social configuration emerged by the mid-thirteenth century, as a whole new group of fortification holders, and even the descendants of ordinary knights, came to enjoy the status and legal privileges reserved for the great families alone one century earlier.

THE KNIGHTS

Knight families are more difficult to analyze because references to them are scarce before the 1170s, and even later it is seldom possible to construct meaningful genealogies of more than one generation. From the local *bailliage* sources it is impossible to provide a definitive answer to the intriguing and central question of whether knights originally descended as younger sons from the old families of counts and barons or whether they derived from the general peasant population, most plausibly from local administrative families on the estates of great lords. It is conceivable that disinherited and adventurous sons of great lords became knights in the retinues of other barons and that younger sons changed their names when they became knights on lesser fiefs, but the *bailliage* evidence does not confirm either alternative as the origin of most knights who appear in the twelfth century.[26] Furthermore, there is no evidence that members of the twelfth-century *domini* families were ever called simply *milites*. Although occasionally an ecclesiastical scribe placed a great lord in a witness list under *de militibus,* that was merely a conventional grouping of lay persons to distinguish them from ecclesiastics, *de clericis.* Never were the *domini* addressed or referred to merely as *milites.*[27] Of course, most male members of baronial families shared the *métier* of fighting and were therefore of the knighthood; as such, they were counted in the *summa militum* of the *Feoda* of 1172, although in the individual registers they were actually accorded the *dominus* title that separated them from all the untitled knights.[28]

The great disparity in status between the old aristocracy and the knights in the first half of the twelfth century is reflected in the usual absence of surnames for knights and in references such as "my knights" and "a certain knight N."[29] Some fragmentary evidence suggests that *milites* and *servientes,* both directly employed by and responsible to the great lords, originally may have shared a comparable level of status; but from the mid-twelfth century, and especially from the 1170s, when knights appeared more often in charters, the term *miles* seems to have become more than just an occupational description and to have acquired a precise tenurial and social connotation, as in the standard formula "N(name), *miles* of X(place)."[30] The *Feoda,* too, clearly shows the knights as a social group distinct from both the baronial administrative agents and the old aristocratic families themselves.

Yet in the last two decades of the century the knights were with increasing frequency termed *domini* in the charters, or variously *milites* and *domini.* The titles were used so indiscriminately that within one generation it is impossible to distinguish the modest from the very powerful families on the basis of title alone, as is the case until the end of the twelfth century. The administrative records from 1200 to 1243, fragmentary as they are, do not follow the charter convention; only in the *Rôles des fiefs* of 1249-52 did the count's scribes finally end the former *dominus-miles* distinction by entitling the fief-holding descendants of both groups *domini.*[31] As this distinction between *domini* and *milites* was being erased in the first half of the thirteenth century,

THE ARISTOCRACY 115

another became accentuated, that between the *domini/milites* and the *armigeri* (or *domicelli, scutiferi*), the nonknighted sons of knight and, to a lesser extent, baronial families. In most cases young men still proceeded from *armiger* to *miles* upon knighting, but the genealogies indicate that by the mid-thirteenth century some men retained the nonknighted status for long periods, often for their entire lifetimes. In the surveys of 1252 and 1275 there were about two *domini* to every *armiger* fief holder (table 15).[32] Despite their slightly inferior status and less valuable fiefs, the *armigeri* shared the same privileges in local affairs with the *domini* and were clearly counted among the aristocracy, as they were in the surveys, by virtue of their tenure.[33] Thus the position of the knights in *bailliage* society underwent a profound transformation from the mid-twelfth century, when they first emerged as distinct lineages, to the mid-thirteenth century, when they and their holdings were systematically inventoried by the count. Yet their changing role as a group does not of itself account for the great diversity in family situations and histories, in which particular combinations of property, marriage alliances, personal initiative, and plain chance defy clear-cut patterns. The most convenient classification for studying the best-documented, noncastellan families in the *bailliage* is in two general categories: the ordinary knight families, which constituted the bulk of fief holders, and the small group of holders of fortified houses, who occupied an intermediate level between the great families and all others.

In the *Rôles* of 1252 the quantitative characteristics of the holders of fortified houses indicate that they formed an intermediate group between the castellan families and the ordinary knights. The fortifications were mostly on fiefs in the 30–99 *l.t.* range, that is, among the 23.1 percent of all valued sole/first fiefs, and were distinguished both by composition and by value from the 69.6 percent of all fiefs that produced under 30 *l.t.* Fortified houses first appeared in number in the early thirteenth century, when the succession crisis probably stimulated their proliferation as well as increased their importance.[34] The councils of 1212 and 1224 explicitly included them with castles as types of fiefs in which the fortification and its immediate justice should pass integrally to one heir. Evidence for the family origins of these holders is not consistent: a few may have derived from *domini* lineages, but others clearly seem to have "risen" from ordinary knight backgrounds. By the mid-thirteenth century the more than twenty fortified houses in the *bailliage* constituted a distinct group of fiefs in terms of incomes (usually over 30 *l.t.*), composition (with justice, and often other rights), and number of rear-fief holders (usually more than four). They were inferior to castle-fiefs, but they were clearly superior to most others (map 7).

Map 7.
Knights of the *Bailliage*

Two families with fortified houses had at least a distant link with older baronial houses. A younger son of the count of Bar-sur-Seine acquired the minor lordship of Ville-sur-Arce by marriage in the mid-twelfth century; it passed again by female inheritance in the early thirteenth century to Robert I of Fontette, who descended directly from an ordinary knight family but who perhaps had remote ties with a *dominus* line. The fief of Ville-sur-Arce was first associated with a fortified house in the *Rôles* of 1252, where it is listed with its forty-hearth village and justice as worth 160 *l.t.* Obviously, such a valuable holding had become the main Fontette fief; the younger son at that time held a 40 *l.t.* rear-fief from the eldest, his wife's dowry of 10 *l.t.*, and another rear-fief of 30 *setiers* of grain, altogether a substantial income, though clearly inferior to his brother's. At Charmont-sur-Barbuise a fortified house is first mentioned in 1233, because its holder had imprisoned some men of Saint-Etienne there and impounded their goods. The fortification was on only half of the village and properties of Charmont (see chapter II), since a collateral line had alienated the other half and was forced to rely on maternal inheritances and even a maternal name. The Charmont family descended directly from Jean I, who was called *dominus* in 1147, but it was not grouped with the other *domini* families in any other reference nor was it granted that title by the count's scribes in the *Feoda* of 1172 (see table 17). The *dominus* title of the Charmont family in the mid-twelfth century remains anomalous. Although both the Ville-sur-Arce and Charmont-sur-Barbuise may have had past ties with baronial lineages, neither was counted among them in the late twelfth century or in the thirteenth century. Moreover, there is no reference to fortifications at either locality before the mid-thirteenth century.

None of the other holders of fortified houses, in spite of some genealogies traceable from the mid-twelfth century, can be linked with any certainty to the old aristocracy. Many appeared first as knights of the count in the *Feoda* of 1172 and continued to owe the originally assigned castle guard even after their own fortifications had been built. The knights of Chervey, for instance, had been followers of the lords of Chacenay from the mid-twelfth century and furnished him a "seneschal" in 1205, but the count of Champagne imposed liegeance on them in 1229, perhaps soon after their fortified house was erected. The fief of Chervey with its fortification was worth 40 *l.t.* in the *Rôles* but did not owe guard (since it had not been a direct fief of the count with that obligation before 1229). Some fortified houses seem to have been built later in the thirteenth century, perhaps as a result of increased wealth. The Rosières, for example, had important commercial properties in Troyes from the late twelfth century and may have been merchants originally, for in 1200 Guillaume I of Rosières was required to convert his alod of a merchant hall into a Champagne fief, and he was probably required to do the same with the village of Rosières. In 1252 Guillaume II held most of that village (house, lands, men, *cens*) as a fief—his brother held only a house and the use of the woods—but only in the inventory of 1265 was a fortified house listed. That fief was not valued in 1252, but Guillaume held also a 30 *l.t.* income from the merchant hall in Troyes, a 30 *l.t.* rear-fief from the lady of Traînel, and another 15 *l.t.* rear-fief, for a total of over 75 *l.t.*; his income was no doubt over 100 *l.t.* His daughter married a man with several fish stalls in Troyes. The Brosse family, on the other hand, was strictly rural. They apparently erected a fortified house on a maternal inheritance, not on their own lands at Brosse. The two Brosse brothers in 1252 shared both paternal and maternal properties, as well as an inheritance from a great-grandmother and an escheat from their uncle. Both brothers married Chappes sisters, one of whom brought part of the viscounty of Troyes as dowry. The Brosses no doubt owed much of their success to Iter II, close advisor to Countess Blanche during the minority crisis, but without their maternal inheritance and dowries and the unexpected escheat of their uncle, who probably died in the East, they would have remained lesser landholders. Most families with comparable incomes possessed a fortification of some sort.

In addition to the more than twenty fortified houses erected in the *bailliage,* there were two castles of recent construction. The castles of Romilly-sur-Seine and Saint-Phal were probably completed by 1200, for both were listed among the great Champagne fiefs, although neither family is included among the old families in other references. Romilly provided 120 *l.t.* in 1252, and its holder owed eight weeks duty in a count's castle, the same amount rendered by his uncle in 1172. Saint-Phal still owed all-year guard at the count's castle in Troyes, but that evident anomaly was rectified by 1265 by the transfer of that service to Saint-Phal itself. Romilly had eight rear-fief holders (worth 85 *l.t.*); Saint-Phal had fourteen. Saint-Phal was represented in the 1314 petition, probably because of its fortunate marriage alliance with a Joinville (Sailly segment) and its blood rather than the position of Saint-Phal itself. Also in that 1314 petition was a descendant of the Clérey family, which had two fortified houses in 1252. Both Clérey and Saint-Phal were ordinary knights in the *Feoda,* but they seem to have acquired considerable properties by the end of the twelfth century; each had two fortifications in 1252, the second secured by marriage, and both appeared among the "nobles" of 1314. Saint-Phal, Clérey, and Romilly are the only examples of families lacking clear filiations with twelfth-century *domini* lineages who appeared at any time among the old families (table 17).[35]

All the new fortifications, like the old castles, were protected from dismemberment by inheritance in the baronial agreements of 1212 and 1224. But the same councils also provided that all heirs of these families would receive equal shares of the estates, exclusive of the fortifications themselves and their immediate rights of justice. That regulation contained a serious portent. Montfey, for example, was a village of about 150 hearths that produced 125 *l.t.* In 1252 it was divided among five children: the eldest son held the fortified house and justice (30 *l.t.*), two other sons each had a house and property (30 *l.t.*), while one daughter had a house (25 *l.t.*), and another had only lands, and rents (8 *l.t.*). Although these were still substantial portions compared with most fief incomes at the time, the logical outcome of such divisions was complete fragmentation, especially on the lower income levels. The village of Buxeuil, for instance, was a single fief with a fortified house, land, *cens,* customs, justice, and other revenues, worth altogether 20 *l.t.* By 1252 Buxeuil had been divided among three brothers and a brother-in-law into four equal shares of 5 *l.t.* The eldest, of course, had the fortified house and justice, but that was small consolation for the 5 *l.t.* income.[36] Dismemberment was occasionally averted by the integral transfer of fortified houses and their estates through marriage: the younger Saint-Phal son, for example, acquired an 80 *l.t.* fief with fortification as his wife's dowry, in addition to three other substantial fiefs. Most portions of these fiefs, even if they did not include actual fortifications, were on the level of fiefs worth over 30 *l.t.* The intent of the baronial council decisions seems generally to have been followed. The holders of fortified houses were distinguished from most other knights as much by their superior incomes and more compact holdings with justice and banal rights as by their distinctive residences, which afforded greater military and social significance.

It becomes progressively more difficult to discuss the mass of ordinary knights who were distinguished neither by prominent ancestors nor by economic or military importance because they are less visible in all documents. Accordingly, the best illustrations of families at the lower levels are all the more important as representative of the bulk of fief holders about whom little can be said except that they appeared in the administrative surveys. Like the baronial families, the lesser fief holders display great variety in lineage development, types of fiefs, and military obligations, and it is usually difficult to evaluate their families, except by comparing them with the quantitative profile of all the fief holders together. Four categories of data are especially valuable as indices for evaluating the lesser families. First, fief holders were distinguished from rear-fief holders. Then there are three quantitative characteristics that are important because the high ratios of response in the *Rôles* makes their determinations especially accurate: the status of the holder was given for 76.7 percent of the fief holders and for 49.8 percent of the rear-fief holders; annual incomes were given for 63.8 percent of the fiefs and for 47.2 percent of the rear-fiefs; and castle guard was mentioned for 68.8 percent of the fiefs.

One of the clearest examples of ordinary knights is the Quincy family. They did not appear in the *Feoda* of 1172 because they were knights of the lord of Nogent, whose castellany was still outside the count's domain. The Quincy family probably held all or most of the village of Quincy, for in 1200 Milo I sold his share of its tithe for the sum of 35 l. for himself and a horse for his son, no doubt in preparation for the Fourth Crusade. The *Rôles* entry for his grandson Milo II lists two fiefs (he was in the 25.4 percent minority of persons who had more than one fief in the survey): the family's traditional holding at Quincy, a house, lands, men, *cens,* and justice, all worth 15 *l.t.*; and his wife's inheritance, or dowry, at Granges, land, *cens,* and *terrage,* worth 8 *l.t.* He owed eight weeks guard for each fief. He also held a "small" rear-fief. His son, however, inherited only the 15 *l.t.* fief because the 8 *l.t.* acquisition went as dowry to the daughter. The main Quincy fief was worth slightly below the median fief value of 20 *l.t.*, but it did have justice, one of the few at that value to have it. The eight weeks guard was comparatively heavy in 1252. The Quincys were probably quite typical of the mid-thirteenth-century fief holders in terms of status, as

well as income: Etienne was a *dominus* (1229), and his son Milo II was
an *armiger* (1230), *miles* (1252), *monsieur* (1265), and *chevalier* (1275).
Other knight families as well acquired entire villages in the second
half of the twelfth century and held them with their concomitant
justice and banal rights through the thirteenth century.[37] The fief of
Macey, for example, a village of thirty hearths with justice, provided its
holder 42 *l.t.* in 1252, a substantial income that had been preserved
from division. And the brothers of Bouy-Luxembourg received their
entire village of thirty hearths in the early thirteenth century; they
shared the house, grange, mill, arable, *terrage,* annual *corvée,* and
justice, and their income was probably about 15 *l.t.* each. Most knights,
however, either because they had never received such large fiefs in the
first place or because the original grants had been fragmented by
inheritances and dowries, held only shares of villages, if any at all. Jean
of Marnay, for example, was a contemporary of Milo II of Quincy and
had a comparable income, but Jean remained an *armiger* for many
years. His fief consisted of one-quarter of the village of Marnay and
contained a house, land, men, fields, *cens,* and justice, worth altogether
20 *l.t.* He owed eight weeks castle guard; two rear-fiefs were held from
him by another knight. Such median-level direct fiefs were not much
different from the more valuable rear-fiefs. The lady of Durnay's eleven
valued (of eighteen) rear-fief holders had incomes ranging from 2 to 70
l.t.; their median of 25 *l.t.* was above the median for all direct fiefs
themselves. The eleven rear-fiefs of the lady of Traînel ranged from 15
to 60 *l.t.*; their median of 20 *l.t.* and their composition were about the
same as for direct fiefs. A 20 *l.t.* fief was about the median for all fiefs
and seems to have been standard as an acceptable grant from the count:
when the count enfranchised his sergeant Gérard of Varennes, he also
gave him a 20 l. rent from the *tonlieu* of the Ypres merchants. [38]
Thibaut IV granted numerous fiefs of 20 *l.t.* in his quest for liege
homages in the second and third decades of the thirteenth century, but
the actual purchasing power of such grants is difficult to evaluate; as
early as 1182 four prebends at Saint-Pierre were each worth 20 l.
annually.[39]

Below the median income, fiefs were usually composed of fragmentary revenues; that is, they did not consist of definite fractions of
villages and did not contain tracts of land, houses with appurtenances,
or other tax or banal revenues. Lesser fiefs were rather minor revenues
collected from scattered sources and were not dissimilar to the lesser
rear-fiefs. The seventeen valued (of nineteen) rear-fiefs held from Jean
of Vallery ranged from 1 to 15 *l.t.*, with a medium of just 3 *l.t.* On this
level fiefs and rear-fiefs were barely distinguishable from peasant tenures. Raoul of Granges, for example, held a direct fief of 1 *l.t.*,
consisting of *cens* and oats payments. Although he appears to have

married into a knight family, he was probably a peasant himself, for the count's scribes noted in the *Rôles* that "he did not do homage but gave faith" for his holding. His son had been "franchised" by a lord in 1246. In another entry, the widow Margaret of Droupt was explicitly identified as a *femina de corpore* of the count and listed for the three fiefs which her father had purchased fifteen to thirty five years before and which now produced 2 *l.t.* from *cens* and 5 *modii* of grain. Rear-fiefs of 2 and 1 *l.t.* were held from her by a *dominus* and a *domina.* Her son Guillaume of Payns (after his father) became an *escuier* by 1275 and held the 3 *l.t.* rear-fief that had belonged to his overlord's brother. Survival must have been precarious on a few *libratae terre,* if these were sole incomes. In 1244 one canon of Pougy donated 15 l. to an abbey in return for a weekly loaf of bread similar to those received by the canons for the son of his brother, a knight.[40]

In addition to the diversity of actual fief values and composition, the family histories reveal the inherent instability of fief tenure caused, not by a failure in some respect by a tenant toward his lord, but rather by family exigencies, such as sudden requirements for ready cash, and the obligation to provide fiefs and dowries for children.[41] Ordinary fiefs, like those with castles and fortified houses, were subject to equal division among direct heirs as long as the main residences passed intact.[42] The threat of steadily diminishing shares must have stimulated an active market in dowries and female inheritances, which could furnish the crucial edge between a modest and a comfortable income. However, those often gave but temporary relief, since a man's own children also required suitable incomes. For example, Hugh of Luyères, *dominus,* had two fiefs in 1252: 10 *l.t.* from men and justice at Onjon and 20 *l.t.* from men, lands, and justice at Montgueux. By 1265 his daughter had the 20 *l.t.* as her dowry, leaving him with only 10 *l.t.*[43] Likewise, Guillaume of Quincy (see above) had to give up his mother's 8 *l.t.* fief as dowry for his sister. Both Thibaut I of Rosières and Milo of Fontette secured 10 *l.t.* fiefs as dowries, although neither had to rely on those for essential income. Occasionally, when a dowry or female inheritance was clearly only an additional income to a man's own property, he would sell the former for ready cash or a rent. The fief of Minay, for example, which probably consisted of the entire village, was divided between a brother and sister at the end of the twelfth century: she took the lesser share (that is, the share without the house) and passed it to her daughter Lacena, whose husband, a knight, held it *ex parte uxoris sue* in ca. 1200. Since the latter's own possessions were sufficient, he sold this acquisition—woods, land, and *terrage*—for 40 l. and 4.5 *modii* grain annually. The other half of Minay was still retained by the male descendants in 1252: Fromond III had a house, land, men, *cens,* and customs, worth 40 *l.t.* income, for which he owed eight weeks guard. He was successively *armiger* (1245), untitled (*Rôles*), *messire* and *chevalier* (1270), and *sire* (1275). Like the great estates, Minay had been divided equally by income between the heirs, but the important components of residence and customs were held by the eldest child.

Dowries and female inheritances were extremely important for those who held their wives' properties as their single fief. Jean of Rigny-le-Ferron, for instance, had been deprived of an inheritance by his ancestors and held only his wife's properties in 1252 (a house, lands, and grain, all worth 20 *l.t.*). A later survey states that he also had fields, woods, and *tonlieu* there and that he did not owe guard. Jean had been a cleric in 1225, without title in the *Rôles*, but *messire* and *chevalier* in 1275. Thanks to his wife's properties, Jean enjoyed an average fief income. Dowries and female inheritances were like other fiefs in composition and value and generally reflected the entire range of fief combinations, including the poorer ones. Milo of Clérey, for example, received only three *setiers* of grain annually as his wife's dowry. Hugh of Maupas' daughter was assigned four *setiers* on a *terrage,* and his son was eventually deprived of his entire inheritance, being forced to rely on his wife's own 4 *l.t.* rear-fief. At this level the dowry of a well-off peasant might seem more satisfactory, were it not for the different tenure and composition and their implications for social status. The dowries of two peasant women who were exchanged by their lords in 1209 in anticipation of marriages furnish a comparison: a dowry of 16 l. cash, 16 *jugera* of land, 60 sheep, 4 oxen, and 4 cows was exchanged for a dowry of 20 l. cash, a house in the town of Méry, 16 *jugera* of land, 4 oxen, and 4 cows.[44] The total value of these peasant dowries was certainly greater than that of small knight dowries, but, of course, the essential difference was in the nature of the property and revenues. Even a low-valued fief produced a fixed annual income and assured some social standing.

The influence of alienations on the fief-holding families is among the most difficult of all evaluations to make. The charters are naturally most sensitive to lay alienations, but seldom is it possible to determine by charter evidence alone the impact of alienations on the lay families themselves. The surveys show a decrease in the total number of fief holders from 1172 to 1275 of about 40 percent. The reason for the disappearance of fiefs and their holders from the Champagne fief system is not evident from the surveys themselves; only the best-documented cases can offer clues. One obvious reason for a mortgage or alienation (the second often followed the first) was for ready cash to support a journey to the East. The steady stream of travelers eastward from the mid-twelfth century seems to have reached major proportions in the last two decades of the twelfth century and the first few years of the thirteenth, for there was a sharp increase in the number of acquisitions by ecclesiastical houses in charters of that period. Most transactions were probably for crusading expenses, although few were explicitly described as such. The great baronial families usually had at least one member on crusade, and they too required money for their retinues: the lord of Ramerupt, for example, mortgaged a large village for 300 l. in 1188, which his creditor (who married his widow) subsequently sold to a neighboring abbey. The count of Bar-sur-Seine sold his *mainmorte* rights in that town for 100 l. in 1198. Both male lines eventually perished in the East. The knights, with fewer resources to begin with, made comparatively more serious commitments. Milo of Quincy (see above) sold only part of his tithe for 35 l. and a horse in 1200, no doubt for the Fourth Crusade, but Hulduin of Villemoyenne, knight, sold all his property to secure 80 l. for his trip to Jerusalem. [45] Hugh Crollebois, knight, took a 40 l. loan in 1198 but then in 1200 had to sell his one-quarter of a village, which he had in alod, for 120 l.; his family is not mentioned after 1208. In 1212 Hagan II of Ervy sold his 8 l. share of a *tonlieu* in Troyes, which he held from the count, for 70 l. because his "sons wanted to go to Constantinople and he didn't have sufficient means for their expenses." None of that family is ever heard from again, and their fief, originally a 10 l. income assigned on the fairs of Troyes, was fully acquired by the chapter of Saint-Etienne. Milo of Beurey, knight, who went East in 1218, promised his tithe, *cens,* and *terrage* to an abbey if he did not return; he was probably unmarried, since there is no mention of his family, and apparently he did not return.[46]   There is no doubt that crusading expenses caused a major disruption in family finances because the necessary cash involved more than a single year's income for most fief holders.[47] Over half of the fiefs in 1252 provided less than 20 *l.t.* income for their holders; to secure at least that amount of cash in advance would have been a major undertaking for the holder and his family. Unfortunately, it is impossible to measure the number of lesser fief holders who either died in the East or lost their properties to cover crusading expenses, although the better-documented cases of baronial families suggest that the decrease in fief holders in the count's records was in fact caused by the disintegration of fiefs and families on all income levels and that the Crusades were one strong factor. Similar financial difficulties in undertaking such expensive expeditions were experienced by townsmen.[48]

There were, of course, many other alienations, often of entire family holdings, which do not seem to have been related to the Crusades. The Bouy-Luxembourg, originally knights of the count of Brienne, had a Champagne fief in the *Feoda* and were rewarded for their support during the succession crisis by another fief of an entire village of thirty hearths, land, a house, a mill, *corvées,* and justice. The two brothers who received it jointly sold it to Larrivour in 1222 for the equivalent of

300 l., and the village became an ecclesiastical prebend. This family does not appear again in the county records, since it had alienated the fief. Although the reason cannot be determined, both the fief and the family disappeared from the Champagne fief system.[49] More explicit is the case of the Ruvigny family, who received their first fief from the count ca. 1190. In 1223 the son Gautier II, *domicellus,* alienated "all his goods both mobile and immobile," which were specified as lands, fields, houses, and *cens.* On his death in 1245 his wife surrendered even the quarter of a vineyard which she had kept and entered the abbey as a convert. The original fief of 1172, reassigned to the Ruvignys in ca. 1190, was completely alienated in 1223/45; neither the fief nor the family appears again in the administrative records or charters. The Vaubercey family is yet another example of how a fief could simply disappear from the count's fief system. Elebaud of Vaubercey had a fief for which he owed eight weeks guard, according to the *Feoda.* In 1173 he converted it into six *modii* (seventy two *setiers*) of grain to be collected annually from an abbey, and in ca. 1200, *Feoda* III, his fief was described by the count's agents as sixty four *setiers* of grain, for which he owed eight weeks guard. In 1201 he gave one *modius* for burial rights, and in 1208 his son Jean sold another for 35 l. to meet expenses for the Albigensian Crusade. At the same time another three *modii* were held from Jean in rear-fief, perhaps because of a dowry for his sister. Thus, in 1218 when Jean left four minor children to fight the Albigensians again, only one of the original six *modii* of grain was left for his direct use. The fief of 1172 and its eight weeks guard were lost to the count. Ecclesiastical houses must have incorporated entire fiefs, either by outright purchase or by default of mortgages, as a matter of course, but there are few explicit examples of foreclosure.[50] Rear-fiefs also were alienated and thus lost to the Champagne fief system.[51]

In a few cases, after fiefs were alienated descendants obtained new fiefs. Milo of Clérey was dispossessed when his father transferred a small fief of a house and several separate pieces of land into an annual three *setiers* of grain (*terrage*) and clothing, which eventually went to Milo's sister as dowry; Milo had to obtain a new holding from another abbey. Renaud of Bouy-sur-Orvin also was dispossessed by his father of a valuable grange and close in 1222, and despite the efforts of Renaud and his overlord, he was unable to regain the property, which an abbey now claimed *de francho allodio.* The lord of Traînel, to whom his father had been a close companion, gave him another holding, but as a rear-fief; he did not hold directly from the count as his father had done. The count, too, was continually reassigning or granting new fiefs to the dispossessed. If the corrections in the Troyes-Isle register of the *Feoda* are indicative, the count reassigned most of the fiefs which fell vacant between 1172 and 1190 to distant or indirect relatives of the original holders (see chapter IV). Gautier of Ruvigny, for example, received his first fief after the decease of its previous holder. The succession crisis in the early thirteenth century forced the countess to reward her supporters with fiefs: the Bouy-Luxembourg brothers were granted an entire thirty-hearth village for their aid. Both the Ruvigny and Bouy fiefs were alienated in the 1220s. More powerful lords were granted incomes from fairs or markets: Jean of Arcis-sur-Aube, for example, received 35 l. from the fairs of Troyes in 1218, but he must have alienated some of that because in 1252 only 22 l. remained. In addition to rewards for past service, the countess purchased support, especially during the second decade, by grants of "augmentation" of fief revenues; that is, new revenues were attached to existing fiefs without the creation of new entities. Henri of Chennegny received 4 l. *in augmentum feodi,* for which he owed six weeks guard, and Milo III of Chervey took over his brother's fief and the 100 s. attached to it "in augmentation," for which he became liege to the count. But after 1230 there are few examples of outright grants of new fiefs or augmentations of income by the count.

Most difficult of all to discuss are knight marriages. Except when a woman explicitly referred to her parents, or where her inheritance or dowry can be traced, she usually cannot be linked with her family, so the genealogies of both lords and knights are most defective with respect to wives and their origins. In the few cases that can be documented, it appears that knight families usually intermarried with other knight families, although there are cases of unions with peasants, townsmen, and baronial families. Robert I of Fontette married the Ville-sur-Arce heiress and secured her major fief, a fortified house and 160 l. annual income, once held by a son of the count of Bar-sur-Seine. The Brosse brothers both married into the old Chappes families, and one obtained a dowry worth 211 l. annually. Undoubtedly there were other cases of knights marrying into the great families, but few can be confirmed by charter evidence. At the other extreme, there were knights who married peasant women. Milo of Quincy, for example, probably married a peasant who was exchanged and franchised by her lord in 1175.[52] Patrick of Chaource, knight, seems to have intended to marry the widow of a tanner of Troyes when he asked the count to free her from *taille* on the count's lands.[53] Thibaut I of Rosières also probably married a peasant of the count's domain: she was given a 10 l. dowry by the countess, and on her death she was entitled *domicella*. Raoul of Granges, who held a very small fief in the *Rôles* of 1252, was probably of peasant origin but seems to have married into a knight family: his son and daughter-in-law were both "franchised" by their lord, a knight.[54] Intermarriage agreements also show the proximity of knights and peasants on private lordships.[55] Other knights were closely related to townsmen, either by direct descent or by marriage: Garin I of Barbet, for example, was a "burger" in 1161 and had a son identified as *miles* and *dominus* in 1194. The Isle-Aumont family which furnished *prévôts* and mayors of Isle in the twelfth century produced a rich Troyen in the thirteenth century who was the first mayor of the commune in 1231. His brother Gautier was also a prominent Troyen, whose widow married a knight, Guillaume of Saint-Benoît, in 1243; her sons took the latter's name: one was an *armiger* who held his step-father's 30 *l.t.* fief (and owed its all-year service in 1252) in addition to his wife's own inheritance of 9 *l.t.*

In spite of the great difficulties in analyzing knight families in the early period, certain traits do emerge from the few cases that can be examined in some detail. In contrast to the count and lord families, useful knight lineages rarely can be constructed before the late twelfth century, and certainly not before the mid-twelfth century. That is to say that although knights appeared in retinues before those times, they did not constitute lineage groups with surnames and were not identified by their particular fief holdings. The knights apparently experienced a sudden rise in prestige and in economic assets during the second half of the twelfth century, and by the turn of the next century they began to enjoy the *dominus* title formerly reserved for the old baronial families. But the knights were not a uniform group in the thirteenth century. They differed widely in the types of their possessions, incomes, military obligations, and marriages. A few families with the highest incomes constructed fortified houses in the early thirteenth century and seem thereafter to have composed an elite just below the old castellan families. Most fief holders, however, had modest residences, not very dissimilar to those of their peasant neighbors, some plots of lands, and a few local rents and revenues. A substantial number of direct, as well as rear-fief, holders had fiefs without residences at all, consisting of only minor rents and grain revenues that provided incomes not much above those of well-off peasants; tenure alone preserved their status. Although most fief holders were probably liege to the count by the 1220s, and all owed him service in time of war, very few owed regular castle guard by the mid-thirteenth century.

Fief holders at all levels were afflicted by inheritance problems. The newly formed regulations requiring all children to receive equal shares of estates, save the main residence and its immediate rights, which went to the eldest, tended to fix family possessions for inevitable dismemberment. Furthermore, alienations for both crusading expenses and unexplained reasons were far more serious for the lesser fief holders than for the great barons because there was no chance for the lesser men without rights of taxation to recoup their losses. The specific cases of family alienations that can be documented confirm the Champagne surveys on the steadily diminishing number of fief holders and their fiefs and the fragmentation of incomes. The 5 *l.t.* fief of Minay, even if it did contain a fortified house, was simply not in the same category as even a fragment of a fief originally worth 100 *l.t.* The great financial disparity also meant that the knights tended to marry at their own income levels, even though intermarriages with great families, townsmen, and peasants were not unknown. In the early thirteenth century the noncastellan fief holders formed a disparate group in terms of titles, incomes, and possessions. Fiefs ranged from the large compact estates just inferior to castellanies to mere collections of assorted minor revenues scarcely distinguishable from peasant incomes. Only half of the count's fief holders were knights, the rest being mainly nonknighted and women; by birth, they were the children of former knights.[56]

CONCLUSION: THE ARISTOCRACY AND THE *COUTUMIER*

The *Coutumier* was composed in the last decade of the thirteenth century as a private collection of recent court judgments and of generally accepted customs regulating rural tenurial and inheritance procedures.[57] As a social group, the "nobles" were distinguished by their titles and tenures from both peasants and townsmen. A *nobles hons* was identified variously as a *vauvassor, chevalier,* and *gentiz honme,* but he was especially defined as one who "held in fief."[58] In the countryside the most obvious social dichotomy was between fief holders and their tenants. Most of the *Coutumier* deals with the points of contact between the two groups, including such relationships as intermarriage, and the customs were explicit in the few cases in which they applied to both "noble ou de poesté."[59] Within the fief-holding group the sole differentiation was between the "castellans and barons," who furnished the fiefs, and all other "gentlemen," who held fiefs.[60] It is not clear whether the holders of fortified houses were included with the castellans at this date, but the appearance of the baronial decision of 1224 as Article I of the *Coutumier* suggests that they were in fact associated with the barons.[61] Yet the priorities and procedures established by the councils of 1212/24 were no longer confined to fortifications but had become standard for all fiefs.[62] Fiefs were distinct from all other tenures, in that they were not available for public acquisition; they were to be granted only "in recognition of the [military] services" rendered by their recipients.[63] Fief tenure was the essential guarantee of aristocratic status by the end of the thirteenth century.

The strong family control over fiefs and the primacy of the immediate family members are evident throughout the *Coutumier*. The
customs make no distinction in status or tenure between fief holders
and rear-fief holders: fief holders were permitted to create rear-fiefs,
but only for their married children.[64] A fief could be mortgaged for up
to three years, with proper notification to the overlord, but it could
not be alienated, since fief tenure was technically only the enjoyment of
assigned revenues, of which the principal was to be preserved.[65]
Children were required to render homage within one year of attaining
majority—age eleven for females, age fifteen for males.[66] The widow
or, if neither parent survived, the eldest child had wardship over
younger children.[67] Finally, relief was not normally owed to the lord
for direct inheritance. The regulations were not advantageous for collateral or indirect transfers, which required the strictly equal division of
a fief among all heirs, irrespective of sex and age, and the payment of
relief, usually one year's income.[68] More serious, the children of
parents who died before the latter had received their own inheritances
were not entitled to anything from their grandparents' estates.[69] Within these broad avenues of fief transfer, fiefs were easily handled at the
will of the immediate holder. Only one principle appears to have been
inviolate: the castle guard assigned to a fief never died. Whether the fief
was subinfeudated or dismembered, proportionate shares of the original
guard were to accompany all fragments of the fief.[70]

The customs and actual court decisions in the *Coutumier* offer a
coherent and reasonably accurate picture of the aristocracy in the late
thirteenth century. The antiquity of the customs, however, cannot be
deduced from the *Coutumier* itself. It is not apparent whether the
customs were identical, or even similar, to those prevailing a century
earlier, and it is not necessarily the case that the society depicted by the
Coutumier is valid for an earlier period. The council decisions of
1212/24 on the transfers of castles and fortifications were obviously
new determinations at the time, efforts to standardize and control
certain critical inheritance processes. The *Coutumier* simply embodied
the text of the second council's decisions as its first article and incorporated the decisions of the first council as its second article. But that
second article of the *Coutumier* also included several later changes; in
particular, the regulations of the original councils for fortifications were
now extended to all fiefs. It cannot be determined when the extension
occurred or whether it was enacted by another council, but the problem of fief disintegration was general in the thirteenth century; at least
by 1269 the count saw fit to prohibit the newly enriched chapter of
Saint-Urbain from purchasing "whole fiefs."[71] Furthermore, the original council provisions for equal shares of revenue for younger children
had been modified in the *Coutumier* to allow a younger brother twice

the share of a younger sister. Both the extension and modification occurred after 1224, so when Article II begins "it is the custom in Champagne . . . ," it is to be understood that the custom was certainly in force in the late thirteenth century but was not necessarily applicable before, in this case, the third decade of the century. As in the case of peasant and community development, the *Coutumier* provisions for fief holders are comprehensible only for the late thirteenth century, for they rest on several crucial developments earlier in the century. The *Coutumier* embodied the culmination of several centuries of social evolution, and it cannot simply be read into or imposed on the earlier period. In fact, the *Coutumier* does not reach beyond the critical period of Thibaut IV's minority (1201-22). The generation of those years saw the preparation for and the failure of the Third and Fourth Crusades. It was the generation that endured the Champagne succession crisis and the resultant insecurity and destruction, which led ultimately to the creation of communes (1230-31) in the most important Champagne towns. At the same time, that generation experienced inheritance problems so severe that baronial councils were called to attempt to solve them. In short, the *Coutumier* portrays the conditions that crystallized in the period 1201-31, but not those of the earlier, less complex age of Henry I.

In the mid-twelfth century the count of Troyes dealt only with his "barons," members of the old count and lord families who with their retinues of agents and military men still exercised virtually independent control of the countryside. Indeed, one of the earliest acts in which young Henry appeared with his father, in 1147, states that "many barons and plebeians of the county" took the cross on their way to the East.[72] In this period the knights were just beginning to emerge as a distinctly titled group but had not yet fully done so. *Armigeri* were scarcely mentioned, and certainly not as underaged fief holders, and the only women to hold properties in their own hands were members of the baronial houses. The rule of Henry I was central to the development of Champagne as a territorial state, for he began the subordination of the great castellan families to a larger territorial unit. The *Feoda* of 1172 reveals the process under way: castellans were organized into new districts, the Champagne castellanies, and listed in administrative registers beyond their control. Their castles were made available to the count on his demand, and when their families failed to produce male heirs, their properties were simply absorbed into the Champagne domain. The imposition of liegeance on their collateral lines in the early thirteenth century continued the subordination.[73] The *Coutumier* only hints at this age when all property and privileges flowed from the old families when it states that fiefs originated with "castellans and barons," who awarded tenures to *gentiz honmes* in return for military service.[74] But the *Coutumier* contains no hint of the great chasm between the barons and the knights in the twelfth century nor of the emergence of knights as a cohesive social group and into distinct lineages in the second half of the twelfth century. Again, the *Feoda* is a milepost in social and political development, for it officially confirmed the significance of the knights by virtue of their tenures and relationship to the count. The *Coutumier* fails to give any indication that only after 1190 did the knights emerge as they were to appear later; that only from the late twelfth century did the knights acquire the title hitherto monopolized by the old families; that only then did the wives of knights begin to hold fiefs in their own right; and that only then did the *armigeri* appear as a separate social group. The *Coutumier* seems to have recognized, by its incorporation of the council decisions of 1212/24, that the holders of fortified houses were treated in the same manner as castellans with respect to inheritance restrictions, but it does not acknowledge that the former had emerged as important property holders in the late twelfth century, and generally after 1200.

The *Coutumier* ignores also the changing role of women, especially in respect to tenure. Among the baronial families women enjoyed the same rights to property as their men, and property passed through both male and female sides, according to the family circumstances (see Ramerupt, Vendeuvre, and Nogent for the transfer of great lordships to women). But the position of women in knight families seems substantially different in the twelfth century, for they do not seem to have had claim to fiefs. The *Feoda* itself indicates that fief tenure was in return for military service, and therefore women of knight families could not hold fiefs in their own right. The corrections made to the original *Feoda* after 1172 and to about 1190 may indicate a change, for 24 percent of the emendations to the Troyes-Isle register mention widows of previous fief holders, and perhaps the 22 percent of replacements by probable relatives were actually to sons-in-law. In any event, the first clear example of a knight family dividing its fief held from the count between a son and daughter is in 1191 for Minay: the fief was split equally, but the son-in-law soon sold his wife's share. By 1252, women represented over 20 percent of the ordinary fief holders, a percentage that remained stable through at least 1275.

It appears that the women of knight families shared the increase in prestige and legal standing of their husbands from the last decades of the twelfth century and came to enjoy the same privileges that women of baronial families already possessed. With the decline in military service in the thirteenth century, there was no longer any objection to fief tenure by those not personally qualified to serve in the field. The control of ordinary fiefs by women seems also to have been accelerated by the council decisions that guaranteed them equal shares of their parents' holdings. The *Coutumier* provision that reduced their shares to half that of a younger brother was introduced at the end of the thirteenth century, and there are no examples of it before 1284.

Two other related and parallel processes occurred in the first two decades of the thirteenth century but were not germane to the *Coutumier* when it was composed: the conversion of alods into fiefs and the imposition of liegeance on all fief holders. Alods existed throughout the twelfth and thirteenth centuries, but their extent and distribution relative to fiefs cannot be determined because the extant documents are concerned essentially with fiefs and ecclesiastical holdings. Alods were defined as being held from no person and being exempt from all obligations: the lord of Traînel defined certain of his woods in 1197 as being "completely free from all exaction, use, and *dominium*"; a knight in 1248 claimed that his men, fields, vines, lands, *cens,* and customs at a certain place were "held from no man and rendered no service, but they were of his alod."[75] In the twelfth century alods were distinguished from fiefs; in the later decades they were contrasted to *cens* as well, and from the mid-thirteenth century alodial properties were often labeled "free alods."[76] The count's policy in the early thirteenth century was to convert important alodial holdings into fiefs: the alod of Rosières, for example, worth about 60 *l.t.* in 1252, and the merchant hall in Troyes that belonged to the Rosières family in alod were converted into fiefs in ca. 1201. In most cases a price was paid for the conversion: one man received 30 *l.t.* for converting one *carrucate* of land, twenty families, and fifty *arpents* of woods, two of vines, and ten of fields into a fief; Pierre of Flacy received 10 l. for his alod conversion; and Hugh of Cléréy probably was simply allowed to have a fortified house in exchange for converting his property at Ervy into a fief in the 1220s.[77] Ecclesiastical institutions also acquired alodial property in this same period.[78] Alodial properties continued to survive, and by the later thirteenth century tenures were carefully distinguished as fiefs, rear-fiefs, *cens,* or alods.[79]

The obverse of the alod conversion policy was the imposition of liegeance. The sharp increase in the count's liegemen from about 47 percent of all fief holders in 1172 to 70–80 percent in the first decade and through the remainder of the thirteenth century was clearly the result of policy. The great collateral lines were of course singled out, since they had special significance during the minority crisis. But the holders of fortified houses also merited close attention: in fact, the countess prevented the concentration of fortifications and large properties by requiring each of several sons to become liege to her directly for the relevant share of the inheritance. The *Coutumier* reports that the younger son of a fief holder had the option of holding his share from the eldest son or directly from the overlord, but that choice had to be made within one year of acquisition.[80] Such an option may have existed in the early thirteenth century, and there is at least one case in which a younger brother was explicitly allowed to be liege either to his brother, the holder of several fortifications, or to the countess.[81] But as the political situation evolved, the countess imposed liegeance in particular cases: in 1219, for example, when Robert I of Fontette converted his alod of 15 l. into a Champagne fief, he also promised to divide his possessions into two fiefs so that each of his then infant sons would be liege to the count. No doubt this was an attempt to keep Fontette's fortification (160 *l.t.*) acquired through marriage separate from his fief acquired from the count (40 *l.t.*).[82] With Thibaut's succession, all important fiefs and fortifications were held directly from him in liege homage. In fact, the count had become so conscious of liegeance that he constituted the income paid for Erard of Ramerupt's surrender of claim to the county in 1221 as a "liege fief."

The *Coutumier* portrait of Champagne fief holders is most accurate for the period of reestablished equilibrium after the 1230s, the actual conditions of which are best described by the *Rôles des fiefs* of 1252. All the fief holders and rear-fief holders in the *Rôles* would be the *nobles* and *gentiz honmes* of the *Coutumier*. But only half of the fief holders were knights in 1252, and the one-fifth who were *armigeri* were not mentioned in the customs, perhaps on the assumption that theirs was a transitional status.[83] Although fief holders were defined by tenure as a fairly uniform group, the great disparities in their economic and political importance, as well as in their origins, were nonetheless apparent. The *Coutumier* identification of castellans and barons as grantors of all fiefs is historically exact. The *Rôles* show further that these same families actually held the great estates with concomitant tax and judicial rights. They held the fiefs worth 100 *l.t.* or more, which represented only 7.3 percent of all fiefs and consumed 39.2 percent of the total available fief revenues. Fiefs in the 30–100 *l.t.* range, most of which had some sort of fortification, constituted 17.4 percent of all fiefs and absorbed 34.6 percent of the accumulated incomes. Thus, one-quarter (24.7 percent) of all fiefs fell into the two categories of castle or fortification fiefs, which together accounted for three-quarters (73.8 percent) of the accumulated fief incomes. They were essentially the same fief holders, 16.5 percent of all holders, who controlled 75.0 percent of all rear-fief holders, most of whom were not related to their lords. The majority of fiefs, the "ordinary" holdings, were distinctly inferior, though governed by the same regulations as the great holdings. Occasionally, a 15 or 20 *l.t.* fief contained on a smaller scale the same full range of components and rights as a great fief, but most fiefs in this range did not constitute estates. And revenues below 10 *l.t.* were mostly from scattered sources, such as grain or minor rents. The lesser fief holders had neither tax nor judicial rights over peasants, nor banal monopolies; they had no base for increasing revenues, and they were powerless to overcome temporary losses. Nor did they have rear-fief holders, except, as provided in the *Coutumier,* when a son or daughter was given part of the fief as a rear-fief on marriage. Most rear-fief holders were in a similar position. Yet, they too were the *nobles* of the *Coutumier.*

Although the *Coutumier* disguises the previous development of the fief-holding aristocracy, it certainly does not present a static image of that society in the late thirteenth century. The customs, both stated and adjudicated, accord well with the general conditions reflected in the *Rôles* of 1252 and with the histories of individual families that can be studied closely. In spite of the diverse histories of the great old families, one general conclusion is inescapable: the small margin between family survival and failure, between economic security and penury, perpetuated family instability. Half of the dozen or so great families of the twelfth century had died out in their main lines by the mid-thirteenth century, in all observable cases the consequence of a lack of male heirs. Properties left to heiresses or indirect heirs were either absorbed into the Champagne domain or carved up among relatives into insignificant holdings. Of the threatened lines, only one (Brienne) was taken over by a collateral line and preserved integrally in title and properties. As the *Coutumier* states, and as individual cases from the twelfth century illustrate, collateral transfers were subject to exactly equal divisions, without regard even for the integrity of fortifications. Although the principles established by the councils of 1212/24 may have eliminated internal family strife (*contentio*) by prohibiting primogeniture and may have guaranteed the unity of fortifications and their immediate properties transferred to direct heirs, they also made inevitable and hastened the dismemberment of the great estates.[84] The emergence of independent segmentary lines from the old families compensated for the loss of great houses, and with few exceptions at the end of the thirteenth century, all replacements were from the same old lines. In the sense that the original twelfth century counts and lords maintained their size and exclusiveness through the two centuries, and in spite of the fortunes of their individual members, they can be said to have formed a local "peerage."

The knights reveal as much diversity as the great families, at least from the late twelfth century, when a few of their families can be observed continuously. The knights, too, were threatened by the volatility of their fortunes, which could be created or destroyed in a generation by family size, marriage, or alienation in the name of piety, economic necessity, or simple adventure. A few knight families increased their revenues by acquiring additional fiefs through purchase, grant, marriage, or escheat, and often these men had the means to erect a fortification. But most knights retained their rather modest incomes and positions. Still others suffered reverses and disappeared entirely from both county and ecclesiastical documents. The regulations on fief transfer and disposition were of course neutral, in that they could be at once beneficial and detrimental, depending on the person involved. Turnover in fief possession was a normal process in the later twelfth century, and the changes in the Troyes-Isle register of the *Feoda* indicate that 12.5 percent of the fiefs in 1172 had been lost to their holding families by ca. 1190. But the total number of fiefs in circulation seems to have remained stable during the period: only four fiefs (three absorbed by the count, one reassigned to an ecclesiastical house) were actually lost from the fifty transfers, or only about 3.2 percent of the 125 fiefs were removed from circulation.

This steady-state situation seems to have changed thereafter. First, the rear-fief holders developed as a new level of tenants: by 1252 they were more numerous than the direct fief holders, and they doubled the number of tenants in the Champagne fief system from 359 in 1172 to 739 (309 direct, 430 rear holders) in 1252. All were subject to similar tenurial regulations, and all were included by the *Coutumier* as the aristocracy. However, the *Rôles* of 1252 make clear that rear-fiefs, despite their similar tenurial regulations, were decidedly inferior in composition and value to the direct fiefs. The few rear-fiefs that were comparable to direct fiefs were rear holdings only because their overlords had been subordinated to the count and their fiefs had become Champagne rear-fiefs (for example, Rosières' holding from the lords of Traînel). The custom reported in the *Coutumier* by which fief holders could create rear-fiefs for their married children probably was a recent option for the knights and certainly did not antedate the thirteenth century; it may have accounted for the many minor holdings in the *Rôles*. Whether the lesser rear-fiefs were ignored by the surveys of 1265 and 1275 because of their meager values or because they had lost their status is not evident, but it would appear that the marginal rear-fief holders had been *déclassés*.

There was also a decrease in the total number of direct fief holders in the thirteenth century, in spite of the vigorous policy of alod conversion, in the range of 20 to 40 percent, and probably closer to the latter. Tied to this decrease was a decline in military service: in spite of the *Coutumier* statement that guard never died, that it passed intact or in proportional part with the fief or its parts, the requirement for castle guard had in fact almost disappeared; the very fragmentation of guard had destroyed its effectiveness. But even more important was its disuse by the mid-thirteenth century: many men had received charters of exemption from all castle guard; others had forgotten how much guard their fiefs owed or simply had never known (7.2 percent of the holders in 1252 were unsure of their obligations); and still others reported to the *enquêteurs* lesser obligations than had been recorded previously.[85] In spite of the *Coutumier* claim, castle guard was no longer the mark of fief tenure or knighthood.

The direct fief holders were a smaller group at the end of the thirteenth century than at the end of the twelfth.[86] Even if the rear-fief holders are included in the aristocracy, the combined numbers of direct and rear-fief holders was still relatively small for a period of strong urban growth and population increase in town and countryside. The great old families no longer had the run of the countryside as they did in the twelfth century. They were effectively curbed by the count's authority and administration and were restricted also by the wholly new set of community institutions, especially the town communes of the largest Champagne centers. The fief holders had lost their *raison d'être* with the disappearance of military service and were condemned to live on decreasing revenues—especially serious for the lesser fief holders, who had fewer resources to begin with—in an age of inflation and new town wealth. Both the great lords and the ordinary fief holders were threatened by identical inheritance procedures. In this context of relatively contracting numbers and diminishing resources, the fief holders maintained, and perhaps as a response to these pressures even strengthened, their social and tenurial solidarity. They preserved their control of the countryside by classifying all tenants as *homes de poesté* with uniform obligations and by attempting to prevent the enfranchised townsmen from acquiring rural tenancies. By insisting on the identification of personal and tenurial status, the *nobles*—the *gentizhonmes*—reserved fief tenure, and its social attributes, for their children alone.

VI

French Feudal Societies
SOME COMPARISONS

Until this century, studies of medieval French society presented either broad overviews of social institutions for all France or extremely local examples in essentially legalistic terms (such as the status and obligations of persons and lands of a particular lordship). The overviews are impressionistic, based on randomly selected cases wrenched from their local environments, while the local studies are so restricted in scope and interpretation as to remain antiquarian. It was the problem-oriented studies of two exceptional scholars—Henri Sée on rural society (1901) and Paul Guilhiermoz on the aristocracy (1902)—which set a new foundation for historical research and which have become reference points for subsequent work.[1] Since that time medievalists have been in the avant-garde of historical studies, especially from 1929, when the *Annales d'histoire économique et sociale* was founded as a forum for the newer social and economic perspectives; in a prodigious number of articles and reviews cofounder Marc Bloch and other contributors attempted to reassess the major problems of medieval history in contemporary, analytical terms.[2] More important than the specific solutions proposed by the various writers at the time was the call by Bloch for a series of local monographs on medieval society and economy from which an ultimate synthesis might emerge; and within a decade of the war's end the appearance of those studies made evident the decisive reorientation of medieval studies to social and economic questions. The first monographs naturally tended to accentuate local and regional peculiarities, since their specific data obviously did not accord exactly with the general conceptual frameworks then current. But now that a quarter-century of research has produced a body of organized evidence for diverse regions of France, the resultant data and interpretations need no longer be restricted to comparisons with theoretical models; they can be compared directly, region by region. Ideally, of course, medieval social history would be constructed from a series of case reports by region and period, but the systematic acquisition of standardized information has been impeded by the fortuitous survival of source materials. Moreover, the great variance in methodologies has resulted in diverse presentations of the local evidence. Since the nature of the extant sources and the variety of models employed to analyze local information seldom make it possible to obtain point-by-point comparisons of evidence and interpretations, these have been distilled by region for the following comparisons with the *bailliage*.[3]

Understanding of the medieval peasantry has not progressed significantly in recent decades. The subject continues to be dominated by discrepant interpretations of serfdom, a result of the diverse types of documents consulted for various regions, dissimilar methods of analysis, and irreconcilable conceptual frameworks formulated by each researcher. Generally, the accepted basic thesis is the one proposed by Bloch and Pierre Petot, which posits two periods of serfdom.[4] In the Carolingian period servile status was little changed from ancient slavery: it was marked by heavy personal obligations, legal incapacity, and the maternal transmission of that status, but the servile population (*servi/ancillae*) was small at that time and virtually disappeared during the next two centuries.[5] By the twelfth and thirteenth centuries a "new serfdom" emerged, but only in certain areas of France, notably Burgundy, Champagne, and the Ile-de-France. It was different from the old, in that it weighed on all members of the rural population, not on individuals or families, and was characterized especially by restrictions on marriage and inheritance. Bloch studied these conditions particularly in the Île-de-France, and although his work was never completed, it has exercised an inordinate influence on the whole question of the medieval peasantry. He concluded that the three traits of serfdom were the head tax (*chevage*), *mainmorte*, and *formariage*; the *taille* for him was a general residence tax without servile connotation.[6] Bloch also detected important changes in the development of peasant status in the thirteenth century, as the *taille* gradually evolved into the single attribute of inferior status. But his interpretation of the community franchises remained ambivalent, for he considered them merely written forms of longstanding customs, yet he credited them with effective enfranchisement from the new serfdom.[7] Neither Bloch nor Petot, however, offered a systematic, local illustration of their models, and certain of their procedural biases have persisted in more recent interpretations of peasant conditions. For example, in spite of the demonstration by Charles Perrin that the community franchises offer a reasonable explanation for structural changes in twelfth and thirteenth century rural society, there is a continued aversion to the integration of those grants in a consolidated chronological framework with the voluminous but discrete information of the private charters. Similarly, the collections of customs that are available for the period have not been fully understood because they have been read in terms of static conditions, in spite of their explicit statements to the contrary. Also, the territorial administrative surveys, with their invaluable standardized information on men and communities in the great principalities, have not been consulted until recently.

In the *bailliage* of Troyes it is clear that after ca. 1120 only a single, undifferentiated peasant population existed; there were neither *servi/ancillae* nor "free" men. Except for the *domini* and *milites,* all rural inhabitants were *homines de corpore* and were subjected to the private justice of a landlord, *taille, mainmorte,* and *formariage.* Bloch's categories would be confirmed if his *chevage* were replaced by *taille* as an essential trait in the *bailliage: chevage* was only exacted from a few residents of some Benedictine estates who also paid *taille* to lay lords, so *chevage* was not universal and not of itself servile, whereas the central role of *taille* is confirmed by the numerous instances in which lords claimed it and by the community franchises which abolished it.[8] All these obligations appeared as the normal concomitant of tenancy, not the result of new impositions in the twelfth and thirteenth centuries, in spite of the late appearance of their formal names—*taille* from the mid-twelfth century, *mainmorte* from the late twelfth century, and *formariage* from the early thirteenth century. The examples of intermarriage exchange agreements from the early twelfth century and the enumeration of these obligations as sources of revenue in the *pariages* prove that the obligations were normal for all tenants but were mentioned by name only when landlords claimed them from persons not resident on their domains. The situation in the *bailliage* conforms not so much to the Bloch-Petot explanation as to the alternate one by Verriest for Hainault: namely, that all peasant obligations, including *taille,* marriage and legacy restrictions, banal monopolies, and justice, were the result of tenancy under a landlord; they were the normal obligations of all tenants, incurred originally to guarantee the viability of the lordship.[9]

Central to the interpretation of peasant conditions in the *bailliage* is the evaluation of the community franchises. First, the franchises were clearly the result of the count's policy, which was itself a response to widespread rural migration already in progress. It was peasant migration that forced landlords to specify their claims by name; a stationary peasantry would not have required the descriptions of their obligations to other lords. Second, the franchises were not codifications of long-standing customs but establishments of new conditions both in newly created villages and in refounded older ones. *Tailles* and marriage restrictions were abolished, exemptions were granted from *péage* and *tonlieu* on the count's domain, fines and military service were regulated—all for a 12 d. hearth tax. Immigration was permitted to all except tenants of local lords. The enfranchised villagers were called *bourgeois* in the late twelfth century, although they were still functionally agrarian. But it was the communes of 1230-31 that had the

greatest impact on social evolution in the *bailliage*. They too were the
result of the count's policy, but for political, not strictly economic,
reasons. They too abolished *taille* and *mainmorte*, controlled military
service, and granted other personal and property privileges, including
freedom of departure (that is, without tax), all in return for a tax on
wealth, the *jurée*. The significance of the *jurée* tax has been obscured
by the institution of the thirteen *jurée* who administered the communes. Most of the self-governing bodies of townsmen failed within a
generation of their creation, but the new tax became a permanent
feature: the *jurée* tax in effect replaced the old tenurial restrictions, as
had the 12 d. hearth tax in the twelfth-century rural franchises, and
created instead large communities of enfranchised persons as a new
social category. The *Coutumier* confirms the development: except for
the enfranchised and the fief holders, all tenants were *homes de poest*
and liable for the old, universal tenurial obligations. In fact, those
requirements were now defined as a "lower condition"; the children of
a noble woman and a nonfranchised man reverted to it and were
responsible for the associated *taille* and *mainmorte*. The equation of
land-man status in the *Coutumier* expressed the historical reality: those
who were not residents of franchised communities at that time were
defined by exclusion as *homes de poest*. Although community franchises were granted periodically through the thirteenth century, usually
by the most powerful lords to their most important communities, the
chances were that tenants not resident in a franchised community by
the mid-thirteenth century were condemned to the "lower condition."
Bloch was correct in isolating the increasing importance of *taille* in the
thirteenth century as the sole definition of a lower status that approxi-
mated "class" conditions, for the *taille* by that time identified all those
who did not share a community franchise.

Conditions and the chronology of development were similar in northern Champagne, even in areas outside the count's direct control. It has
been shown, for example, that the *homines sanctuarii* so common in
the north were in fact ordinary tenants on ecclesiastical lands who were
subjected to the same triad of obligations—*taille, mainmorte,* and *formariage*—as other peasants: their special name reflected only their
tenancy on ecclesiastical lands and had nothing to do with a "servile"
status.[10]   An important event in the north was the charter of Beau-
mont, issued in 1182 by Count Henry I's brother, William of White
Hands, archbishop of Reims. It was especially important as a model for
small village franchises in the thirteenth century, and in Luxembourg its
influence has been assessed as the stimulant of major social and economic developments.[11]   It provided for open immigration (not to be
challenged after one year and one day), exemptions from taxes and
tolls, fixed judicial procedures and military requirements, and internal

village administration, in return for a fixed 12 d. hearth tax. It was similar to the franchises issued by Count Henry in the *bailliage* in the same period, except that it was far more detailed, being itself modeled on the Reims city charter, and included specifics on village administration. From the 1230s the four largest towns in Luxembourg received more extensive grants, like the contemporary Champagne commune grants. Just to the east, in Lorraine, the community franchises also had a significant impact on rural conditions. From the 1170/80s there were several hundred grants, mostly by lay lords, which fixed *tailles*, limited military obligations, standardized legal proceedings, and granted economic privileges and some local autonomy. As a type of document, the franchise replaced the older domainal document, the *censier*, which no longer accurately reflected rural conditions, especially after the breakup of the old domainal organization in the twelfth century. It is not coincidental that the first formal intermarriage agreements for tenants come from 1179. The villages not enfranchised were later accounted for in the *rapports de droit*, which were analogous to the *pariages*, in that they recorded only rights and revenues of landlords in communities still held strictly under their control.[12]   Again, the mix of conditions and the chronology of franchise grants are close to those in the *bailliage*. They also appear to have been similar in Alsace: there are no references to *servi* in the twelfth century; all tenants except nobles and clergy were liable to the same restrictions, which were clearly the result of tenancy. The spread of community franchises in Alsace seems to have consolidated rural communities as entities with a wide range of self-administration and economic privileges.[13]

South of the *bailliage* in Burgundy, especially in the closely studied Mâconnais, conditions were likewise similar: *servi* were not mentioned from the early twelfth century, and all tenants were liable to *taille* thereafter; there were few community franchises, but those granted— from the 1170s—clearly abolished the *taille* and *mainmorte*, fixed judicial and military requirements, and granted some economic privileges.[14]   Lands of the Church of Lyon and the county of Forez reveal the same: the absence of *servi* from the twelfth century, obligations incurred by tenancy, and the spread of community franchises in Forez from the 1220s as a result of the count's policy. As Duby has demonstrated, the variance in peasant conditions formerly attributed to geography or lordship is now seen as a function of chronology.[15]   In sum, the entire eastern area, from northern Champagne to southern Burgundy and from Luxembourg to Alsace, would support a single, unified explanation of peasant social development, with the exception of some discrepancy in chronology, the result of the policies of individual princes.

Directly west and north of Champagne, in the royal domain, Picardy, and the Belgian provinces, the community franchises have been far less appreciated and studied. Although comparisons are difficult, generally the data appear remarkably similar to those in the *bailliage*. The customs of Lorris (1155) that abolished *taille,* tolls, and arbitrary fines were the model for numerous community franchises on the royal domain and certainly must have had some impact on the countryside, but they have yet to be studied on a regional level.[16] Perhaps the best example in the Paris region of how the integration of franchises with the other charter information can determine the evaluation of social development is the study of the burg of Saint-Germain-des-Prés.[17] In the twelfth century the abbey's men (*homines*) were liable for marriage and legacy taxes in ordinary charters; in 1174 they were exempted from *taille* in return for an annual 3 s. hearth tax, and in 1252 they were freed from *mainmorte,* marriage tax, and all *servitium.* These privileges applied to all residents of the community, irrespective of where they had been born (that is, under whose lordship), and to natives who had emigrated but had not yet married. The abbot retained only banal monopolies and the right to collect royal aides. There was no reference to *chevage* here, and there were few such references for other localities in the Paris region. Thus, the two partial franchises did in fact alter the obligations of ordinary residents. The situation is not as clear in Picardy, where the absence of references to *mainmorte, formariage,* capitation, and heavy *corvées* is seen as an indication of the lack of serfdom. *Taille* is interpreted as a banal imposition without reference to personal status, but the reading is contradictory because the *homines de corpore* are considered "free," and the cases of *taille* commutation in the early thirteenth century have not been fully analyzed. Furthermore, the over two hundred extant community franchises in Picardy, most of them from the years 1190 to 1250, have been evaluated as simple codifications of longstanding customs, and their influence on peasant and community development has not been determined.[18]

Least attention to rural conditions has been paid in Belgium, dominated as it has always been by an interest in towns and commerce; in spite of excellent studies on individual monastic houses, regional studies like Verriest's on Hainault have been few. The situation in Flanders, for example, has been obscured by various concepts of serfdom and by the propensity to see an advanced "agrarian freedom" as a complement to urban development. In fact, the evidence on rural conditions accords with that in other areas both as to peasant conditions and as to the chronology of the count's community franchises (from the 1160s and early 1180s). The franchise of 1254 for residents on the count's domain is similar to other grants at that date, for instance in the royal domain. Ultimately, however, rural conditions were as complex in Belgium as elsewhere, and traditional domainal organization with heavy tax and labor service existed contemporaneously and under the same lordships as villages with few obligations; no case can be made for peculiar Flemish conditions of advanced liberties.[19] Perhaps the mid-thirteenth-century survey of the count of Namur's domain furnishes the best description to date of northern rural obligations: all tenants had the same requirements as those on the Champagne domain—marriage and legacy restrictions, justice, and military service. Again, however, community franchises from the twelfth century have not been fully integrated with the other evidence in Namur, although they have been linked to the breakup of the old domainal organization.[20] In spite of dissimilar methods of analysis, evidence for the royal domain, Picardy, Flanders, Namur, and Hainault generally agrees with that for the eastern areas.

In western France rural conditions have been most closely studied in Poitou. There, as in most areas, the terms *servus, ancilla,* and *mancipius* disappeared from the charters in the early twelfth century; tenants were normally obligated for rents, taxes, occasional services, and *questa,* a fixed 6 d. hearth tax. The absence of references to *chevage,* heavy *corvées,* and marriage taxes, in addition to the abundant references to widespread land clearing from the eleventh century, has led to the conclusion that this area was devoid of serfdom. Yet, the community franchises that appeared from the late twelfth century and through the thirteenth century have not been integrated with the other charter references; those grants in fact provided exemption from *tailles* and taxes on legacies and marriages, freedom of immigration, fixed military service and schedules of fines, and other economic privileges. Numerous later confirmations of these grants suggest that they represented special privileges not shared by the rest of the rural population; so the relative conditions of the franchised and nonfranchised remain to be determined, although none of the data seem out of context in more eastern and northern areas of France.[21] Indeed, a close study of the priory of Chapelle-Aude confirms the absence of *servi* but also shows that it was a franchise of 1249 that freed tenants from *mainmorte* and marriage restrictions, converted their *tailles* into a wealth tax, and guaranteed free movement of persons and free disposition of property.[22] Similar discrepancies in interpretation occur in Normandy: it has been assumed that serfdom disappeared early there also, yet the only in-depth study of domainal organization reveals that ordinary villagers throughout the duchy in the twelfth and thirteenth centuries paid taxes for marriage and burial rights, owed *corvées,* and paid a residence tax of 12 d. (converted *taille*).[23] It is not clear how the privileges of the communes that spread in large urban centers in the second half of the twelfth century compared with those in the countryside.

In southern France conditions were the same at least on the great territorial domains. In the Dauphiny, for example, the last reference to *servi/ancillae* was in 1117, and all peasants were subjected to the triad of obligations, as well as *corvées* and military service. It was the policy of the count at the end of the thirteenth century which eliminated or regulated those obligations on his own domain, usually in the most urbanized areas; but as in the north, the count retained justice, military service, and extraordinary taxation over all, and the nonfranchised villagers continued to pay the old obligations as well.[24] The inquest on the count's domain in Provence (1252) offers an exceptionally accurate picture of normal rural conditions also: tenants were held to the same obligations as in the Dauphiny, Namur, and Champagne. Although the important Provençal towns gradually acquired exemptions and privileges through the twelfth and thirteenth centuries, so did the smaller, less visible communities.[25] Conditions in the rest of the Midi have not been adequately analyzed, and preliminary results are confusing. Language is a major obstacle, and the Languedoc terminology must be better understood before further advance is possible in the area of social development. Although there are no references to the triad of peasant obligations in the Toulouse area, the franchises show that in the Lauragais, directly south of Toulouse, *tailles* were abolished, open immigration was allowed, and a 12 d. hearth tax was imposed as the universal form of taxation in even the smallest communities in the thirteenth century; no doubt this was, as in the north, the commutation of the previous tenant obligations. The presence of consulates in some twelfth-century towns has obscured the significance of the later franchises to much larger segments of the population; the franchise of 1242 to Fanjeaux, for example, applied to its entire castellany and was remarkably similar to the northern franchises.[26]

The variety of sources, methods of analysis, and conceptual frameworks in the numerous monographs preclude systematic comparisons of many facets of rural social development, but from even this brief extraction of data and conclusions it would appear that peasant and community development were essentially similar and underwent parallel changes throughout France. *Tailles* and marriage and bequeathal restrictions were universal and were associated with tenancy; military service and subjection to a particular private justice were likewise standard; and the various other obligations, including banal monopolies and *corvées,* were also normal for most peasants, although their specific forms were determined by local customs. None of these impositions was associated with "servile" status. Nor were they imposed in the twelfth and thirteenth centuries as new obligations. Rather, they became differentiated by name in the twelfth century as tenant mobility broke the traditional, unwritten identification of tenants and their obligations.[27] From the mid-twelfth century, and especially from the 1170s, great landlords in all regions began to issue community franchises that abolished the old tenurial obligations in favor of a minor hearth tax in an attempt to control larger populations of tenants in certain communities, of which only a small number were in fact newly founded villages. They granted the same basic points: freedom of movement, property transfer, and marriage (without tax); the conversion of all taxes into a single, fixed hearth tax; and some economic privileges. The franchises created islands of privileged communities throughout the kingdom, and they must be linked with changes in the general social and economic environment from the mid-twelfth century. The monographs now seem to reveal not so much regional diversity of rural conditions as essentially chronological disparities. Some of the geographical variation was due of course to the relative economic developments of various areas and to the special policies of territorial princes; but the absolute contrast between the eastern area of serfdom and the northern, southern, and western areas of early peasant freedom simply does not hold—it is the result of a scholarly aberration that sees the normal conditions of tenancy in one area as the traits of "serfdom" in another. A uniform method of analysis of the sources shows that by the mid-thirteenth century a general checkered pattern of strictly-held and of franchised communities prevailed throughout the kingdom.

The medieval aristocracy, unlike the peasantry, is a rapidly developing field of research, with increasing precision in quantitative methods and interpretation. The essential problem of the definition of the aristocracy remains, but specific questions now focus on the relationship of aristocracy to knighthood, the composition of the aristocracy in terms of families, and the method of transmission of aristocratic status. [28] Until the past decade the unchallenged formulation of aristocratic development was that of Guilhiermoz, especially as modified by Bloch and Duby.[29] It offered the equation liberty=aristocracy=knighthood, which is to say that those persons who retained their personal liberty in the Carolingian period became the aristocracy in the "feudal" period (the eleventh and twelfth centuries) and assumed knighthood in accordance with their military functions. Bloch added that the Carolingian-descended aristocracy had died out by the mid-twelfth century and was replaced by a new elite of knights and vassals; it was the new aristocracy that lost its military functions in the thirteenth century and became a group defined by birth alone, now with legal sanction.[30] This basic thesis was further refined by Duby, who showed that in the Mâconnais, Carolingian families, as well as institutions, survived the dark period and into the eleventh century, when they and the knights who first emerged at that time constituted a two-tiered aristocracy. It was closed to outsiders, status was transmitted through the male line, and the families intermarried and shared a common *genre de vie*.[31] By the thirteenth century their aristocratic status was detached from their military functions and was assured by birth alone. In spite of the tendency to defer to Duby's model as a working framework—it was the first fully documented local demonstration available—recent studies have confirmed, rather, an alternate thesis of aristocratic development, first fully documented by Genicot for Namur.[32] This thesis maintains that the great Carolingian families not only survived as lineages but also preserved their social exclusiveness into the thirteenth century. Their status was never dependent on anything other than birth and was transmitted through both male and female lines; and only those families had control of economic, political, and military functions. In eleventh-century Namur, for example, the lords were a closed group of about fifty families that remained basically stable to the mid-thirteenth century, when under a variety of biological and financial pressures they were forced to accept the knights as their social equals. The knights were traditionally a group apart, identified essentially by *métier*; their status owed nothing to high birth, and they were not linked to the great families. Only from the late twelfth and early thirteenth centuries did the knights begin to acquire aristocratic status and gradually fuse with the old families to form an enlarged aristocracy as far as titles, attributes, and privileges were concerned. By the end of the thirteenth century the aristocracy was quite different in composition and significance from what it had been in previous centuries.

The central issue in the evaluation of aristocratic development is the relative position of the knights and the castellan families. The most intense investigations have been conducted on the Belgian aristocracies, which in general conform to Genicot's model for Namur and supply a wealth of additional information. Perhaps the most penetrating study of any medieval aristocracy for the ninth through the thirteenth centuries is that by Ernest Warlop for Flanders.[33] A meticulous comparison of chronicle with charter references, supported by a file of several hundred genealogies, has proved conclusively that *nobiles* was a term with a long tradition and specific meaning, referring to a restrictive group of families which constituted the aristocracy. All the eleventh-century officials, peers (great landlords), and all castellans but one (the Erembald of the 1127 crisis) were descendants of the Carolingian aristocracy. They were sharply distinguished from the knights, who first appeared from the mid-tenth century and who remained a group defined by *métier*, as opposed to the aristocracy, which was defined by family. Although the great families took up knighthood, they represented an officer-corps and were never identified simply as knights. A leveling occurred in the twelfth century, and by the early thirteenth century even the knights carried the *dominus* title; the two groups assimilated and by the fourteenth century constituted a new aristocracy set against the rest of the Flemish population. The same picture holds for Hainault, Brabant, the northerly duchy of Guelders, and the county of Zutphen: the twelfth-century knights were only armed retainers who shared neither social status, military importance, nor economic resources with the old aristocratic families; the latter were endogamous and preserved their standing solely by virtue of their bloodlines.[34] Only from the late twelfth century did the prestige and privileges of knights suddenly increase; within a generation they had intermarried with aristocratic families and joined them in checking the encroachments of townsmen on fief tenure through marriage and purchase. By the late thirteenth century the Belgian aristocracies encompassed a wide spectrum of conditions, wealth, and political and military functions; and as knighthood became less important, a new internal division developed between the knighted and nonknighted within the newly enlarged aristocracy.

Evidence from the *bailliage* of Troyes confirms the general Belgian thesis, although here, as with the peasantry, the methods of interpretation, presentation, and especially the quantitative results make impossible an exact comparison with other regions. It is clear that in the *bailliage* in the twelfth century both the private charter references and the Champagne administrative records acknowledged the fundamental distinction between the counts and lords and the knights. The genealogical reconstructions, imperfect as they are for this period, seem to confirm that separation of families. The same basic divide is observable still in the thirteenth century, in spite of recent title changes: the knight-descended fief holders are easily identified by the values and compositions of their fiefs; the old families alone had the great estates with full local powers, in spite of their general subjugation to the count of Champagne in the political and military spheres. It seems that the knights acquired their fiefs and hereditary control over them in the second half of the twelfth century, shortly before they assumed the *dominus* title. There was a wide range of castle guard owed for their fiefs, but over half of the count's knights owed no regular guard at that time. The first three decades of the thirteenth century witnessed important changes. The great families and their collateral lines became liege to the count of Champagne, and their castles were made fully renderable to him at his request. The count(ess) insisted upon liege homage from most fief holders during the succession crisis and even purchased alods to be converted into Champagne fiefs. A new level of holders emerged with the construction of fortified houses at the same time. An entire layer of rear-fief holders also seems to have developed:

by virtue of their tenures they were of the aristocracy, but most of their holdings were small, so insignificant in fact that by the end of the century the count's *enquêteurs* no longer inventoried them. Perhaps the most serious common experience of the great and humble fief holders was the constant threat to their holdings of fragmentation. When they failed to produce heirs, the great families lost entire castellanies to the count of Champagne or to their indirect heirs; the knights saw their much smaller fiefs divided for dowries, debts, or extraordinary expenses, such as for crusades. The *Coutumier* gives evidence of the potential turbulence inherent in normal fief tenure, but the *Rôles* of 1252 furnish the most immediate examples of the extraordinary range of conditions among fief holders not observable from the narrative or legal documents; noteworthy are the relatively low levels of income and authority of the great majority of fief holders.

Despite the various interpretations, the evolution of aristocracies close to the *bailliage* was similar. Most notably in Burgundy developments parallel those in Champagne in several important respects. Ducal territorial authority was consolidated only during the twelfth century, and liege homage was the main technique for subordinating the castellans. Knights of the castles seem to have settled on land only in the late twelfth century; thereafter a two-month guard obligation was common. The duke actively stimulated the conversion of alods into fiefs from the late twelfth century, as did the bishop of Langres and the archbishop of Lyons, both of whom had great financial resources to support such a policy. Fortified houses also proliferated in Burgundy in the early thirteenth century, about the same time that the *domicelli* emerged as a stable new group. There is also evidence that the great lords, the duke in particular, married at lower levels in order to consolidate specific properties and rights; no doubt lesser lords married at correspondingly lower levels, that is, with members of knight families.[35] Even in the Mâconnais the evidence is essentially in agreement with that in the *bailliage* for the twelfth and thirteenth centuries: in ca. 1100, for example, only the castellans (and abbots of Cluny and Tournus, both of whom had castles nearby) carried the *dominus* title; knights did not acquire that title until ca. 1190, at the same time that they also acquired control over rural tenants. Fortified houses also appeared in the first half of the thirteenth century.[36]

Substantially the same picture emerges from western France. In Poitou the descendants of the Carolingian aristocracy became the "independent castellans" of the eleventh century; occasionally qualified as *nobiles*, they maintained an exclusiveness vis-à-vis the knights, some of whom were recruited from the peasantry and from the ecclesiastical *familiae*. The knights, originally full-time residents of castles, settled in the countryside in the twelfth century, and by the thirteenth century they were liable for only fifteen days annual castle guard. Most knights had small fiefs, often only a manse with some revenues and lesser privileges; a few had alodial lands of their own as well. Especially revealing on the local level are the lords of Parthenay: one of the ten great families of Poitou, they were the only family in their area to have the *dominus* title in charters and also the only one to have a genealogy traceable from the early eleventh century. The other eighteen local aristocratic families (castellans and landlords forced into homage) appeared only from the late eleventh century, but they too were always distinct from the knights and were not qualified as *milites* until the late twelfth century; the Parthenays avoided that attribution until 1269. The knights, on the other hand, had only weak personal bonds with the castellans and possessed small fiefs which were often liable for grain rents and which were scarcely distinguishable from peasant tenures. Only from the late twelfth century did they assume the *dominus* title, and thereafter they became indistinguishable by title and tenure from the old families. By the mid-thirteenth century the sons of both groups delayed taking up knighthood, instead remaining *valets* for most of or even their entire lives without losing their status.[37] In Normandy, too, an aristocracy possessing political and military authority existed separately from the body of knights which supplied military service but exercised no command functions. The 1172 ducal inquest indicates that at least on the ducal domain, as in Champagne, the distinction between the great fief holders, such as counts, barons, and abbots, and the simple knights was still recognized. The so-called "two levels of feudalism" remained distinct until the knights acquired jurisdictional rights over their lands and tenants (probably in the late twelfth century because the *coutumier* of ca. 1200 shows that certainly by then ordinary knights enjoyed the same privileges as barons in matters of jurisdiction and were bound by the same restrictions in fief disposition). But similar social and legal standing did not erase the reality of substantial economic and political differences: in certain cases the rate of fine for a knight was 20 l., compared with 100 l. for a baron. In the bishopric of Bayeux, for instance, knight fiefs were small (15 l. relief in the twelfth century) and scattered and seem to have experienced outright disintegration in the thirteenth century when the importance of knight service declined.[38]

A similar picture applies to the Ile-de-France. Barons and knights were associated in the same system of fief tenure, incurred similar obligations, and enjoyed like exemptions, but the economic and political importance of the barons persisted: they alone were protected by restrictions on fief transfers, and for certain offenses they were assessed a standard 30 l., as opposed to the 10 l. for knights. Knights owed forty days service annually, although that obligation was gradually commuted in the thirteenth century. Only a few fiefs had castles; most knight fiefs contained simple rural structures, and there were many poor knights who lived almost like peasants.[39] Likewise, in Brittany, the fragmentation of small knight fiefs into pieces so small that they were distinguishable from peasant tenures only by their inheritance procedures was also observed.[40] Although there was a single social and legal group of Breton *gentilshommes* by the end of the thirteenth century, few owed military service, and fewer still had properties even remotely resembling lordships with justice, ban, and other rights.

In southern France the situation is difficult to evaluate in the absence of systematic regional studies like those available for the north. Although the Midi is supposed to have had markedly different institutions, the recent revision in our understanding of northern society has considerably reduced the differences. From preliminary investigations it appears that in the Midi the great Carolingian-descended families remained distinct from the knights until the twelfth century. The oaths of fidelity taken among the aristocracy were on the level of political alliances; fidelity was independent of tenure, and castles were usually on alods. Fiefs, which were not much different from peasant tenures, were granted in return for service to agents of the aristocracy; and a basic social divide separated the aristocracy from its armed retainers and administrative agents. A study of Templar implantation in Rouergue from ca. 1140 has revealed that knights tended to coalesce around the new military order and its ideals, whereas the older, more powerful families kept their distance. In Savoy and the Dauphiny the continuity of the Carolingian families which were the great alodial holders independent of the knights is clearly seen in their genealogies; unfortunately, the knights have not been closely studied in those areas.[41]

Perhaps the best comparisons for the *bailliage* evidence are with the two areas which have also been subjected to quantitative studies, Forez and Picardy. The county of Forez, although deficient in early documents, possesses a large collection of carefully edited thirteenth-century charters, which are the basis for the first reliable figures on the survival rates and income levels of the Forez aristocracy and which provide the best quantitative comparisons with the *bailliage*.[42] Forez is also the southernmost aristocracy to have been closely analyzed to date. In the mid-thirteenth century the count of Forez was by far the wealthiest man in the county (with an annual income of 12,000 l. annually). Immediately below him were a few great lords with several castles each (1,000–2,000 l.) and then twenty or so castellans (100–500 l.); at the lowest level were the numerous ordinary knights, most of whom had modest if not meager incomes (25 l.). The knights were obviously not in the same league with the great families, and the perspective of other local studies for the twelfth century makes clear that the mid-thirteenth-century income levels in Forez reflected the diverse origins of the fief holders and especially the great gap between simple knights and the few barons. In spite of the different documents and methods of analysis, the income levels are substantially parallel to those in the *bailliage*.[43] Equally important as a quantitative determination is the high rate of extinction of these families: fully one-third of the 215 families mentioned at one time or another in the thirteenth century had disappeared by the end of the century; the rate of disappearance increased to 50 percent in the next two centuries, a loss that is not the reflection of insufficient documentation. This information compares very closely with the disappearance of 20–40 percent of Champagne fief holders in the *bailliage* from 1172 to 1275. A corollary thirteenth-century development in Forez was the increase in the number of nonknighted members of the aristocracy: by 1250 over half of the count's fief holders were nonknighted *donzeux*. In the *bailliage* there was one nonknighted *armiger* for every two *domini*.

In Picardy there was a fundamental distinction in the late twelfth century between the families of lords, who held command powers and whose status could be transmitted through the female line, and the knights, who were professional men-at-arms. The knights first appeared with the spread of castles from the late tenth century but remained a group defined by *métier* and did not secure hereditary possession of lands until the twelfth century. Bonds of fidelity did not constitute a "feudal system," and fief tenure was regulated only in the late twelfth century, at the same time that the knights were first called *domini*; they soon merged with the old families that until then had had exclusive claim to that title. The old aristocracy, identified solely by family origins and never called "knights," was made up of about fifty families by 1190.[44] By 1240, thirteen of these had disappeared, while forty five new families had joined the group; although many of the new men have traceable genealogies from the twelfth century, they did not carry the *dominus* title until the thirteenth century. By 1290, twelve additional families had the title, but thirty of the older families had disappeared. Thus by 1290 only twelve of the original twelfth-century aristocratic families survived in that position, constituting only 24 percent of the entire group at that date; sixty four other families were relative newcomers. Although the total size of the group remained stable, the composition of families had changed drastically. The study of Picardy is important because it demonstrates how "nonfeudal" elements were in fact the crucial ones of the medieval aristocracy: birth, wealth, and command positions were the determinants; power derived not from fiefs or the services rendered for them but from patrimony and in-

herited rights. Aristocratic life predated and only gradually accommodated itself to "feudal" organization, and the knights did not share the
aristocratic lifestyle until the thirteenth century.

The great body of evidence from many areas overwhelmingly confirms the Belgian thesis, which can no longer be challenged by variant
readings of some scattered and fragmentary texts. In spite of some
hesitation for the Midi (where conditions should be clarified soon),
virtually all the close studies of the last decade, irrespective of the
varying quality of their sources, of differing methodologies, and of
individual emphases, reach similar conclusions. Indeed, recent works
based on the older assumptions, as that on the aristocracy of Alsace,
can be successfully challenged now on methodological grounds. [45]
Duby himself once acknowledged that he had followed Bloch too
closely; he accepted Genicot's formulation and even expanded it into a
model of "cultural diffusion," by which he offered a fluid definition of
the aristocracy to replace the static ones: the aristocracy at the end of
the twelfth century was that group of men which enjoyed the titles and
prerogatives that two hundred years earlier had been reserved for a few
great families which then possessed what had been exclusively royal
rights two hundred years before that.[46] Thus, ordinary knights were
excluded from the aristocracy before the late twelfth century, when
they were not yet socially, politically, or militarily important, but they
were included in the thirteenth-century aristocracy, after an increase in
prestige furnished them with titles and rights over their holdings.

Most threatened by the recent local studies is the very concept of
"feudal society." Bloch's several criteria for medieval feudal society
were: fragmented political authority, a specialized class of warriors that
dominated society, the grant of fiefs in return for military service,
personal ties of obedience and protection that were the nexus of social
relationships, and a subject peasantry.[47] The monographs have modified Bloch's framework in two general ways. First, medieval society has
been somewhat "demonarchized." The traditional concentration on a
royal perspective, even when royal authority and power were only
theoretical in most of the kingdom, and the view that the princes and
barons were divisive forces in medieval society are simply not pertinent
at the regional or local level. What appears as political fragmentation
from the royal point of view was actually political organization on a
smaller scale and independent of the king. It was the territorial princes,
not the king, who provided the crucial leadership in medieval society
and in the development of state organization before the thirteenth
century. They subordinated the old aristocracy of castellans, they
consolidated fief tenure and liegeance into a hierarchical system, and
they guaranteed the general rise of the knights from the late twelfth

century. Royal influence was incidental or nonexistent during the development of the basic political, social, and economic institutions in most of the realm.

The second general revision of Bloch's perspective is that medieval society has been substantially "defeudalized." The germs of that process were planted by Duby (1953), who found that the Mâconnais did not fit the model of feudal society that had been postulated for the Loire-to-Rhine area, and it came to a logical conclusion when Fossier (1968) found scarcely any trace in Picardy of what is usually taken as "feudalism." There is no longer an obsession with homage and fief tenure per se, as their chronological development becomes more precise and as their formal aspects have become submerged in a host of interpretative questions. It is now clear that the specialized class of warriors developed only from the late tenth and early eleventh centuries and that they were merely armed retainers and did not dominate society until perhaps the late twelfth century; only then did they acquire the requisite titles, economic assets, and hereditary rights over their tenancies. Fiefs were not the sole basis of knight incomes until perhaps the thirteenth century; the determined policies of princes in many areas to convert alods into fiefs testifies to the survival of alods among even the lesser families into the thirteenth century. Indeed, alods were the basis of aristocratic power, and the subordination of the great alodial holders by the territorial princes was a major accomplishment of the twelfth century. It facilitated the subsequent incorporation of the principalities by the next higher organization, the kingdom. The oath of fidelity is no longer seen as an effective method of control—it was essentially a bilateral political agreement—and the link between fidelity and tenure now seems to have been weak. There is no evidence for anything comparable to a pyramidal social structure even on the royal domain before the mid-twelfth century.[48] The *bailliage* evidence suggests that a hierarchical organization was being imposed from 1172 but had not matured before the mid-thirteenth century. Furthermore, all evidence suggests that the fiefs of knights were generally minor holdings throughout the kingdom; the quantitative determinations both in the *bailliage* and in the county of Forez confirm it. That explains why the thirteenth-century fief holders—and their overlords—placed such emphasis on the distinction between fief tenure and all other tenures: since the privileges derived from fief tenure were no longer justified by military service, nor the style of life assured by sufficient revenues, fief tenure itself became the guarantee of fief-holding status and its legal privileges. Although there is greater caution now in the use of technical terms, some muddleheadedness persists, as "vassal" is rendered for a variety of terms and "feudal" is applied to mottes, warriors, kings, and regimes.[49] Finally, a subject peasantry now seems dubiously static in the light of the numerous examples of continually evolving conditions of persons and communities. The normal obligations of peasant tenure do not appear to have been exceptionally burdensome; they were inconvenient and prevented the accumulation of great private fortunes in the countryside, but tolerable rural conditions were assured by the threat of peasant migration. The now-documented gradual evolution of communes and consulates makes even the traditional urban-rural dichotomy untenable. In short, the local studies have demonstrated that the previous exclusive concentration on the peculiarities of tenure and personal relationships distorts the image of medieval society.

APPENDIX
Family Histories

*Arcis-sur-Aube	*Dampierre (Aube)	Payns (knights)
Barbet	*Durnay	*Plancy
*Bar-sur-Seine	*Ervy (lords)	*Pont-sur-Seine
Basson	Ervy (knights)	*Pougy
Bouy-Luxembourg	*Esternay	Quincy
Bouy-sur-Orvin	Fontette	*Ramerupt
*Brienne	Granges	Rigny-le-Ferron
Brosse	Isle-Aumont	Romilly-sur-Seine
*Chacenay	*Jully-sur-Sarce	Rosières
Chapelle-Geoffroy	Macey	Ruvigny
*Chappes	*Marigny-le-Châtel	Saint-Maurice-aux-Riches-
Charmont-sous-Barbuise	Marnay-sur-Seine	Hommes
Chennegy	Maupas	Saint-Phal
Chervey	*Méry-sur-Seine	*Traînel
Clérey (lords)	Minay	*Vendeuvre-sur-Barse
Clérey (knights)	Montfey	*Villemaur-sur-Vanne
Crollebois	*Nogent-sur-Seine	Ville-sur-Arce
	*Payns (lords)	Vaubercey

Note: Families are located on maps 6 (lords) and 7 (knights); other villages are on map 4.
*Old Aristocracy

INTRODUCTION

The purpose of this Appendix is twofold: to furnish the references for statements made in the text, especially in chapter V, about particular individuals and families; and to illustrate how the Champagne registers of fiefs measure certain qualities of the aristocracy. Consequently, the following histories highlight certain patterns of family development and do not provide definitive documentation for the families, many of which could well be the subject of separate studies. Specific citations are given only for the most important events, characteristics, and relationships; other details and the references for statements not documented here can be found in Alphonse Roserot, *Dictionnaire historique de la Champagne méridionale (Aube) des origines à 1790*, 3 vols. (Langres, 1942-48). Although he ignored the technical problems of changing terminology and of information from different types of sources in the medieval period, Roserot remains an essential and generally reliable reference. He carefully checked, revised, and summarized the contributions of earlier local historians on the great baronial families, and I have verified his work by independent genealogical reconstructions directly from the sources. However, the *Dictionnaire* is not satisfactory for the numerous less important families, many of which were ignored altogether, and most of their genealogies and histories are based entirely on my own reconstructions. The lesser families are documented in greater detail than the baronial ones described in the *Dictionnaire*. Biographical material on the count's officials, most of whom had roots outside the *bailliage*, for the twelfth century is in Benton, "The Court of Champagne under Henry the Liberal," chapters 3–4.

Source references follow the conventions described in the list of abbreviations. The genealogical tables furnish only the dates, titles, and appropriate reference in the Champagne registers. The dates, of course, are not inclusive and refer solely to the documents in which the persons are mentioned. The date of birth is almost never known, and the date of death is approximate, being taken from the earliest reference to the deceased or his widow or to the assumption of the inheritance by the heirs. The following symbols are employed in the tables:

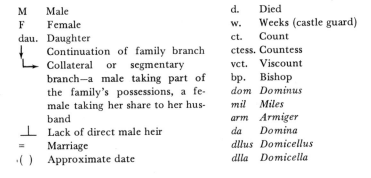

M	Male	d.	Died
F	Female	w.	Weeks (castle guard)
dau.	Daughter	ct.	Count
↓	Continuation of family branch	ctess.	Countess
↳	Collateral or segmentary branch—a male taking part of the family's possessions, a female taking her share to her husband	vct.	Viscount
		bp.	Bishop
		dom	*Dominus*
		mil	*Miles*
		arm	*Armiger*
⊥	Lack of direct male heir	*da*	*Domina*
=	Marriage	*dllus*	*Domicellus*
·( )	Approximate date	*dlla*	*Domicella*

Names set in upper case type are cross-referenced in the genealogies and family histories.

*Arcis-sur-Aube

The line of Arcis lords became independent of the Ramerupt-Arcis house in the 1120s (see Ramerupt and its genealogy). Its activities before 1172 are not clear, and Roserot's genealogy for this period is doubtful, but from the 1170s all the county records and local charters agree in treating Arcis as an important separate lordship.

JEAN I: Listed in *Feoda*, Troyes, 1885; *dominus* in 1189,StL,101; died probably in Acre in 1190. He was married to Elisant, daughter of the viscount of Joigny.

JEAN II: Liege for Arcis and all its appurtenances in *Feoda* II,2449; holder of a "great fief" in *Feoda* IV,2938. Member of the 1212 baronial council; knight banneret in 1214. 1215,CB,66v: swore to support young Thibaut against the Briennes, to whom he was distantly related. 1218,Arch. Aube,27 H 3: received from the countess a fief of revenues (35 l.) *in portis* of Troyes, which seems to have been a reward for his pledge for 200 l. on her payment to the Briennes in the same year (1218,Th,108r—109v). Died by 1222,B,19, when his widow Marie referred to the 35 l. assigned *in nundinis* of Troyes.

GUY: Succeeded as *dominus* of Arcis in 1222,Ch,18 (= Th,294r–v), when he assigned to his brother Anseric a share of the inheritance (escheat): 43 l. annually

Arcis-sur-Aube

André, 1082, 1123

RAMERUPT | ARCIS

Alice = BRIENNE, Erard I   F
ct.
d. 1125

Jean I = Joigny, Elisant, dau. of vct.
Feoda
1189 *dom*
d. (1190)

Jean II = Turney, Maria *da*
1200, 1214
d. 1222

Guy = CHACENAY, Matilda   Anseric
1222 *dom*   treasurer,
1228   deacon Laon
Rôles: castle   1222, 1226

Jean III
Rôles: dom, castellany
d. 1273

Jean IV   Erard   Guillaume   F   Helisand
1273 *sire*   1273 *escuier*   1273 cleric   1273: 200.l dowry
Rôles B
1282

Jean V
d. 1293

on the *péage* and *prévôté* of Arcis; Jean II's widow claimed that this source used to yield 200 l. (the same amount for which her husband was pledge in 1218). Guy appeared in the 1228 retroban(*Feoda* VI,4299). In 1230,*Histoire*,2077, he acquired the fief of Guillaume of Vertus and promised the count that if he had two sons, one would hold this fief, and the other would have Arcis. He was in debt for 300 l. to Jean of Soissons in 1238,*Histoire*,2473. Apparently he was on his deathbed in 1252 (*Rôles*,Troyes,1140), for he sent the count's *enquêteurs* a letter stating that he held the castle of Arcis, several neighboring villages, and twenty three rear-fief holders, all of which constituted a single fief (probably worth, exclusive of rear-fiefs, close to the 200 l. annual revenue mentioned in 1222).

JEAN III: In an emendation to his father's entry in the *Rôles*, he replaced his father for the "castle and castellany" of Arcis and for a 22 l. income from the fairs of Troyes (*Rôles*,Troyes,1147).

JEAN IV: In 1273,Ch,178 (eighteenth-century copy), it was decided that Jean IV, *chevalier*, would be *sire* of Arcis and that his two brothers, Erard, *escuier* (see also chapter II, n. 146, for Erard), and Guillaume, cleric, and two sisters would hold other properties (he promised sister Helisand 200 l., or one year's income from Arcis, for her dowry). *Sire* of Arcis in *Rôles B*,Troyes,6462. In 1282 he and his cousin Erard of Chacenay sold the village of Lusigny, which they held as alodial property, with tenants, justice, and *mainmorte* rights; Jean's half of the sale price was 800 l. (see also Chacenay).

Barbet

GARIN I: (1161),*Histoire* III, p. 452: Witness; 1174,M,65: witness under *de burgensibus Trecarum*. He was dead by 1181,M,81, when his widow Eschiba quarreled with the abbey over his inheritance: the 4 s. *cens* that she owed was abolished, in return for which she gave the 2 *arpents* of vineyard that a knight, Gautier of Courcelles, held for an 8 d. *cens*.

GARIN II: Appeared with his mother in 1181 and approved the arrangement. 1194,R,102r(ix): *miles, dominus*. This family was probably related to those of the same name who married into the knight family of Curia, but their exact relationship cannot be determined.

*Bar-sur-Seine

The counts of Bar-sur-Seine are well covered by Roserot (his table II is simplified here). There is some disagreement on the Carolingian roots of the family; the best résumé is by Maurice Chaume, "Notes sur quelques familles comtales champenois, X^e–XIe siècle," *Recherches d'histoire chrétienne et médiévale* (Dijon, 1947). There was a *castrum* (1103,Mol,244–245), to which a *burgus* and *villa* were later attached (1218,Mor,77). The count of Bar-sur-Seine headed the Bar-sur-Aube register of the *Feoda*,62. In *Feoda* II,2433, he was qualified as a *dominus*, and his castles were held *juraturum*; in *Feoda* IV,2917, he was listed *de magnis feodis*. The area of this county is described in 1197,Mor,42: it extended from the Seine at Bar to Courteron (12 km), out to Essoyes (8 km), and back to Bar via Chervey; it was a fairly small but compact area of strategic importance in controlling the southern Seine approach to Troyes. In 1198,M,131, Milo IV sold his claim of *mainmorte* on his men of Bar for 100 l., probably to support his expedition to the East; in 1210 he

Bar-sur-Seine

Milo II
9th century = Ermengarde

Milo I
ct. Tonnerre(III) m. Agatha de Bar-sur-Seine
ct. Bar(I), d. (1046)

Hugh-Renaud
ct. Bar
bp. Langres, 1065–85

Eustace = BRIENNE, Gautier I
1080, ct. Brienne and Bar

BRIENNE
Erard I

BAR-SUR-SEINE
Milo II
1085–1111

Guy = CHACENAY
ct. 1125, 1147

Renaud
abbot Cîteaux
1134–50

Herbert = VILLE-SUR-ARCE,
d. 1169

Milo III = Baudemont
ct. 1147, 1151

Manasses
ct. 1151–68
bp. Langres
1179–92

Petronilla = Puiset (vct. Chartres)
ctess. 1168, 1174

Milo IV = ?Joingy, Helisand
ct. 1189–1219

Gautier = Courtenay, Elizabeth
1197
d. 1219

Guillaume
grand master of Temple,
d. 1218

Agnes = DURNAY, Jacques I
1219, 1233

extended the same privilege to his men of Essoyes, Merrey-sur-Arce, and Neuville-sur-Seine (charter in Petal, *Essoyes*, p. 508). Milo took an oath of loyalty to Blanche in 1215,CB,68r. Both Milo and his two sons died in the East in 1218-19, and the county of Bar-sur-Seine was then purchased by young Thibaut IV: he acquired the dowry share of Milo's widow Helisand in 1225,*Histoire*,1677 and the share of Jacques of Durnay's wife in 1223 (see Durnay). Thibaut must have secured all Bar-sur-Seine by 1227 when he reissued the 1198 *mainmorte* exemption to the townsmen; in 1231 he issued his own communal franchise to the town (see chapter III). In 1252 Bar-sur-Seine was a castellany fully incorporated into the Champagne domain (see the quantitative analysis of the *Rôles* in chapter IV).

Basson

THIBAUT (NARROES): Liege and owed guard for his fief at Basson(*Feoda*, Villemaur,334).

HENRI I: Did liege homage to the count (*Feoda* II,Villemaur,2216), but he claimed in *Feoda* IV,Villemaur,2888 that he did not know whether he was liege; he was required to report back by All Saints' Day. 1216,V,19r–v: on his departure for the Albigensian Crusade he gave the abbey some grain but retained the justice over it; he must have perished on that expedition because two years later, in 1218,R,95 (xvi), his wife and three sons gave another abbey an annual one *modius* of grain from the Basson mill. The three sons, Thibaut II, Geoffroy, and Guillaume, were still *domicelli* in 1230,StS,221r, when they gave a woman and her children with her 15 s. annual payment (*taille*) to Saint-Etienne. The next year, in 1231,R,95(xvii), they were *domini* of Basson; their dispute with Larrivour, which stemmed from their mother's grant in 1218, was settled by 1233,R,96(xv): they retained justice over all *seculari*, but not the *conversi*, in the pastures of Basson, an arrangement approved by their overlord, Guy of Méry. In 1229 Thibaut II was listed for half of the property he held at Basson in *Feoda* VI(Knights of the Countess' Dowry),4003: this seems to have been the same fief held by his father and grandfather; he also held a fief in Nogent. The Villemaur register for the *Rôles* of 1252 is unfortunately missing. Perhaps it was Thibaut II's son Jean of Basson, *escuier*, who held half of the house and arable and seventy six *arpents* of woods there in *Rôles B*, Villemaur, 6600.

Bouy-Luxembourg

ESTOLD I: Witness as a *miles* of the count of Brienne in (1166),BF,3; listed in *Feoda*,Troyes,1965. He and his brother, *milites* of the count of Brienne, were witnesses in (1180s),StL,69 and 1186,R,53(iv). He was called a *dominus* in 1197, Arch.Aube,27 H 3 but was probably already dead because he had been replaced in the *Feoda* by ca. 1190 by Gilo.

GILO: Probably son of Estold I; the father of Estold II in 1209,M,257, when he and nine of his *homines* gave up all use of a woods to an abbey; this act was confirmed by his brothers Renaud and Hugh, *milites*, in 1214,M,276–77. As *dominus* in 1212,R,7(xxxvi), Gilo sold the tithe of Assencières, worth three *modii* annually, for 100 l. and half the *redditus* of Bouy for 8 l. Gilo and Hugh were given the village of Bouy sometime in the early thirteenth century by Countess Blanche in return for their services, but they sold and donated it in 1221-22. Hugh sold two-thirds of his share for 100 l. in 1222,R,65(xix): all his "rerum . . . exceptis

Bouy-Luxembourg

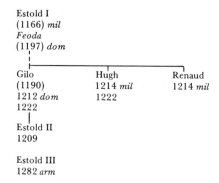

Estold I
(1166) *mil*
Feoda
(1197) *dom*

Gilo	Hugh	Renaud
(1190)	1214 *mil*	1214 *mil*
1212 *dom*	1222	
1222		
Estold II		
1209		

Estold III
1282 *arm*

hominibus suis, et justicia et corveiis," that is, what he sold consisted of all the *terrage*, half of the mill, half of the house, half of the grange, and the rest of the property. Gilo, on the other hand, sold everything, including the annual *corvée* and his fifteen *familiae hominium* in 1222,R,65(xx): his possessions were further identified in 1223,R,65(xxi) as sixty *jugera* of land and half of the justice, mill, and pool, all of which had been granted originally by the countess *in recompensationem* for service *tempore guerre mea* (the countess). Thus, the brothers had a village of thirty hearths, one hundred twenty *jugera* of land, one house, one mill, waters, annual *corvée*, and justice, for which the sale price was equivalent to 300 l. The entire village was then given to Eudes, cleric of Bouy, in 1223,R,66(xxiv) to hold for life for three *modii* rent to the abbey.

ESTOLD III: The fief of Estold, *armiger*, was exempted from the sale of Lusigny by the Chacenay family in 1282,Ch,185.

Roserot is in error in identifying Jean of Briel with this line rather than with the main Briel line: the sale of Bouy in 1222 effectively eliminated the main property of this family, and no descendants appear in the surveys.

Bouy-sur-Orvin

PIERRE: Held two distinct fiefs in *Feoda*(Méry,2033; Pont, 1691: twelve weeks guard), which he continued to hold through the early thirteenth century in "plain homage" (*Feoda* III,Méry,2568; *Feoda* V,Pont,3149). The second fief, at Méry (Marpigny or Malpigny, today destroyed, located on the Barbuise River) probably came from his wife. He was probably originally a knight of the lords of Traînel, for in 1217,S,63r, he was as *dominus*, executor of the testament of Garnier III (of Traînel), lord of Marigny. In 1219,StP,145, as *vir nobilis* he bequeathed the tithe of the castle of Marigny, three and a half *modii* of wheat, to the Hôtel-Dieu and the Léproserie of Marigny. In 1219,S,30r, he gave, without reason, his main holding of Clos (today Clos-Mâcon, near Bouy)—"hospitatis et clausa cum grangis"—to Sellières with the understanding that his wife would hold it for her lifetime; then, if the abbey did not want the property, it would revert to his heirs. Such an arrangement was unique and created many conflicts after his death. Pierre gave seven *setiers* of grain and 26 s. *in nummis* for the support of his daughter, a nun in Paraclet (done before his death but not recorded until 1229,P,199). He died by

Bouy-sur-Orvin

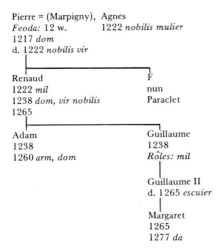

Pierre = (Marpigny), Agnes
Feoda: 12 w.   1222 nobilis mulier
1217 dom
d. 1222 nobilis vir

Renaud   F
1222 mil   nun
1238 dom, vir nobilis   Paraclet
1265

Adam   Guillaume
1238   1238
1260 arm, dom   Rôles: mil

                              Guillaume II
                              d. 1265 escuier

                              Margaret
                              1265
                              1277 da

1222,S,30r–v, when his widow and son Renaud, *miles*, surrendered the grange (although that was not the agreement) for a life rent of six *setiers* of grain. His widow Agnes, *mulier nobilis*, *domina* of Bouy, had difficulties collecting the grain; she died by 1241,P,235.

RENAUD: Called variously "of Bouy" and "of Marpigny." In *Feoda* VI,4056, of 1229, he held a rear-fief from Dreux of Traînel at Pont, but the Clos property escaped his control, in spite of the efforts of both Renaud and his overlord Dreux to reclaim it. Dreux said in 1235,S,31v–32r that Clos was his fief, but the abbey said that the property was held now *de francho alodio* and that Pierre himself while living had so testified, as had many others; Traînel was forced to drop the claim. Renaud kept up the challenges (1238,Arch.Aube,9 H 125: he was *dominus, nobilis vir*) but finally gave up "omne jus et omne dominium" in 1252,S,35r–v; he still claimed, unsuccessfully, in 1265,Arch.Aube,9 H 132, that his father had given the grange in return for the tithe. Thus, the family fief of Bouy had been effectively alienated, and that property was not accounted for in the *Rôles*. Apparently Renaud was given another holding by Dreux of Traînel at Marigny, but in 1237,P, 200,219, Renaud, *miles* and *dilectis et fidelis* of Dreux, surrendered all that he had there in fief from Dreux to Paraclet. Although his maternal inheritance at Marpigny remained intact, in 1251,*Documents* I, p.xxv, n. 3, he agreed to hold that property, including a mill, waters, and men, as a rear-fief from Isabel of Caves. Thus, two Champagne fiefs of 1172 had become one rear-fief in the accounting of 1252.

ADAM: Son of Renaud in 1238; an *armiger* and *dominus* of Bouy in 1260,S, 38v–39r, but it is not clear whether he actually held property there because he is not listed in the Champagne surveys; perhaps he held a fief from the abbey.

GUILLAUME: Son of Renaud in 1238; he was a *miles* who held a rear-fief of six *setiers* of grain (? the same secured in 1222) in *Rôles*,Provins,810.

GUILLAUME II: Probably son of Guillaume I; *escuier* who died in 1265 and whose daughter Margaret (*Hommages*,Meaux,5741) was still called *domina* of Bouy in 1277,S,38r, when she held justice over ten *arpents* of land there.

Brienne

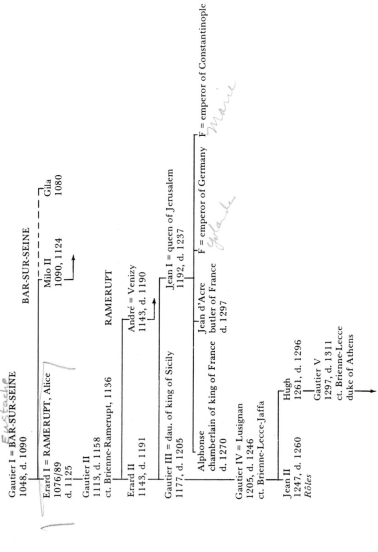

Engilbert I–IV
950–1027/31

Gautier I = BAR-SUR-SEINE *Eustache*
1048, d. 1090

BAR-SUR-SEINE

Milo II
1090, 1124

Gila
1080

Erard I = RAMERUPT, Alice
1076/89
d. 1125

RAMERUPT

Gautier II
1113, d. 1158
ct. Brienne-Ramerupt, 1136

André = Venizy
1143, d. 1190

Erard II
1143, d. 1191

Gautier III = dau. of king of Sicily
1177, d. 1205

Jean I = queen of Jerusalem
1192, d. 1237

F = emperor of Germany *Yolande*

F = emperor of Constantinople *Marie*

Alphonse
chamberlain of king of France
d. 1270

Jean d'Acre
butler of France
d. 1297

Gautier IV = Lusignan
1205, d. 1246
ct. Brienne-Lecce-Jaffa

Jean II
1247, d. 1260
Rôles

Hugh
1261, d. 1296

Gautier V
1297, d. 1311
ct. Brienne-Lecce
duke of Athens

*Brienne

The Brienne family is well-documented and has been fully studied by Roserot, from whom this table is extracted. Jean I (d. 1237), who married the queen of Jerusalem, was an important supporter of Blanche and Thibaut against his own cousin Erard (of Brienne, Ramerupt branch) when he wrote in 1213,CB,3v—4r that it was an ancient custom in the kingdom of France that no one under twenty-one years of age could appear in court (that is, be in legal majority), and therefore young Thibaut's possession of Champagne could not be legally challenged. Jean reported that he had heard from the testimony *multorum nobilium virorum* that Count Henry II had left his lands to his brother Thibaut III, and Jean concluded that the daughters of Henry had no better claim to the county than the sons of Thibaut III. In 1252 Jean II was probably overseas, for the county of Brienne was administered by a guardian, the lord of Reynel, and Jean II was listed simply for *plura homagia* in the *Rôles*,Troyes,1139.

Brosse

ITER I: Probably the same as Iter li Burs, who was liege, owed guard, and held land at Brosse and Ervy in *Feoda*,Ervy,303. His son Henri was in *Feoda*,Ervy,302 and *Feoda* II,Ervy,2199.

ITER II: Held the house (? fortified) of Guillaume of Lasson from the latter in *Feoda* IV,Ervy,2881. Executor of the will of his maternal grandfather, Bartholomew of Polisy, in 1218,Mol,307—8. Iter II was an important councillor to Blanche and Thibaut IV and probably received compensation for his services, yet his most important properties were Polisy and Villiers-le-Bois, both from his mother's side. 1219,Mol,308: *miles, dominus*; 1239,N,93: *nobilis vir.* 1233,*Histoire* V,2264: he built a house in the Jewish quarter of Troyes. His eldest son seems to have been Bartholomew, who was in *Feoda* VI,Saint-Florentin,4010 for his grandmother's

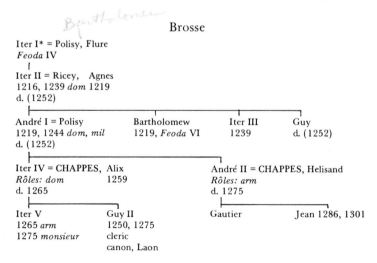

Brosse

Iter I* = Polisy, Flure
Feoda IV
|
Iter II = Ricey, Agnes
1216, 1239 *dom* 1219
d. (1252)

André I = Polisy	Bartholomew	Iter III	Guy
1219, 1244 *dom, mil*	1219, *Feoda* VI	1239	d. (1252)
d. (1252)			

Iter IV = CHAPPES, Alix		André II = CHAPPES, Helisand
Rôles: dom 1259		*Rôles: arm*
d. 1265		d. 1275

Iter V	Guy II	Gautier	Jean 1286, 1301
1265 *arm*	1250, 1275		
1275 *monsieur*	cleric		
	canon, Laon		

*Iter li Burs
Feoda: liege, guard

property at Mussey-le-Servens, for which he owed four weeks guard. Another son, André I, also appeared in 1219 and 1239; in 1244,Mol,359-60 as *miles, dominus,* he held Polisy. He had purchased three fiefs at Montigny by 1252 (*Rôles,*Bar-sur-Seine,90), but he was already dead then because his widow appeared with her sons (*Rôles,*Ervy,382).

ANDRE II and ITER IV: The brothers shared their father's lands and also their uncle Guy's escheat. There were four distinct holdings: (1) the Brosse lands of their father and some properties purchased by him; (2) Villiers-le-Bois and Polisy from their great-grandmother; (3) Riceys from their grandmother; and (4) lands at Brosse from their uncle, Guy. The properties were listed as four fiefs (*Rôles,*Ervy,385) and also as two fiefs, the Brosse properties versus all the rest (*Rôles,*Ervy,367,368). The *Rôles* entries are confusing because both André I and his brother Guy died shortly before the *Rôles* were drawn up (in the quantitative tables, André II, not his father, is counted for all properties that he had just inherited; his mother is counted for her share as widow). Furthermore, Iter IV, *dominus,* was in the East, so his wife responded for him, although there was also an official guardian for his children (*Rôles,*Ervy,382,383,385,386); André II was still an *armiger.* Both brothers married Chappes sisters, and Iter IV received as dowry part of the viscounty of Troyes, which he sold to the count for a 211 l. rent in 1259.

ITER V: Was in financial difficulties when he sold back to the count, in order to liquidate some debts, lands that the count had given him (1265,StS,41r–v). By *Hommages,*Bar-sur-Seine,5409, he held only one-third of Polisy from his inheritance. He was listed as *monsieur* in *Rôles B,*Bar-sur-Seine,6522.

ANDRE II: Still held the fortified house of Ricey and his Chappes dowry (*Hommages,*Chaource,5402).

It seems that the Brosses put together a sizable collection of properties in the first half of the thirteenth century. Iter II's role as councillor to the countess may have been important, especially because he was on the winning side of a serious conflict, but the major part of the total family holdings in mid-century, in addition to their father's and uncle's lands, was the maternal inheritance. By the 1275 *Rôles,* however, there is the impression, in spite of the paucity of information in both the 1265 and 1275 surveys, that the Brosse fortune had been substantially dissipated.

*Chacenay

The Chacenays appear from the late eleventh century in the company of the most important lords of the *bailliage* but were not designated *domini* in the extant charters until 1137/38. Milo, for example, was one of the *viri illustri* along with the counts of Brienne and Bar-sur-Seine who permitted an abbey to acquire from their *casamenti* and *feodi* in 1103,Ch,10. Anseric II's widow Hubelina was entitled *domina* in 1137,R,20(xlvii); her son Jacques was the first male of that line to be qualified *dominus,* in (1138),Ch,23. His son Erard I is listed three times in the *Feoda*: Villemaur,322;Troyes,1890 bis: liege and guard; Bar-sur-Aube,63: *dominus* of Chacenay. Chacenay is qualified as a "castellany" in 1165 (1175, see chapter III, n. 4),M,53.

ERARD II: On the eve of his departure for the East in 1218,M,294, he promised not to exact a *generalem talliam* from the abbey's men living in his "castellany," but he expected an *auxilium* on four occasions: the knighting of his eldest son, the marriage of a daughter, ransom for his capture in war, and support for a crusade. He was a *nobilis vir* in 1218,M,300. As one of the most ardent supporters of Erard of

Chacenay

```
Anseric I
1076
 |
Milo
1103 vir illuster
 |
Anseric II = Hubelina
d. 1137     1137 da
 |_____
 |                    |                    |                    |
Jacques = ?BRIENNE   Thomas I            Anseric III         F = BAR-SUR-SEINE
(1138) dom           abbot Clairvaux     1147
d. 1158              1171–75
                                         DURNAY
 |_____
 |                    |            |
Erard I              F = BAR-SUR-SEINE   Thomas II
Feoda: dom, d. 1191                      |__→
 |_____
 |                        |
Erard II = Broyes        Jacques II
1203, 1212
d. 1236
 |_____
 |            |              |                    |
Hugh         Erard III      Alix = Forez, ct.     Matilda = ARCIS, Guy
d. 1245      d. 1249        d. 1278               |__→
 |__          |__            |
                            Erard IV
                            1281 mil
```

Brienne's challenge to the count of Champagne, he was subjected to many ecclesiastical sanctions, but he finally did homage to Thibaut IV in 1221,CB,49v. Both he and his two sons died in the East at mid-century, and his estate was divided among the six children of his two daughters. The relatives agreed to a division in 1273, Ch,178 and in 1281/82,Ch,183–185, but disputes continued (a summary of the divisions and disputes is in *Coutumier*, p. 163, n. 4; however, the genealogies are not correct: Alix's son Erard IV was specifically mentioned in 1281; Matilda, not Alix, married Guy of Arcis; and Jean IV, not Jean III, was designated lord of Arcis; see the Arcis genealogy). Erard IV sold his half of Lusigny, which he had from his mother *de franco allodio*, in men, justice, and *mainmorte*, for 800 l. (1281,Ch,183-84), and his cousin Jean IV of Arcis did the same.

Chapelle-Geoffroy

Geoffroy of Chapelle-Geoffroy was mentioned with his mother in (1147),V,105v and alone in 1161,V,104r–v. This family and its lands were at the time under the lord of Nogent, whose castellany remained independent until 1199, when it became a direct Champagne castellany and its fief holders became direct Champagne fief holders. The probable descendant of Geoffroy was Milo, who in *Feoda* VI,4198 did liege homage for his fief at Chapelle-Geoffroy and for eight rear-fief holders, for which he owed twelve weeks castle guard at Nogent. His widow held the wardship for their children in *Rôles*,Nogent,676: a fortified house, justice, and woods, all worth 50 *l.t.*, and eight rear-fief holders, for which twelve weeks guard was owed (the edited version of "13 months" is probably an error for "3 months," the amount rendered in *Feoda* VI). This family was under the lord of Nogent in the twelfth century and therefore was not inventoried in the *Feoda* of 1172; its absence from the ca. 1200 registers is inexplicable.

Chappes

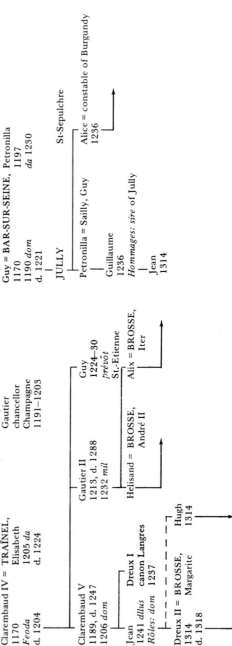

CHAPPES   PLANCY   JULLY-SUR-SARCE   JULLY   St-Sepulchre

Gila
(1082)

Gautier I
1085, d. 1114

Hugh I

Ponce
1121

Clarembaud I = ? BRIENNE
1121, d. 1136

Clarembaud II–III
1137 dom, d. 1184

Clarembaud IV = TRAÎNEL,
1170   Elisabeth
Feoda   1205 da
d. 1204   d. 1224

Gautier
chancellor
Champagne
1191–1203

Guy = BAR-SUR-SEINE, Petronilla
1170   1197
1190 dom   da 1230
d. 1221

Petronilla = Sailly, Guy

Alice = constable of Burgundy
1236

Clarembaud V
1189, d. 1247
1206 dom

Gautier II
1213, d. 1288
1232 mil

Guy
1224–30
prévôt
St.-Etienne

Guillaume
1236
Hommages: sire of Jully

Jean
1314

Jean   Dreux I
1241 dllus canon Langres
Rôles: dom 1237

Helisand = BROSSE,
André II

Alix = BROSSE,
Iter

Dreux II = BROSSE,
1314   Margarite
d. 1318

Hugh
1314

*Chappes

The Chappes first appeared in a reference to Gautier of Chappes, son of Gila, *mulier nobilissima,* who held in fief from Gautier I of Brienne in (1080),Mol,225. The Chappes genealogy has been worked out in great detail by Roserot, whose table is simplified here. There was an *oppidum* in 1117,M,20; Chappes was a "castellany" in 1165,M,53 (see chapter III, n. 4).

CLAREMBAUD II–III (probably a single person, not two as indicated by Roserot): First of his line to be qualified as *dominus,* in (1137),M,27. *Feoda,*Troyes,1886: liege of two fiefs, Chappes and Gyé-sur-Seine, and the viscounty of Troyes, for which he owed *estagium* (the viscounty was already in the family's possession in 1121,M,16, when Ponce assigned some revenues on it). *Feoda* II,2441: *dominus* of Chappes, one of the "great fief" holders, liege for both Chappes and Plancy (now held by a collateral line; see Plancy).

CLAREMBAUD IV: He assigned some revenues from the viscounty of Troyes (1178,L, pp. 100–101); he sold 100 l. worth of property and left his wife and three children to go crusading in (1189),M,83; he probably also went on the Fourth Crusade (1205,R,13[vi]).

CLAREMBAUD V: Succeeded as *dominus* of Chappes in 1206,M,223; in 1206,M, 226, he donated the great tithe of Chappes for an annual memorial service for his father.

GAUTIER II: Brother of Clarembaud V, who could have started a collateral line if he had not left only two daughters. Gautier was a *miles* in 1232,R,37(xxxv). In 1242,*Histoire,*2603, he mortgaged all his possessions to Jacques, the Jew of Dampierre, for three years for 160 l. Both his daughters married Brosse brothers, and Helisand took part of the viscounty of Troyes and part of Chappes itself to her husband (*Rôles,*Troyes,1124,1145). Gautier's brother Guy was *prévôt* of Saint-Etienne in 1230,StS,68v–69r, when the share of the viscounty of Troyes was assigned to Gautier's daughters as dowries.

JEAN: *Domicellus* in 1241,StS,228v. As *dominus* in 1252 he held the main family possessions, two distinct fiefs: the castle, castellany, and village of Chappes and the village of Gyé-sur-Seine and other scattered revenues; there were forty three rear-fief holders (*Rôles,*Troyes,1132; Isle,463). He had the same holdings in *Hommages,*Troyes,5314. His son Dreux appeared in the 1314 petition.

Charmont-sous-Barbuise

DREUX (HUREPEL): Sole *miles* witness to a charter of the count of Troyes in 1103,StL,4.

JEAN (HUREPEL)I: *Dominus* in an agreement over the village of Charmont in 1147,StL,17 (see chapter II for a detailed analysis); but in *Feoda,*Troyes,1904, when he was liege and owed guard, he was without title. His daughter Emeline had a unique entry in *Feoda,*Troyes,1995; she was liege for her fief as dowry, which could not be sold or diminished, or it would revert to the count. There were two family lines from Jean I: one continued as lords of Charmont and retained the fortified house there, the other alienated its share of Charmont and was forced to rely on maternal acquisitions.

MILO: Although there is no reference that explicitly connects him with Jean (Hurepel) II, he was probably the brother, for in 1199,StP,91, as *miles,* he gave up

Charmont-sous-Barbuise

Dreux (Hurepel)
1103 *mil*

Jean (Hurepel) I = Alaïde
1147 *dom*
Feoda

Emeline   Bovo   Jean (Hurepel) II = Rouilly-Sacey, Beliard   Milo = Emenard 1233 *da, nobilis mulier*
Feoda   1193 *mil*   1200, 1226 *da*   1199 *mil*
                        d. 1226   *nobilis mulier* d. 1232   d. 1225 *dom*

Iter (Hurepel) of Rosson   Henri of Rosson   Adeline = Robert of Maignay   Bovo
1225 *mil*   1229 *dom*   1232 *da*   1232   1225 cleric
                             Rôles   1233 *dllus*
                             Hommages

                                          Milo   Philip of St-Etienne-sur-Barbuise   Perrin
                                          1233   1233 *dom*   *Rôles: arm*
                                                                                           Hommages: seigneur

                                                                                           Anselm
                                                                                           Rôles B

half the tithe of Charmont both on fiefs and on other properties ("vel nomine casamenti vel alio modo"); this was probably a result of his brother's alienation in 1193 (see below). He was a *dominus* at the time of his death in 1225,M,343, when his widow and sons disputed with the abbey over the escheats of men and women of the Church of Charmont who died without heirs: the abbey would have the mobile goods, the family would retain the immobile ones. In (1233),StS,315r–v, his widow, Emenard, *domina, nobilis mulier*, claimed the escheat of a certain Lambert, *homo* of the chapter, but she had to give up the claim to both mobile and immobile possessions because he resided on a free plot and was immune from all control and *bannum*, except to the deacon and chapter (see the provisions of the 1147 accord analyzed in chapter II); the parties also agreed to share equally the men and women intermarrying there.

BOVO: A cleric in 1225, but he had succeeded to his father's properties by 1233,StS,220r–v, when as a *domicellus* he seized some men of Saint-Etienne, imprisoned them in his *domus fort* at Charmont, and confiscated their goods; he was forced to release them by the episcopal official of Troyes.

PERRIN: *Rôles*,Troyes,1105: *Armiger* who held at Charmont his father's possessions, including the fortified house, no guard; and at Fuligny his mother's inheritance of a house, land, woods, men, justice, worth 50 *l.t.*, no guard. He was still a *domicellus* in 1256,StS,240v–241r but also a *dominus* of Charmont. In *Hommages*, Troyes,5339, he was *seigneur* of Charmont, and the fortified house was called a "fortress."

ANSELM: Probably son of Perrin. *Rôles B*,Troyes,6455: he held the fortress of Charmont.

JEAN (HUREPEL) II: 1193,R,63(vii): *Miles*, who gave up whatever he possessed and all *juris* that he had over his father's "hereditate . . . in omnibus locis," in woods, plain lands, and other properties, in return for which the abbey promised him food and clothing ("in victu et vestitu necessaria ministrat") for life and reception as a convert on his death. When he died in 1226,StS,214r, his widow Beliard, *domina, nobilia mulier*, agreed not to claim any escheat or *formariage* over the men of Saint-Loup and Saint-Etienne who resided there in her justice. There is no further mention of rights or properties at Charmont for this branch, so the 1193 alienation was probably for his entire share of the inheritance. Jean secured other property from his wife, and in 1200,M,171 he allowed the abbey to use his woods at Rosson for building and for heating at its grange at Rouilly-Sacey.

ADELINE: (1232),R,67(xxviii): *Domina* of Charmont and daughter of Jean, *dominus*, although there is no reference to their properties at Charmont: she gave up claim to one-fifth part of one-twentieth of the woods of Rosson, its *funda* and justice, and one-fifth of the justice of Rosson and Gérault, for 20 l. and an annual seven *setiers* of grain; her husband had claimed these rights as part of her inheritance, but the abbey said that her father had already surrendered them. In 1232,R,67(xxviii), she gave up two *setiers* of grain from the *terrage* of Rouilly-Sacey for her mother's soul. It was probably her sons Phillip of Saint-Etienne-sous-Barbuise, *dominus* and *miles*, and Milo who in 1233,R,22(lx) disputed with the abbey over their inheritance at Rosson, which they claimed had been a gift (*donum*) from their grandfather, but they were forced to surrender it: three-twentieths of the woods of Rosson, the *fundus* and justice over it, and also three-twentieths of the justice and *terrage* of Rosson and Gérault, for 18 l.

ITER (HUREPEL) OF ROSSON: Probably brother of Adeline. In 1225,R,87 (xxxiv), as *dominus* he gave up one-fourth of the pasture, woods, and other property at Rosson and Gérault, but his five children were allowed to build houses in the woods, and the monks would not have pasture rights within those enclosures; he also retained rights of land clearing in the woods and agreed to praise the grant of one-fourth of the pasture by Jean.

HENRI OF ROSSON: He seems to have been the son of Beliard, rather than of Emenard, as Roserot has. In 1229,R,6(xxxii), as *dominus* he gave the abbey half a *modius* annually from his *terrage* at Rouilly-Sacey and use of all the pastures there. *Rôles*,Troyes,1120: he was without title, though he would have merited the *dominus* title, and he held at Rosson house, lands, fields, and woods, worth about 100 *l.t.* and owing twelve weeks guard; and at Montgueux land, but he didn't know about guard; his niece held 17 *l.t.* in rear-fief, obtained from her husband's inheritance.

Chennegy

The name Chennegy, taken from the forest of Chennegy, which was shared by three men, was used only from the late twelfth century. One was Dudo of Saint-Mesmin, a *miles* in 1131,Lalore,IV (Chartes d'Andecy),161, who gave use of the woods to an abbey in 1147,N,7. Dudo owed four weeks castle guard in *Feoda*,Pont,1688, but he was replaced by his son Thibaut by ca. 1190.

HENRI (of Chennegy): A former *clericus* and apparently second son of Dudo of Saint-Mesmin, whom he replaced in *Feoda*,Troyes,1998; Payns,1645, by ca. 1190. He was in *Feoda* IV,Méry,2900. 1200.L, p. 114: *miles*, with his wife Verderine and mother Alice, *domina* of Chennegy: they were *nobiles* who had *dominium* over the woods of Chennegy. In 1204,StP,107, he sold his justice and certain customs over three villages "in potestate etiam et hominibus" which Henri claimed to have leased to the abbey for twelve *modii* of oats annually; he surrendered all claim over villages and men for 90 l. cash and only six *modii* annual payment; he retained only one fief that was held from him and a few peasants. 1222,L, pp. 121-22: he assigned 15 s. from customs, 7 d. *cens*, and three *modii* of *terrage* grain to the abbey: these revenues had constituted a fief held from him by a knight. *Feoda* VI,4021: in return for 4 l. annually, which he received from the count *in augmentum feodi*, he owed six weeks castle guard at Villemaur. 1228,MLC,265: *nobilis vir*. His holdings apparently passed to his daughter, for in the *Rôles*,Troyes,1119 Jean of Vallery held property, including houses, at Chennegy and Saint-Mesmin via his wife; there were eight rear-fiefs at Chennegy, of which seven were valued in *libratae terre* (1,1,3,3,3,5,8) for a total of 23 *l.t.* In all, there were nineteen rear-fiefs held from this family, of which seventeen were valued, for a total of 75 *l.t.* (average of 4.4 *l.t.*).

Chervey

MILO I: 1146,Ch,30: Witness as *miles* of the lord of Chacenay.

MILO II: 1204,Mor,51: *Miles.* 1206,M,229: took his wife's fief of three *setiers* of grain, forcing Milo of Clérey to seek elsewhere for a fief (see Clérey knights). 1205,M,221: called the "seneschal" of the lord of Chacenay. 1206,Ch,78: *dominus.* He entered a monastery in 1223,Mol,314.

MILO III: 1211,Mol,301: 1215,Ch,87. *Feoda* VI,3744: Did homage to the count, but he didn't know whether he was liege.

ERARD: 1229,Ch,130: Received from the count the fief that had been held by his brother Simon plus the 100 s. granted "in augmentation" by the count on the market of Bar-sur-Seine; "because of this, he [Erard] became my [the count's] liege man, save liegeance to the lord of Chacenay." This act was the basis for the entry in *Feoda* VI,4069. He also appeared in 1238,Mor,100 and in 1249,Mor,114.

ACHARD: Probably the son of Erard. *Rôles,*Bar-sur-Seine,85: the fortified house of Chervey, lands, fields, and a vineyard, worth 40 *l.t.*; no guard.

Chervey

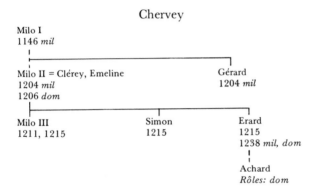

Milo I
1146 *mil*

Milo II = Clérey, Emeline   Gérard
1204 *mil*   1204 *mil*
1206 *dom*

Milo III   Simon   Erard
1211, 1215   1215   1215
                                 1238 *mil, dom*

                                 Achard
                                 Rôles: dom

Clérey (lords)

HUGH (JOSLAIN): 1157,Chapin,*Villes de foires*, appendix 1: One-third of his (? merchant) house in Troyes was given by Count Henry I to accompany the foundation of Saint-Etienne. *Feoda,*Payns,1680; Troyes, 1903: liege and guard. He died by (1172),R,102(x), leaving his widow, *domina* Laura, and son Eudes.

EUDES (JOSLAIN): He replaced Renaud of Verzy and his brother for two fiefs by ca. 1190 (*Feoda,*Sézanne,1972) and also replaced Gérard of Clérey, who was liege and owed all-year guard (*Feoda,*Troyes,1940). In 1195,L, p. 105, he gave an abbey five *setiers* annually from his arable at Créney, and in 1198,M,132, he sold his house in Troyes (? the rest of the above) for 260 l. He was identified as the son of Hugh (Joslain) in 1199,M,142, when he, his wife Alice, and his brothers sold a *platea* in Troyes which he had "free from all custom, *tonlieu*, and taxes of the viscounty" to the abbey for 20 l. Another charter identified him as a *miles* and the *platea* as a house next to Saint-Jean-en-Chastel (1200,M,120). In 1199,M,147, he

Clérey (lords)

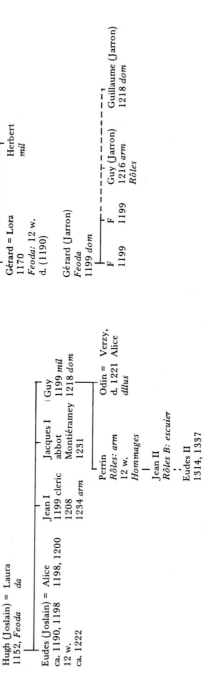

Hugh (Joslain) = Laura
1152, *Feoda*   *da*

Eudes (Joslain) = Alice
ca. 1190, 1198   1198, 1200
12 w.
ca. 1222

Jean I
1199 cleric
1208
1234 *arm*

Jacques I
abbot
Montiéramey
1231

Guy
1199 *mil*
1218 *dom*

Odin = Verzy, Alice
d. 1221 *dllus*

Perrin
Rôles: arm
12 w.
Hommages

Jean II
Rôles B: escuier

Eudes II
1314, 1337

Gérard = Lora
1170
Feoda: 12 w.
d. (1190)

Herbert
mil

Gérard (Jarron)
Feoda
1199 *dom*

F   F   Guy (Jarron)   Guillaume (Jarron)
1199   1199   1216 *arm*   1218 *dom*
                  Rôles

announced the solution to a dispute which he, Gérard (Joslain), and the other *domini* of Clérey agreed to: the abbey would have one-third of the justice and *dominium* of Clérey. In *Feoda* IV,Troyes,3588, he was liege, and in *Feoda* VI,4184, of after 1222, he did liege homage for the fortified house of Clérey and for things at Chéu, and he "posuit . . . in feudum" what he had at Ervy.

JEAN I: A cleric in 1199. 1208,MLC,264: he approved his father's gift to the abbey. 1227,MLC,69: *domicellus*, he was judged seven years in arrears for four *setiers* of grain which he owed the abbey from the *terrage* of Clérey. 1231,M,356: as an *armiger* he gave one-eighth of the tithe of Clérey to the abbey, at the request of his brother Jacques, the abbot.

GUY (JOSLAIN): *Miles* in 1199 and *dominus* in 1218 when he and Guillaume (Jarron) forfeited to the abbey half of the "lordship and justice" of Clérey for not appearing at court (see below). His son Odin, *domicellus*, had died by 1221. Guy may have been the brother of Eudes mentioned in 1234,*Histoire*,2340 as having been promised the fourth vacant prebend at Saint-Etienne by Thibaut IV. Guy may still have been living in 1265 *Hommages*,Isle,5373: he was referred to as the father of Pierre, viscount of Ligny-le-Châtel.

PERRIN: *Rôles*,Troyes,1110,1132; Isle,438: He held the same properties which his uncle Eudes had in *Feoda* VI: (1) at Créney: land, *cens*, and justice, worth 25 *l.t.*; 2) at Clérey: men, woods, and other property; and 3) at Chéu: the fortified house, worth 50 *l.t.* All this gave him a minimum of 80 *l.t.*, for which he owed twelve weeks guard. He also had two rear-fiefs at Clérey, a house with justice from the lord of Chappes and men with justice from the lord of Saint-Phal. In *Hommages*,Troyes, 5373, he was *monsieur* Pierre, viscount of Ligny-le-Châtel, who had just died.

JEAN II: *Hommages*,Troyes,5445: Son of the above, liege of the fortified house, the mill, and 19 *l.t.* at Clérey, plus the fortified house of Chéu. In *Rôles B*,Isle, 6499, as *escuier* he held the same properties. It was probably Jean's son Eudes II who appeared in the 1314 petition.

The second branch of Clérey seems to have been related originally to the above line.

GERARD: Witness in 1170, R,14(xvii) and in several other charters of the 1170s; he was identified as a *miles* in 1173,R,26(iii). *Feoda*,Troyes,1940: liege and twelve weeks guard at Isle; in a second listing his heirs were also liege and owed twelve weeks guard (*Feoda*,Villemaur,341). In (undated),V,82v–83r, he gave the abbey whatever he held in fief from his father-in-law, *dominus* Herbert Crassus, at Crelly; one of his two brothers was identified as a *miles*. He may have died without a direct heir, since one of his fiefs was acquired by (? his cousin) Eudes (Joslain) by ca. 1190 (*Feoda*,Troyes,1940).

GERARD (JARRON): *Feoda*, Troyes, 1958: *Homo*, perhaps the son-in-law of Gérard of Clérey (Gérard Jarron was not the same as Gérard of Clérey: if he were, the duplicate listing of a single person within one register would have been unique for the entire *Feoda*.). (1189),M,82: *dominus*. 1199,M,147: one of the *domini* of Clérey disputing the *justicia et dominium* of the place of which the abbey took one-third by default. 1201,M,179: acted with Baldwin Crassus, an uncle or cousin, in surrendering certain lands in a forest. His sons were probably Guillaume (Jarron), *miles* and *dominus* in 1218,M,298 and Guy (Jarron), *armiger* in 1216,M,289 who in the *Rôles*,Isle,441 was listed for a house at Lantage, from his mother, and a house, lands, and other properties, and two rear-fief holders (with 13 *l.t.*).

Clérey (knights)

ROBERT: *Feoda*,Troyes, 1959: [R] obert of Clérey, liege; replaced by his widow by ca. 1190. 1202,M,198: *laicus*, with his wife Aceline and his sons Milo, Etienne, and Robert II, gave the abbey seven separate pieces of land and his *ochia*; he agreed to hold the rest of his land, on the condition that he could neither sell nor mortgage it without the consent of the monks, in return for which he received annually for his and his wife's lifetimes three *setiers* of grain, one pair of shoes, one tunic, and one cape.

MILO: *Miles*, probably son and heir of Robert, stated that he had a *casamentum* of three *setiers* of grain in *terrage* from the abbey that went to his sister Emeline in marriage (1206,M,229). In fact, Milo probably never had the holding and had already secured another *casamentum* from Mores in 1204, when he was a *miles* (1204,Mor,51). He was also listed in *Feoda* V,Troyes,3614 as liege, but it is not clear whether he did hold a fief from the count at this date (1210/14) or whether the register was simply a copy of an earlier list because his father seems to have mortgaged the Champagne fief by ca. 1190/1202 (for the Crusade?). There are no later listings in the county registers for anyone of this family or for the holding in Clérey.

Crollebois

The Crollebois family may have originated near Provins, where two brothers of that name were listed in *Feoda*,Provins,1576,1613, but there is no early information on the family described here. Hugh and Pierre shared (probably with other relatives also) the village of Magnant and the revenues of several nearby villages apparently as alods; only the *cens* of Magnant did they hold from another person, the lord of Vendeuvre (1190,M,87). In 1198,M,135, Hugh, *miles*, gave all his share of Magnant in men, lands, fields, justice, and other rights as collateral for a 40 l. loan, which he could redeem during his lifetime; the next year both brothers gave up the *cens* of Magnant, as well as all they had in the villages of Villemoyenne and Courbeton (1199,M,150). Pierre may also have given his share of Magnant and may have died soon thereafter, for all subsequent conflicts involved Hugh alone. In 1200,M,176, Hugh's share of Magnant was defined as one-quarter of the village, which he held "jure hereditario a patre suo," and he now surrendered full possession for 120 l. cash; the abbey described the property: "in omnibus emolumentis, et absque ulla retentione, scilicet in hominibus, in omni justicia, in corveiis, in decimis, in pasturis, in nemoribus et pratis et in omnibus aliis." Apparently the abbot attempted to get by with less than the designated price because Hugh stated that if the abbey didn't have the full sum, *quod non credat*, he would give the difference as a gift (1200,M,197). Hugh shared an alod with a knight relative at Villemoyenne and Courbeton, described as a *tenementum* of two plots of two *jugera* each, which Hugh claimed "jure hereditario pertinere in alodio" and which he apparently had already given to the abbey with the approval of the lord of Chappes (1207,M,234–35; 1208,M,239). The Crollebois and Villemoyenne families were probably the offshoots of great alodial holders; the former disappeared after 1208, and the latter were eventually incorporated into the count's fief-holding system.

*Dampierre (Aube)

The Dampierre genealogy has been worked out by Roserot from a cartulary of Montier-en-Der (Archives Haute-Marne); Benton has noted some revisions in his "The Court of Champagne," p. 81. There was a *castrum* by 1120,Arch,Aube,20 H 5. Guillaume I was a *dominus* in 1152,CP,11; he was constable of Champagne and appeared as witness in the count's charters, in one instance among the count's *milites* (1170,*Histoire* III, pp. 458–59). His son Guy II was liege and owed custody for the viscounty of Troyes in *Feoda*,Troyes,1889; although there is no evidence that he was ever constable (Benton), he held several castles in the early thirteenth century (*Feoda* II,2462,2482; *Feoda* VI,3806). In 1213,Liber principum,344r–346r, his son Guillaume II promised good faith to the countess as liegeman for all his lands and required his *milites et homines* of the burg of Dampierre and his *vavasores* of the castellany of Dampierre also to swear an oath of support. He accepted the constableship, but without hereditary claims, in Feb. 1220,Liber principum, 343v–344r; in May 1220,Th,204r–v, he gave up the viscounty of Troyes. The Dampierres were lords of Saint-Just and Saint-Dizier as well. Because of the high level of their marriages, the Dampierre properties passed intact to younger sons, until the last direct male heir died ca. 1309; his sister took the lordship to her husband Gautier IV of Châtillon.

Dampierre (Aube)

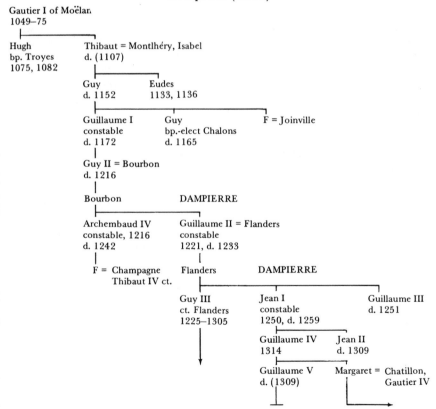

Gautier I of Moëlan
1049–75

Hugh   Thibaut = Montlhéry, Isabel
bp. Troyes   d. (1107)
1075, 1082

Guy   Eudes
d. 1152   1133, 1136

Guillaume I   Guy   F = Joinville
constable   bp.-elect Chalons
d. 1172   d. 1165

Guy II = Bourbon
d. 1216

Bourbon   DAMPIERRE

Archembaud IV   Guillaume II = Flanders
constable, 1216   constable
d. 1242   1221, d. 1233

F = Champagne   Flanders   DAMPIERRE
    Thibaut IV ct.

                    Guy III   Jean I   Guillaume III
                    ct. Flanders   constable   d. 1251
                    1225–1305   1250, d. 1259

                                        Guillaume IV   Jean II
                                        1314   d. 1309

                                        Guillaume V   Margaret = Chatillon,
                                        d. (1309)   Gautier IV

*Durnay

The Durnay family was a collateral of the Chacenay line. Although they seem to have had access to considerable money and to have made good marriages, they made few gifts to local monastic houses and were not prominent in *bailliage* affairs. The family faded from the 1270s and failed to appear in either the 1304 convocation or the 1314 petition. The actual location of Durnay is not known.

THOMAS II: Brother of Erard of Chacenay; appeared first in 1158; he never took the Durnay title but was always "of Chacenay." He was not listed in the *Feoda* because Durnay was strictly a rear-fief of Chacenay. In 1171,Ch,46, Thomas built the new village of Saint-Usage (see chapter II, n. 114). 1179,Ch,54: *dominus* of Chacenay, from whom a *casamentum* was held.

JACQUES I: 1199,M,139: *Miles;* he had men at Saint-Parres and Laubressel in 1199,M,140. 1214,Mor,71: he permitted Mores to acquire mobile but not landed possessions without his permission at Quercy and Beaufort. 1219,*Histoire*,1247: paid 300 l. relief to the count for his wife's share of the Bar-sur-Seine inheritance, but in 1223,*Histoire*,1586, he sold it to Thibaut IV for 500 l. Attended the baronial council of 1224, perhaps as a replacement for his cousin Erard of Chacenay. He and his son Gérard were in *Feoda* VI,4217 as *homines* of the count.

GERARD I: 1206,M,233: Son of Jacques; 1218,R,29(xiii): *miles, dominus.* 1244, Ch,150: his brother Jacques II was a monk at Clairvaux. In 1244,Ch,155, he bought all that Eudes of Broyes had in "eritages, en demoines, en fiez, en totes gardes" at Vendeuvre for 4000 l. He had died by 1252, when his wife Margaret, *domina*, was listed in the *Rôles*,Troyes,1122 for her Vendeuvre inheritance and other properties, worth 200 *l.t.*, in addition to eighteen rear-fief holders (worth 240 *l.t.*); this probably represented two Vendeuvre shares, hers and her brother's. She was probably the "*domina* of Vendeuvre" who held the castle and village and all men in the justice there in *Hommages*,Troyes,5317.

JEAN: 1249,M,114: *Dominus. Hommages*,Troyes,5313: "*dominus* Johannes, *dominus* of Durnay" was listed for: (1) "Vendeuvre and its castellany," which his father had purchased from the lord of Broyes, (2) Ville-sur-Arce, and (3) at Bar-sur-Seine. In 1268,M,416, as a *miles*, he purchased part of Vendeuvre from Milo II of Pougy. He died by 1272, and his widow Guillema was *domina* of both Durnay and Vendeuvre in 1285,M,427.

JACQUES III: Liege of several properties, especially Gronay, in *Hommages*,Bar-sur-Aube,5755.

GERARD III: Franchised the men of Durnay and Vendeuvre from arbitrary *taille* in 1271, Vallet de Viriville, *Archives historique*, p. 368, note b (notice).

Durnay

CHACENAY   DURNAY

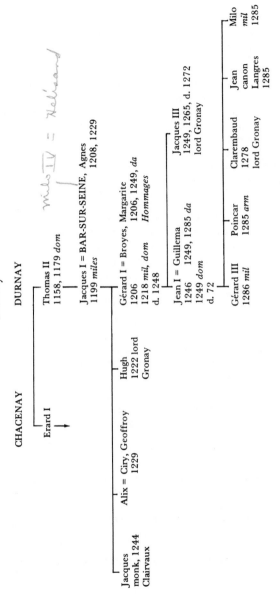

Erard I →

Thomas II
1158, 1179 *dom*

Milo IV = Holland

Jacques I = BAR-SUR-SEINE, Agnes
1199 *miles*   1208, 1229

Alix = Ciry, Geoffroy   Hugh
1229   1222 lord
                         Gronay

Jacques
monk, 1244
Clairvaux

Gérard I = Broyes, Margarite
1206   1206, 1249, *da*
1218 *mil, dom*   *Hommages*
d. 1248

Jacques III
1249, 1265, d. 1272
lord Gronay

Jean I = Guillema
1246   1249, 1285 *da*
1249 *dom*
d. 72

Gérard III   Poincar   Clarembaud   Jean   Milo
1286 *mil*   1285 *arm*   1278   canon   *mil*
                                 lord Gronay   Langres   1285
                                                   1285

*Ervy (lords)

Men who seem to have been lords of Ervy are mentioned from the late eleventh century, but the first positively identified as *dominus* of Ervy is Milo II in (1160/70),V,81v, where he appeared with *militibus suis*. He or his son Milo (III) is simply listed, without title, at the head of the Ervy register of the *Feoda* (Ervy, 295). It was probably Milo III who was *dominus* in *Feoda* IV,Ervy,2870 of ca. 1204/10. In 1214,CB,144r–v, he sold his house, land, and all possessions inside Ervy to the countess. The *Extenta*,Ervy of 1276/78 states that originally the count of Champagne had only half of the justice of Ervy and that he (probably Count Henry II in 1187–90; see chapter III, n. 23) purchased the other half. In fact, the count of Champagne did homage to the duke of Burgundy in 1143 for Ervy, which appeared as a Champagne castellany in the *Feoda* of 1172 and in later surveys. It would seem that the count used Ervy as a castellany center while he possessed only half of it directly in his hand. The count's acquisition of full control by, say, 1197 might well explain the grant of the customs of Lorris to the residents of Ervy in 1199, the only castellany town to receive any such grant in the *bailliage* (see chapter III, Community franchises). The family of Ervy lords may have survived in the thirteenth century, for *Rôles*,Ervy,333 refers to a fief held half from the count, half from the lord of Ervy, and *Rôles*,Ervy,373 states that a fief was held from the count alone, with no part from the lord of Ervy. The Ervy family, however, does not appear in the thirteenth-century documents.

Ervy (knights)

HAGAN I: *Feoda*,Troyes,1992; Payns,1651; *Feoda* IV,Ervy,2871: Liege, listed directly behind *dominus* Milo of Ervy (see Ervy, lords). Witness to several acts in the late twelfth and early thirteenth centuries. 1205,StS,59r: *dilectus et fidelis* of the countess, from whom he held a *feudum et casamentum* of 10 l. annually from the *tonlieu* of Troyes; of this income he gave the chapter 20 s., and another 20 s. in 1207,StS,59v–60r. He was a *miles* in 1208,N,22.

HAGAN II: 1212,StS,79r: Approved his father's gift of 40 s. from the *tonlieu* of Troyes (identified here as from the merchants of Ypres), and sold the remaining 8 l. of it for 70 l. cash, since his sons Henri and Guy "vellent Constantinopolim perficisci, non haberet expensas que eis ad viaticum sufficere." In the same year he surrendered, after a dispute, four parts of the tithe on wine in several villages for 60 l.; that was praised by his son Guy at the Feast of John the Baptist, "in quo factus fuit novus miles apud Paentium[Payns]" (1212,StS,61v). It may have been the same four parts or another share which was mortgaged for 65 l. to the bishop of Troyes, who retained the produce until redemption,(undated),StS,129v.

The 10 l. fief of revenue that was progressively alienated in 1205, 1207, and 1212 was probably the fief accounted for in the *Feoda* of 1172; nothing further is known of this family from either charters or county registers.

*Esternay

Esternay was a segmentary line of Marigny, which was itself a collateral line of Traînel (see Marigny and Traînel, as well as the latter's genealogical table), but it retained the Traînel name into the fourteenth century. Dreux I was liege in *Feoda* VI,Villemaur,3777, but Esternay seems to have been held still by his brother

Anselm, the constable, in *Rôles*,Sézanne,1075. It was probably Dreux II who first had Esternay as a separate holding (*Rôles B*,Pont,6612). Dreux III appeared in the 1314 petition.

Fontette

The Fontette line appears to have been an offshoot of the Briel family which was prominent in the early twelfth century. Hugh of Fontette referred to his grandfather Pierre of Briel in 1164,Ch,43; this Pierre was a *dominus* and had a *domina* wife and three sons, including a "Wido," who may have been "Guido," Hugh's father in (1076/1111),Mol-I,71.

HUGH I: Appeared as joint witness with and was probably the brother of Pierre in 1180,Mor,24. Hugh was probably the elder; he was still a boy as the son of Guy in (1147),Ch,31 but had become a *miles* by 1158,Ch,58,140. In *Feoda*,Troyes,49, he was liege and owed guard.

PIERRE I: First appeared in *Feoda*,Laferté,17; Bar-sur-Aube,90: he owed twelve weeks guard and possessed one-third of the viscounty of Bar. He was witness as *miles* in 1179,Ch,54; he gave Clairvaux the tithe of Autreville in 1204,Ch,74. He was called Pierre le Gros in 1211,Ch,85 and was still living in 1215,Ch,87 as *dominus*, when he approved of what his son Guy I, *miles* of Noé (just down the road from Fontette), had granted to Clairvaux.

HUGH II: Seems to have been the successor to Pierre; in 1236,Ch,150, he and his brother Robert were *domini.*

ROBERT I: Still a minor in 1204; as a *miles* in 1206,Mor,56 he made a successful marriage with the heiress of Ville-sur-Arce (see Ville-sur-Arce). In 1219 he promised Thibaut IV that he would break up his possessions into two fiefs so that each of his two infant sons would hold one in liege homage from the count; Robert also converted his alod worth 15 l. annually into a Champagne fief; he owed six weeks guard at Bar-sur-Seine (1219, Petel,*Ville-sur-Arce*,no. 4). This action in 1219 may have been caused by the disintegration of the house of Bar-sur-Seine with the death of its male heirs in that year; in 1225 the widowed countess of Bar-sur-Seine sold her entire share of that county, with the exception of Robert's fief, to Thibaut IV. Robert was dead by 1250,Mor,115; his widow Emeline, who had brought him Ville-sur-Arce, was still alive in 1252, when she was listed in *Rôles*,Bar-sur-Seine,55 for the *domus fort*, lands, men, and justice at Ville-sur-Arce, worth 160 *l.t.* and owing four weeks guard.

PIERRE III: A minor in 1219; *armiger* in 1236,MLC,93, when he quarreled over his wife's inheritance of *terrage* at Clérey; *miles* in 1246,Mor,106. In *Feoda* VI,4229, he was given a fief from the count worth 40 l. annually, an entire village near Bar-sur-Seine; he still had it as a *dominus* in *Rôles*,Bar-sur-Seine,56 and owed four weeks guard; his mother held her Ville-sur-Arce inheritance in her own hand. In 1263,Mor,126, he was Pierre (Baras), *chevalier;* in *Hommages*, Bar-sur-Seine,5413, *monsieur.* He died by *Rôles B*,Bar-sur-Seine,6516, when his widow referred to his fief as the *maison fort* of Ville-sur-Arce and forty hearths of men; his brother Milo held a rear-fief from him. Pierre and Milo together held a house and three *setiers* of grain in rear-fief from the lord of Durnay (*Rôles*,Troyes,1122).

MILO: *Rôles*,Bar-sur-Seine,56: *Dominus*, held 40 l. revenues from Pierre; also 10 *l.t.* from his wife's dowry at Courbeton and thirty *setiers* of grain as a rear-fief from the lord of Jully-sur-Sacre (*Rôles*,Bar-sur-Seine,84; Isle,436).

Fontette

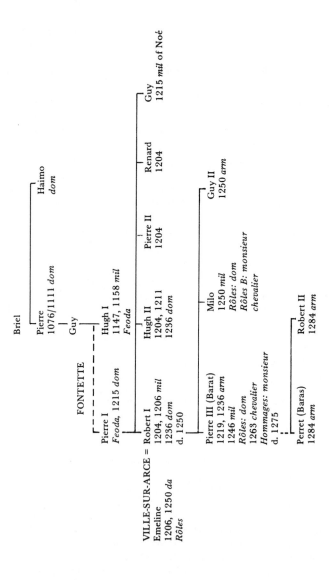

Briel

Pierre
1076/1111 *dom*

Guy

Haimo
dom

Hugh I
1147, 1158 *mil*
Feoda

FONTETTE

Pierre I
Feoda, 1215 *dom*

Hugh II
1204, 1211
1236 *dom*

Pierre II
1204

Renard
1204

Guy
1215 *mil* of Noé

VILLE-SUR-ARCE = Robert I
Emeline   1204, 1206 *mil*
1206, 1250 *da*   1236 *dom*
Rôles   d. 1250

Milo
1250 *mil*
Rôles: dom
Rôles B: monsieur
    chevalier

Guy II
1250 *arm*

Pierre III (Barat)
1219, 1236 *arm*
1246 *mil*
Rôles: dom
1263 *chevalier*
Hommages: monsieur
d. 1275

Perret (Baras)
1284 *arm*

Robert II
1284 *arm*

GUY II: Brother of Pierre III and Milo; still an *armiger* while his brothers were *milites* in 1250,Mor,115. In *Rôles*,Bar-sur-Seine,69, he was without title and held two vineyards and one man, worth 3 *l.t.*, from his father's inheritance.

PERRET (BARAS): He and his brother Robert II, *armigeri,* were probably sons of Pierre III in 1284,M,425.

Granges

RAOUL: 1242,M,376: Without title; husband of Mabile, whose brother was Iter of Payns, *armiger,* and whose sister was Sibile, wife of a *miles.* 1246,LP,175r: Raoul's son Herbert and his wife and heirs were "franchised and liberated" by Jean of Marcilly, *miles;* this charter may have been drawn up long after the event because the past perfect tense is used. *Rôles*,Payns,754: Raoul held a 20 s. fief of oats and *cens* at Vilercel and Payns; this fief had been held from Simon of Hunbauville, who sold it to the count, so now Raoul held directly from the count: "non fecit homagium sed dedit fidem, ut dicit." This might well illustrate the case of an overlord who chose not to accept a low-born man as fief holder (*Coutumier,* Article VI [undated decision]). See also chapter II and the Payns family. The Granges and Payns families are the rare ones in which low birth is alluded to in the *Rôles;* they have been coded as nontitled for the quantitative tables.

Granges

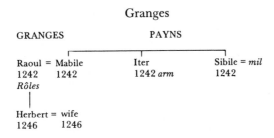

GRANGES   PAYNS

Raoul = Mabile   Iter   Sibile = *mil*
1242   1242   1242 *arm*   1242
Rôles

Herbert = wife
1246   1246

Isle-Aumont

ROBERT I: *Prévôt* in 1114; appeared also in 1100,M,18 and in 1122,M,24. His brother Jean I was a *miles* in 1138,M,31; both he and Gérard appeared in 1140,M,32.

MAURICE: *Miles* in 1138,M,31 and mayor of Isle in 1146,Arch.Aube,20 H 9.

ROBERT II: Probably in the direct line of Robert I and Maurice. Mayor of Isle in 1169,HD,23v. Listed in *Feoda*,Payns,1656. *Villicus* of Isle in 1184,StL,75 and a *prévôt* in 1186,MLC,135.

GAUTIER: Gautier of Isle in 1184 and probably the same as Gautier Melitarius, as suspected by Chapin. He appeared in (1180/90),L, p. 102. Dead by 1243,HD,82r, when his widow married Guillaume of Saint-Benoît, *miles, dominus.* Gautier was a *civis trecis* when his sons disputed a gift of wine to the Hôtel-Dieu.

GERARD (II): Simply Gérard of Isle in 1203,L, pp. 115-16 and in 1205,L, pp. 117-18. Gérard Melitarius, *prévôt,* in 1217,Arch.Aube,5 bis H l. Mayor of the

Isle-Aumont

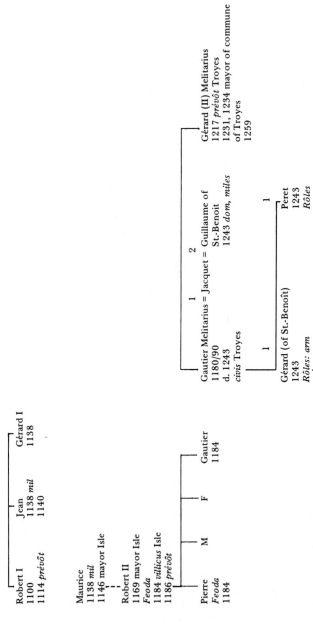

Robert I
1100
1114 *prévôt*

Jean
1138 *mil*
1140

Gérard I
1138

Maurice
1138 *mil*
1146 mayor Isle

Robert II
1169 mayor Isle
Feoda
1184 *villicus* Isle
1186 *prévôt*

Pierre
Feoda
1184

M

F

Gautier
1184

Gautier Melitarius = Jacquet = Guillaume of
1180/90   St-Benoit
d. 1243   1243 *dom, miles*
civis Troyes

                    1   2

Gérard (of St.-Benoît)
1243
Rôles: arm

                    1

Peret
1243
Rôles

                    1

Petronilla = JULLY
1263 *da*

Gérard (II) Melitarius
1217 *prévôt* Troyes
1231, 1234 mayor of commune
of Troyes
1259

commune of Troyes in 1231, Chapin,*Villes de foires*, appendix 7 and in 1234, StP,197. Simply *civis* of Troyes in 1236,N,78 and 1259,Arch.Aube,13 H 114.

GERARD III (of Saint-Benoît): Took his stepfather's name. In *Rôles*,Nogent,681, he was an *armiger* and held 30 *l.t.* income at Chapelle-Geoffroy for all-year service; this holding also probably came from his stepfather. He was listed in *Rôles*, Méry,580 for his wife's inheritance at Payns: 8 *l.t.* and no guard. Therefore, his total income was 39 *l.t.* His daughter Petronilla was a *domina* and married into the Jully house. His brother Peret acted with him in the 1243 dispute over their father's grant; Peret seems to have held only a rear-fief of 2 *l.t.* from the lord of Romilly in *Rôles*,Pont,785. There is no information on Guillaume of Saint-Benoît's family.

*Jully-sur-Sarce

Jully-sur-Sarce was a collateral line of the Chappes family (see the Chappes genealogy).

GUY: First appeared as *dominus* of Jully in 1192,M,97, when he held his properties (*de feodo et casamento*, 1209,StS,68v) from his brother Clarembaud IV of Chappes. He took the cross in 1199 and had returned by 1206,Liber principum, 102v−103r, when the castle of Jully was officially made renderable to the countess, although it was held directly from the lord of Chappes. Jully was still considered to be a rear-fief of Chappes in *Feoda* II and was not listed as a great fief. Guy attended the council of 1212 and was a knight banneret in 1214. In 1215,Th,242r, the countess referred to him as a "noble" in the court of Champagne. He died by 1221,Liber principum,108v, when the countess fulfilled his testament. Since he left only two daughters, Jully went integrally to one of them, while the additional holding of Saint-Sepulchre, also held from the Chappes family, went to the other as dowry for her marriage to the constable of Burgundy.

GUILLAUME: Probably the younger Sailly son who inherited his mother's property. He was first mentioned in 1236; in 1265 he was *monsieur* Guillaume, *sire* of Jully, who held two fiefs: the Jully properties and the minor revenues at Sailly (*Hommages*,Bar-sur-Seine,5433). It was probably his son Jean who appeared in the petition of 1314.

Macey

GEOFFROY: *Feoda*,Troyes,1913: guard. (1169-80),MLC,45: *dominus*.

GUILLAUME: Probably direct descendant of Geoffroy, for whom no other relative can be found; 1247,MLC,100: *miles, dominus*. By 1252 he had died, and his widow *domina* Isabel held as her dowry the justice of Macey, worth 2 *l.t.*, for which she owed two and one half days guard (*Rôles*,Isle,427).

FLORA: *Domicella* and probably daughter of Guillaume and Isabel who held the main fief: house, lands, fields, vines, men, *cens*, and use of woods, worth 40 *l.t.*, for which she owed unspecified guard; there was also one rear-fief holder (*Rôles*, Isle,430). She was still *domicella* in *Hommages*,Bar-sur-Seine,5427.

GEOFFROY II: Perhaps the younger brother of Flora; *monsieur, chevalier*, who held the justice of Macey (Flora's mother's dowry in 1252) in *Rôles B*,Isle,6511. The village of Macey had thirty hearths in ca. 1290,*Etat des bois*.

In 1252 the village of Macey, of about thirty hearths, provided 42 *l.t.*, but the main 40 *l.t.* fief was without justice because that had been assigned in dowry.

Macey

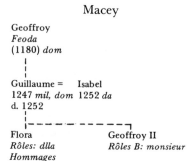

Geoffroy
Feoda
(1180) *dom*

Guillaume =   Isabel
1247 *mil, dom* 1252 *da*
d. 1252

Flora   Geoffroy II
Rôles: dlla   *Rôles B: monsieur*
Hommages

*Marigny-le-Châtel

Marigny-le-Châtel was a segment of the Traînel family (see Traînel and its genealogy). Garnier II (d. 1195) "of Traînel" or 'of Marigny" was seneschal of Nevers. Marigny was not mentioned in the *Feoda* probably because it was still considered to be a rear-fief of Traînel, but in *Feoda* II,2451, the *dominus* (Garnier III) of Marigny was liege to the count and held the castle there as a "great fief." He attended the council of 1212 and was a knight banneret in 1214. Garnier IV attended the council of 1224 and was listed in *Feoda* VI,3865, where he promised the count that if he had two heirs, one would hold Marigny, and the other would have Maraye and Saint-Medard. In 1228,Th,336r–v, he sold 1,200 *arpents* of woods to the countess. As *dominus* in the *Rôles*,Troyes,1131; Sézanne,1076, he held both Maraye and Esternay; the latter soon became itself a segment (see Esternay). His widow, the *dame* of Marigny, held the lands and castle in *Rôles B*,Pont,6609. This family also produced an archdeacon of Laon, Guy, who died bishop-elect of Verdun, and a constable of Champagne, Anselm, lord of Voisons and Soligny. But the direct line failed when Garnier V left only four daughters, three of whom had died by 1290; the surviving daughter took Marigny to her husband (details of the transfer are not clear). By 1304 Guillaume of Thil had acquired the lordship, and in 1314 he appeared as the lord of Marigny along with the other "nobles." The Thils appeared in the mid-twelfth century, holding fiefs from the counts of Brienne. Ansculf was viscount of Bar-sur-Aube in *Feoda*,Bar-sur-Aube,89, and it was probably his descendant Jean who appeared in the same capacity for both Bar and Laferté in *Feoda* V,Bar-sur-Aube,2817. The Thils were also related somehow to the Mérys, for in 1207,Mol,298–99, Jean obtained the escheat of Milo le Bechu (of Méry) of one-fourth of the tithe of Méry and Saint-Dulph.

Marnay-sur-Seine

Jean of Marnay was liege for lands, fields, woods, justice, and men at Marnay in *Feoda* VII,5206 (see also chapter IV, n. 20). In 1252 he was still an *armiger* and held at Marnay, specified as a house, land, men, fields, *cens,* and justice, worth 20 *l.t.,* and he owed eight weeks castle guard. A knight held two rear-fiefs from him, worth 20 *l.t.* and 3 *l.t.* (*Rôles*,Nogent,663). In 1265 he was liege and owed eight weeks guard for the same property, now equated with one-quarter of the village of Marnay (*Hommages*,Nogent,5548).

Maupas

HUGH: 1223,V,8v: *Miles,* owed eight *setiers* of grain from the *terrage* of Maupas to the abbey, but he still had the justice over the *terrage;* both his son and daughter had claims on the grain, but she surrendered hers (her dowry). Hugh died by 1229,V,15r–v, when his wife married Herbert, *miles* of Villeneuve. In (undated), V,40r, her daughter Helisand gave up her entire inheritance, which was: the woods and lands, but not the men, of Lailly, Poisei, and Courgenay, to the abbey. 1229,V,15r–v: Agnes, *nobilis mulier,* gave the abbey one *modius* of grain, 4 s., twenty loaves of bread, and twenty chickens from her custom, which was from the fief of Jean of Fontaine, *miles,* and Iter, son of Henri of Thorigny, *miles.*

JACQUES: *Rôles,*Ervy,358: *Dominus,* held entirely in rear-fief from Geoffroy of Survanne, 4 *l.t.,* which came from Jacques' wife's inheritance. It would seem that Jacques had a single holding, since the overlords of his mother did not list him for a holding in 1252.

Maupas

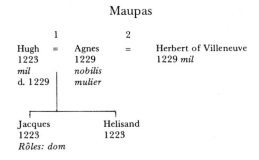

```
            1              2
   Hugh    =   Agnes    =   Herbert of Villeneuve
   1223        1229         1229 mil
   mil      ┌─ nobilis
   d. 1229  │  mulier
            │
      ┌─────┴─────┐
   Jacques      Helisand
   1223         1223
   Rôles: dom
```

*Méry-sur-Seine

The many scattered references to the Méry family unfortunately cannot be fitted into a meaningful genealogy. There was a *dominus* of Méry in 1097/1104,Mol,234: both he (Geoffroy) and later his son (Otrannus) were *dapiferi* of Count Hugh of Troyes; they were also qualified as *nobiles* in the early twelfth century. None of their direct successors had comparable titles from the mid-twelfth century but appeared rather as *milites.* In any event, Méry appeared as a Champagne castellany in the *Feoda* of 1172. There is also evidence that the chapter of Saint-Pierre had a fortification there: its *honor* of Méry was confirmed by the king in 1177,StP,29, and its fortress there was the object of a dispute between the chapter and the countess in 1220,LP,25v–27r.

Minay

ALUIS: 1166,S,24v: He mortgaged all his lands at Mesnil to the church of Joy for an annual thirty two *setiers* of grain; he received 10 s., and his brothers received 20 s., for approving the transaction. Perhaps he was the *dominus* Aliquidus in 1191 (*vidimus* of 1513),Arch.Aube,9 H 125. His son may have died young because nothing is known of his line until 1245; the daughter Emeline seems to have had half of his property.

EMELINE: Her husband Hulduin, also of Minay, had property at Minay and Hauterive in *Feoda*,Pont,1701, for which he was liege and owed twelve weeks guard; when he died in ca. 1190 he was replaced in the *Feoda* by his son-in-law Milo of Balloy. In 1189,Arch.Aube,9 H 21, Emeline and Hulduin with their *pueri* sold a house to Sellières for 15 l.; Emeline's children were: Hugh, *miles*, in 1189 and in *Feoda* III,Bray,2637, where he was liege and owed guard, and Milo, who was liege for his wife's property in *Feoda* V,Pont,3144; Sézanne,3547.

LACENE: Her husband Milo of Balloy had his own fief in *Feoda*,Bray,1352 for which he owed eight weeks guard. He replaced his father-in-law in the original *Feoda* ca. 1190 and was listed for that same property in *Feoda* III,Pont,2489: he was liege and owed the same twelve weeks guard; the fief, *ex parte uxoris sue*, was described as half of Minay and what was mortgaged to Sellières (that is, the land mortgaged in 1166 by Aluis). Milo was also listed for his father-in-law's holdings at Hauterive in *Feoda* V,Provins,3113. However, in 1200,S,24v–25r, Milo, *miles*, sold all the property in Minay "tam in terris quam in teragis et nemoribus exceptis hominibus et censibus suis et hostisia una de vineis" for 40 l. and four and a half *modii* of oats in *cens*; his wife received 40 s. for approving, and his overlord Milo Regis also approved (1200,S,25r). The other half of Minay was probably still held by the other branch, represented by Fromond III.

FROMOND III: 1245,Arch.Aube,9 H 64: His father, Anselm, *scutifer*, was dead, and his uncle was prior of Notre-Dame of Pont; Fromond, *armiger*, gave two *setiers* from his *terrage* at Minay (which was his mother's). In *Rôles*,Pont,780, he was without title, but his fief was described as: a house at Minay, one *carrucate* of land, men, *cens*, and customs, worth 40 s. (? error for 40 *l.t.*); he owed eight weeks

Minay

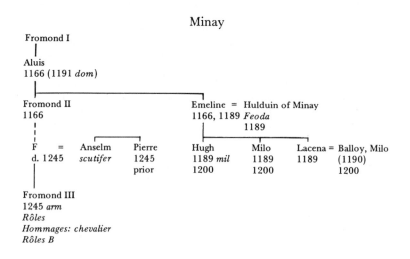

```
Fromond I
|
Aluis
1166 (1191 dom)
|_____
Fromond II                    Emeline = Hulduin of Minay
1166                          1166, 1189 Feoda
 |                             |        1189
 |                             |_____
 F    =  Anselm    Pierre      Hugh     Milo    Lacena = Balloy, Milo
 d. 1245  scutifer  1245       1189 mil  1189    1189     (1190)
 |                  prior      1200     1200             1200
 |
Fromond III
1245 arm
Rôles
Hommages: chevalier
Rôles B
```

guard. Three rear-fiefs were held from him: 1 *l.t.*, 20 *l.t.*, and one-half *modius* of grain. The same entry is in *Hommages*,Pont,5518. In 1270,S,27r–v, he was *messire* Fromon of Minay, *chevalier*. In *Rôles B*,Pont,6629, he was *sires Fromons, chevalier*. In *Extenta*,Pont, he had a house in front of the merchant hall of Pont that owed 35 s. *cens*. Several other persons from Minay cannot be linked with this family.

Montfey

The Montfey family is scarcely encountered in the ecclesiastical acts. According to the ca. 1290 *Etat des bois*, the village had 150 hearths, and the *Rôles* of 1252 accounted for the village as six Champagne fiefs, together worth 125 *l.t.*: there were a fortified house, three other houses, lands, fields, men, and justice, for which a total of forty days guard was owed (*Rôles*,Ervy,372). The village was divided among two brothers (30 *l.t.* each), a relative who was probably a brother (30 *l.t.*), and two sisters (25 and 8 *l.t.*).

GERARD: *Armiger*, had the fortified house, lands, fields, men, and justice, worth 30 *l.t.*; he owed eight days guard (*Rôles*,Ervy,338). He was still an *armiger* in 1271,*Documents* II, p. 35, n. 1.

HUGH: Had a house, justice, lands, and fields there, as well as men at Saint-Liebault; the two holdings seem to have constituted a single fief worth 30 *l.t.* owing eight days guard (*Rôles*,Ervy,337). He also had 160 *arpents* of land in Bray (*Rôles*,Bray,122).

HERBERT OF PUISEAUX: *Dominus*, perhaps brother of the above. His main holding was 30 *l.t.* from his wife's dowry; the house and 30 *l.t.* at Montfey were held from him in rear-fief by Geoffroy of Montfey, *armiger*, who may have been a younger Montfey brother (*Rôles*,Ervy,343). It is not clear why Herbert had any of Montfey, but it seems that he allowed a younger brother to hold his share, since he had a comparable holding from his wife. Geoffroy also had a 2 *l.t.* rear-fief there from Hugh, so in all Geoffroy had 32 *l.t.* at Montfey.

The two sisters of Montfey took their shares of the village to their husbands: Milo of Saint-Loup-de-Naud had 25 *l.t.* and a house there, for which he owed two weeks guard (*Rôles*,Ervy,356); Pierre of Saint-Oulph, *dominus*, had 8 *l.t.* in lands, fields, men, and *cens*, but not a house, and owed two weeks guard, but his own main holding was 20 *l.t.* from the *péage* and oven of Méry (*Rôles*,Méry,576). Thus, there were four fiefs approximately equal in income, but only two of them had rights of justice, and only one of them had a fortified house.

*Nogent-sur-Seine

MILO I: *Vir illuster* in 1127, A. Catel and M. Lecomte, eds., *Chartes et documents de l'abbaye cistercienne de Preuilly* (Montereau, 1927), no. 5. In 1138,MLC,25, land was held from him at Chapelle-Geoffroy. 1144,P,49: *dominus*. 1146,P,52: he sold one-third of the tithe of Chalautre-la-Grande for 120 l. and approved the acquisitions by Paraclet from *milites de feodo suo* and his *rusticis*. There was a castle at Nogent from the mid-twelfth century, (undated),V,41v. Milo may have used the 120 l. in 1146 to finance his expedition to Jerusalem, where he probably died; his son Renaud (mentioned in 1147,P,6) may have died there also, for by 1161,V,104r–v, Milo's son-in-law was *dominus* of Nogent.

GERARD: *Dominus* in 1164,V,101v–102r; in 1171,P,61, he gave Paraclet 40 s.

Nogent-sur-Seine

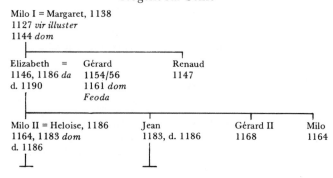

Milo I = Margaret, 1138
1127 *vir illuster*
1144 *dom*

Elizabeth = Gérard   Renaud
1146, 1186 *da* 1154/56   1147
d. 1190   1161 *dom*
                 Feoda

Milo II = Heloise, 1186   Jean   Gérard II   Milo
1164, 1183 *dom*   1183, d. 1186 1168   1164
d. 1186

annually from the *forum* of Nogent with the count's approval, but that act, like the one in 1182,P,15, was probably drawn up after his death.

MILO II: He was probably the *dominus* of Nogent and liege in *Feoda*,Provins, 1399; Bar-sur-Aube,71. 1183,V,102r: *miles,dominus;* his brother Jean was still unmarried.

Both brothers were dead by 1186,P,75, when their mother Elizabeth, *domina*, gave Paraclet 14 l. annually from the *péage* and *tonlieu* of Nogent and all that she had at Poisy for their souls (the charter of 1194,P,83 that referred to Milo was probably drawn up after his death). She appeared again as *domina* of Nogent in 1189,Arch.Aube,9 H 21 and for the last time in 1190(*vidimus* of 1250), Arch.Aube,G 988. Another charter, (undated),V,101v, calls her the "former lady" of Nogent. In 1199,*Histoire*,485, Thibaut III gave Nogent to his wife Blanche as part of her dowry, and in *Feoda* III of ca. 1200 Nogent was a Champagne castellany with ten knights: a notation in the register explains that this was the first time that they were included in a register. In 1226,*Documents* I, p. 476, Thibaut did homage to the abbot of Saint-Denis for the castle and lands of Nogent; he also paid 2,000 l. for the return of the gold cross and altar of Saint-Etienne, which were being held as security.

*Payns (lords)

NOCHER: 1161,V,83v: He and his wife gave the abbey use of part of the woods of Droupt-Sainte-Marie. *Feoda*,Payns,1686: the wife of Nocher (of Payns) is listed for his fief. There was a reference to his son-in-law in (undated),R,101(iii).

PIERRE: *Feoda*,VI,3721: Pledge for a knight; 1225,MLC,175: *dominus, miles*, pledge for another knight. 1240,Arch.Aube,22 H 1614: *dominus, miles*, with his wife Gila, *domina*, agreed to hold their house on the road of Payns with all its appurtenances from the abbey; after their deaths the entire holding, as well as part of the oven of Payns, would go to the abbey. *Rôles*,Troyes,1108,1122: held two rear-fiefs, 3 *l.t.* from the lady of Romilly and 7 *l.t.* from the lady of Durnay.

Payns (lords)

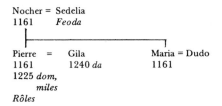

Nocher = Sedelia
1161 *Feoda*

Pierre = Gila Maria = Dudo
1161 1240 *da* 1161
1225 *dom,*
  miles
Rôles

Payns (knights)

GUILLAUME: 1229,Th,356r: his daughter Agnes, *femina de corpore* of the count, was given by the count to the bishop of Troyes. Guillaume's widow, Margaret of Droupt, *femina regis* [of Navarre] *de corpore*, is listed in *Rôles*,Méry,571: her status may have prevented her from doing homage, for the entry notes that *non fecit homagium*. Her holding consisted of three revenues: 40 s. in *cens* and arable, four *modii* of oats, and nine *setiers* of oats, all purchased by her father from fifteen to thirty five years before from two knights, one of whom was Pierre of Bouy (see Bouy-sur-Orvin). She had three rear-fief holders: a *dominus* held 40 s.; a *domina* held 20 s. in land, *cens*, and customs; and a nontitled person held another 20 s. She owed guard for six weeks. It was probably a direct relative, Pierre of Droupt, *major communie de Meriaco*, who held one-third of her listing in the *Rôles* from her. Perhaps it was her son Guillaume of Payns, *escuiers*, who held the 60 s. rear-fief that had been held by his lord's deceased brother, a *chevalier*, in *Rôles B*, Troyes, 6469. See also the Granges family for another low-born fief holder in the *Rôles*.

*Plancy

The first reference to Plancy was in (1080),Mol,225: the *castrum* of Plancy was held by Gila, *mulier nobilissima* (see Chappes).

HUGH I: First known member of the Plancy family, which always held its castle from the Chappes family and which therefore was most likely a collateral line of the Chappes. In 1099,Mol,235–36, he was a *dominus* and his wife a *nobilissima* woman, when they donated part of an alod; the act was witnessed by six men identified as their *milites*.

HUGH II: 1138,M,31: Witness as a *miles;* (1060),Mol,276: *dominus*. He was liege in *Feoda*,Troyes,1892.

HAICE/HATO: Appeared in 1160,MLC,30; *laicus* in 1167,L, pp. 99-100; deacon in 1182,StP,36; bishop of Troyes and chancellor of Champagne, 1191-93.

GILO: 1189,P,77: *Dominus*. In 1190,M,88, he set out for Jerusalem, and the monks later complained that his wife did not carry out his order not to burden the men of the abbey with "exactions."

PHILIP I: One of the "great fief" holders in *Feoda* II,2450, but he was liege to the lord of Chappes. 1206,Arch.Aube,G 988: *dominus*. Member of the council of 1212 and a knight banneret in 1214. Apparently he had supported the Brienne faction because in Apr. 1221,Th,215v–216r, Clarembaud V of Chappes had to guarantee to the count that the castle of Plancy, held *immediate* from Chappes, would be used

Plancy

CHAPPES

Gila
(1080)

PLANCY

Gautier

Hugh I = Emeline
1090, 1099   1099 *nobilissima*
dom

Hugh II = TRAÎNEL, Isabel
1138, d. 1189
Feoda

Haice
1160 bp. Troyes
chancellor Champagne
d. 1193

Gilo = Hodieard
1189   d. 1215 *da*
dom
1190 crusade

Capraine

Philip I = BAR-SUR-SEINE, Agnes
1203, 1206 *dom*   1210, 1218 *da*
d. 1235   1234

Dreux
1204 canon
1209 crusade

Thibaut
1234, d. 1250 *dom*

Philip II
1234
Rôles: canon

Jacques
1234, 1240 *dom*
Rôles, Hommages

Hugh III
1234, d. 1274

Margarite = St.-Florentin, vct.

Philip III
1314, d. 1317

for good purposes only (that is, not against the count) for the next five years. Gilo's alliance with the Briennes may have necessitated his journey to the East in 1218,StP,144. Member of the council of 1224. In 1224,M,333, he made a *pariage* over four villages on the Barbuise river (see chapter III, Communities).

DREUX: Perhaps the brother of Philip I. Canon of Saint-Pierre (1204,StP,109r); *capicerius* of Saint-Etienne in 1209,StS,145v–146r, when he went to Jerusalem.

JACQUES: 1240,Arch.Aube,G 988: *Dominus.* Listed twice in the *Rôles:* for the castle and castellany of Plancy, held from Jean of Chappes (Troyes,1132), and for the fortified house of Praslin and the *conductus mercati* of Plancy (Isle,466). He was *monsieur, seigneur* of Plancy, and liege of Praslin in *Hommages,*Isle,5397.

PHILIP II: A minor in 1234; a cleric in *Rôles,*Troyes,1138; Isle,467 who held the escheat of his brother *dominus* Thibaut that yielded 68 *l.t. Hommages,*Troyes, 5354: *monsieur,* canon of Saint-Pierre of Troyes.

PHILIP III: Appeared with the "nobles" of 1314; died by 1317, but his line continued.

*Pont-sur-Seine

There is only one reference to simply a lord of Pont (1101,Mol-I,17). In the late eleventh century Philip of Pont was bishop of Troyes, and Garnier I was lord of Pont and Traînel, both of which had castles, in 1110,Mol,253–54 (see Traînel and its genealogy). It is possible that the lands and castle of Pont were taken from the Traînels before a viable collateral line emerged; in any case, the seemingly substantial personages named "of Pont" in the early twelfth century cannot be linked. The count had a *prévôt* of Pont in 1153,S,23v–24r, and Pont was fully in the Champagne domain in the *Feoda* of 1172. But the fact that the old Traînel family actually had Pont before the Marigny branch had segmented in the twelfth century is proved by the sale in 1208,Th,235r–v and in 1209,Th,238r–v, in which Anselm III of Traînel and his cousin Garnier III of Marigny sold their rights of *péage,* men, woods, and land at Pont; that is, they must have had a common ancestor who held the rights originally.

*Pougy

Although the origin of the Pougy family is obscure, their sudden presence in high positions in the mid-twelfth century points strongly to a link with a distinguished old family. There may even have been a link with the count's family itself: in 1154 Count Henry I fulfilled a vow by establishing three canons at Pougy (see Roserot); Henry of Carinthia, bishop of Troyes and relative of Thibaut II's wife, addressed Manasses of Pougy, the future bishop of Troyes, as *dilectus filius* (1158,StL,27); finally, the names of the Pougy brothers are very similar to those in the count's family (Hugh, the count of Troyes, and Eudes, last son of Thibaut II).

EUDES I: Constable of Champagne, 1152, 1169. Lord of Pougy, Avant-lès-Ramerupt (see chapter II for the pact of 1169 over this village), Marrolles-sur-Seine, and Mesnil-Lettre. He was in the *Feoda,*Rosnay,203; he died in 1182. For him in particular, see Benton, "The Court of Champagne." His brothers Manasses I and Hugh, *dominus:* 1153/56,Mol,273; *Feoda,*Troyes,1895; *Feoda* III,Troyes,2515; Hugh as *vir nobilis* in 1206,L, pp. 118-19.

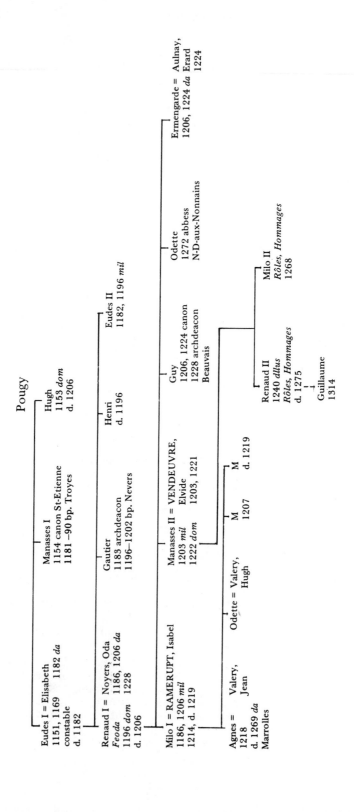

Pougy

RENAUD I: *Feoda*,Troyes,1894; Rosnay,201: owed twelve weeks guard. 1196,StP,81: he and his brother Eudes II gave an anniversary for their brother Henri. Renaud was *dominus* of Marrolles (1196,Liber principum,107r); *nobilis vir* (1203,StL,139). *Feoda* II,2476: *dominus* of Marrolles and a "great fief" holder for both Marrolles and Pougy. *Feoda* IV,Rosnay,2848: twelve weeks guard for the justice of Saint-Léger. Died by 1206,StL,146.

MILO I: Appeared by 1186. He shared the escheated viscounty of Saint-Florentin by ca. 1190 (*Feoda*,Troyes,2000); *miles* in 1206,StL,146. Attended the council of 1212; knight banneret in 1214.

MANASSES II: Appeared in 1203. *Dominus* in 1222,M,340, when he approved the sale by his brother-in-law Erard of Aulnay of half the justice, *taille*, woods, *corvées* of Mesnil-Lettre, as well as one-third of the safeguard, for 300 l.; Erard had the property through his wife's dowry. Attended the council of 1224. Before 1252 he sold the entire *villa* of Courgerennes and a house (*Rôles*,Troyes,1114.)

GUY: 1201,StS,108r: *Miles*, gave a woman and her land to the chapter. *Feoda* IV,Rosnay,2845: liege and three months guard. Canon of Auxerre (1224,M,330); archdeacon of Beauvais (1228,M,348).

RENAUD II: *Domicellus* in 1240,*Histoire*,2544. In 1252 he held 20 *l.t. in bursa* and 30 *l.t.* revenue at Pougy and in several villages (*Rôles*,Troyes,1130), which he still had as *monsieur* in *Hommages*,Troyes,5316. In *Rôles B*,Troyes,6461, it was probably his widow, *madame*, who held them.

MILO II: Younger son of Manasses II and Elvide of Vendeuvre, so he took his mother's property: the fortified house and part of the castle of Vendeuvre, as well as seven rear-fief holders (*Rôles*,Troyes,1125). He was listed for the same possessions in 1265 (*Hommages*,Troyes,5338), but he sold them to Jean of Durnay in 1268,M,416.

GUILLAUME: Appeared in 1287 and among the nobles in 1314 as the lord of Pougy, but his relationship to the Pougy family is not known (Roserot suspects that he may have married into the family).

Quincy

SIMON: 1156/58,P,11: He sold land and use of the woods at Quincy to Paraclet for repairing its mill.

MILO I: 1200,P,207: He sold his share of the tithe of Quincy to the abbey for 35 l. to himself, a horse to his son, and 20 s. to his wife and daughter. (Milo may have been related to Aitor of Quincy, who sold his *totum tenementum*, including rents and *terrage*, to the abbey for 100 l. in 1194,P,84 and in 1198,P,21.) Milo is probably the Milo Sanctus who in 1194,P,83 gave half the oven of Quincy, which he held from *dominus* Milo of Nogent, and a vineyard for the support of two daughters as nuns in Paraclet. It appears that he married Margaret, daughter of Benoît of Pont, who was franchised in 1175 because Benoît's fief of Saint-Parres in 1172 was sold by Milo's son in 1218 and because Milo's granddaughter was also named Margaret (see chapter V, n. 52).

ETIENNE: 1218,P,161: *Miles*, sold all his *cens* and the justice over it at Chalautre-la-Grande, Saint-Ferréol, and Saint-Parres for 35 l. The transaction was confirmed by Thibaut IV in 1229,P,199, when Etienne was a *dominus* (this fief was probably the one held by Benoît of Pont in *Feoda*,Pont,1728).

Quincy

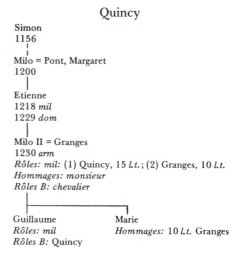

Simon
1156

Milo = Pont, Margaret
1200

Etienne
1218 *mil*
1229 *dom*

Milo II = Granges
1230 *arm*
Rôles: mil: (1) Quincy, 15 *l.t.*; (2) Granges, 10 *l.t.*
Hommages: monsieur
Rôles B: chevalier

Guillaume   Marie
Rôles: mil   *Hommages:* 10 *l.t.* Granges
Rôles B: Quincy

MILO II: 1230,P,201: *Armiger*, sold the *terrage* of Tremblay and Avant-lès-Marcilly. *Rôles*,Nogent,671: *miles*, liege, and he held: (1) at Quincy: a house, lands, men, *cens*, and justice, worth together 15 *l.t.*; and (2) at Granges (from his wife): land, *cens*, and *terrage*, all worth 8 *l.t.* He owed eight weeks guard for each fief. His sister Mathilda held eight *setiers* from his *terrage* in rear-fief, and Milo himself held a *parvum feudum* in rear-fief from Guibert of Courbeton (*Rôles*,Pont,760). *Hommages*,Nogent,5533: *monsieur*, liege. *Rôles B*,Nogent,6630: *monsieur, chevalier*.

GUILLAUME: *Rôles*,Sezanne,1083: *Miles*, held the escheat of his grandfather G. of Granges. *Rôles B*,Nogent,6634: land, men, customs, and *terrage*, of which one-third was held in rear-fief by his sister; he owed eight weeks guard.

MARIE: *Hommages*,Pont,5527: She held her mother's inheritance at Granges, 10 *l.t.*, for which she owed eight weeks guard in another listing (probably an emendation: *Hommages*,Nogent,5544).

The Quincy family did not appear in the *Feoda* of 1172 because they were still under the lord of Nogent. The family's main holding of 15 *l.t.* passed to the son; the 8 (later 10) *l.t.* acquisition passed out by dowry to the daughter.

*Ramerupt

Counts of Ramerupt-Arcis appeared from the end of the tenth century (see Roserot).

ANDRE I: The last count of both places (1100,M,18); he may still have been alive in 1123,Arch.Aube,20 H 8. A *castrum* was mentioned in 1100,M,16. André had the Ramerupt-Arcis properties because they were considered less valuable than the Roucy holdings that had been acquired by marriage and held by the eldest brother. All André's sons predeceased him, so his two daughters divided his lands: one took Arcis as an independent lordship (see Arcis), and the other took Ramerupt to her Brienne husband.

GAUTIER II: Son of Alice of Ramerupt and Erard of Brienne; became count of

Ramerupt

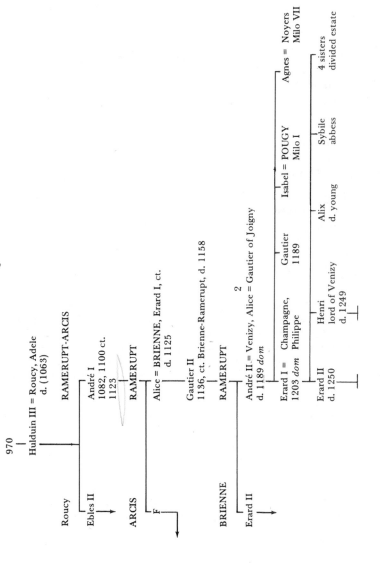

970

Hulduin III = Roucy, Adele
                d. (1063)

Roucy   RAMERUPT-ARCIS

Ebles II   André I
               1082, 1100 ct.
               1123

ARCIS   RAMERUPT

F   Alice = BRIENNE, Erard I, ct.
                       d. 1125

               Gautier II
               1136, ct. Brienne-Ramerupt, d. 1158

BRIENNE   RAMERUPT

Erard II   André II = Venizy, Alice = Gautier of Joigny
                          d. 1189 dom
                                    2

               Erard I = Champagne,   Gautier   Isabel = POUGY   Agnes = Noyers
               1203 dom Philippe   1189   Milo I   Milo VII

               Erard II   Henri   Alix   Sybile   4 sisters
               d. 1250   lord of Venizy d. young abbess   divided estate
                          d. 1249

Brienne after his father's death in 1125. He was also called "count of Brienne and Ramerupt" in 1136, the last reference to Ramerupt as a county.

ANDRE II: As a younger son in the Brienne family, he received the lesser property, Ramerupt, which was now only a lordship, and held as a rear-fief from his older brother Erard II of Brienne in *Feoda*,Troyes,1884 and in *Feoda* II,Troyes, 2447. In 1176,Arch.Aube,20 H 11, André purchased a mill from one of his *homines* for 50 l. and gave it to the priory of Notre-Dame of Ramerupt. He had the title *dominus* of Ramerupt first in 1189,Arch.Aube,20 H 11. He must have died shortly thereafter, perhaps on a crusade; his mortgage of Nogent-sur-Aube in 1188 for 300 l. to Gautier of Joigny was then sold to Montiéramey in 1195,M,109 for 300 l., plus 40 l. for the revenues (see the analysis of the charter in chapter II, Communities). Gautier probably married André's widow, for he appeared as *dominus* of Ramerupt.

ERARD I (styled "of Brienne"): *Dominus* in 1203,M,207, when he made an arrangement with the abbey over the administration and revenues of Nogent-sur-Aube, which his father had mortgaged. In 1208,StP,122, with the assent of his stepfather Gautier, he sold the *gîte* of Trouan-le-Petit for 100 l. and sixty *setiers* of oats annually, which was assigned to the men there, who if they did not pay were fined at 15 d. per *setier*—all of which was approved by the count of Brienne, from whom the fief moved(1208,StP,123). Erard was liege to the count of Champagne for Ramerupt in *Feoda* V,Troyes,3590. Thereafter he became the storm center of the succession crisis: his marriage to Philippe, daughter of Count Henry II of Champagne and the queen of Jerusalem, gave him a claim to the county itself, and he dominated the second decade of the thirteenth century in the *bailliage* by his expeditions, temporary truces, and excommunications. A bull of Innocent III, (undated),Th,84r, referred to the situation as a "scandalia . . . tam in oriente quam in occidente." Finally, on Thibaut's coming of age, Erard and his wife gave up all claims: they received 5,000 l. cash and a rent of 1,200 l. in Nov. 1221,Th,15v—19r; 19v—22v; 25r—v: the payment constituted a *feodum ligium;* Erard was allowed to build a "fortress" with a moat, but with only plain (not reinforced) walls and without a tower. On the eve of the attack by the French barons in 1229,*Histoire*, 1991, Thibaut forced Erard to surrender the castles of Ramerupt and Venizy and required all Erard's men to swear allegiance to the count, especially against the duke of Burgundy and the counts of Boulogne and Bar-le-Duc. In 1234,*Histoire*, 2329, Erard gave his daughter 140 l. annually as a dowry in her marriage to Anselm of Dampierre's son.

ERARD II: Little is known of him. In 1248,M,383, he sold his grange and the remaining share of all *terrages, corvées*, rents, and arable at Nogent-sur-Aube to Montiéramey for 257 l., obviously for crusading expenses; he died two years later at Mansourah. His brother Henri, lord of Venizy (from his mother), also died there in 1249. The two brothers left no heirs, and their four sisters (one other had died young, and another was abbess of Pieté) divided the Ramerupt estate. The count's *enquêteurs* listed Erard in the *Rôles*,Troyes,1091 for 20 *l.t.* at Ramerupt "de assisia comitisse" and 5 *l.t.* at Troyes "in praeria," and they thought that he held Isle-Ramerupt; they listed the three rear-fiefs held from him as worth 250 *l.t.* After Erard's death was known, the scribes listed the shares of his estate held by the daughters and their husbands, one-quarter each: (1) Isabel and Henri VI, count of Grandpré, (2) Margarite and Thierry of Bièvre, (3) Jeanne and Mathew III, lord of Montmorency, and (4) Marie and the lord of Nanteuil-la-Fosse (*Rôles*,Troyes, 1126,1127,1143; Meaux,548). The count of Grandpré seems to have acquired at least another quarter, for he subsequently called himself lord of Ramerupt. But the Ramerupt line was effectively at an end.

Rigny-le-Ferron

GODIN I: *Miles* in 1206,V,58v; his wife Bancelina was termed a *nobilis mulier* (1225,V,10r–v).

GODIN II: Appeared in 1225; *domicellus* in 1228,Arch.Aube,10 H l. Although neither brother appears in the Champagne surveys—either they held all their property from an abbey or they had alienated it by 1252—they probably held their family's main properties, since their sister Lucia's son had his properties from his own wife.

JEAN: A cleric in 1225,V,64v–65r. In *Rôles*,Isle,445, he was without title; he held from his wife's side a house in Fontaine, lands, and one *modius* of oats annually, altogether worth about 20 *l.t.*; the one rear-fief held from him was worth 5 *l.t.*, and he did not owe guard. In *Hommages*,Isle, 5389, he was liege for a house, lands, fields, *tonlieu*, and woods at Fontaine; he held the same in *Rôles B*,Isle,6483 as *messires* Jean, *chevalier*. Jean is an example of those fief holders who held their sole fief from their wives' families.

Rigny-le-Ferron

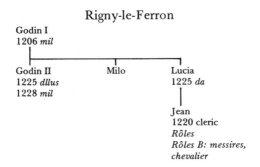

Godin I
1206 *mil*

Godin II   Milo   Lucia
1225 *dllus*   1225 *da*
1228 *mil*

Jean
1220 cleric
Rôles
Rôles B: messires,
chevalier

Romilly-sur-Seine

In 1104,Mol,250-52, Count Hugh of Troyes gave Molesme all his rights in the village of Romilly, effective after his death: arable, fields, woods, waters, *servi*, *ancillae*, justice, and all usages. Nothing further is known of Romilly until the appearance of the brothers Hugh and Eudes of Romilly in 1171.

HUGH I: Appeared with his brother in 1171,V,77v. He headed the Pont register in *Feoda*,Pont,1687; he also was listed in *Feoda*,Troyes,1888; Chantemerle,1290 and owed eight weeks guard; his brother did not appear and may have been underage. Hugh died by ca. 1200,*Feoda* II,2459, when Romilly was counted among the important Champagne fiefs and was held in guardianship by an agent of the count, Robert of Milly. By *Feoda* V,Troyes,3589, ca. 1210/14, Hugh's brother Eudes had taken charge.

Romilly-sur-Seine

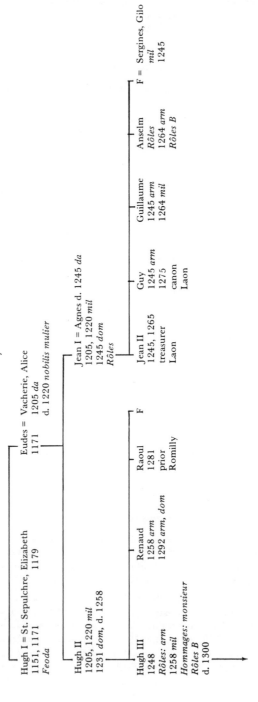

Hugh I = St. Sepulchre, Elizabeth
1151, 1171   1179
Feoda

Eudes = Vacherie, Alice
1171   1205 *da*
             d. 1220 *nobilis mulier*

Hugh II
1205, 1220 *mil*
1231 *dom*, d. 1258

Jean I = Agnes d. 1245 *da*
1205, 1220 *mil*
1245 *dom*
Rôles

Hugh III
1248
Rôles: arm
1258 *mil*
Hommages: monsieur
Rôles B
d. 1300

Renaud
1258 *arm*
1292 *arm, dom*

Raoul   F
1281
prior
Romilly

Jean II
1245, 1265
treasurer
Laon

Guy
1245 *arm*
1275
canon
Laon

Guillaume
1245 *arm*
1264 *mil*

Anselm
Rôles
1264 *arm*
Rôles B

F = Sergines, Gilo
    mil
    1245

HUGH II: Appeared with his younger brother Jean in 1205,S,20v. They were both knights on the death of their mother, *nobilis mulier*, in 1220,MLC,142, when they assigned 7 l. revenues (5 l. from the *péage* of Ervy and 40 s. *cens* from the mill at Vanne) to the abbey. Hugh did liege homage in *Feoda* VI,4057. In 1248,S,15v, he and his brother, *milites, domini,* disputed with the abbey over some common pastures. Hugh died in 1258,Arch.Aube,9 H 59, when his son executed his testament.

HUGH III: Took his father's lands while still an *armiger* in *Rôles,*Pont,785: the castle of Romilly, lands, and revenues, all worth 120 *l.t.* There were also eight rear-fief holders: his uncle Jean I for 60 *l.t.;* two holdings of 10 *l.t.*, one each at 3 *l.t.* and 5 *l.t.*; and three persons shared a mill. Those eight holdings were worth together 85 *l.t.* He owed four weeks guard each at Troyes and Pont. He was a *miles* by 1258. In *Hommages,*Méry,5495, he was *monsieur;* he also held a fief from his wife, the daughter of Lyon of Sézanne, knight. In *Rôles B,*Pont,6621, his holdings were described as: the castle and lands of Romilly; his wife's lands at Conflans; 5 *l.t. péage* at Cele; the fortified house of Lechières and one hundred *arpents* of land; plus eleven rear-fief holders, including his cousins Anselm and Guy. In 1281,Arch. Aube,9 H 116, he was called *miles et castellanus* and brother of Raoul, prior of Romilly. He made his will in 1300,LeClert,*Romilly, pièce justicative,* no. 1. Hugh's younger brother Renaud remained an *armiger* all his life. Hugh's son Hugh IV carried the line into the fourteenth century.

JEAN I: As younger brother of Hugh II, he developed a collateral line. He appeared in 1205 and was a knight in 1220. In *Feoda* VI,4223,4235, ca. 1222-43, he held from his brother fiefs of one hundred *jugera* of land, men, a house, and lands at Pars-lès-Romilly. In *Rôles,*Pont,785, he was a *dominus* and held in rear-fief from his brother 60 *l.t.* at Romilly and Pars.

JEAN II: He was probably the eldest son, but all his brothers held in rear-fief from their uncle Hugh II. Jean was the treasurer, and his brother Guy was a canon of the Church of Laon in 1245,Arch.Aube,9 H 64. He was still treasurer in *Hommages,* Provins,5652. His brother Guillaume was an *armiger* in 1245 and a knight in 1264,StU,162. Anselm was an *armiger* in 1264 and an *escuier* in *Hommages,* when he still shared property with Jean II (as they had in the *Rôles,*Provins,1376). In *Rôles B,*Pont,6621, *sires* Guy (the canon) and *armiger* Anselm held fiefs from their cousin Hugh III.

Rosières

The alod of Rosières was acquired by Montier-en-Der in 1140/50,MD,81, and the village seems to have remained under ecclesiastical control through the twelfth century; there is no mention of a fief there in the 1172 *Feoda.*

GUILLAUME I: First of the Rosières family to be mentioned. *Feoda* III,Troyes, 2537: liege for his house at Rosières and for his entire alod in Troyes (later identified as a merchant hall), which he now converted into a Champagne fief and received back as an "augmentation of fief" by doing homage. 1224,MLC,115: he, *dominus,* and his sister Elizabeth, *domina,* sold the 6 l. annual revenue from the house of a rich Troyen, which she held for a 2 d. *cens* from the abbey; she received 60 l.

THIBAUT I: Probably related to, most likely as brother of, Guillaume. His wife Auda seems to have been a peasant woman of the countess of Champagne, for the

Rosières

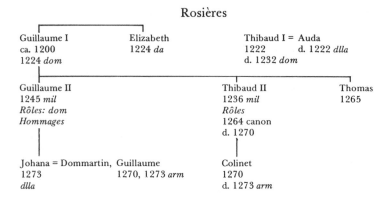

latter granted her a 10 l. dowry on her marriage to Thibaut; in 1222,H,21(Saint-Bernard), she was entitled *domicella* when she gave away 20 s. of that 10 l. assigned on the fairs of Troyes. Thibaut was not listed in any of the fragmentary *Feoda* registers of the early thirteenth century, but he was probably a knight of the count. 1232,MLC,16: he was *dilectus et fidelis* of the count; he sold all he had in the village of Jeugny: house with appurtenances, men, lands, fields, *cens*, customs, justice, *gîte*, fiefs, and other revenues to the abbey; the sale price was 265 l., which the *bailli* of Troyes had to collect because Thibaut died after the sale but before the payment (1232,MLC,174,178).

GUILLAUME II: It is difficult to decide when Guillaume II begins and his father ends; in 1245,P,242, he seems to be the son because he referred to his father's possession of tithe and other revenues. *Rôles*,Troyes,1104: *dominus*, he had four distinct fiefs: (1) at Rosières: a house, land, fields, justice, and men (this was probably worth the same 30 *l.t.* as his brother's share of the village); (2) at Troyes: houses next to the Temple, where the merchants of Douai sold their goods, and *cens*, worth together 30 *l.t.;* (3) a 30 *l.t.* rear-fief from the lady of Traînel, who entitled him *messires* in her letter in Old French to the *enquêteurs* (*Rôles*,1357); and (4) a 15 *l.t.* rear-fief at Cortevrot (*Rôles*,Provins,893). His total income was over 75 *l.t.*, and he did not owe guard. He sold several properties in this period, including a fief of a *terrage* and tithe worth eight *setiers* of grain and 7 s. *cens* annually, which was held from him by an *armiger* in *Rôles*,Troyes,1137. *Hommages*,Troyes,5321: there was now a fortified house at Rosières; his brother Thomas held in rear-fief from him.

THIBAUT II: 1236,N,78: *Miles*. In *Rôles*,Troyes,1104; Vertus,1183; Troyes, 1121, he held: (1) a 30 *l.t.* rear-fief from his brother (see above); (2) a house at Ecury, which he obtained from his wife's dowry: justice, ban, and men, for which he owed eighteen weeks guard; and (3) at Rosières, a house and use of the woods. In 1264,StU,17, he was canon of Saint-Etienne and sold his half of the hall in which the merchants of Douai sold their cloth to Saint-Urbain for 500 l.; the chapter was purchasing all land in that area for the construction of its church. He died by 1270,StS,269v–270v, when his son Colinet sold a fief to Saint-Etienne for 70 l. Colinet, *armiger*, died by 1273,L, pp. 166-67, so his cousin and her husband Guillaume, *armiger* of Dommartin, sold the *cens* on several houses in Troyes. Guillaume was involved in several commercial properties in Troyes, from which he collected rents; in 1264,StU,50, as *escuier*, he sold a 6 l. *cens* on the sales of a fish stall for 130 l.

Ruvigny

GAUTIER I: He was assigned the fief of Elias of Laubressel, whom he replaced in the *Feoda,*Troyes,1912 by ca. 1190.

GAUTIER II: *Domicellus* who with his wife gave the abbey "omnia bona sua tam mobilia quam immobilia" for their souls, plus the use of one-quarter of a vineyard during their lifetimes (1223,MLC,153); another charter identified their goods as lands, fields, houses, *cens,* and other revenues (1223,MLC,85). He died by 1245,MLC,80, when his wife gave up the vineyard and entered the abbey as a *conversa.* Two years later the vineyard, identified as having belonged to Gautier, *armiger,* was exchanged for one *mine* annually of grain from Larrivour (1247, MLC,138). The original Champagne fief of 1172 had been reassigned by ca. 1190, mostly alienated by 1223, and finally eliminated by 1245.

Saint-Maurice-aux-Riches-Hommes

HUGH I: 1198,*Documents* I, pp. 467–68: Pledge to Phillip Augustus for Count Thibaut III's homage for Champagne lands held from the king. 1198,Th,46v: witness to Thibaut's grant of a fief. 1208,L,p.119: with the praise of his wife Ameline, he gave the abbey three *mines* annually on his mill at Chantelou. He attended the 1212 baronial council but was not listed in any other register of fief holders. It would appear that he was a financier, perhaps creditor of Thibaut III; at least he had to have important financial assets to appear as pledge for the count.

HUGH II: 1224,V,30r: *Fidelis* of Thibaut IV. 1234,Arch.Aube,23 H 9: *miles,* with the assent of his wife, *domina* Margaret, he donated one-fourth of all his possessions in arable, fields, waters, vineyards, woods, men, and justice, plus an annual grain supply and rents, to support the newly founded (by rich Troyens) Notre-Dame-des-Prés; the grains and revenues were very small and from scattered sources, suggesting a piecemeal acquisition. He died by 1247,L, pp. 143-44, when his widow, *nobila* Margaret, dame of Savières, disputed some of the grain gift. In *Rôles,*Méry,584, she was identified as the widow of *dominus* Hugh, and she held: (1) her dowry at Savières of a mill, waters, vineyard, *cens,* justice, men, and lands, and (2) scattered rents, men, justice, lands, and vineyards in the *prévôtés* of Troyes, Nogent, and Villemaur; her entire income was 35 *l.t.,* and she did not owe guard.

GUY: Perhaps son of Hugh II and Margaret; was *messire* in *Hommages,*Méry,5491.

Saint-Phal

MILO: *Feoda,*Troyes, 1891: Liege and all-year guard. 1186,MLC,47,135: *miles,* one of the "discreet" arbitors of a dispute between Montier-le-Celle and Mores. Died by 1196,N,112, when his son Pierre approved what he, the *dominus* of Saint-Phal, had agreed upon with the abbey; the transaction was described in 1196(*vidimus* of 1263),Arch.Aube,22 H 1514 and in 1196(*vidimus* of 1309),Arch.Aube,22 H 1513: the abbey retained all justice within the villages of Fays-la-Chapelle and Chamoy; Milo had justice outside the villages and was required to act through the abbey's mayor for any problem inside.

PIERRE: Liege in *Feoda* III,Troyes,2519 and a "great fief" holder in *Feoda* IV, 2930, perhaps because of a newly built castle there, first mentioned in 1252.

ANDRE I AND EUDES: André (probably) or his brother Eudes was the *dominus* of Saint-Phal and liege to the count before all persons in *Feoda* VI,4266; both

Saint-Phal

Milo
Feoda: liege, all-year guard
1186 *mil*
d. 1196 *dom*

Pierre
1196

Eudes
1217 *dom*
d. 1240

André I
1228 *dom*

Guillaume
1239 canon Laon

Josbert
1236 *dom*
d. 1250

Jean = Pringy, Margaret *da*
1227 *dllus*
1234 *dom*
Rôles, Hommages: monsieur

André II
Rôles: arm, all-year guard
Hommages: monsieur
d. 1291

Margaret
Hommages: dlla

André III
1287 canon
d. 1302 deacon
St.-Pierre

Etienne
1291, 1297
canon St.-Pierre

Pierre
1310
prior Nesle

Isabel
1292–1301
abbess N-D-aux-Nonnains

Guy = Sailly
1302, 1318 *dom*

Etienne
1314

brothers were in the 1228 rear-ban (*Feoda* VI,4350,4351). Eudes was excommunicated for his support of the Brienne faction in 1217,*Histoire* V,1068. André I was a *miles* in 1228,MLC,70, but he must have died before 1252, for he certainly was not the *armiger* André in the *Rôles* (as Roserot says).

ANDRE II: Probably the son of André I. *Rôles*,Isle,461: *armiger* and owed all-year guard, as his grandfather did in 1172; but he also held the castle of Saint-Phal, mentioned here for the first time, as well as many other properties, and had fourteen rear-fief holders. In *Hommages*,Isle,5398, he was *monsieur;* he explained that he did not owe guard at Isle but had exchanged it against time at Saint-Phal, which he claimed was a prerogative of those living at Isle. He probably lived a long life, for his sons entered the Church: the eldest, Guy, however, married a Sailly (Joinville segment), and his own son Etienne appeared in 1314 as lord of Saint-Phal; his appearance in that petition was perhaps due more to the Joinville than to the Saint-Phal blood.

JOSBERT: 1236,MLC,75: *Miles, nobilis vir;* 1243,LP,174r: *miles, dominus,* sold one hundred and twenty *arpents* of woods at 12 s. per *arpent* to the count. *Rôles*,Troyes,1115: *dominus;* in fact, he was dead: his widow was listed for her dowry at Rivière-la-Corps: house, lands, men, and other revenues, worth 30 *l.t.*, and one rear-fief holder for 5 *l.t.;* she did not owe guard. These lands were her husband's and should have passed to his brother Jean, who claimed that he *debet tenere* Rivière as escheat from his brother (*Rôles*,Troyes,1112).

JEAN: 1227,HD,95v: *Domicellus,* sold four *jugera* of land for 8 l., and each *jugera* was liable for 18 d. *cens* and 4 d. *terrage* annually. 1234,HD,108r–v: *miles, dominus,* sold a *terrage* on fourteen *arpents* of land for 7 l. and a 4 d. *cens.* 1247,*Histoire* V,2816: he sold fifty *arpents* of woods to the count for 65 l. In 1252 he held four distinct fiefs (*Rôles*,Troyes,1112; Payns,755; Vitry,1218): (1) the escheat of his brother, worth 30 *l.t.* (see Josbert); (2) at Payns, 40 *l.t.* in fields, *cens,* and men, for which he owed four weeks guard; (3) at Pringy, the fortified house, worth 80 *l.t.*, no guard; and (4) at Savières, a rear-fief from André (II) of Saint-Phal. His total income was at least 120 *l.t.* (or 150 *l.t.* with his brother's property), for which he owed one month guard. In *Hommages*,Troyes,5332, he was *monsieur* and owed four weeks guard for possessions at Rivière and Payns.

Roserot placed Margaret of Pringy and Chamoy in 1247,*Histoire* V,2816 as the widow of Eudes, but Pringy is clearly listed under Jean in the *Rôles*, so she was probably his wife; her presence in the 1147 act was to approve of what Jean had sold. Her daughter Margaret of Saint-Phal appeared as *demiselle* in *Hommages*, Payns,5506 for 140 *l.t.* at Payns (equal to Jean's worth in the *Rôles*). In any case, the sizable fortune put together by Jean consisted of his own fief, a rear-fief, his brother's fief, and his wife's inheritance.

*Traînel

The Traînels were one of the most important and stable aristocratic families in the *bailliage,* and their history has been fully worked out (this table is simplified from Roserot). In the early twelfth century they possessed a sizable collection of lands between Troyes and Sens, the Seine and the Armançon, but in the next two centuries much of it was carved up as dowries for daughters and lordships for younger sons. They succeeded in projecting two collateral lines into the highest level (Marigny and Esternay), but they also lost two castellanies to the count of

Traînel

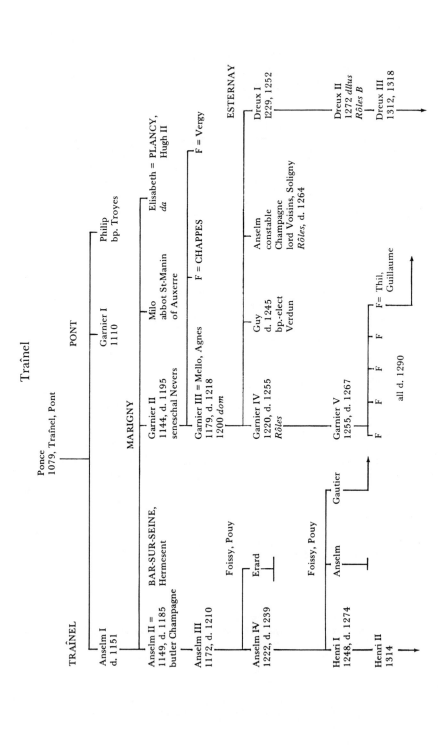

Ponce
1079, Traînel, Pont

TRAÎNEL

Anselm I
d. 1151

PONT

Garnier I
1110

Philip
bp. Troyes

MARIGNY

Anselm II =
1149, d. 1185
butler Champagne

BAR-SUR-SEINE,
Hermesent

Garnier II
1144, d. 1195
seneschal Nevers

Milo
abbot St-Manin
of Auxerre

Elisabeth = **PLANCY,**
da Hugh II

Anselm III
1172, d. 1210

Foissy, Pouy

Garnier III = Mello, Agnes
1179, d. 1218
1200 *dom*

F = CHAPPES

F = Vergy

Anselm IV
1222, d. 1239

Erard

Garnier IV
1220, d. 1255
Rôles

Guy
d. 1245
bp.-elect
Verdun

Anselm
constable
Champagne
lord Voisins, Soligny
Rôles, d. 1264

ESTERNAY

Dreux I
1229, 1252

Henri I
1248, d. 1274

Anselm

Gautier

Foissy, Pouy

Garnier V
1255, d. 1267

F   F   F   F   F= Thil,
Guillaume

all d. 1290

Dreux II
1272 *dllus*
Rôles B

Henri II
1314

Dreux III
1312, 1318

Champagne (see Pont-sur-Seine, and chapter V, n. 15, for Saint-Florentin). The main Traînel family had close relations with the count's family in the twelfth century and held several high offices, but in the thirteenth century little distinguished them except the steady succession of male heirs who maintained a "presence" in *bailliage* affairs and continued their line. Although they appear in numerous charters, few acts reflect their own personal affairs.

ANSELM I: Cofounder of Vauluisant as a *nobilis vir* in 1127,V,49r; witness under *de militibus* in 1136,M,31. There was already a *castrum* at Traînel (1110,Mol, 253–54).

ANSELM II: He and his brother Garnier II (of Marigny) were called *domini* of Traînel in 1151,L, pp. 92-93. He was a witness under *de militibus comitis* in 1161,M,47. He was *dominus* and liege in *Feoda*,Troyes,1887. But most important, he was butler of Champagne and confidant of Count Henry I.

ANSELM III: Probably the lord of Traînel listed in *Feoda* II,2452 as holder of a "great fief." In 1208 he sold the last Traînel possessions in Pont (see Pont-sur-Seine). He must have died by 1210/14 because his widow was *domina* of Traînel in *Feoda* V,Troyes,3580.

ANSELM IV: Listed in *Feoda* V,Troyes,3585, but he may still have been a minor because he did not attend the council of 1212. Knight banneret in 1214; he failed to attend the council of 1224, but his cousin Garnier IV of Marigny did. He died in the East in 1239; his widow, *dame* Sibile, wrote a letter in French to the count's *enquêteurs* in 1252 describing her thirteen rear-fief holders and their possessions worth 380 *l.t.* (*Rôles*,Traînel,1357). Their son, *monsieur* Henri, was listed in *Hommages*,Nogent,5541, but he died in 1274 and did not appear in the *Rôles* of 1275. His own son appeared in the 1314 petition.

*Vendeuvre-sur-Barse

The Vendeuvres first appeared in the late eleventh century; a *castrum* was mentioned in (1107),M,18.

HULDUIN I: 1121,M,23: He and his brother Roscelin, *domini*, gave Montiéramey all they had except *feodi laicorum* in three *villae*: justice, woods, fields, arable, and waters, and the abbey was allowed to acquire there anything it could from their fiefs. The charter states that the brothers feared Count Hugh of Troyes for having negotiated this sale, so the abbey gave them two excellent horses, 40 s. for each of their wives, and the village of Longpré, on the condition that they return it if they ever recovered their *castrum et honorem*, which Count Hugh held in mortgage for 300 l. Hulduin last appeared in 1159,R,53(ii).

ROSCELIN BRANCH: Roscelin's children appeared in 1121,M,23. Geoffroy I was liege in *Feoda*,Bar-sur-Aube,64; he died by 1206,M,233. His son André was *dominus* of Vendeuvre in (1200),M,161 but had died by 1202,M,200; his brother Geoffroy II was *domicellus* in 1202,M,194. Information on this branch is spotty and runs out in the early thirteenth century; although André seems to have merited the same *dominus* title as the descendants of the other Vendeuvre branch, the actual properties of this line appear to have been few and in no way comparable to those of the other branch.

LAURENT BRANCH: Laurent appeared in 1143,M,41; his brothers Hulduin II (1153,M,41) and Eudes I (1172,Mor,17) were younger. In *Feoda*,Troyes,1897, his

Vendeuvre-sur-Barse

Thibaud
(1075)

Hugh I
(1103, 1107)

Hulduin I
1121 *dom*

Roscelin
1121 *dom*

Geoffroy I
1121, 1163 *mil*
Feoda

Thibaud II
1121

André
1179
(1200) *dom*
d. 1202

Geoffroy II
1202 *dllus*
1206

Eudes I = Cirey
1172   Beatrice
d. 1198   1197
          1200 *da*

Euda = Broyes
1197   Hugh IV
d. 1234

Broyes

Hugh V

Eudes II
1233
sold 1244

Margaret = DURNAY,
1206, 1252 Gérard
Hommages d. 1248

Laurent = Oda
1143   *Feoda: da*
d. 1172

Bochard
1145, 1197 *mil*
1208

Hugh II = Helviz
1172   d. 1194
1193 *dom*

Hulduin III
1197
deacon
Langres

Elvide =   POUGY
1203, 1221 Manasses II

POUGY

Renaud II
1242, d. 1275

Milo
1249, 1269
sold 1268

Ermengart = Clefmont
1200, d. 1246 Simon III
da   1200 *dom*
              d. 1238

Eudes
1200, d. 1253
Rôles: 240 l.

Clefmont

Simon IV
1200, 1235 *dom*

Simon V
1265

Guillaume
1265 *dllus*
d. 1309

heir was liege and owed guard; his wife remarried by 1177,R,85(xxi), when Galeran was acting for his stepson.

BOCHARD: Probably the elder, since he was mentioned in 1153; he was probably the "heir" of Laurent in the *Feoda*. He was a *miles* in 1197,R,28(x); in 1208,M,248, he agreed with the abbot of Montiéramey that their men and women in three parishes could freely intermarry, with the children going to the lords of their fathers.

HUGH II: 1193,M,99: *Dominus;* he and his uncle Eudes I mortgaged for 25 l. the woods, fields, lands, *terrages,* and men of two villages, and the abbey would enjoy all revenues until redemption. His son Hulduin III was deacon of Langres (1197, M,123). On his death in ca. 1200, Hugh's estate was divided equally between his two daughters. Elvide, who married Manasses of Pougy, inherited the fortified house and part of the castle of Vendeuvre; her second son, Milo, was listed for it in *Rôles,*Troyes,1125 and in *Hommages,*Troyes,5338, but he sold it to the lord of Durnay in 1268 (see Durnay). Hugh's other duaghter, Ermegart, took her share of Vendeuvre to the Clefmont family. Simon III of Clefmont was in *Feoda,*Laferté,56; he was a *dominus* in 1200,M,48; in 1217,*Histoire* V,1068, he was excommunicated for his support of the Brienne faction. It was probably his son who mortgaged all he had at Laferté to the count for 72 l. in 1233,*Histoire* V,2290. Simon IV was a *dominus* in 1235,Mor,98. He held a 200 l. rent from the count, but not as a liegeman, and his castle of Clefmont was renderable at the count's need (1245, *Histoire,*2697). His brother Eudes was a *miles* (1246,Mor,107) and was listed in *Rôles,*Troyes,1123 as a *dominus* who held Vendeuvre, Longpré, and other properties, worth 240 *l.t.,* and had four rear-fief holders (his brother Simon carried on the main Clefmont line). Eudes's son Simon V was liege for one-eighth of the castellany of Vendeuvre, excepting the castle, of which half came from his mother's dowry (*Hommages,*Troyes,5349).

EUDES I BRANCH: Eudes was liege in the *Feoda,*Bar-sur-Aube,66; his wife, the *domina* of Cirey, held a house there (*Rôles,*Troyes,1899). He was *dominus* in 1190,M,87 and one of the *domini* of Vendeuvre in (1200),M,161. He died by ca. 1200, for his wife was liege of Vendeuvre in *Feoda* II,Vitry,2219.

HUGH IV OF BROYES: Married Eudes I's only daughter, Euda, who was listed in *Feoda,*Troyes,1899 for her mother's property. His mother-in-law had died by ca. 1204/10, for he was liege for Vendeuvre in *Feoda* III,Troyes,2529; he was also listed in *Feoda* IV,Bar-sur-Aube,2782 and in *Feoda* VI,Troyes,3654 (he is occasionally called Hugh Commarcis). The main Broyes property passed to Hugh V and his descendants, while the Vendeuvre acquisition was split between the younger Eudes II and his sister Margaret. In 1233,Mor,97, Eudes II was *dominus,* and in 1244,Ch,155, he sold his share of Vendeuvre to Gérard of Durnay (see Durnay), his brother-in-law, who already had Margaret's share. In *Hommages,*Troyes,5317, Margaret had half of the castle, the village, justice, and all men of the castellany of Vendeuvre.

The history of the Vendeuvres clearly illustrates the interplay of inheritance procedure, marriage alliance, and the consequence of the lack of male heirs. Hulduin left half of a very large estate in ca. 1170 to each of his two sons, but their direct lines soon consisted of only heiresses married to other distinguished families. Eudes I left only one daughter, and since her husband's family of Broyes was substantial in its own right, her inheritance passed to a younger son and a daughter, whose husband (Durnay) eventually purchased her brother's share of the Vendeuvre estate; her son acquired another quarter of the estate. Laurent's descendants also

Ville-sur-Arce

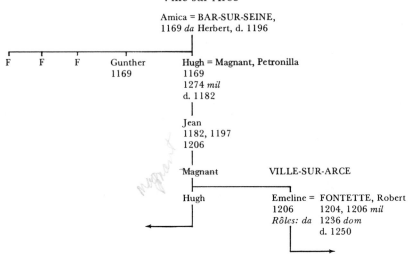

ended with two heiresses (the heir was already in the Church), both of whom made favorable marriages; each passed her one-fourth share of Vendeuvre to younger sons. The dismemberment process was halted when the Durnays attempted to reconstitute the estate; although they failed to put the original estate together, they did manage to control most of the Vendeuvre income.

*Villemaur-sur-Vanne

Roserot's genealogy is the best possible, although it is not complete. The Villemaur family had several concurrent branches in the twelfth century, and often they failed to use the Villemaur name. They may have been independent lords originally, but by 1143 Villemaur was in the county of Troyes and in the count's direct domain. The Villemaur family did not continue as a prominent one to the thirteenth century. Manasses I was a *dominus* in the early twelfth century; his sons Eudes (*vir nobilis*) and Dreux were mentioned in 1127,V,49r. Manasses II was listed by his first name only at the head of the Villemaur register of the *Feoda;* his widow was *domina* of Villemaur in his place in ca. 1200 in *Feoda* II,Villemaur,2208: a notation indicates that she held only a house there. She held the *péage* there in 1197,P,97. It was probably a direct descendant Erard, *dominus* of Villemaur, who in 1219,Th,216v–217r exchanged all his possessions in that town (justice, men, oven, mill, customs, and other revenues) in return for possessions elsewhere from the countess. This appears to be similar to the cases in which the Pont (Traînel) and Ervy families surrendered what remained in their former castellanies to the countess in 1208 and 1214, respectively.

Ville-sur-Arce

It is not clear whether Ville-sur-Arce was a segmentary line of the counts of Bar-sur-Seine originating with Herbert of Bar-sur-Seine or whether it was a separate line that Herbert acquired by marriage; in any case, as younger son of the Bar-sur-Seine family Herbert became head of the Ville-sur-Arce line. His wife was *domina* when he died in 1169,Mor,15. Their son Hugh (Goriard) was mentioned in 1169, was listed in *Feoda,*Laferté,21 for two months guard, and was a *miles* in 1174,Mor,19. Hugh married Petronilla, heiress of neighboring Magnant, and died by 1182,Mor,26. His own son Jean (Goriard), variously "of Ville-sur-Arce" and "of Magnant," inherited both properties. In 1197,Arch.Aube,27 H 3, he put one of his daughters into Foissy as a nun. His son inherited Magnant, and his daughter took Ville-sur-Arce to her husband, Robert of Fontette, whom she had married by 1206,Mor,56 (see Fontette for the subsequent history of Ville-sur-Arce).

Vaubercey

Vaubercey probably is today in Blaincourt (Roserot).

HUGH: A *miles* in (1166),BF,3. He was probably the *ille* of Wauberce who was liege and owed guard in *Feoda,*Bar-sur-Aube,122. He was in *Feoda* III,Wassy,2692 owing eight weeks guard, but he was replaced by ca.1190 by his son Elebaud.

ELEBAUD: He owed eight weeks guard in *Feoda,*Vitry,505. In 1173,R,26(iii), he converted all that he had in plain lands and woods into a six *modii* (seventy two *setiers) annone* from the abbey. In *Feoda* III,Wassy,2580, he owed eight weeks guard for sixty four *setiers* of grain. In 1201,R,27(vi), he gave up one *modius* for burial privileges. In 1209,R,26(v), his son Jean sold another *modius* for 35 l. for expenses for the Albigensian Crusade; another three *modii* were held from him by Herbert of Laferté (in rear-fief, perhaps as dowry). Thus, the count's fief of 1172 was converted into grain revenues in 1173 and was then alienated for burial rights, crusading expenses, and as a rear-fief by 1209, when Jean left four minor children to go south to fight; either one *modius* (of the original six in 1172) or only four *setiers* (of the sixty four in ca. 1200) remained to his family.

NOTES

Abbreviations and the form of documentation in the notes are described in the List of Abbreviations.

I. Introduction

1. An overview is given by René Crozet, *Histoire de Champagne*, 2d ed. (Paris, 1933). The best introduction to the medieval period is Jean Longnon's chapter "La Champagne," in *Histoire des institutions françaises au mogen âge*. I. *Institutions seigneuriales*, eds. F. Lot and R. Fawtier (Paris, 1957). However, the standard work is still Henri d'Arbois de Jubainville, *Histoire des ducs et des comtes de Champagne*, 7 vols. (Paris, 1859–69). The most recent presentation of the twelfth century is John F. Benton, "The Court of Champagne under Henry the Liberal and Countess Marie" (Ph.D. diss., Princeton University, 1959), of which part appears as "The Court of Champagne as a Literary Center" in *Speculum* 36 (1961): 551–91. A brief history of the diocese of Troyes within the general ecclesiastical history of Champagne is Joseph Roserot de Melin, *Le diocèse de Troyes des origines à nos jours (IIIe siècle-1955)* (Troyes, 1957).

2. All that is known about the counts of Troyes from the ninth to the mid-tenth century, including a plausible genealogy, is in Georges Duhem, "Les comtes de Troyes au début du Xe siècle," *Annuaire de l'Aube*, 1932, pp. 17–24. See also the genealogical table of counts from the mid-tenth century in Michel Bur, "Remarques sur les plus anciens documents concernant les foires de Champagne," in *Les Villes*, Publications de l'Université de Reims, Faculté des Lettres et Sciences Humaines, no. 3 (Reims, 1972), p. 56.

3. Brief histories of the Vermandois and Blois houses are in Arbois de Jubainville, *Histoire*, I, books 3–4. The problem of the transfer of the county of Troyes from the last local count (Richard, 926) to the Vermandois house (Robert I, 956) has been reworked by Karl F. Werner, in "Untersuchungen zur Frühzeit des französischen Fürstentums (9.–10. Jahrhundert)," *Die Welt als Geschichte* 20 (1960): 107–11.

4. Jean Richard, *Les ducs de Bourgogne et la formation du duché du XIe au XIVe siècle* (Paris, 1954), pp. 30–31. The charter of 1143 (Archives Côte d'Or, Chambre des Comtes de Dijon, Cartulaire B.10432, fol.67, printed in *Documents* I, p. 466) refers only to the *Comitatus Trecarum* and other lands for which the count did homage, but the undated charter which immediately follows it lists all the places that the count held from the duke. Richard concludes that after the localities named in both charters are canceled, those left in the undated charter constituted the "county of Troyes" in the act of 1143. It is not clear when the duke reestablished his control over the county, but he retained it throughout the twelfth and thirteenth centuries.

5. The *Livre des hommages* of 1264–65; see also below and nn. 6 and 20.

6. For the *bailliage* of Troyes, the *Livre des hommages* contains nine castellany registers; the register for Ervy, which should have been included, is probably lost. The *Rôles des fiefs* ten years later do contain a register for Ervy in the *bailliage* (see also nn. 20 and 21). The main differences between the *bailliage* of Troyes in 1265 and the modern *département* of Aube are:

1) The *bailliage* included lands to the south and west of Saint-Florentin, including the viscounty of Joigny and the lordships of Champlost and Venizy, areas which are in the present-day *département* of Yonne. I have been unable to consult the archives of Yonne (especially for genealogies), but the fief holders located there and

212

listed in the Saint-Florentin registers of the printed administrative surveys have been included in the quantitative analyses of chap. IV.

2) In the *Rôles des fiefs* of 1275 the *bailliage* contained the nine castellanies already included in the *Livre des hommages* and two additional ones: Ervy, which was certainly in the *bailliage* in 1265 (see above), and Provins, which lacks both geographical and historical affinities with the Troyes-centered area and which has been excluded here.

7. The chronicle of Aubri of Trois-Fontaines, *Chronica*, in *Monumenta Germaniae Historica, Scriptores* XXIII, ed. Paul Scheffer-Boichorst (Hanover, 1874), contains few references to strictly local events in the *bailliage*. The nature of this study precludes any consideration of purely literary works.

8. See chap. II, n. 1.

9. This is true for nothern Burgundy, where the increased documentation of the twelfth century was due to the spread of Cistercian houses and to the increase in episcopal and collegial cartularies, but it contrasts with southern Burgundy, where the number of charters is slight at this time; see Richard, *Les ducs de Bourgogne*, p. xxviii.

10. Such an environment is ably recreated in several papers in *Bernard de Clairvaux*, Commission d'histoire de l'ordre de Cîteaux, III (Paris, 1953): Jean Richard, "Le milieu familial," on geography and society in eleventh-century northern Burgundy (pp. 3—15); and Robert Fossier, "Le plateau de Langres et la fondation de Clairvaux" (pp.67—75) and "L'installation et les premières années de Clairvaux" (pp. 77—93).

11. The involvement of the Cistercian houses in the Forest of Othe (southwest of Troyes) in clearing land and supplying wood for village construction and in exploiting iron deposits is discussed by Heinrich Rubner, *Untersuchungen zur Forstverfassung des Mittelalterlichen Frankreich* (Wiesbaden, 1965), pp. 26—35.

12. The numerous charters of Clairvaux in the archives of Aube have been generally excluded because most of those acts concern localities and families just beyond the *bailliage*. The Clairvaux collection, insofar as it concerns the development of the abbey, has been analyzed in several articles by Fossier (see n. 10).

13. The only cartularies composed by the count's scribes—the "Cartulaire de Blanche," the "Cartulaire de Thou," the "Liber pontificum," and the "Liber principum"—were concerned mainly with Thibaut IV's minority: they are records of homages received, negotiations about loyalties, and copies of letters from powerful lords, mostly prelates, who supported Blanche and her son.

14. The "Grand Cartulaire" of the town of Troyes is a manuscript of 1377; the "Petit Cartulaire" dates from the fifteenth century.

15. Printed in Auguste Longnon, ed., *Documents relatifs au comté de Champagne et de Brie (1172—1361)*, 3 vols. (Paris, 1901—14), I, *Les fiefs*; a discussion of the manuscripts and dates is on pp. xi—xix. The text of the *Feoda* printed here was reconstructed by Longnon from two manuscripts: ms. 2227 of the Bibliothèque de Troyes, and ms. P 1114 of the Archives Nationales, a defective French version that he originally printed as the "Livre des vassaux du comté de Champagne et de Brie," in volume 7 of Arbois de Jubainville, *Histoire*.

16. The foundation charter of 1157 is in Elizabeth Chapin, *Les villes de foires de Champagne* (Paris, 1937), appendix 1. Another generous gift is in 1173,StS,32v. Countess Marie referred to the revenues which Henry I had given to the chapter for *custodibus thesauri* (1186,StS,56v).

17. Text in *Documents* I, p. xiii, n. 2. The young countess was in complete ignorance of Champagne administrative affairs and so sought the advice of the two former officials who wrote: "Intimamus vobis preterea quod scripta feodorum vestrorum sunt in ecclesia Sancti Stephani Trecarum . . . ad tradendum vero scripta feodorum in ecclesia Beati Stephani, ego Milo Brebanus interfui, et comes Henricus secum tulit exemplarium ultra mare." The letter is undated, and Jean Longnon, *Recherches sur la vie de Geoffroy de Villehardouin* (Paris, 1939), p. 98, places it

before 1209. It seems incredible that Blanche could have remained in ignorance of such a basic document for eight years (1201–8). A date closer to 1201 would be more reasonable: if Geoffroy of Villehardouin wrote the letter in 1205, the first year in which he appeared as "marshal of Romania," that would allow a four-year hiatus. In either case, the statement suggests that there may have been a conspiracy to keep the countess unaware of the existence or whereabouts of the document, proof again of the power of a document which could not be disputed by later oral testimony.

18. They are printed as *Feoda* I–VII in *Documents* I.

19. Auguste Longnon, ed., *Rôles des fiefs du comté de Champagne sous le règne de Thibaut le Chansonnier (1249–52)* (Paris, 1877). A discussion of the manuscripts and their dates is in *Documents* I, pp. xxiii–xxviii. See also chap. IV, n. 20, for an example of the increasing precision of the registers.

20. "Livre des hommages faits à Thibaut V," in *Documents* I. The original Latin register for Villemaur is extant (Arch.Aube,Laisse E 467); the other castellany registers survive in a French copy of 1326.

21. "Rôles des fiefs rédigés sous la régence de Blanche d'Artois," in *Documents* I. Blanche was the widow of Count Henry III (d. 1274); in 1275 she married Edmond of Lancaster, who held the county in custody for her daughter Jeanne until 1284. The original document survives in the Archives Nationales, J 196 no. 43. Longnon concluded that it was drawn up from September 1274 to December 1275.

22. Printed in *Documents* I.

23. Ibid.

24. P. Portejoie, ed., *L'ancien coutumier de Champagne (XIIIe siècle)*, (Poitiers, 1956); a discussion of the composition and dating is found on pp. 7–11. However, the entire picture of the Jours of Troyes in the late thirteenth century has been revised: there was no such institution as a "court of barons" that rendered judgments independently of the official Jours of Troyes; see John F. Benton, "Philip the Fair and the Jours of Troyes," *Studies in Medieval and Renaissance History* 6 (1969): 281–302.

II. The Peasantry and Rural Communities

1. The lack of charters makes impossible a close study of peasant conditions before the twelfth century. The approximately one hundred extant acts before 1100 contain little beyond the formalized references to *villa* components. Only the abbey of Montier-en-Der, just outside the *bailliage*, possesses the documents of which a special study would produce significant results on the earlier period.

2. (After 1080),Mol,227–28. A glance at any early charter of Molesme or Montier-en-Der shows how similar the phrasing is; only the right of justice was a recent addition to the old formulas.

3. A few examples: 1101,Mol,242–43; 1103,Mol,244–45; 1115,Mol,261: *servi* and *ancillae* in a *villa* were considered *in dominicatu*, no matter where they resided.

4. Several early-twelfth-century charters seem to equate the terms; for example, in (1111),M,18: "si homines Sancti Petri [Montiéramey] uxorem ex ancillis comitis acceperint, infantes ipsorum invicem partiantur; et si servus comitis ancillam Sancti Petri duxerit, similiter partiantur." The scribes may have themselves confused the terms in the transitional period of the early twelfth century, when both *homines* and *servi* were current.

5. There were, of course, a few aberrants. For example, there was a reference to an *ancilla* as late as 1190,StP,56: the bishop's *prévôt*'s son married an *ancilla* of the chapter (who was the stepdaughter of a *civis* of Troyes). Also in 1177 (see chap. III, n. 8) there were *famuli et ancillae* at Montiéramey. These seem to have been servants or domestics in the service of great households; they were mentioned in reference to intermarriages, not to tenure or tenurial obligations. The other few references to the older social categories were clearly cases in which scribes copied the old formulas, as in 1177,StP,29, a royal confirmation of all possessions,

including *servis et ancillis,* in the old manner (see above, nn. 2, 3). There are a few references to *liberi,* as in (1100),StL,3, but it would be impossible to read into them anything more than antiquarian usage. *Rusticus* occurs occasionally to mean "peasant": 1146,P,52: the lord of Nogent allowed the abbey to acquire donations from *rustici* who held lands from him; 1154,*Histoire* III, pp. 443—44; 1203,R,55(xx): the count of Brienne referred to his *rusticus;* 1210,CB,45r—v: *rustici* of the countess of Champagne; *Rôles,*Isle,468: *rustici* held lands from a fief holder. The term *villanus* occurs seldom, as in (1089),StL,2; also in 1200 (see n. 6). It should also be noted that in Montier-en-Der's ninth-century *polyptique,* 732 of the 811 (90 percent) manses on its 22 domains were of free status; text in Charles Lalore, ed., *Le polyptique de l'abbaye de Montier-en-Der* (Paris, 1878).

6. 1200,Mor,48. The Champagne administrative surveys and a very few charters also use *homo* and *homo ligius* in the sense of fief holder; for example, in (1189),M,82 the lord of Chappes referred to his *homo,* Thibaut of Fresnay, *miles.* When referring to peasants and used without qualification, the term occurred only in the plural as *homines,* not in its singular form. I have translated it throughout as "men" or "peasants," although its actual significance did change: originally it included all inhabitants, irrespective of the size of the community (hamlet or town) and of the privileges bestowed by the lord; but after the community franchises, and especially the commune grants of 1230—31, it most properly referred to those residing outside the larger towns who had not received franchises (see chap. III).

7. 1200,*Documents* I, p. 469; 1225,B,25: "exceptis feodis militum et justicia feodorum, et exceptis hominibus meis de corpore cum rebus mobilis et hereditatibus eorum."

8. 1234,StP,196.

9. 1226,Ch,128.

10. 1216,StS,132r—v; 1208,M,245: a man, "sacramento prestito, fecerat fidelitatem [to the abbot], . . . tanquam homo proprius ecclesie."

11. 1220,V,64v.

12. 1171,O,lv—2r; 1233,Mol,330—33. (see also n. 79); other examples from the franchised communities are in chap. III.

13. 1221,M,315.

14. 1225,M,336: "sub poteste, dominio, justitia, et jurisdictione," and he owed an annual maximum of 30 s. *abonationia* (commuted *taille;* see below).

15. 1238,M,373: a woman swore "fidelitatem . . . [as a] femina de corpore et de capite" and paid her *taille;* 1251,StS,235v—236r: the wife of a tavernkeeper "asserted" that she was *de corpore* of Saint-Etienne and not of another lord; 1264,B,69: a woman recognized an *armiger* as her lord and surrendered all her goods to him in what appears to be a case of an unsustained appeal for justice over his head to his overlord; she lost all her possessions (see n. 152).

16. There are examples of men becoming "legitimate" or "legal" for certain responsibilities: 1242/62,MLC,50: two *legitimi homines* swore fidelity to representatives of two churches that they would collect a disputed tithe on wine; 1165, Mor,9: the chaplain and two "legal" men of Landreville were to serve official notice whenever the abbey's animals trespassed on certain pastures.

17. The community regulations could, of course, require oath-taking on other occasions, such as when the persons of officials or lords changed, as in the example from 1250 cited in n. 132. See also chap. III, n. 48, for the men of Courlon-sur-Yonne, who were required to take an annual oath.

18. 1145,StL,13; 1192,M,95: several men denied the *dominium et homagium* of the abbey and fled first to the canons of Saint-Pierre, then to the count of Champagne; 1256,StS,240v—241r: the chapter claimed the children and property of a man, *ratione domini.*

19. 1114,StL,5: the lord of Chappes surrendered *omne dominium* over lands, woods, and persons to the abbey; 1196,O,14v: "homines de corpore . . . qui homines de potesta vocantur"; see also nn. 14 and 18.

20. 1110,Mol,253—54: customs ran *per dominatum castrorum* of Traînel and

Pont-sur-Seine; (1218),M,295: the count of Bar-sur-Seine guaranteed the safe travel of horses and wagons to Montiéramey and "omnes alias qui sub dominio et potestate mea consistunt"; 1223,V,36v: the count of Brienne gave the abbey use of all woods and lands under his *dominio et potestate;* 1236,M,366: certain lands and houses were "in villa, finagio, et dominio [of Fravaux]."

21. 1173,R,4(xii): certain property "tam de dominio quam de feodo"; 1201,M,178: a knight sold all that he possessed "tam in feodo quam in dominio" (the same phrase in 1201,MLC,168); 1220,R,59(xx): Hugh of Broyes gave up what he possessed in a certain place in *cens, terrage,* and tithe, and he also gave up whatever he had in his *dominio* except fiefs; 1263,P,269: Dreux of Traînel approved the sale of lands, to be free "ab omni jure feodi sive domini"; 1277,S,21v: Hugh III of Romilly-sur-Seine permitted Sellières to acquire property in Romilly village and in all his "*dominio,* justice, fiefs, rear-fiefs, and *cens.*"

22. 1199,M,147: a dispute over the *justicia et dominio* of Clérey between the abbey and the *domini* of the place resulted in the abbey's acquisition of one-third of the justice; 1172,M,62: the count of Champagne gave Saint-Jean-en-Chastel "all justice and *potestate*" over its property within the walls of Troyes; 1194,M,104: Geoffroy Furnerius gave the abbey all he possessed *in potestatibus* in two villages "tam in hominibus quam in justiciis, proventibus, et terras"; 1204,StP,107: Henri of Chennegy gave up all the justice, customs, men, and *potestate* in three villages for 90 l. and an annual 6 *modii* of grain; 1246,StS,61r–v: the lord of Marigny approved the sale of wheat from a mill in his "land, justice, and *dominio*"; 1264,P,267: half a mill, with *jure dominio et justitia,* was given the abbey. The count's scribes distinguished carefully between *dominium* (rights over persons and property) and *jurisdictionis* (control of justice).

23. 1203,M,207: "in his omnibus non habebit abbas dominium plus quam ego, nec ego plus quam abbas"; similarly in the *pariage* of Pargues, 1209,M,260, the countess declared that "nec huis habebo potestatem vel dominium plusquam abbas, nec abbas plus quam ego." A similar definition of *dominium* as the total collection of rights over property is contained in the statement by the count's scribes in the *Extenta* for a village on the Champagne domain in which the count had no rights at all (text is in chap. III, n. 15).

24. 1170,StL,43.

25. 1176,StL,52; 1208,M,244: "quos etiam tenebat de alodio suo sine particione alicuijus"; 1184,L, p. 107: the countess gave the abbey a certain Gérard, who had been purchased by young Count Henry (I) for 18 l.; 1206,StL,126: a man and his heirs were sold by the lady of Pougy for a 20 s. rent; 1201,StP,100: the lord of Traînel gave up his claim to a family, which the abbey also claimed, for a 4 l. 10 s. rent at each fair of Marigny; 1223,B,22: the lord of Joigny gave "Belinum hominem suum, uxorem ejus, et heredes eorum, et totum tenementum illorum."

26. 1187, in Vallet de Viriville, *Les archives historiques du département de l'Aube* (Troyes, 1841), p. 375, n. C: the men of Onjon paid the count 30 l. so that " . . . eos nulli dabo nec a manu mea eos alienabo."

27. 1225,StP,173: a man and his wife were the object of a dispute between the count and the chapter, each of whom claimed the man as a *homo*; as a result of the conflict the man fled, and now the count freed him from all obligations, including military service, but the man's children would be shared by both lords; 1196,O,14v: *exactiones* were defined as *mainmorte* and marriage restriction.

28. 1290,B,86.

29. In the first half of the twelfth century it seems that justice was associated only with persons and that a lord's claim to justice followed them; 1102/1125, Mol,244: "omnes predicte villa [Essoyes] habitores, ipsius comitis homines vel ejus justicie subjecti"; 1113,M,18: the count granted the abbey justice over three villages, so that if the abbey's men committed crimes against the count's men, the latter would seek justice from the abbot or his *prévôt;* 1161,StL,32: the count exempted the abbey's men living "in justicia mea in civitate et potestatem Trecensi" from his administrative officials, except for major crimes (assault, rape,

murder); 1173,StS,32v: the count granted the chapter "omnem iustitiam in hominibus vestris qui vobis censum debent ubicumque sint." But it seems that in the
second half of the twelfth century there was a greater appreciation for the conflict
caused by the physical mobility of persons between tenurial and personal justice,
and an effort was made to be explicit in such claims: 1177,StL,56: the count of
Brienne granted the justice of four manses which owed *cens*; 1187,StS,89r–92r: a
papal confirmation of all justice "over men and lands which owe you *cens*,
wherever those men may be"; 1207,MLC,7: a knight had justice over his men and
their lands that owed him *cens* and customs, but all other men in the village
(Ruvigny) were in the abbey's justice. See also references in n. 22.

30. See below and chap. III for the control of justice in communities.

31. 1153,*Histoire* III, pp. 442–43; 1158,StL,29 (full quotation is in n. 72).

32. 1238,M,373; 1260,Arch.Aube,22 H 1451: "femina erat ut dicitur de corpore" and owed 12 d. annually on All Saints' Day.

33. On occasion it was collected in kind: 1229,Mol,318: a knight collected 6
modii of wine from a village *in tallia*. In a few cases *taille* was used in the sense of
general taxation: 1177,StP,29: the count collected 15 *modii* of grain for "safeguard" from the abbey's village of les Grandes-Chapelles—the abbey's agents collected the *tallia*, although the marshal of Troyes could be present, and the count
promised not to collect any other *talliam* or *consuetudines*, although he retained
military service; 1181,StP,34: the count agreed not to take more than 200 l. from
the men of the bishop of Troyes when the see was vacant; 1172,M,63: the count
would not " . . . gistium in eadem villa [Fravaux] accipimus vel pro gistio villam
illam talliabimus"; 1187,*Histoire* III, p. 479: the "*tailles* of *gîte* and safeguard"
were owed by all residents of Luyères who did not possess *liberi cartas*;
1205,Th,240r: Hugh of Broyes promised that his *prévôt* would take a *tallia* on his
mother's lands if her ordinary income were not sufficient to pay her creditors 360 l.
annually for four years. Finally, in 1218,M,294, Erard of Chacenay, departing for
the East, promised not to exact a "generalem etiam talliam in hominibus vel feminis
[of the abbey] in chastellaria mea manentibus," but he still expected it from
certain villages on four occasions: the knighting of his son, the marriage of his
daughter, his ransom in war, and *auxilium* for an expedition to Jerusalem. The Jews
were subject to a special *taille*, a large, all-purpose tax; for example, in 1222,
Th,317r, one man and his son paid 160 l. for their *taille*.

34. 1200,LP,169v. There are few references to arbitrary *taille* by name:
1175,O,2v–3r: the abbey and the count shared the village of Puits, in which women
were taxed a yearly maximum of 5 s., while men could be taxed *per arbitrario
talliam* by their respective lords (see n. 59 for how their children of mixed
marriages were divided); 1205,CB,138v–141r: "homo suus de capite et de corpore
et quod ipse ad voluntatem suam talliabat eum." The references to general taxation
(n. 33) probably meant arbitrary *taille*.

35. 1191,StL,106: if she died before compensation was made, her children
would be shared by both lords; see below for the marriage arrangements.

36. For *taille* transferred with the woman, see 1231,StS,118r–v; retained by
original lord, 1194,StS,116r and 1229,StS,168v; shared by both lords, 1219,N,139;
1237,StS,165r; and 1263,StS,25r–v: the chapter cont nued to receive 10 s. annually for *taille* from its woman who had married a tow..man of Troyes.

37. 1225,M,336 (see above, n. 14).

38. *Extenta*,Troyes: "sunt ibi quidam homines abonati per cartas dominorum
[counts of Champagne], quidam ad vitam, quidam perpetuo." The total payments
from these in the castellany of Troyes were only 70 l. in 1276/78, compared with
the farm of justice alone of 611 l.

39. 1211,Mol,301–2. The commutation of *taille* did not include, the abbey was
careful to specify, the other obligations of *mainmorte, corvées, cens, terrage*, tithes,
and all other revenues, nor did it include justice or safeguard; however, the men
were free from marriage restrictions (see quotation in n. 53). *Extenta*, Rumilly-lès-
Vaudes: each man owed 3 s. for *abonament* plus 3 s. per draft animal.

40. 1233,Mol,330–33. Revenues from *tailles* and commuted *tailles* were treated as a single type of revenue: three knight brothers sold their "tallias, abonamenta et redditus hominum suorum" in their village, saving only *cens* and justice from them (1231,Mol,325); the lord of Traînel transferred a 20 s. gift assigned on a *cens* and customs to revenue "juramentorum seu talliarum hominum meorum" (1263,P,270).

41. See chap. III for analysis of the community franchises. Another tax, the *chevagium*, is often confused with *taille*, but it was quite different. The few examples of it in the *bailliage* are from the period 1189–1222 and involve payments to Benedictine houses. 1189,StL,99: the abbey collected a lifetime *chevagium* from any of its men settling in certain villages; 1200,LP,169v: the bishop of Troyes had 4 d. in *chevage* from three men who owed Philip of Assenay *tailles* of 12 s., 9 s., and 6 s; 1202,StL,134: the abbey's rights in certain villages were listed as *terrage*, tithe, customs, *cens*, and *chevagis hominum*; 1216,M,285: Montiéramey gave up "omnia chevagia hominum et feminarum nostrarum et heredum suorum" in two villages to the lord of Jaucourt, who in return allowed his men to migrate from his village to settle in the abbey's two villages; 1222,M,323: in the *pariage* over four villages on the Barbuise River, Montiéramey collected a 4 d. annual *chevage* on each house lot (*masnagium*), while the lord of Plancy retained justice, military and plowing services, and *tailles* (see also below, Communities). Since some men paid both *taille* and *chevage* to different lords, it would appear that the latter was rather a hearth rent than a personal tax.

42. *Extenta,* Bar-sur-Seine: except for members of the commune of Bar, the count had "mainmorte sur ceux où il prant taille"; 1279,Arch.Aube,23 H 184: Notre-Dame-des-Prés claimed that a certain woman "erat femina de capite et de corpore et de manumortua."

43. *Extenta,* Troyes: the count's scribes furnished a definition: the count had "quodam jus sive deverium quod vocatur manus mortua, racione cujus capit dominus [the count] omnia bona hominum decedencium sine liberis, vel sine cognatis vel agnatis eisdem debentibus succedere, et omnia bona hominum male natorum decedencium."

44. 1243,L, pp. 140–41: the custom of the castellany of Villemaur was defined as: "quando aliquis tenens ouchiam aliquam ad costumam decedit sine herede de corpore suo manente cum eo, ouchia revertitur ad dominum de quo dicta costuma movet." Josbert had married the sole heiress and claimed all her father's property, half as his marriage share, half as escheat; he had to return the half of escheat. Similarly, in 1294,L, pp. 174–75, the abbey allowed a man to hold a plot of land for 8 d. *cens*, on the condition that if he died without children, it would revert to the abbey.

45. 1222,M,323; 1218,Mol,307–8: a tenant of the lord of Villair who had moved to Molesme was not permitted to inherit at Villair.

46. The first mention was in 1194,StP,69, in which *manus mortua* was defined as a *consuetudo* (see full quotation in n. 50, below). Although the term had not been employed earlier, the restriction was common. An agreement in 1139,MD,77 provided that "si homines monachorum prefate ecclesie mortui fuerint in mea [the count's] terra vel in mea justicia sine herede ac sine pare, qui non sit de eodem dominio, pecuniam hominis mortui vel mulieris haberunt monachi."

47. 1219,N,22: two children and a son-in-law each received one-third; the phrasing of the agreement suggests that the abbey retained the major share of the property and bought off the children's claim at a small fraction of the total value.

48. 1223,N,52.

49. 1238,StL,259(extract): the abbey claimed both the land and the movables by reason of *excasure*; 1263,StS,40v–41r: the chapter bought off a woman's claim to her mother's and uncle's properties (both belonged to the chapter) for 40 s. and 20 l. respectively.

50. 1194,StP,69: the *consuetudo* called *manus mortua* was lifted " . . . ita quod omnes eorum [its men living in the suburb of Troyes] possessiones in edificiis et

tenementis et omnibus aliis mobilibus ubicumque fuerint, ad heredes propinquores libere et sine contradictione deveniant, si homines fuerint ecclesie nostre et manentes infra dictam banleugam."

51. 1198,Ch,68; the same exemption was extended to his men of Essoyes, Merrey-sur-Arce, and Neuville-sur-Seine in 1210 (the text is in Auguste Petel, *Essoyes. Histoire et statistique avec pièces justicatives inédites* [Troyes, 1893], p. 508); 1244,StP,204: the bishop of Troyes sold a *mainmorte* exemption to his men there; 1228,StS,139r–v: the chapter abolished *mainmorte* and escheat in the village of Giffaumont.

52. For example, Simon of Clefmont prohibited Mores from acquiring lands, fields, and vineyards and other immovables (*hereditate*) from his own men, but he did allow the acquisition of movables (1200,Mor,48); 1225,M,343: the abbey was permitted to have the movables of its deceased men who held lands from the lord of Charmont, and the latter retained their lands. In the countryside there was a sharp difference between land and immovables on the one hand and personal possessions and movables on the other; even the *Coutumier* deals with the distinction at length when it involved *mainmorte* claims. In urban areas, where there was more wealth invested in movables, the count's franchises devised a more efficient system of taxation (see chap. III).

53. There are few references to *formariage* as such: 1211,Mol,301–2: "homines de Villery possint maritare filias suas ibi voluerint, sine formaritagio inde persolvendo" (see also n. 39 for their *taille* commutation); 1216,N,33; 1226,StS,214r: the lady of Charmont agreed not to claim "escheat or *formariage*" from the men of Saint-Etienne and Saint-Loup living under her justice (see the situation in Charmont village, chap. II); 1222,M,323: marriage to outsiders was called *mesmaritagio*; 1233,Mol,330: Montier-la-Celle granted *licentia et permissione* to its women to marry men of Molesme; 1242,Mol,358–59: the lady of Pars allowed a woman freely *ad nubendum*; 1180,N,8: a man paid the abbey 5 s. for permission to marry one of its women.

54. 1194,StS,116r: the abbey retained "jure et justicia et tallia nostra in eadem mulier"; 1220,StL,207: the chapter had retained its claim over a woman who married a miller of Saint-Loup, which now settled the account by giving a woman of its own to the chapter; 1229,StS,168r: in an exchange of women with Saint-Loup, the chapter retained the *taille* of its own women; 1235,Mol,339: a man promised to pay 2 s. annually for life for his wife, who belonged to that abbey. But in 1232,M,357, the abbey and Saint-Etienne allowed their men and women in the counties of Troyes and Brienne to intermarry freely, but they and their children's "talias per mediam partiemur."

55. 1183,StL,72: "cum tota familia sua et cum toto tenemento suo"; 1200,Mol,291–92: a woman, her children, and all her *res*; 1227,MLC,11: a woman with all her *hereditas*. But in 1231,Mol,324, only the women, not their inheritances, were transferred. 1251,StS,235v–236r: the chapter threatened to excommunicate Milo of Auxerre for trying to recover rights over his *femina de corpore*, who had married the chapter's man Coutelet of Troyes, a tavernkeeper; her rights had probably been transferred to the chapter on the occasion of her marriage.

56. 1216,Arch.Aube,22 H 145; (1207),StP,117: "unam de feminis suis ad valentiam istius"; 1219,N,42: "10 s., more or less"; 1241,Arch.Aube, 22 H 1598: "ad valorem dicte Emeline [20 s.]."

57. 1191,StL,106: a woman continued to pay her 5 s. *taille* to her original lord until her husband's lord exchanged a woman for her; 1236,N,156: a man promised to pay his wife's *servitium* until her original lord had been compensated by another woman; 1236,Arch.Aube,22 H 1669: Notre-Dame-aux-Nonnains claimed its rights "tam in tallia quam in heredibus" of a woman who married an outsider until the latter's lord furnished a replacement; 1237,StS,165r: until it was compensated by a woman of equal value, Montier-la-Celle would continue to collect half of the *taille* and "service" and would have claim to half the children of a woman whom it gave to the chapter.

58. 1192,StS,116r; 1218,StP,142; 1227,Arch.Aube,22 H 1576.

59. 1186,StL,82; 1189,StL,101: the abbey and Jean of Arcis each took two sons; 1175,O,2v–3r: children of mixed marriages in the village shared by co-lords were allotted as follows: the first child to the father's lord, the second and third to the mother's, the fourth and fifth to the father's, and so on; 1206,N,18: in a complicated division, three sons and one daughter were equated with two daughters, one of whom had children.

60. 1145,StL,13: the lord of Traînel sought to halt the practice by which his women married men of Saint-Loup and escaped their personal taxes; henceforth, he claimed, he could collect *servitium* (i.e., *taille*) from the men involved. 1145,MLC,34: the abbey's man married the sister of the count's *serviens*; half the children would be assigned to each lord; 1173,StS,35r (confirmation of the 1157 foundation charter): the men of Saint-Etienne were probably the count's originally, having been given by him on the occasion of the foundation. Since ca. 1111 the count had allowed his men to intermarry with those of Montiéramey (see above, n. 4).

61. 1180,M,8. Similar arrangements allowing intermarriages but requiring the equal division of the children were made between: the chapter of Saint-Etienne and Montier-la-Celle (1187,StS,164r); Saint-Loup and Saint-Pierre (1189,StL,99); Saint-Loup and Saint-Etienne (1193,StL,112); Saint-Etienne and Montiéramey (1232,M,357).

62. 1205,Arch.Aube,22 H 1490: Notre-Dame-aux-Nonnains and Anselm of Courcelles-sur-Voire allowed their men to intermarry; 1208,M,248: the abbey and Bouchard of Vendeuvre reached a similar agreement over three villages near Lusigny; 1216,Th,192v–193r: the abbot of Saint-Germain-des-Prés and the countess of Champagne agreed that in return for 12 l. annually the abbot would not *prohibere* marriages between their respective men and women in several Champagne castellanies; 1224,StS,63r: the chapter and the wife of Garnier of Faiel agreed over the men of Faiel and several other villages; 1264,StS,71r: the children of intermarriages, "ubicumque se transtulerint vel mansionem fecerint," would be divided equally between their respective lords. Some of the *pariages* contain similiar provisions between lay lords. No doubt there were other such arrangements, though few have been preserved; some of those between lay lords were perhaps made orally.

63. (1084/1107),Mol-I,66: a lord gave his alod to the abbey to construct an *atrium* and to *rustici hospitari* in plots of 40 feet for an 8 d. rent; (1100),StL,3: a reference to men coming *ex aliis locis* to settle in the abbey's villages; 1121,M,23: the abbey gave up its village of Longpré-le-Sec to the lord of Vendeuvre, but its men could *ad dominos suos redire* if they wished; 1161,StL,32: the count allowed the abbey's men, no matter where they came from, to settle in Troyes and be exempt from his administrative control; 1177,StL,56: on giving the abbey six manses, the count of Brienne stipulated that if for any reason the present *possessor* left, the abbey would hold it directly until someone else arrived who was willing to pay the customary rent (2 s. 6 d. or 3 s. 6 d.). See also the case in 1139, n. 46 above.

64. 1197,StP,86; 1165,StS,71r; 1209,StS,60v–61r: the chapter concluded an agreement with the lord of Jully-sur-Sarce whereby it surrendered to him its men at Fouchères in return for exemption from another payment owed him; by claiming customary rights over its men who subsequently migrated there, the chapter effectively prevented emigration to that village of its men who expected to secure better conditions from the lord of Jully. See also references in n. 60.

65. 1206,M,230.

66. 1213,Th,61r–v; 1259,StS,245r–v: the chapter freed a family but required the son, "quando erit sui juris et a patre suo separatus," to pay the same one *mine* of grain which his father had paid.

67. 1204,Mol,292–93; 1158,*Histoire* III, p. 448: the count gave his rights over a brother and sister who had emigrated to Wassy, two brothers who had come from

Vitry, and a woman who had come from Payns—all five had migrated to Troyes before being transferred by their lord, the count, to another lord.

68. 1223,R,43(i): this was part of an ultimate solution (a temporary agreement had been reached in 1209,R,15–16[xxv]) to the longstanding dispute over the woods of Dosches between the Méry family and the abbey, which sought to prevent the villagers from taking excessive firewood and from clearing the trees for arable and pasture; the abbey now had the exclusive use of one thousand *arpents* of woods, and the villagers had the rest for themselves. The custom by which only residents enjoyed the woods was also defined in 1219,R,88(xli): "qui exit de potestate Doschie amittit usuarium ejusdem nemoris, et quia idem S[ilvestre Taille-bose] exierat de potestate illa, ut dicebant, usuarium illud amiserat."

69. 1172,MLC,28: both *homines* and *hospites* were subject to the prior's court; 1176,*Histoire* III, pp. 465–66: *hospites* shared the same privileges as the *homines* in a village; 1179,StL,64: the abbey was allowed to receive *hospites* on some lands, on the condition that they pay the safeguard tax and be liable to justice like the other residents of Hugh of Vergy; the abbey was exempted from paying their safeguard tax if they departed and left the land vacant; 1186,StL,81: the lord of Pougy allowed any *hospes* to reside on a vacant *ochia* in Molins; 1188,StP,46: newcomers as well as natives were liable to the safeguard custom of fifteen *modii* of oats, which was allowed to the monks of Chapelle-aux-Planches whenever they demanded (*ad voluntatem*); 1204,M,209: the plowing *corvées* of *hominum albanorum* who held lands at Rouilly-Sacey were owed to the two lay lords of the land; 1221,Th,338r–v: among the four *domini* and other *burgenses* who swore that the castle of Joigny was renderable to the count of Champagne, even if the lord of Joigny refused, was Stephen, *albus*; 1236,Arch.Aube,20 H 11: two *albani* married *feminae de corpore* and so themselves were liable to exchange by the lords wishing to balance their accounts of exchanged persons.

70. 1179,StL,64: the lord of Traînel required only justice over newcomers if they settled in new lands but imposed justice and safeguard if the newcomers settled elsewhere.

71. 1177,*Histoire* III, pp. 467–68: the *hospites* who settled in Notre-Dame of Oulchy's lands came under its jurisdiction, unless they were merchants, in which case they came under the count's jurisdiction; 1228,MLC,2: the count's officials gave them fifteen days in which to take down the temporary structures (*logis et stallis*) which they operated for the abbey on the fair grounds; 1259,S,65v: *hospites* had permanent stalls in Méry.

72. 1158,StL,29: "quod si quis eciam predictorum sex hospitum meus sit [he cannot be seized by the count's agents on that account]; . . . sciendum tamen quod exactionem quo vulgo tallia dicitur, propter libertatem furni, de homine meo non perdam."

73. (1152/80),L, pp. 94–95: the bakers on the Léproserie's *furni mansionarii* were exempted from the count's officials and military service, but if the men owed the count *taille*, he retained that; 1199,HD,24r: Thibaut III freed the Hôtel-Dieu's bakers from all customs, justice, and his officials, "excepto hoc quod si homines mei mansionarii predicti fuerint de illis tantummodo talliam meam michi retinui."

74. 1162,StL,33: he gave the abbey land near Les Noës and the "hospites qui in ea manerint, ab omni servicio sive justicia sive consuetudine michi debita, dumtaxit homines mei non sint, perhenniter emancipavi." See chap. III for the community franchises.

75. The *Extenta*,Payns, refers to a payment exacted for a permission to migrate: "appelatur 'eschief' quando aliquis redimit se a domino suo, ut possit remanere sub dominio juridicione alterius dominio" (see also chap. III, n. 36). Payments ranged from 2 s. to 10 s. annually; examples are in the *Extenta* for Nogent.

76. 1236,Arch.Aube,20 H 11: he also gave her children and all possessions, mobile and immobile. The lord of Ramerupt was one of the few lay lords openly to induce the immigration of men of other lords: in the *pariage* over Nogent-sur-Aube, he and the abbot of Montiéramey, co-lords, accepted all *homines*, no matter where

they came from (that is, no matter who their lords), to settle there (1203,M,207; see below). There were surprisingly few disputes over the possession of *hospites*, perhaps because it was very complicated to locate and then prove a prior relationship with men, especially beyond a few day's journey. One of the rare recorded disputes is in 1164,StS,32r: the two lords claimed a certain David the Lotharingian, *qui albanus erat*; the count's court decided that the man would swear fidelity to one of the lords, who in turn would pay the other lord 12 d. annually (*taille* ?), but after the man died, his wife and children would go to the second lord.

77. In 1250,Mor,115, the widow of Robert I of Fontette attempted to reclaim two of her tenants who had taken the religious habit at Mores without her permission (see Appendix). There is also an interesting case from the 1190s: two brothers who had been under the *dominium et homagium* of Montiéramey rejected that lordship and became men of the canons of Saint-Pierre of Troyes; they fled again and sought "protection" from the count, becoming his men. But the count ordered an inquest, which revealed that the men and their children actually belonged to Montiéramey and that the canons of Saint-Pierre had accepted them without questions; the count did not accept them (1192,M,95). The canons apparently kept them, but three years later those two brothers were formally transferred back to Montiéramey in a general exchange of tenants (1195,M,106).

78. 1157,Chapin, *Les villes de foires*, appendix 1: "omnes homines albanos apud Trecas, Pruvinum et Pontes sub dominio ecclesie vestre, si infra annum et diem ibidem remanserint omnino liberos"; 1187,StS,89r—92r: a papal confirmation of that act listed by name twenty three Troyens who belonged to the chapter and rephrased the original grant to "homines albanos quicumque apud Trecas, Pruvinis, Pontes sub dominio ecclesie vivere infram annum et diem remanserint liberos." Of course, newcomers still had the option of leaving within the year, and as another charter put it, by remaining they were in effect choosing a lord: 1159/88,StS,36r: "si voluerint sub eadem libertate [Pont] ibidem remaneant."

79. 1171,O,1v—2r; 1233,Mol,330—33: there were two types of newcomers in Essoyes and its three associated villages: the count's men who came there would be shared jointly by the count and the abbot, and the abbey's men from its other villages who came there "through marriage or otherwise" remained under the abbey alone, especially for *mainmorte*.

80. 1194,StP,69: "homines qui albani nuncupantur et in dominium ecclesie se transtulerunt eodem libertate [*mainmorte* exemption] gaudebunt."

81. 1172,M,62 and 1178,M,69: new settlers were allowed to build houses on the priory's land in Troyes, and they came under the prior's, not the count's, jurisdiction; 1187,StL,87.

82. 1204,Th,32r; 1205,Th,194r; 1208,Th,205r—v: another Champagne baron on the border region agreed not to claim "servitude" from outside men coming to live in his castellany unless he could prove by sworn witnesses or judicial duel that they had previously owed him service; that is, the count's men could settle there without being subjected to arbitrary personal taxation.

83. 1209,*Histoire* V,710.

84. 1215,Th,30v; 1217,Th,232r: they agreed to hunt down criminal suspects in each other's lands and to return them for judgment; 1220,Th,231r: the countess agreed with the count of Bar-le-Duc not to permit their men to settle on each other's lands. But perhaps the critical situation which prompted the count's men to move off the Champagne lands had been halted by 1222; once again there was an agreement by which the count would not accept men of another lord on his lands, an indication that the flow of men had been reversed: 1222,Th,157v: Thibaut IV would not accept (*retinere*) men on his lands from the village of Joncreuil, which the bishop of Langres announced he would hold for his lifetime.

85. The 1230—31 communal charters (see chap. III) did not allow men of the count or of his fief holders to enter the communes; but the *Extenta*,Troyes, of 1276/78 stated that they could enter: any man could leave a fief or rear-fief of Champagne and settle in Troyes; "similiter est de hominibus albanis quod sunt

homines comitis, si [cum uxore] manent Trecis per annum et diem [et] alium dominum non fecerint." The change in policy probably occurred after the failure of the commune of Troyes in 1240.

86. The use of specific terms, such as *hospes* or *albanus*, to cover these men in transit may also have protected the lords from accusations of enticement by other local lords; a lord was free of responsibility until he formally accepted a man's oath.

87. The best examples of the roles and privileges of mayors and *prévôts* in local communities are in the formalized arrangements between lords on shared community organization (see below). *Villici* were the key resident agents in the early twelfth century, as in (1104),M,18; they were seldom mentioned in the twelfth century, although one appears in a witness list in 1187,M,79. 1113,M,18: the *prévôt* of the abbot rendered justice in three villages; 1196,N,12: the mayor exercised justice over the abbey's men at Fays; 1260,Ch,170: Alix of Chacenay reassigned a 100 s. bequest of her brother to the *taille* on her men of Bligny, which was to be collected and delivered by the mayor there.

88. The case of Saint-Loup is illustrative: in 1159,StL,30, it secured the "liberty" of its mayor of Luyères from all the count's agents and justice; in 1161,StL,32, it further secured the privilege for mayors, "sub-mayors," and *servientes* in all its villages: they were exempted from *péage* and *tonlieu* whenever they went to market.

89. For examples of sons of mayors inheriting their fathers' offices: (early twelfth century),Arch.Aube,20 H 10; 1177,V,106v; 1240,Mol,355–56; of a son-in-law: 1146,*Histoire* III, pp. 433–34; of *majorissae*: 1224,M,329; 1231,StP,192.

90. For examples of daughters of mayors exchanged for marriage: 1202,Th,12r–v; 1202,StP,102; 1215,Mol,305; 1225,StL,226. 1211,M,266: the lord of Chacenay deposed his mayor because the local prior had customarily appointed the mayor in that village to act for both parties; 1227,StS,148r: Gilo, formerly mayor of a knight, took a similar position with Saint-Etienne as mayor of Pars, but he had to make a public recognition that he had become a *homo* of the chapter.

91. Also called *ministeriales, ministri*, and occasionally *nuncii* or *receptores*.

92. The case of Saint-Loup is illustrative: in 1103,StL,40, three of its *servientes* secured immunity from the count; in 1153,StL,22, there were six agents, and in 1154,StL,24, there were seven; 1169,StP,75: the abbey's *servientes* were immune while in office.

93. 1187,MLC,35; 1185,P,75: Paraclet's *receptores* took an oath eight days before they were to collect 14 l. from the *péage* and *tonlieu* of Nogent to render the exact amount collected; 1153,*Histoire* III, pp. 442–43: the count's *servientes* collected taxes and customs from his villages; administrative agents also collected rents in kind: 1168,StL,39; 1204,StP,107; 1209,M,257; 1210,M,261.

94. 1103,StL,4; 1235,P,46; 1161,StL,32; (undated),Th,166v–167v: four of the count's *servientes* in Chablis were exempted from *tallagium* and other customs.

95. 1212,StP,130; 1197,StL,121: two knights offered to have their *ministeriales* eject unwanted persons from a priory; 1209,StL,153: the lord of Traînel's *servientes* would levy a 5 s. fine on any of the abbey's men caught in certain villages.

96. In 1172 the count's *servientes* were to inquire about who held the fief of Gérard of Savoy that should have reverted to the count (*Feoda*,Troyes,1895); 1228,MLC,2: they were to dismantle the stalls and booths left up after the Provins fair. In August 1201 the countess specified the duties and privileges of all her *prévôts* in a standard "contract": for example, they had one-fifth of fines, the remainder going to her; they could not accept gifts or bribes, except food; and they had to swear to preserve her rights (*Feoda* V,2985).

97. In the twelfth century there are some references which seem to put the agents on the level of knights: 1110/13,M,18: the abbey could acquire property from the count's men, "sive miles sive serviens"; 1147,Arch.Aube,20 H 10: the count of Brienne allowed Sainte-Marie of Ramerupt to acquire property from his *homines* (fief-holders?) and *servientes*. Even in the late twelfth century the count of Bar-sur-Seine conducted his councils "coram militibus et ministerialibus meis"

(1165,Mor,6 and 1197,Mor,42). By the thirteenth century, however, there was a clear divide between knights and administrative agents: 1217,StS,63r: the countess gave her *serviens* to the deacon of Saint-Etienne "in homine [and] . . . in perpetuam possidendum"; 1262,S,61r: the lord of Marigny gave oxen and a *terrage* to his *serviens* to hold for a 7 d. *cens*, on the condition that the man and his heirs remain *homines mei de corporibus.*

98. 1145,StL,3: women in Traînel's *potestate* passed by marriage under the abbey's *jus et dominationem*; Traînel obviously was presented with a *fait accompli* and had to acknowledge that the women were *manumissas*; but he also stipulated that if such a situation recurred, the men of the abbey would owe him "service" for any woman of his they married. Also, 1145,MLC,34.

99. 1161,StL,31; 1219,StS,177r: "manumissit [and] . . . in perpetuum quitavit"; 1162,StL,33; 1165,StL,38; 1173,StL,47; 1189,StL,76; (1217),StL,187: the lady of Chappes manumitted a woman and "eam liberam et absolutam concedo Beati Lupo Trecensi." "Manumit" was to transfer rights over a person; "emancipate" was to exempt the person himself: in 1170,StL,143, for example, the count emancipated any man to be picked by the abbot from the count's justice, customs, taxes, and other obligations in the castellany of Pont; the man was to be a personal agent for the abbot and thus required the exemptions, but he himself enjoyed no such privileges from his own lord, the abbot.

100. In the late thirteenth century there are a few cases of manumission in the sense of *taille* commutation, but they are all from one abbey, Sellières: 1281,Arch. Aube,9 H 116: the abbey "manumitted" a man from *taille* for 2 s. annually; 1285,Arch.Aube,9 H 116: another for 1 s. annually. It would appear, in view of the heavy use of the term by Saint-Loup in the twelfth century and by Sellières in the thirteenth century, that stylistic influences played an important role in the meaning of the word.

101. 1187,*Histoire* III, p. 479: the residents of Luyères who had *liberi cartas* (from Count Thibaut II) were exempted from the *gîte* and safeguard tax, which were now commuted to 6 l. annually for the rest of the village; 1165,*Histoire* III, pp. 350–51(notice).

102. 1215,Th,144v: he and his wife were "liberos ab omni tallia, tolta, demanda et exactione"; (1220s),Th,309r.

103. 1205,StS,59r.

104. (1220s),Th,308v.

105. 1223,Th,300r; 1222,Th,291v: two merchants of Sienna received a like compensation.

106. (1220s),Th,300r; 1222,Th,249v.

107. 1222,Th,310r–v; (1220s),Th,291v: a *serviens* of the count was freed for life from personal taxes and military service, unless he wished to volunteer in times of crisis; 1222,Th,312v: Thibaut "manumitted" Jean Bernay, his *serviens*, and his wife, a *domicella* of the countess, *ab omni servitutis* as reward for "long service."

108. In form, these franchises are remarkably similar to those issued by Philip Augustus for merchants; for example, see the two grants of 1180: *Recueil des actes de Philippe Auguste*, vol. 1, ed. H. F. Delaborde (Paris, 1916): 1180, no. 5 (for *servientes*); 1180, no. 16 (for a converted Jew). Charters of exemption may well have been developed first for merchants and then extended for general use (see also a notice of Count Henry I in 1165, *Historie* III, pp. 350–51).

109. *Extenta,*Pont.

110. The communal charters contain a clause that invited the count's agents who had already secured individual franchises to join the communes (see chap. III, n. 36).

111. The private lords also later copied the count's grants of community franchises (chap. III). Only a few examples of individual exemptions survive: for example, in 1259,StS,245r–v; a man, his wife, and son acknowledged themselves to be *homines* of the chapter and agreed to remain under its justice; the chapter then "franchised" them from *taille*, toll, exaction, and *mainmorte* for an annual one *setier* of grain. See also n. 100.

112. 1194,StP,69.
113. 1117,M,20; 1102/25,Mol,244.
114. See n. 21 on *dominium*. Of course, a uniform situation did not necessarily prevail, and the old "domainal" organization probably survived longest under ecclesiastical and conservative lay lords. 1171,Ch,46: the lord of Durnay agreed to demolish his "new village" of Saint-Usage, which he was in the course of building, because it was close to an abbey's grange and threatened the latter's interests; he promised also not to build any more villages in the vicinity; 1195,V,55v: a *villa* used to exist where a grange now stood; 1226,B,3: papal permission was granted to *edificare* villages, churches, and cemeteries in *loca deserta*. The best study of the early *villa* is Gabriel Fournier, *Le peuplement rural en Basse Auvergne* (Paris, 1962), chap. 3: Fournier concludes that by the eleventh century, *villa* meant "village," not "seigneurie" (pp. 232–38). Although Auvergne may have been less impressed with the domainal organization, the meaning was the same even in the north by the twelfth century; see Henri Dubled, "Quelques observations sur le sens du mot *villa*," *Le Moyen Age* 59 (1953): 1-11, and Camille J. Joset, *Les villes au pays de Luxembourg (1196–1383)* (Brussels, 1940), p. 23.
115. *Etat des bois*, in *Documents* I, pp. 190–92 (Villemaur), 193 (Ervy), and 194–95 (Isle). The scribes gave hearth sizes for eighty-four villages and left blanks for others for which they did not have information. A possible bias in this sample is the disproportionate number of small villages nestled around a large wooded area. Another sample of about the same size (eighty villages) for northern Champagne— the sergeantry of Porcien—in ca. 1300 gives an average of eighty to one hundred hearths, and in that area there were also many villages of over two hundred hearths and even one of one thousand (*Documents* I, pp. 418–21). The very size and importance of Troyes in the *bailliage* probably resulted in fewer medium-sized towns.
116. Edouard Baratier, *La démographie provençale du XIIIe au XVIe siècle* (Paris, 1961), is the most comprehensive study of medieval populations. After a detailed analysis of the best available town and rural hearth figures, Baratier concludes that considerable fluctuations make it impossible to fix an exact hearth coefficient; his reluctant best estimate is 4.5 (pp. 58 ff.).
117. See chap. III for castellany towns, esp. n. 56.
118. 1147,StL,17; see also the history of the Charmont family in the Appendix.
119. 1163,StL,36; 1226,StS,214r: the lady of Charmont gave up all "pretense" to the claim of escheat and marriage tax over the men of Saint-Loup and Saint-Etienne living there; 1233,StS,220r–v the *domicellus* of Charmont was fined by the episcopal official for imprisoning some of Saint-Etienne's men in his *domus fort* (the first reference to a fortress there) and impounding their goods; (1233),StS, 315r–v: the lady of Charmont had to surrender the goods of a certain Lambert, who had just died, because he lived on the immune house lot (his property was exempted from her claim of *mainmorte*).
120. (1169),M,55. Seloncourt has since disappeared.
121. 1225,M,340: the abbey purchased from Erard of Aulnay, who held them in fief from Manasses of Pougy, one-half of the justice, *tailles*, and *corvées* and one-third of the safeguard tax and other revenues, all for 300 l.
122. Puits is now in the *département* of Marne. 1171,O,1v–2r; (1170s),O,3r: the count notified his *prévôt* of Vitry that now the abbot of Oyes would share the exemptions which the mayor of Puits used to have; 1175,O,2v–3r.
123. 1196,O,14v: Eustace of Conflans-sur-Seine sought the "forismaritagio et manumortua [over] . . . homines de corpore in villa Puits . . . qui homines de potesta vocantur que de iure meo esse dicebam."
124. 1196,N,12: the renewal of certain customs in two villages between the lord of Saint-Phal and the abbey (its archives had burned in the 1188 fire in Troyes): in Fays-la-Chapelle the abbey had justice, exercised by the mayor of the abbess there (it had been granted by the count and confirmed in 1189,N,7), and in Chamoy the abbey also had justice, but the lord had a mayor there who supervised the measuring of wine and wheat with the abbey's mayor, and both officials had police

powers; furthermore, the lord had a ban in Chamoy by which only his *homines* and *hospites* could sell at a certain time; 1204,M,209: the abbey and Milo of Sormery shared mayors, *corvées*, and escheats in Rouilly-Sacey; Milo had the plowing *corvée* of *albani*, and the abbey collected *terrage* on uncleared lands as its *corvée; the* abbey claimed all inheritances except house lots; the two mayors were *omnimodis liberi*, but Milo's man owed the abbey *terrage* all the same. 1205,CB,83v—84r: Renaud, deacon of Villemaur, associated the countess over his lands and granted her half of the *taille* of his men and justice in several villages. 1211,M,266: the prior of Chacenay customarily appointed the mayor of a village, who was to represent both the prior and the lord of Chacenay. 1225,MLC,175: the abbey and the lord of Lirey agreed over Courcelles: each had full justice over his own men and lands; only those men who were holding in *cens* were shared jointly for justice, harvesting, and fines.

125. 1222,M,323: the villages of Saint-Etienne, Saint-Rémi, Nozay, and Saint-Martin (disappeared).

126. 1195,M,109.

127. 1203,M,207, renewed 1222/23,M,320.

128. 1248,M,383: the abbey paid 457 l. for the other half.

129. Since only ecclesiastical houses maintained archives, they are present in virtually all the extant *pariages*. One of the earliest examples of *pariage* in Champagne is the 1206,CB,112r—113r agreement between the countess and the abbot of Saint-Remi of Reims over Villeneuve-Fraxines: each party had a *prévôt*, and both *prévôts* chose the mayor and *scabini* of the village, who took oaths to the *prévôts;* justice was shared, but taxes, rents, banal ovens, and tithes remained the abbot's. The fact that this agreement was copied twice (1206,Th,181v—182r and 274v—275r) and modified once to cover marriages and *mainmorte* (1212,CB,128v—129r) indicates its importance to the count's scribes. Another association of the same year was between the countess and the dean of Villemaur over the *tailles* and justice of two of the dean's villages (1206,*Histoire* V,644).

130. 1233,Mol,300—330(=1234,*Documents* II, pp. 62—63): the monks associated the count and his heirs; 1234, in Petel, *Essoyes*, p. 504: the count announced to his *prévôts* and *baillis* that he had entered into a *societas* with the abbey over these villages and ordered them not to disturb the places. The situation at Essoyes was rather complicated, for the lord of Chacenay had at least some interests there which seem to have been snatched by the abbot; 1229,Mol,319: the lord of Chacenay and the abbot agreed to the intermarriage of their men there, with the children to be divided (the case here was of eight women); (1230), Petel, *Essoyes*, p. 503: the count promised the lord of Chacenay that he would never take Essoyes, that it was Molesme's, and that if Chacenay was able to acquire it, he would hold it from the count "in augmentation" of fief. 1231,Mol,325: the abbey purchased from its knights Guillaume and Jeremia of Verpillières all *tailles*, commuted *tailles*, and revenues of the men of Verpillières, except justice and *cens*, for 68 l. The actual "association" between the abbey and the count may have occurred in 1231, when the count was issuing franchises to his castellany towns (see chap. III) because in 1231,Ch,139, the three brothers of Chacenay made a *communitate* of their own at Bertignolles and claimed that they were copying the Essoyes model; in 1232,Mol, 325—26, the lord of Chacenay made a similar "custom" for his men of Poligny after he sold his possessions (mill, house, all his justice) at Essoyes to the abbey. Only part of Essoyes ever belonged to the abbey; the rest had been held by the count of Bar-sur-Seine, who in 1210 had given the men there a *mainmorte* exemption like the one he had given Bar-sur-Seine in 1198; his share of Essoyes passed to the count of Champagne in the 1220s (see the history of the Bar-sur-Seine family in the Appendix).

131. *Extenta,* Rumilly-lès-Vaudes.

132. 1250,*Documents* II, pp. 60—62: a few of the provisions were more specific than the ones of the 1234 charters; for example, when the person of the abbot or the count changed, the villagers had to take a new oath of fidelity; and all military

expeditions were to be led by a sergeant chosen by both parties. Léon Gallet, *Les traites de pariage dans la France féodale* (Paris, 1936), pp. 198 ff., suggests that Molesme followed a similar policy under abbots Isambard (1227—38) and Christopher of Essoyes (1239—52); however, the device was a general one, and Montiéramey had a number of *pariages* even earlier.

133. Charles-Edmond Perrin, "Chartes de franchise et rapports de droits en Lorraine," *Le Moyen Age* 52 (1946): 17—18, considers the "associations" as forms of franchise; this is clearly not the case in the *bailliage* (nor in Luxembourg; see Joset, *Les villes au pays de Luxembourg*, p. 30). There is only one example of an agreement that served both as an association and a franchise (for Chaource, see chap. III).

134. Gallet, *Les traites de pariage*, p. 13, concludes that *pariages* were simply a method by which ecclesiastical houses reacted against safeguard claims of laymen, but only a few examples in the *bailliage* could be explained in this way: one is in 1235,MLC,20, when the count exempted the abbey's men in three villages from work at his castle in Méry, in return for which the abbey "associated" him over its men at Droupt-Sainte-Marie: all revenues except *cens* and customs were to be shared; the count still claimed his *captagium* and *mainmorte* there in the 1276/78 *Extenta*, Méry.

135. Perhaps the most difficult immigration with which lay lords had to cope was of men into ecclesiastical houses, either into orders or simply as tenants. Montiéramey and Sellières, for example, had papal permission to "receive" and "retain" men "fleeing" the world, a privilege which allowed broad interpretation (1178,M,70; 1186,S,4r—5r—grants of similar phrasing). The count allowed his men to assume the religious habit at Montiéramey and Foissy (1158,M,45; 1159, Arch.Aube,27 H 3), and the count of Brienne allowed his men to do the same at Andecy and even to take all their possessions with them (1135, Lalore IV [Chartes d'Andecy], 165). In 1219,H,2(Saint-Nicholas), the chapter of Saint-Pierre allowed its man André and his wife to give four *jugera* of arable, one-half an *arpent* of vineyard, and one-half of a field to Saint-Nicholas and to enter as a convert there; 1231,R,22(lvii—lviii): Humber of Ayllefou, his wife, and son gave all their lands and worldly goods to Larrivour in return for being supported by the abbey for their lives while they tilled the same lands. Most ecclesiastical houses probably absorbed immigrants without publicity, although an enraged lay lord could make a scene by claiming his men (see n. 77).

136. See chap. I, text and n. 24. Portejoie's edition is based on a collation of nine manuscripts from ca. 1295 to ca. 1600; in cases of variant readings I have used the first (*A*) version, or, in lieu of that, the second (*B*, early fourteenth century).

137. As stated in Article XVII, a decision dealing with the wardship of orphaned children, the arrangements were valid for either "noble ou de poesté" (*B*: "noble ou non-noble").

138. Articles LXV; XIV: "hommes ou femmes qui soient de mainmorte ou soient hommes taillaubles." See chap. III, n. 67, for the term *serf* in the *Coutumier*.

139. Article XXVI: "Coustume est en Champagne, au leuz ou les mainzmortes sunt, que III chouses partent honme de poesté. C'est asavoir aages, mariages, feux et leux, et y puet panre li sires mainmorte quant il uns de ses gens muert."

140. Article XVII (1289 decision); XII: the younger brother must decide within one year of coming of age ("dedanz l'an qui seront aagié") whether to hold directly from his brother or his overlord.

141. *Eschiet* and *mainmorte* were used interchangeably: Article XXVII: "eschiete ou mainmorte." The distinction is that *mainmorte* concerned property with no surviving direct heir, whereas *eschiet* included other situations, such as heirs living away from home or claims by indirect heirs. In 1219,N,42, the *escasura et manumortua* of a deceased's property was claimed by the children; and in 1228, StS,139r—v, the chapter gave up claims to *manus mortuas sive excasuras* over its men of Giffaumont.

142. Article LXV.

143. Article XXVII: "herritaiges qui movient de censives ou de coustumes. [The lord had to regrant the lands to] ... tex gens qui soient de la condicion que cil estoient de qui l'escheoite vient." Article XXVI: he could not take *mainmorte* if the sole survivors were underage children, although he could take the portions of any of them who died.

144. Examples from the charters illustrate: 1219,Arch.Aube,23 H 300: Erard of Villehardouin gave a fief to two men, on the condition that they not transfer it "into the hands of tailleable persons"; 1258,StS,241v–242r: the chapter required a woman to become its *femina de corpore* in order to hold one-half of her grand-father's property—she was to return it if she did not; 1262,S,61r: Garnier V of Marigny gave his *serviens* Guy of Marigny and his heirs an oven in Echemines with an enforced ban in the area, and a *terrage* in the month of July, for a 7 d. *cens*; Garnier allowed it to pass to Guy's heirs, so long as they remained *homines mei de corporibus*.

145. Article XIV (undated decision).

146. Article X (1284 decision).

147. Article LVIII (1295 decision).

148. A possible example of this is in 1216,N,33: a woman was allowed to "remain freely" under the abbey's custody without being liable for *taille*, marriage tax, or *mainmorte*, for a 6 s. rent. In 1263,StS,251r–v, the chapter permitted its *femina de corpore* Alice to marry Jean Troilin, *civis* of Troyes, under these conditions: that she pay 10 s. annually for *taille* and that she be quit of *mainmorte* unless she died without heir, in which case her possessions would revert to the chapter; if her husband should die, she could not remarry without the chapter's permission.

149. Article VI (undated decision): the children "sievent la peour condicion." A possible example of a child of such a marriage is in 1219,Th,352v: Count Thibaut IV enfranchised a man because he was born of a count's *femina de corpore;* the implication is that the man's father was either enfranchised or a fief holder.

150. Portejoie notes (*Coutumier*, p. 24, n. 61) that the right of a child of such a mixed union to "choose" his mother's status was mentioned in 1494 as a custom in the area bounded by the rivers Seine and Aube, Seine and Yonne, that is, precisely the area of the *bailliage* of Troyes.

151. Article XXXV: the tenant could claim judgment in the lordship where he "couche et lieve et ay . . . demorance."

152. Article XXXVI includes a formal request to be used by a lord seeking to "extradite" a man who had appealed to another lord for justice; Article LXIV (1295 decision) provided for the loss of all possessions after an unsuccessful appeal to an overlord.

153. Article LXIII.

154. Article XXXVI: "Coustume est en Champagne que hons de poesté ne peut avoir franchise ne ne droit ne se peut appeler frans, s'il n'a dou don dou signor lettres ou privilaiges."

III. Franchised Communities

1. A purported attempt to look at the entirety of southern Champagne, but which is nevertheless essentially confined to Troyes, is Théophile Boutiot, *Des institutions communales dans la Champagne méridionale au XIIe et au XIIIe siècle* (Troyes, 1865).

2. A possibly earlier franchise was for Saint-Martin, just south of Troyes: in 1172,M,62, the count allowed the men of Saint-Jean-en-Chastel to settle there, build houses, and live according to the *libertate* which his ancestors had granted to "the men of Saint-Martin." The village remained entirely in the count's hands and had forty hearths in ca. 1290, *Etat des bois.*

3. 877,M,6; 896,M,12.

4. 1165,M,53, which contains the confirmations of 1263 and 1412. Professor

John F. Benton has advised me that the actual date should be 1175. *Exactiones* were defined as *mainmorte* and marriage tax in 1196,O,14v. The locations of Chaource and Metz-Robert on map 4 have been inadvertently reversed.

5. For a discussion of these standardized fines and for the customs of Lorris in general, see Maurice Prou, "Les coutumes de Lorris et leur propagation aux XIIe et XIIIe siècles," *Revue historique de droit français et étranger* 18 (1884): 139–209, 267–320, 441–57, 523–56.

6. The county castellanies of Troyes, Isle, Saint-Florentin, and Ervy and the castellany-fiefs of Chacenay and Chappes.

7. The witness list includes two men who were "at that time *prévôts* of Chaource." The 1177 *pariage* also refers to the "*prévôts* of Chaource."

8. 1177,*Documents* II, p. 64, n. 4(=1177,M,68).

9. The abbot's own men were restricted: "nulli de hominibus ipsius abbatius . . . retinebuntur, nisi assensu ipsius abbatii." *Retinere* means "to allow to remain," as in the original franchise's statement that immigrants proved to belong to knights of the neighboring castellanies "in villa deinceps non retinebuntur" (see also chap. II, n. 84). The castellanies listed in 1177 were the same as those listed in 1175, except that Villemaur (the count's) replaced Chacenay (private). Also, three knights, instead of the original two, and four local residents were now required to prove that a man belonged to another lord.

10. 1209,M,260; confirmed by Thibaut IV in 1222,M,316. The grant was both a franchise and a *pariage*: the abbey associated the countess over half of the revenues (customs, justice, *tonlieu*, sales taxes) and administration (two *prévôts* to act jointly in holding court, summoning men, collecting fines) in this grant of a "free village." The abbey retained all tithes and *terrage* (constituting together one-sixth of the harvest), churches, and banal ovens; no other ecclesiastical house was allowed in the village, not even to build a grange. Immigration was prohibited to men of the abbey, of the countess, and of her direct fief holders in the six neighboring castellanies; immigrants who were proved to be *de capite et de corpore* by seven men (three knights, three villagers, and one resident of the man's former village) to be tailleable *ad voluntatem* were given a fifteen-day safe-conduct in which to leave. Anyone who lived one year and one day without challenge ("nisi dominus suus eum infra annum et diem coram prepositis de Pargis reclamaverit") could be *burgensis* like the others, provided that he resided in the village.

11. *Extenta,*Chaource.

12. Baratier, *La démographie provençale*, pp. 40–41, found that the total number of tailleable men was about 20 percent greater than the number of hearths; six hundred members at Chaource would give about five hundred hearths. Chaource produced 480 l. from its *prévôté* in 1276/78 (*Extenta,*Chaource), which was shared between the count and the abbot.

13. 1173,*Histoire* III, pp. 462–63; the 1198 charter is in *Extenta*, Saint-Mards. The 1173 grant to Maraye was undoubtedly earlier than the one to Chaource because the latter clarified immigration procedures, no doubt at the request of local lords who had experienced difficulties with the pull of franchises on their own men.

14. *Etat des bois*: Saint-Mards' hearths were not recorded. See also table 2.

15. *Extenta,*Saint-Mards: "dominus non habet ibi aliqua in dominio suo, scilicet neque terras, neque furnos, neque molendina, neque mercatum, neque tholoneum, neque pedagium, neque manum mortuem, neque aliqua(m) prisam, preterquam illam que continetur in transcripto franchisie dicte ville . . . sed bene dicunt quod dominus habet ibi omnem omnino juridictionem."

16. *Extenta,*Villeneuve-au-Chemin.

17. Villeneuve had been created a "new" village in 1178,M,69 when the count and the prior of Saint-Jean-en-Chastel agreed to share the revenues. The count had assigned some of his share here to Erard of Brienne in 1233,M,327, but he reacquired it in 1271/73, as reported by the *Extenta*, Villeneuve. In 1276/78 the count had half the village, as in 1178, so the entire village consisted of 130 tenants and perhaps a hundred hearths.

18. The text is in *Extenta*, Pont-sur-Seine.

19. For duels in the absence of the *prévôt*: if a composition was made first without the *prévôt* but then with his approval, the fine was 6 d., but if pledges had already been taken before a composition was made, the fine was 7 s. 6 d.; the victor of any duel in which death occurred was fined 100 s. On market days anyone causing injury was fined 60 s., and if injury was caused by arms, the perpetrator was at the count's mercy.

20. *Extenta*,Pont-sur-Seine: the situation was as follows: if there were four or more sons living at home, they could enter the community by paying 12 d., just as strangers did; each was required to "jure sur sains à garder la franchise et les droits de la ville. Et, pour que li sont jure, requieront la sairement dou prevost de la vile, quar il ont heu par lonc usaige des prevos qui ont esté sa en arriars en la dicte ville par election dou comun de la vile, Et est crehuz par son sairement seux eux."

21. Ibid; " . . . nec miles ne(c) allius hominum aliquem pro conventione aliqua velalia de causa ad eadem villa revocare possit, nisi suus homo fuerit de corpore, vel in eo antiquam et talliabilem commendacionem hab(ue)rit, pro qua in ipsa sectam habere debeat."

22. There were, of course, other completely new villages, for example, the one established by the lord of Durnay in 1171,Ch,46, which had to be destroyed because it threatened a nearby abbey (see chap. II, n. 114).

23. The *Extenta*,Ervy text says that "King Henry" purchased the other half. The royal title was correct only after the 1234 acquisition of the kingdom of Navarre, so the earliest king-count of that name was Henry III (1270–74). Had the lords of Ervy retained their share until that period, they would have been inventoried in the county administrative surveys, especially the *Rôles* and *Hommages*, from which they are absent. Perhaps the *Extenta* reference was a lapse for Henry II; a purchase during his active rule, 1187–90, would explain the franchise in 1199, just after Thibaut had succeeded, as well as the 1214 sale by the Ervy family of its possessions in the town (and the family's sudden disappearance afterward). It was common for new lords to reissue the grants of previous lords; see Bar-sur-Seine in the Appendix.

24. The text is in *Ordonnances des rois de France de la troisième race*, 22 vols. (Paris, 1723–1849), VI, pp. 200–202. According to Prou, "Les coutumes de Lorris," p. 301, the spread of this type of charter was ephemeral in the last decade of the twelfth century, and only Ervy (in the *bailliage*) had even a modified form of its franchise. Prou notes that many other franchises had similar clauses, especially for judicial fines, and that it would be difficult to isolate the Lorris charter as the sole influence.

25. *Extenta*,Ervy.

26. These chronological limits are not due merely to the lack of other documents. Charters of the count were numerous from the mid-twelfth century through the thirteenth century, but the franchises were confined to a few narrow timespans. Moreover, the franchised communities were mentioned in the *Extenta* of 1276/78; if other communities had received grants whose texts are now lost, there would have been at least a reference here (Villeneuve-au-Châtelot's franchise, for example, appears only in the *Extenta*).

27. See chap. 1, n. 17.

28. 1209,*Histoire* V,718.

29. 1213 Oct,LP,85r–86r; see also the charter of Jean of Brienne of 1213 in the Appendix. Twelve thirteen was the year in which the four-year royal wardship over Thibaut IV expired (see n. 28). Other charters concerning Thibaut's minority are in *Documents* I, pp. 471–75.

30. The "Liber pontificum" contains numerous acts from 1214 by prelates supporting Blanche and Thibaut; they show as well the active roles played by Innocent III and Honorius.

31. The "Cartulary of Blanche" is the secular counterpart to the "Liber pontificum," in that it collects the acts of Champagne overlords and important barons

who supported Thibaut. The Assembly of Meaux, 1216 July,CB,9r–v, was the occasion of many charters attesting support for Thibaut. However, a truce was not arranged until 1218 June,CB,41r–42r.

32. 1220 Dec.,Th,158v–159r.

33. 1222,LP,83r–85r, and in many other places: their capitulation was carefully recorded.

34. The details of Thibaut's politics and personal relations with the queen and the French barons are in Sidney Painter, *The Scourge of the Clergy: Peter of Dreux, Duke of Brittany* (Baltimore, 1937).

35. Aubri reports the events in general and gives these figures for the years 1229–30.

36. Texts: for Troyes, Chapin, *Les villes de foires*, pp. 288–89; for Saint-Florentin, Villemaur, and Bar-sur-Seine, the texts are appended to their respective *Extenta* registers in *Documents* II. Differences in the texts are limited to the following: In the latter three grants, the count stated that he could send an overseer during tax collection, a correction of an obvious oversight in the first grant. In the Villemaur charter the area of the *prévôté* was defined as excluding Vauchassis, which already had a franchise (see above). The charter of Bar-sur-Seine has a special provision allowing any of the count's men "in Champagne and in Brie" to "escheat" there; the *Extenta,*Payns, defines this: "appelatur 'eschief' quando aliquis redimit se a domino suo ut possit remanere sub dominio juridictione alterius domin." This provision was probably added because until about 1227 Bar-sur-Seine had been a county under its own counts (see chap. V and the entry on the Bar-sur-Seine family in the Appendix). Finally, the only clauses not discussed in this section are: the requirement that the count's men use his mills and ovens—the mayor of each community would assign other mills and ovens in the event that the count's facilities were not adequate—and permission for the count's sergeants who already had individual franchises to join the above communities.

37. The 1267 reissue of the Bar-sur-Seine charter states that the count's "receiver" would choose the thirteen men on the first of May; the text is in Lucien Courtant, *Histoire de la ville et de l'ancien comté de Bar-sur-Seine* (Bar-sur-Seine, 1855), pp. 93–94.

38. "Et cil XIII nomé jureront sore sainz que ma droiture et celi de la comune de Troies garderont et governeront la vile et les afaires de la vile a bone foi." The count's men in Troyes had an internal administration from the twelfth century, but it was closely controlled by the count. The count had a *villicus* of the "community" in 1197,H,21(Saint-Bernard); the *prévôt* and *scabini* in 1215,MLC,81 issued a charter.

39. A seal of the commune of Troyes depicts a seated man surrounded by twelve heads, with the legend: "sigillum majoris et juratorum communie trecensis" (Boutiot, *Des institutions communales*, pp. 12 ff).

40. *Feoda* V,2985, dated 1201.

41. The reissue of 1242 is printed in Vallet de Viriville, *Les archives historiques du département de l'Aube*, pp. 370–74. The commune actually ended in 1240 when ten prominent townsmen took over the finances for five years: the *jurée* was suspended and a sales tax imposed on all transactions without exception, but this arrangement failed after two years. A discussion of the main developments is in Chapin, *Les villes de foires*, pp. 162–72.

42. There is outside evidence as well that these communes continued: for example, the mayor of the Bar-sur-Seine commune is mentioned in 1259,Mor,117, and he issued a charter in 1272,Arch.Aube,14bis H 21.

43. Reference to a castle in Isle is in 1097/1104,Mol,234; to mayors of Isle: 1158,Arch.Aube,27 H 3; 1165,M,53; 1170,M,60. In both *Feoda* IV,2852 of 1204/10 and *Feoda* VI,4203 of ca. 1222 fiefs are listed as being *in majorica insularum*. Bochard was mayor in 1220,StL,21 and mayor of the commune in 1235,MLC,180.

44. *Rôles*,Méry,572: Pierre had one-third of the fief of Margaret of Droupt, a

woman of the count and probably related to Pierre; see also the entry on the Granges family in the Appendix.

45. Vauchassis, which shared the 1198 Maraye franchise (see above), was explicitly excluded from the *prévôté* of Villemaur, which included the 1231 commune provisions (see n. 36).

46. See the entry on the Nogent family in the Appendix.

47. See the entry on the Pont family in the Appendix.

48. Various sections of the 1230–31 grants were borrowed from earlier charters. For example, in 1220,Th,44r, the count's franchise provided that four *jurati* of a village "preserve the count's *iure et vila*," a phrase similar to that sworn by the *jurée* in 1230–31. Closest in form to the commune charters is the 1228,Th,133v–134r grant to the men of Courlon-sur-Yonne: they paid a tax of 4 d. per pound value of lands (*libre valoris teneure sua*) in return for *taille* exemption and other privileges. An earlier attempt to evaluate the commune charters in the context of previous franchises is by René Bourgeois, *Du mouvement communal dans le comté de Champagne aux XIIe et XIIIe siècles* (Paris, 1904).

49. A fine review of the later municipal development of Troyes is by Françoise Bibolet, "Le rôle de la guerre de cent ans dans le développement des libertés municipales à Troyes," *Mémoires de la Société Academique de l'Aube* 99 (1939–42): 295–320.

50. "Comes Campanie communias burgensium et rusticorum fecit, in quibus magis confidebat, quam in militibus suis" *Monumenta Germaniae Historica, Scriptores* XXIII, p. 929.

51. Ervy's franchise of 1199 applied to the count's men in the entire castellany. The June 1231 charters for Bar-sur-Seine and Villemaur also included their castellanies; in fact, in 1258, Courtant, *Bar-sur-Seine*, p. 92, Thibaut IV referred to men of Villeneuve and Celles-sur-Ource as being "of the community and of the justice" of Bar-sur-Seine, and in the 1328 *Prisée* (*Documents* II, pp. 378–380) there were forty-one villages sharing Villemaur's commune. The *Extenta* for Payns reports that its *jurée* covered men in the castellany as well as in the town. It would appear that the September 1230 franchise of Troyes was the only grant limited to townsmen and that in the later grants the count was led to extend their scope to cover all his men in each castellany. Of course, only his own men were included.

52. A good description of the various impositions falling on peasants is by Henri Sée, "Etude sur les classes serviles en Champagne du XIe au XIVe siècle," *Revue historique* 56 (1894): 225–52, 57 (1895): 1–21. With the exception of a few evaluations, such as the importance of *corvée* or the significance of the *hospites*, Sée's presentation holds up well.

53. There is no evidence that peasants were excluded from the clergy as a matter of principle; see the examples of peasants as clerics in chap. II, n. 135. Also, 1228,V,37r–v: the abbey received from a local lord a family of peasants consisting of husband, wife, and children, one of whom was a cleric.

54. 1234(seventeenth-century copy),Ch,145: Erard of Chacenay franchised his men of Vitry-le-Croisé from "tolls and *tailles*." 1255(seventeenth-century copy), Ch,170: the count of Forez, husband of one of the Chacenay heiresses, enfranchised the men of Chacenay itself from all tolls and *tailles* in return for a tax of 1 d. per pound value of land and 3 d. per pound value of movables (precisely one-half of the count's rate in the communes); he further sold them the *prévôté* and justice of the place for an annual 15 l., in effect granting them an internal self-administration; he retained justice over major crimes, heretics, Jews, ecclesiastics, and *gentils-hommes* (the same exceptions retained by the count of Champagne in the commune grants). 1255(authentic copy of 1576 of a *vidimus* of 1396), in Vallet de Viriville, *Les archives historiques*, pp. 362–68: the lord of Durnay's franchise for Villeneuve-au-Chêne.

55. Dannemoine is an example of a village under the full control of a lay lord at the end of the thirteenth century; it was exceptionally well described because it entered the count's domain in 1273 (*Documents* II, p. 47, n. 4). In 1276/78,

Extenta,Dannemoine, it had 105 hearths and produced 18 l. from *tailles*, about 6 l. from *mainmorte*, and 40 l. from justice annually; altogether these revenues produced two-thirds of the reported revenue of 90 *l.t.* in the 1252 *Rôles*,Ervy,339; see also chap. IV, n. 31.

56. Baratier, *La démographie provençale,* chap. 7, uses the following classification: 250–400 hearths constitute a small town, 400 or more a medium or average (not in the statistical sense) town, and 1,000 or more hearths a large town. His definition of urban—requiring 400 hearths (p. 37)—would exclude the *bailliage* castellany towns as urban centers, if size alone were the criterion; in fact, the slightly smaller castellany towns assumed the functions of the 400-hearth towns in Provence. Troyes was so large and exercised such a strong influence in the *bailliage* that towns of Baratier's medium size did not develop (although there were large agrarian villages). There are no reliable figures for the population of Troyes. Provins had at least 10,000 in the early fourteenth century, if its roll of residents (2,700 persons) is assumed to reflect hearths; see Marie-Thérèse Morlet, "L'origine des habitants de Provins aux XIIIe et XIVe siècles d'après les noms de personne," *Bulletin philologique et historique du Comité des Travaux Historiques et Scientifiques,* 1961, pp. 95–114. It is unlikely that Provins, in spite of its important cloth industry, had a much larger population in the thirteenth century than Troyes, which had similar economic functions but which was more important as an administrative and cultural center. J. C. Russell, *Medieval Regions and their Cities* (Bloomington, Ind., 1972), places the population of Troyes at about 14,800 (p. 148, table 19).

57. *Extenta*,Troyes: "habet dominus merum et mixtum imperium et omnem omnino jurisdictionem in ominibus personis, preterquam in privilegiatis et preterquam in hominibus ecclesiarum illarum Trecensium, que vel privilegio vel usu longevo in suis hominibus habent consimilem potestatem."

58. For example, in 1258,StS,241v–242r (see also chap. II, n. 144), a *femina de corpore* inherited half of her grandfather's possessions, which owed altogether 12 d. rent (the average paid by the count's tenants in Villeneuve-au-Chemin; see above); she had a house (3 d. rent) and land (3 d. rent). If she had had to pay a *taille* of 5 s. in addition, her payments would have been substantially heavier.

59. 1050,MD,35: the count of Brienne defined his "customs" to include *corvées* (see also n. 63).

60. 1153,P,7: the sale of four *arpents* each of land and fields included *corvées;* 1195,R,5(xxv); 1207,M,234: Hugh Crollebois, knight, gave what was probably his alod at Magnant, including *corvée* (see Appendix). Champagne fiefs also included *corvées:* the new fief of Bouy-Luxembourg had an annual *corvée* from "all the village" of thirty hearths (see Appendix); see also the villages of Mesnil-Lettre in 1222 (under Pougy in the Appendix) and Nogent-sur-Aube in 1248 (under Ramerupt in the Appendix).

61. 1196,N,12: Milo of Saint-Phal shared the *corvées* at Rouilly-Sacey but retained all the plowing *corvée* owed by the *albani* there (see chap. II, n. 124); the lord of Plancy likewise had the plowing service, among other rights, in the *pariage* over four villages in 1222,M,323 (see chap. II). The abbot of Molesme preserved the *corvée* owed on his lands in three villages in 1233 (see chap. II, n. 130) and insisted on it from the villagers of Villery, whose *taille* he commuted (1211,Mol,301–2). When Courcelles was divided in 1225, the residents who paid *cens* were shared in respect to justice, fines, and harvest duties (see chap. II, n. 124).

62. The countess franchised her chaplain's sister and brother-in-law from all obligations, including *corvée,* in ca. 1220 (see chap. II, n. 106).

63. The count of Brienne defined the "customs" that he no longer required of an abbey to be justice, *corvées,* road and castle work, and ban, which was distinguished from the others (1050,MD,35). 1102/25,Mol,244: *per consuetudinarum bannum* referred to baking at a certain oven; 1196,N,12: the lord of Saint-Phal had a ban at Chamoy by which only his men and *hospites* could sell at a certain time.

64. See above, n. 36, for the ban in the count's communes, and chap. II for

Nogent, where the count also had a ban on wine, by which he alone could sell wine during the month after Easter, worth 30 l. annually (*Extenta,* Nogent).

65. For example, Coursan with eighty hearths in 1290 (*Etat des bois*) contained *hommes taillables* who together paid an annual 37 l. in 1276/78 (*Extenta,* Ervy), or an average of 10 s. per hearth.

66. See the example of Montfey, a village of 150 hearths, divided into six separate fiefs (see the Appendix).

67. Article X (decision dated 1284 but assigned to 1285 by Benton, "Philip the Fair," p. 310, n. 8): the reference to "men of *mainmorte* and of *serve condition*" appears only in the rubric, not in the body of the article; the latter refers rather to men and women who are "of *mainmorte* and *tailleable.*" If ms. *A* was written ca. 1295, then the introduction of the term *serve* in contemporary matters could be closely dated to the last decade of the century. This would be confirmed by the second *Coutumier* reference, Article LVIII (a decision dated 1295), in which a *femme serve* married a *franc homme.* For both decisions the court contained royal officials, masters of the Parlement of Paris, who may have been responsible for the new terms. In none of the other *Coutumier* articles dealing with peasant tenure is *serf* used in any form. This evidence tends to support the observation by Pierre Petot that *serf* and *servage* were the result of translations from the Justinian Code of *servus* and *servitus* and that the translators failed to understand the distinction between ancient slavery and their own rural conditions; see Petot, "L'évolution numerique de la classe servile en France du IXe au XIVe siècle," in *Recueils de la Société Jean Bodin* II. *Le Servage,* 2d ed., (Brussels, 1959), p. 164, n. 1. The difficulties of "serfdom" as a concept for comparative purposes are discussed in Alexandre Eck, "La notion du servage à la lumière de la méthode comparative," in ibid., pp. 339–42.

IV. The Fief Holders

1. See chap. I for an evaluation of charters as a source.

2. See chap. I for the historical context of the surveys.

3. The validity of figures based on a few hundred cases, with percentages carried to the first decimal, may seem questionable, but the results from the *bailliage* compare very closely with those from the entire county (see also n. 52). Furthermore, in most instances the *bailliage* registers have lower ratios of omitted data than those for any other area. For both reasons—very close comparative results and higher ratios of response—the *bailliage* results can be taken as an accurate approximation for the entire county. All calculations are based on revised raw figures, so that where several categories (such as income or status) have been regrouped after initial computations for presentation here, the total percentages may not always be 100.0 percent.

4. The summation at the end of the *Feoda* gives a total of 2,030, which the editor claims should be in fact 2,036. However, by using a very cautious procedure for identifying persons in the *Feoda,* I have eliminated over 100 duplications; the number of actual persons is below 1,900 (see also nn. 5 and 6).

5. I have considered the possibility that the scribes were counting fiefs instead of persons and that the duplications of persons represented additional fief holdings; but if that were the case, the sum of raw and duplicate entries (fiefs) would be equal to the *summa militum,* whereas this is true for one castellany only (Saint-Florentin). The sum of the raw and multiple entries (men), on the other hand, exactly equals the *summa* for Méry, Pont, and Villemaur and is very close for Troyes-Isle, Saint-Florentin, and Payns, leaving only Ervy to be explained as a deviation. The ambivalence of counting men and fiefs is inherent in the document itself: entitled *Feoda,* its summation is of *milites.* The same point is made in Milo Breban's letter to the countess (ca. 1205) in which he refers to the *scripta feodorum* but gives a total of knights, not fiefs (see below, n. 9).

6. Ten persons without surnames have been identified. For example, the Manasses who heads the Villemaur list was obviously Manasses of Villemaur (see the Appendix). Twenty-three others without surnames can be positively identified; although about half of them seem to be duplications, no adjustments have been made in the calculations. That even contemporary scribes were somewhat confused is shown by the entry for Robert Fayel, after which is added: "This Robert is the same as the above Robert of Biautel" (*Feoda*, 1209 and 1255). Three duplications in Troyes and Payns have been arbitrarily subtracted from Payns because of its shrinkage as a castellany in the thirteenth century (see table 15). Only a couple of the remaining identifiable duplications have been arbitrarily assigned to one castellany over another.

7. See the histories of knight families in the Appendix.

8. Of the 313 persons, only one has a duplication of military service: Geoffroy Regis owed two months in Méry and four in Pont; he is assigned to Pont.

9. This 41–45 percent does not accord with the statement by former county officials in ca. 1205 that the count had 2,200 *milites*, of whom 1,800 (82 percent) owed guard (they were *tam ligii quam munitionis observatoris*); on this letter, see chap. I, n. 17, and on the spread of liegeance in the early thirteenth century, see below, Trends and n. 59. On the Payns register, see below, n. 11.

10. See below and n. 12.

11. That the failure to mention guard is in fact proof that no regular duty was required is shown by two entries. In the Provins register, in which only 24 of the 237 knights owed regular guard, an explanation appended to the register reads: "The custom of Provins is that if war breaks out near the castle of Provins, all knights from the limestone road to the woods of Aliot and from the woods of Joy to the River Seine will come to stay at Provins, except those knights who are in the castellany of Bray-sur-Seine" (*Feoda*, 1643). Likewise, in the castellany of Montereau-faut-Yonne, where only 3 of the 29 knights owed regular guard, all knights were required to stay at the castle if hostilities occurred in that vicinity (*Feoda*, 1285). The Payns register is unique among all *Feoda* registers in mentioning neither castle guard nor liegemen; it is possible, unlikely as it may seem, that there was no obligation for regular duty at that time in Payns. An interesting specific case: Henri Crosart was simply listed in *Feoda*, Saint-Florentin, 272 without guard; in *Feoda* IV (of 1204/10), Saint-Florentin, 2867, he was excluded by name from a list of fief holders who owed eight weeks guard at that castle (therefore, the failure to mention guard in 1172 meant that he owed none).

12. If, on the other hand, "guard" is interpreted as a neutral notation without reference to a specific term of service, the accumulation of duty-time could be based on the median of specified service (5–6 weeks) instead of 4 weeks; the accumulation would increase from 204 to 306 weeks, and the percentage of duty-time performed by those owing "guard" would increase from 17.9 percent to 23 percent, but this increase would not affect the overall ratios in table 4-B.

13. That the absence of notation on liegeance actually meant that a person was not liege to the count is shown in specific cases: for example, Pierre of Bouy-sur-Orvin was listed twice in *Feoda* but without reference to liegeance; in *Feoda* III and V, however, he was noted for "plain homage" (see the Appendix). See also the example in n. 11.

14. If "guard" is calculated as the median (maximum of six weeks), the percentage rises to 65.4 percent. Or, if "guard" is dropped altogether from the calculation, the percentage drops to 61.2 percent. In either case, the deviation is small.

15. See above, n. 9.

16. *Feoda*, 1083, 1797, 1856, 1006 (a knight who in 1172 owed eight weeks guard lost his fief ca. 1192 when the bridge on which his revenue was assigned collapsed).

17. Scribes in the early thirteenth century referred to *testimoneo scripti, sicut in scripto*, and *ut in scripto* (*Feoda* III, 2412, 2528, 2539). The *liber feodorum*

mentioned in *Feoda* VII, 5270, dated after 1243, probably still referred to the *Feoda* of 1172, the only full survey of fiefs to that date. Even in 1252, *Rôles*, Bray, 152, a man was held to eight weeks guard, *sicut scripta dicunt*.

18. The *Feoda* III register (ca. 1201) for Nogent, which had entered the Champagne domain in 1199, states that the fief holders in Nogent had been previously listed neither *in scripto patris comitis Henrici neque in scripto filii*. The statement implies that an effort had been made to compose an entirely new survey under Henry II.

19. Indeed, these registers may have been recorded in the count's presence as homages were given: *Feoda* VII, 4146 refers to Henri, *cambellanus meus*, as pledge for a certain relief.

20. The entries for Jean of Marnay furnish a comparison. In *Feoda* VII, 5206, of after 1234: he did liege homage for arable, fields, men, woods, and justice at Marnay; some property there was held from him by *dominus* Jacques of Pont. The entry in *Rôles*, Nogent, 663 (drawn up in 1249) is more precise: Jean was now identified as an *armiger;* he had a house at Marnay in addition to the above-mentioned properties, and all were valued at 20 *l.t.*; he also owed eight weeks castle guard. Apparently Jacques of Pont had died by 1249; now Jean Albigeois, *miles*, held two rear-fiefs from Marnay: 20 *l.t.* at Marnay and 3 *l.t.* at Pont. See the later entry for Marnay in the Appendix.

21. Thibaut IV sent a letter in 1250 to his *baronibus, castellanis, militibus et aliis feodatis* requesting that they tell the *enquêteurs*, a knight and a canon, about their fiefs and rear-fiefs (*Layettes du Trésor des Chartes* III, ed. Joseph de Laborde [Paris, 1875], pp. 122–23). The registers of 1249 and 1252 are considered to represent a single date in the calculations, and all adjustments have been made in favor of greater information rather than for one date or another.

22. On *librata terre* as a unit of income, see below and n. 30. Hereafter it appears as *l.t.*

23. *Rôles*, Nogent 660,668,683,684.

24. *Rôles*, Nogent,681; Méry,580.

25. *Rôles*, Pont,766; Nogent,664; Sézanne,1020. *Feoda* VI,3971.

26. The *dominus* category here includes ninety *domini*, thirteen *milites*, and one *dominus-miles*. In fact, *miles* is used in only three registers: Pont has six *milites* and one *dominus*, Nogent has five and three respectively, and Bar-sur-Seine two and fourteen. In the early-thirteenth-century charters, *dominus* generally became a substitute for *miles*, with the use of one term over the other at the preference of the particular scribe, and occasionally both titles were employed. The fact that Thibaut IV addressed his *milites* (see above, n. 21), whereas the *Rôles* referred predominantly to *domini* rather than to *milites*, establishes the equivalency. An example within the *Rôles* itself confirms the synonymous use of *dominus* and *miles*: Hugh of Montfey was entitled *dominus* for his direct fief (Ervy,337) and *miles* for his rear-fief (Bray,122). Also interesting are the cases of scribal corrections of *dominus* (i.e., *dominus* equivalent to *knighted*) to *armiger* (Meaux,512) and of *armiger* to *miles* (Sézanne,1026); both changes illustrate the importance of correct status attribution when known. See chap. V for discussion of the evolution of titles.

27. *Rôles*, Nogent,660; *Feoda* VI,3941; 1263,P,268. Also, Jean of Rigny-le-Ferron was without title in *Rôles*, Isle,445 but was *messire* and *chevalier* in *Rôles B*, Isle,6483. Fromond II of Minay, who was without title in the *Rôles*, was an *armiger* in 1245 and a *chevalier* in 1270 (see the Appendix). The holder of a rear-fief, Seger of Fontvanne, was without title in *Rôles*, Isle,445 but was an *armiger* in 1264, StU,34, when he sold that rear-fief for 20 l.

28. The elimination of entries without status assumes that they are random, caused by scribal ignorance or negligence, and not related to status as such. Also, in cases where a minor heir is listed by Christian name only and also without status, but where the father's full name and status are given, the entry is coded as if it were still the father's, with his status rather than his son's blank counted.

29. The percentage may actually be slightly below 56.5 percent, since several entries note that rear-fiefs would be recorded at a later time.

30. The *librata terre* was a standard unit of value employed throughout the county and did not refer to a specific coinage. In fact, the moneys of Provins and Troyes were probably equal, and in 1165 money of Meaux was made equal to both of them (Martin Bouquet, *Recueil des historiens des Gaules et de la France*, XVI, [1814] p. 702). The earliest reference to a unit of assessment is in *Feoda* II,Rosnay,2164, of ca. 1200, for Oudard of Aulnay, perhaps just before he became marshal of Champagne: he was listed for *quindecim libratis terre*. The 1212 council on the regulation of female succession to castles and fortifications required that heiresses receive equivalent shares of such estates, which presumed a standard unit of assessment (see chap. V). An alternate expression is in *Rôles*,Bar-sur-Aube,10: "que omnia valent circiter sexaginta libras annuatim."

31. The council decision of 1212 on equal shares among direct heirs directed that the calculations omit the values of the (rear-)fiefs held from the estate; see *Coutumier*, p. 146, n. In most cases a clear distinction is made between the direct holder's income and the revenues assigned to his rear-fief holders, but in some cases adjustments must be made. For example, Isabel of Dannemoine, *domina*, held the entire village of Dannemoine and some other possessions for a total of 120 *l.t.* as her fief. But one-third of that village, valued at 30 *l.t.*, was held from her by Henri of Esclaville in rear-fief, and another rear-fief was assigned on her other revenues, so that her actual income was 80 *l.t.*, which is the value coded here (*Rôles*,Ervy,339).

32. *Rôles*,Isle,435.

33. There is no way of checking whether fief holders undervalued their fiefs, but presumably the *enquêteurs* would be able to spot flagrant violations, especially if testimony was taken in the presence of local officials.

34. *Rôles*,Bar-sur-Seine,55,68; Troyes,1120,1140. See also n. 51.

35. Two men held rear-fiefs from Guillaume of Leignes and *ipse nihil tenet in manu sua* (*Rôles*,Bar-sur-Seine,88). The same with Robert of Saint-Mards, though he may have entered the church by this time (*Rôles*,Méry,590), for in 1265 he was a canon of Laon still holding his inheritance in the *bailliage* (*Hommages*,Villemaur, 5487).

36. The most valuable of the multiple fiefs are coded as "first" fiefs, except in the case, say, of nonvalued castles or fortifications, which take precedence over less important but valued fiefs.

37. This 63.8 percent response ratio for 178 sole or first fiefs for all nine castellanies is actually the second best ratio of response available, ranking after the much smaller sample for the castellany of Saint-Florentin (72.2 percent).

38. *Rôles*,Ervy,339. *Extenta*,Dannemoine; see chap. III, n. 55, and above, n. 31. Also, the 60 *l.t.* fief of Lasson in *Rôles*,Ervy,336 was not listed with justice, but in *Rôles B*,Ervy,6657 that fief was listed by components, including justice.

39. For example, the 40 *l.t.* fief of Flora, *domicella*, of Macey seems to have included the entire village of Macey (thirty hearths in ca. 1290, *Etat des bois*) except justice: house, lands, fields, vines, men, *cens*, use of woods; the justice, worth 2 *l.t.*, had been assigned to her mother as dowry and was listed in another entry (*Rôles*,Isle,427,430; see also the Appendix).

40. An excellent example to prove that the *enquêteurs* indeed included all important parts of most fiefs is of the village of Montfey: it was divided among five brothers and sisters in 1252 and had five separate entries in the *Rôles;* yet only one of them, the eldest brother with the fortified house, had justice there (see the Appendix).

41. Examples of fiefs in the castellany of Bar-sur-Seine: parts of an oven, worth 3 *l.t.* each (*Rôles*,61,62); two vineyards worth 3 *l.t.* (*Rôles*,69); *terrage* and *cens* worth 5 *l.t.* (*Rôles*,72); whereas two 50 *l.t.* fiefs each contained arable, fields, ovens, mills, and justice (*Rôles*,75,76).

42. *Feoda* IV,Ervy,2881, of ca. 1204/10: Iter of Brosse held his *domus* render-

able to the count (see the Appendix). *Feoda* III of ca. 1201 contains a section entitled "Hec sunt castella jurabilia et reddibilia, et domus similiter."

43. This finding is corroborated by archaeological evidence that castles, fortifications, and large (fortified) houses were held only by the very small minority of wealthy lords, whereas knights lived in houses similar to those of peasants: see Pierre Héliot, "Les demeures seigneuriales dans la région Picarde au moyen âge: châteaux ou manoirs?" in *Recueil de travaux offert à M. Clovis Brunel*, 2 vols. (Paris, 1955), II, 574—83. The quantitative results for the *bailliage* here exclude a few references to granges and one to a merchant hall.

44. The breakdown by status of those owing service gives percentages which ranged ±6 percent from the overall averages: 39.6 percent of the *dominae* and 27.8 percent of those without status gave service, compared with the overall average of 33.6 percent (the *domicellae* and others, with only five persons each, are of course excluded). There is likewise a ±6 percent variation from the average 28 percent of fief holders not owing guard.

45. Of the fiefs with explicit terms of service, 76 percent were worth less than 30 *l.t.*, compared with 74.8 percent of fiefs without guard. An example of the disassociation between fief value and length of service is for the village of Montfey: divided among three brothers and two sisters, the village provided incomes and terms of service of: 30 *l.t.* (eight days), 30 *l.t.* (eight days), 30 *l.t.*(held as a rear-fief, no guard), 25 *l.t.*(two weeks), and 8 *l.t.* (six weeks). In this case there was even a reverse relationship (see also n. 40 above and the Appendix).

46. Huet of Romilly owed the eight weeks which his grandfather's brother had owed in 1172. André of Saint-Phal owed unspecified "custody," although his great-grandfather had owed service all year in 1172 (see chap. V and the Appendix).

47. Some aspects of this frontier are discussed in Jean Lemarignier, *Recherches sur l'hommage en marche et les frontières féodales* (Lille, 1945), chaps. 4 and 5. The appearance of the fortified houses in the early thirteenth century and their location in forested areas, as opposed to sites of the older castles on commanding terrain or at river junctions, was true in northern Champagne also. See the fine study that integrates archaeological and documentary evidence by Michel Bur et al., *Vestiges d'habitat seigneurial fortifié du Bas-Pays Argonnais,* Cahiers des Lettres et Sciences Humaines de l'Université de Reims (Reims, 1972).

48. *Hommages,*Isle,5398; see also the Appendix.

49. Table 11 is derived from tables 7-B and 12.

50. As with fiefs, the rear-fiefs are tabulated by single and first fief in order to facilitate cross-tabulation with status. Since only 8.3 percent of the rear-fief holders had more than one rear-fief, the sole/first calculations are obviously similar to those for all individual rear-fiefs.

51. Of the fifty-two rear-fiefs held by direct fief holders, twenty-six (50 percent) are valued, about the same proportion as for all rear-fiefs (47.2 percent). A table of values of rear-fiefs held by direct fief holders follows:

l.t.	frequency	accumulation
120	2	240
70	1	70
60	1	60
50	1	50
40	1	40
30	2	60
20	5	105
10	5	67
1	8	31
	26	723[a]

[a]Average value, 27.8 *l.t.*

Twenty-six of the fifty-two fiefs were not valued.

52. See Theodore Evergates, "The Aristocracy of Champagne in the Mid-Thirteenth Century: A Quantitative Description," *The Journal of Interdisciplinary History* 5 (1974): 1–18.

53. Fifty-four (of 178 valued) fiefs and thirty-two (forty, less the eight main-holders, of valued) rear-fiefs were worth 30 *l.t.* or more. Their respective accumulations of income were 3,563 *l.t.* and 1,468 *l.t.* (see tables 8 and 13).

54. For the definition of the *bailliage* as used in this study, see chap. I.

55. There are a few instances of persons who appeared in charters through the period 1265–75 and who were listed in either the *Livre des hommages* or the *Rôles des fiefs* (1275) but not, as would be expected, in both. I have not resolved these individual omissions with the fact that several castellany registers do not show any decline in total numbers.

56. Both the ⁻20.4 percent (1172–1252) and the ⁻43.1 percent (1172–1275) are based on very good totals. The interpolated figures to cover lacunae are: in the first case, Villemaur, a very stable castellany, is given a count of thirty in 1252; in the second case, Méry, also exceptionally stable, is assigned seventeen in 1275. The only reason for rejecting the ⁻43.1 percent would be a problematic manuscript tradition; in fact, the original register of the *bailliage* of Troyes is extant for 1275, and although slightly mutilated at the beginning, it is by no means incomplete (see chap. I, n. 21).

57. The only extant register of the *bailliage* from the *Livre des hommages* (1265) is for Villemaur, and it employs the same Latin titles as the *Rôles* of 1252. The equivalence of the Latin and French titles is clear by mid-thirteenth century: Hugh of Saint-Aubin was entitled *dominus* by the scribes in the *Rôles*,Nogent,674 and *messire* by the lady of Traînel who sent the *enquêteurs* a report in the vernacular on her rear-fiefs (*Rôles*,1357).

58. The status breakdown in table 15 is based on the total of known status in each survey; the refinement in status provided by nonsurvey sources for the *Rôles* of 1252 (table 6, in brackets) was not performed on the later surveys because of their limited data (see above, especially nn. 26–27).

59. The fragmentary registers *Feoda* II/III and IV/V have been combined; the results give a *bailliage* total percentage of liege versus nonliege for the entries taken as a whole, without regard to castellany. *Feoda* VI/VII are not organized by either castellany or *bailliage*, so the total county results are used here. The figure of almost 80 percent liegeance in the first decade of the thirteenth century agrees with Milo Breban's claim (ca. 1205) that 1,800 (82 percent) of the count's 2,200 knights were both liege and liable to castle guard (see n. 9 above).

60. *Feoda*,Laferté,2774.

61. *Feoda* V,Troyes,3590.

V. The Aristocracy

1. The fact that (very) occasionally *domini* were listed in the early-twelfth-century witness lists under *de militibus* does not prove the equivalence of *dominus* and *miles*. Such a grouping was intended to distinguish the warriors (*de militibus*) from the ecclesiastics (*de clericis*) or, in a tripartite distinction, the warriors from the canons and monks. The *domini* were of course qualified warriors, but they were not entitled simply "knights" (see below, The Knights, and nn. 27 and 28).

2. See chap. IV, n. 26.

3. This is an interesting problem which I have not solved. It would seem that the failure to mention status in this period was related, not to the family's status as such, but rather to the scribal conventions of particular ecclesiastical houses or even of orders.

4. The editor affixed the heading "great fiefs" to this register because it occurs in a similar register in *Feoda* IV.

5. The contemporary Norman inquest (1172), the only administrative survey in

France comparable to the *Feoda,* reveals a similar basic division between the lords and the knights; see Jacques Boussard, "L'enquête de 1172 sur les services de chevalier en Normandie," in *Recueil de travaux offert à M. Clovis Brunel,* 2 vols. (Paris, 1955), I, pp. 193–208.

6. The text is in *Coutumier,* pp. 145–46, n. 1, and in Teulet, *Layettes du Trésor des Chartes,* I, no. 1031: although the seals of those who approved are missing, their names had been written above their respective seals. Several persons in the council of 1212 have been omitted from table 17 (see below, n. 35).

7. The text is in *Coutumier,* pp. 142–44, n.

8. The text is in *Documents* I, pp. 437–38.

9. In the *Livre des hommages,* for example, Durnay, Plancy, and Dampierre are entitled *"dominus* N, *dominus* of X" (translated in the Old French as *"monsiegneur* N, *seigneur* of X"), whereas Chappes, Pougy, and Traînel are simply *"dominus* of X." In the *Rôles des fiefs* (1275) Chappes and Arcis are *"sire* of X."

10. The text is in *Documents* I, pp. 440–41.

11. The text is in *Documents* II, pp. 515–16.

12. Several men who did not belong to the old aristocracy appear in a few of the lists; see below, The Knights, and n. 35.

13. It was Lalore who first stressed the importance of these *seigneurs de second ordre* in local society, and he envisioned a series of monographs on their families in order to analyze their role in medieval society; see his "Documents pour servir à la généalogie des anciens seigneurs de Traînel," *Mémoires de la Société Académique de l'Aube* 34 (1870): 177–271.

14. Genealogies and all references are in the Appendix under the appropriate names.

15. The evidence for Pont is given below and in the Appendix. Although I have not been able to consult the archives for Yonne, in which Saint-Florentin is now located (see chap. I, n. 6), the evidence seems to indicate that the Traînel family originally held Saint-Florentin, as well as Pont. A charter of Count Thibaut II in 1151,L, pp. 92–93 deals with the gift by Hugh Adhenches to the Léproserie of what he possessed in a certain place which was *de feodo* of the *domini* of Traînel, Anselm II and his brother Garnier. The scribe states that this transaction took place in the presence of the brothers at the bridge of Nasellis (Natiaux), *sub castro* of Saint-Florentin, *quoniam de feodo eorum erat.* The use of *quoniam* here is not only a needless repetition but also a *non sequitur.* The sentence would be meaningful if *quoniam* were an error for *quondam:* the castle of Saint-Florentin was "formerly" the fief of the Traînels. An analogous phrase was applied to the "former" lady of Nogent in ca. 1190 when the castle of Nogent was absorbed into the count's domain (see the Appendix).

16. The term "segmentation" is borrowed from anthropology. There is some discussion on how strictly the term should be applied in defining "segmentary societies," but a general statement of the concept is in John Middleton and David Tait, eds., *Tribes Without Rulers: Studies in African Segmentary Systems* (London, 1958), esp. pp. 3–8.

17. This conclusion from charter references has been confirmed by narrative statements of contemporaries that show their own perceptions of their families' genealogies; see Georges Duby, "Structures de parenté de noblesse. France du Nord. XIe–XIIe siècles," in *Miscellanea mediaevalia in memoriam Jan Frederik Niermeyer* (Groningen, 1967), pp. 149–65.

18. The definitive proof that the "nobles" of the charters actually constituted a precise group of families, the aristocracy, has been demonstrated by a meticulous comparison of terminology in the various types of sources, especially the chronicles, in Flanders by Ernest Warlop, *De Vlaamse adel voor 1300,* 3 vols. (Handzame, 1968).

19. For the figures see chap. IV, table 7.

20. See the Arcis genealogy in the Appendix.

21. In the *Rôles,* Margaret (of Broyes), widow of Jacques of Durnay, held her

inheritance at Vendeuvre, valued at 200 *l.t.*, plus eighteen rear-fiefs worth at least 240 *l.t.*; this entry may have included her brother's share of one-quarter of Vendeuvre, which he sold to her husband in 1244. It was this half of Vendeuvre that was called the "castle" of Vendeuvre in the *Hommages* of 1265. Her son Jean purchased probably another quarter in 1268 from Milo II of Pougy, who in 1252 was listed for part of the castle, the fortified house, and seven rear-fief holders there. Thus, Vendeuvre in its entirety in 1252 would have constituted a direct income of ca. 400 *l.t.* and thirty two rear-fiefs providing another 400 *l.t.* See Vendeuvre and Durnay in the Appendix.

22. See the Pougy genealogy in the Appendix.

23. The charters are of course biased in favor of high-level marriages, as only those spouses would usually appear in transactions with an abbey. Even so, the names of many wives of great families are not known, and it is almost impossible to find evidence for children who married out of their social level. Mixed marriages did occur, as the *Coutumier* recognized; see chap. II and its notes 148 and 149.

24. See below, n. 26.

25. Exact references are under the appropriate names in the Appendix. Marigny: *Feoda* II, VI: if there were two heirs, one was to take Marigny, and the other would have other property. Ramerupt: *Feoda* V: its first listing as a direct fief; hitherto it had been a rear-fief of Brienne. Pougy: *Feoda* IV. Dampierre: its holder had been liege for part of the viscounty of Troyes in the original *Feoda*, but in 1218 liegeance was imposed for all Dampierre itself. Esternay: *Feoda* VI. Holders of less important fiefs often had the choice of whether to hold directly from the countess or from an elder brother. However, Simon of Châteauvillan was not allowed to hold his castle from his older brother; the countess gave him a 30 l. rent to soften the order to hold in liege homage directly from her (1208,Th,205r–v). See also n. 82 below for the Briennes and the Appendix for the Jully family.

26. Name changes are difficult to control, and even contemporaries must have experienced some confusion. A county scribe remarked that the Robert Fayel listed in the *Feoda* was the same person as the previously mentioned Robert of Biautel (*Feoda*,1209,1255). Only a slight stretch of the imagination might also see scribal pique in the entry "Bartholomew of Polisy, Ricey, Vilede, and Vilers" (*Feoda* III,Troyes,2602). Other entries in both the *Feoda* and the *Rôles* show that it was not unusual for sons to adopt surnames from their fiefs in cases, for instance, when they inherited their sole holding from the maternal line; but the preference by collateral lines of the great families of retaining the main family name for even several generations indicates that the sons of those prestigious families did not readily give up those identities. See above and the Appendix for the lords of Ramerupt (Brienne), Marigny and Esternay (Traînel), Jully (Chappes), and Durnay (Chacenay).

27. The count of Brienne, for example, was included among the *milites* in a witness list in 1146,Ch,29.

28. One of the few references, outside of witness lists, to the fact that great lords were also formally part of the knighthood is in 1203,Ch,73: *dominus* Erard II of Chacenay referred to a gift that he had made *nondum miles*. He also was the one who had the right to collect a "general *taille*" in several villages on four occasions: the marriage of his daughter, his ransom in war, his journey to Jerusalem, and "ad meam vel filii mei novam militam."

29. 1099,Mol,235–36: "these are his [Hugh of Plancy's] knights," seven men of whom only two had surnames; 1101,Mol,242–43: "a certain *miles* of Bar, called Retroversus"; 1107,Mol,252: the lord of Traînel and *ejuis militibus*; 1151,L, pp. 92–93: Anselm and Garnier of Traînel referred to Pierre of Tornel, *eorum miles*; (1160/70),V,81v: the lord of Ervy referred to "my knights," as did the count of Brienne (1179,StL,60); 1146,P,52: Milo of Nogent praised whatever the *milites de feodo suo* gave to Paraclet. 1200,Mor,48: a lord defined his *homines* as *milites, burgenses,* and *villani*. In 1194,P,83, a scribe who recopied the charter of 1146,P,52 wrote *homines* in place of the original *milites* and *rustici* (see also n. 30).

30. (1182),MD,54: the count of Brienne required that the abbey feed him and "ten or fifteen" of his *milites* and *servientes* if he should pass in the vicinity. 1100/1113,M,18: the abbey could acquire property from the count's men *sive miles sive serviens*. 1160,*Histoire* III, p. 451: the count of Champagne guaranteed Molesme that "nemo hominum meorum, neque miles neque clericus neque aliquis de servientibus meis" would be permitted to request food or accommodation at certain of the abbey's villages; only those traveling with the count's party and those summoning men to military service were entitled to such hospitality. The distinction between knights and administrative agents was quite clear on the count's lands in the *Feoda* of 1172, but the old proximity was preserved longer on the private lordships; for example, the count of Bar-sur-Seine conducted his councils *coram militibus et ministerialibus meis* in 1165,Mor,6 and 1197,Mor,42.

31. See chap. IV and its note 26.

32. There are few references to *armigeri* in the twelfth century. In 1154,P,55, two *armigeri*, Hato and Obert, were in the household retinue of the count of Blois; they were listed among the witnesses after two *milites*, the *panetarius*, the *camerarius*, and the *hostiarius*. In the negotiations which Geoffroy of Villehardouin, the chronicler, undertook with the Venetians for the transport of the Fourth Crusade, provisions were made for 4,500 *milites* with one horse apiece, 9,000 *scutifers*, and 20,000 footsoldiers (agreement of 1201, in Longnon, *Recherches sur la vie de Geoffroy de Villehardouin*, no.59), suggesting that in the early thirteenth century there was still a precise difference between knighted and nonknighted. There are few explicit references to the progression from nonknighted to knighted status: in 1206,M,232, Jean of Buxeuil confirmed an approval which he had made "before he was a knight." In 1248,Mor,109, a knight confirmed the sale which he had made *adhuc armiger esset, et necdum erat uxori obligatus* (see also the example above in n. 28, and chap. IV for a quantitative determination of the *armigeri* in the surveys).

33. Ca. 1290,*Etat des bois*(Villemaur): the custom of the woods of Montigny-les-Monts was enjoyed by both *chevaliers* and *escuiers*, as well as by ecclesiastical institutions.

34. The first reference to fortified houses as a distinct type of fortification was in ca. 1200, *Feoda* III: both castles and fortified houses were renderable to the count ("Hec sunt castella jurabilia et reddibilia, et domus similiter"). In 1176,*Histoire* III, pp. 465–66, Hugh of Saraceny agreed with the prior of Celle-sous-Chantemerle not to build a *domum firmum* with a wall or moat in the village.

35. The discrepancies in table 17 are few. The lord of Charmont (1147) does not appear as such elsewhere; the Clérey and Saint-Phal appearances in 1314 may have been due to marriages with older, more distinguished lineages; Romilly in ca. 1200 was a great fief along with Saint-Phal because of a new fortification. Omitted from all consideration here are the Villehardouin-Aulnay lineages: in spite of some properties within the *bailliage* of Troyes, their lands were always inventoried in castellanies of the *bailliage* of Chaumont; an excellent study of the family and its holdings is Longnon, *Recherches sur la vie de Geoffroy de Villehardouin*. Finally, Hugh of Saint-Maurice-aux-Riches-Hommes is omitted from the list of those in the council of 1212. He appeared in 1198 as pledge for Thibaut III to Philip Augustus but is not listed in any other Champagne register. He was probably a financier, perhaps creditor, of Thibaut; he was certainly not a great lord, nor even a knight. His son became a knight, and the latter's gift in 1234 to the newly founded Notre-Dame-des-Prés, sponsored by rich Troyens, was of small and scattered revenues (equaling one-fourth of his income), which suggest piecemeal acquisitions; that is, it appears to have been a merchant's acquisitions of lands and revenues in the countryside. His widow had a total fief income of 35 *l.t.* in 1252 (see Saint-Maurice in the Appendix). Thus, in the council of 1212 there were three men without ties to the old families who appeared among the "barons": the marshal Oudard of Aulney, his uncle Jean of Villehardouin, and Hugh of Saint-Maurice. They were evidently close advisors of the countess and attended in that capacity, not as representatives of the baronial families whose approval was sought for the new rules of inheritance.

36. *Rôles*, Bar-sur-Seine,67.
37. In the 1175 franchise to Chaource the count prohibited the "men of the villages of knights" from emigrating to Chaource. In (1186),BF,7, the count of Brienne referred to churches in *villis militum ad comitatum meum pertinens*. In the thirteenth century there are cases of knights selling entire villages: Thibaut I of Rosières sold the *villa* of Jeugny, which he seems to have held from the abbey of Montier-la-Celle, for 265 l.: it consisted of his house, men, lands, fields, *cens*, customs, justice, *gîte*, and rear-fiefs (1232,MLC,16). Similarly, in 1230,M,353, a knight sold the entire village of Saint-Saturn—men, justice, customs, *cens, terrages, ochii*, the mill, and other revenues—for 450 l.
38. 1222,Th,310r–v (see also chap. II, n. 107).
39. Richard, *Les ducs de Bourgogne*, pp. 276—77, remarks on the apparently standard 20 l. value of Thibaut's grants of fiefs, but he also correctly notes that there was no apparent relationship between fief value and length of required service. 1182,StP,36.
40. 1242,Arch.Aube,1 H 41(17v–23v): Gérard, canon of Pougy, gave to Basse-fontaine certain *terrages* and revenues over tenements and added 15 l. cash so that his brother (*miles*) Guillaume's son Gilo would have one loaf of bread weekly for his life to be collected at the abbey.
41. In one of the few cases of fief transfer for other than family requirements, Erard I of Ramerupt compensated the abbey of Molesme for damages caused by his agents by transferring control (*feoda et homagia*) of the fiefs of André of Brosse and Thomas of Ricey to the abbey (1244,Mol,359—60). In another case, Gilo of Plancy required a fief holder on his mother's own lands which passed to his sister by inheritance to be liege to him instead of to her (1189,P,77). Both cases are exceptional.
42. The *Coutumier*, Article II, provides that all fiefs be subject to equal division among heirs, save that the house pass undivided to the eldest. This custom was analogous to that applied to castles and fortified houses (councils of 1212 and 1224); and it was probably in force from the same period, the early thirteenth century, although there is no way of knowing whether a formal council decided the regulation or whether it became customary by analogy.
43. *Rôles*,Troyes,1100; *Hommages*,Troyes,5342.
44. 1209,Mol,300: the lord of Plancy exchanged a woman and her dowry for one from Molesme.
45. 1201,MLC,74: he sold "all his possessions from Clérey to Chappes, in land, men, and in all things" for 200 l.: 80 l. for his journey, 80 l. for the redemption of his father-in-law's house, and 40 l. for the abbey to rebuild its church. It is not clear whether he sold his entire rights over Villemoyenne, which was in the area between Chappes and Clérey, but his probable son Simon, *dominus*, had only a rear-fief from the lord of Chappes in *Rôles*,Troyes,132; perhaps it was Simon's mother who had her dowry in Villemaur (*Rôles*,Bar-sur-Seine,92).
46. Milo's father was a *dominus* (1190,Mol,36). Milo himself was a *miles* in 1216,Mor,74, when it was decided that he would hold his *casamentum* (land, woods, revenues) from the abbey instead of from the lord of Chacenay, who claimed it; Milo *recognovit se fuisse hominem* of the abbey. In 1218,Mor,78, he headed East and promised that if he did not return the abbey should have his tithe, *terrage*, and *cens* revenues. His uncle Raoul had gone East in 1190,Mor,36.
47. This is true even for knights who did not hold from the count. For example, Menard of Maizières, *miles*, with the approval of his wife, two sons, and daughter, sold both the fief which he held from the abbey and what he had *in dominio* (that is, as alod) at Mesnil for 90 l.; no member of the family appears in the Champagne surveys or any other charter.
48. In 1214,StS,63v–64r, the two sons of Mathew Corrigiarius, "citizen" of Troyes, gave up their rights to their mother's inheritance, a stall in Troyes, for 37 l. because they "had just taken the cross and set out [for the East] almost on the same day."
49. It is not clear whether the family retained a fief from the count of Brienne

because the latter failed to enumerate his rear-fiefs in the *Rôles*. A descendant in 1282 held a fief from the lord of Chacenay, but that may have been a later acquisition.

50. Ecclesiastical houses with ready cash may have followed the count's example, purchasing fiefs from other lords and converting alods into fiefs in the early thirteenth century; one case is from 1207,Mor,58: Thomas of Buxières absolved two of his rear-fief holders from homage to him and permitted them to transfer that homage to Mores and the Temple.

51. 1222,V,14r: Pierre, *armiger*, of Fontenay gave the abbey the rear-fief which he held from Henri Gasteblé, *miles*; the latter freed him from homage and all other obligations, including a *cens*, that went with the holding. See also the example in chap. IV, n. 35.

52. Benoît of Pont, an agent of the count, had a daughter, Margaret, who was exchanged by the count as a peasant for another woman from Saint-Loup in 1175,StL,48. She was to marry a man of the abbey, and Benoît was to hold the man's fief until the marriage occurred (1175,StL,49). Apparently it did not take place, and she seems to have married Milo of Quincy, although she is never mentioned with Milo by name. Milo's son Etienne in 1218 had Benoît of Pont's fief, which had been listed in the *Feoda* of 1172; moreover, Milo's granddaughter was also named Margaret. It appears that Milo married Margaret and took her father's fief. See also Quincy in the Appendix and Benton, "The Court of Champagne," pp. 168–69, for Benoit.

53. 1229,Th,321r: he requested that Lora, widow of the tanner Die of Troyes, be freed from *taille* on county lands.

54. See Granges in the Appendix and the mayor of Méry in Chapter IV.

55. For example, Garnier(Choars) of Laubressel was one of the *homines* of Larrivour who approved the agreement on the use of the woods of Dosches in 1230 (see chap. II, n. 68 also). In that same year, 1230,R,104(xv), he was betrothed to a woman of Montier-la-Celle, the daughter of a knight of that abbey; the abbey surrendered claim to the woman in exchange for a woman of the same *valore* whenever a man of Montier-la-Celle would want to marry a woman of Larrivour; in the meantime, each party was to have half of her *tallias et servitia* and her children.

56. There were, of course, knights of other origins: (1180/90),MLC,55: the knight Hugh, identified only as "formerly a monk," may have been of peasant origin, since he was not identified by family; 1209,StL,154: Thibaut, knight, was a converted Jew; the Jean of Poanz, *homo* and *serviens* of the countess, who was given in perpetuity to Saint-Etienne in 1217,StS,63r may have been the Jean of Poainz, *miles*, who held a fief from the chapter in 1219,StS,210v.

57. See chap. I, n. 24, and chap. II, n. 136.

58. Articles II, IV, VII, and XI.

59. Article XVII and chap. II, nn. 148 and 149.

60. Article XI.

61. Article I: a French translation of the 1224 decision, in which the "barons and castellans" seem to have been equated with those who held castles or fortified houses. No other *Coutumier* article explains the relative position of the latter.

62. Article II, which extended the Article I provisions to all fief holders and appears to have incorporated the provisions of the council of 1212 for daughters, with a change in the relative weight of younger sons and daughters.

63. Article XI.

64. Ibid.

65. Article IV.

66. Articles V(decision of 1278 on majorities) and XII.

67. Articles V and XVII.

68. Articles XV(decision of 1289/92 on relief) and L(decision of 1285 on collateral inheritance).

69. Article VIII.

70. Article XIII.

71. 1269,P,286; see also below, n. 78.
72. 1147,Arch.Aube,20 H 9: one *miles* appeared in the witness list, along with a *serviens*, a *prévôt*, and several unqualified persons. The count's *curia* was conducted in the presence of his "barons" in this period (e.g., 1125/51,Mol,263).
73. See above, n. 25.
74. Article XI.
75. 1196,P,99: the lord of Traînel gave certain woods "as his alod, that is, free . . . ab omni exactione et usuario, et dominio absolutum"; 1248,Mor,109: "omnia que in supra dicta locus habebat, a nullo homine tenebat, et nulli servitium reddebat, set erant de alodio suo"; in 1153,CP,12, Nevel, *miles*, of Ramerupt gave his entire alod to an abbey.
76. 1112,Lalore IV(Chartes de Beaulieu),181: the count of Brienne's men holding either "by fief or by alod" could donate property to the abbey; 1175,Mor,21: the alod of Buxières consisted of manses, *cens*, *terrage*, and tithe; 1182,Mor,26: the *prévôt* of Bar-sur-Seine gave from his alod, fief, and *cens* in Villenesse; 1233, V,91r-v: a 25 s. *cens* was "liberum et de alodio"; 1256,Mor,121: "ex libero allodio"; 1264,StU,27: a 27 s. rent was "de franco alodio"; 1281,Ch,183: the village of Lusigny, men, justice, and revenues "de franco allodio" was sold for 800 l.
77. *Feoda* V,3394,3956. See also chap. IV, Trends. Richard, *Les ducs de Bourgogne*, p. 267, has aptly described the situation during the minority crisis as "une véritable course aux fidélités."
78. See the Crollebois family's alienations in the Appendix.
79. 1269,P,286: Count Thibaut praised what Saint-Urbain had acquired from his "fiefs, rear-fiefs, *cens*, alods, or *dominium*"; he allowed them to purchase up to 300 *l.t.* from these possessions, but *feudum integrum nullatenus acquirat*. Thibaut used the same expression for the various types of tenures in several charters (e.g., 1269,Mor,132). 1273,H,21 (Saint-Nicholas): the property of a knight, "movanz . . . soit à terrage, à coutume, à censive, ou de fiau, ou de arrière fiau ou à autre servitude."
80. Article XII.
81. *Feoda* IV,Méry,2903: Hago of Saron held three fortified houses; his brother, whose fief is not described, was allowed to hold directly from Hago, but if he chose not to, he was required to hold from the countess.
82. See the Appendix: in 1252 the younger brother actually held in rear-fief from the eldest. In *Feoda* VI,3733, the count of Brienne was required to keep his county as a fief distinct from his other possessions, so that if he had two sons, each would be liege to the count of Champagne for a separate fief. See also above, n. 25.
83. Since military service was the reason for fief tenure, all fief holders were presumably qualified knights in theory, and the *Coutumier* could assume that fief holders were *chevaliers* as well as *gentiz hommes*. The *Rôles* of 1252 show that about one-fifth of the fief holders were actually *armigeri*. The case of Thibaut II of Basson is illustrative: he was called a *domicellus* in a private charter of 1230 but was listed among the "Knights of the Countess' Dowry" in 1229 by the Champagne officials (see the Appendix).
84. One of the few examples of internal family contention over inheritance portions is for Alice of Loge's children: her sons Jacques, *miles*, and Dreux, Jean, and Guillaume, *domicelli*, disputed the share of their eldest brother Hugh, canon of Saint-Pierre (April,1220,StP,151). It was decided that Hugh would have the possessions inside Troyes (several stalls and lodges) on the condition that the other son, Etienne, *miles*, approve on his return from overseas; he did approve in May, 1221,StP,157.
85. *Rôles*,Bar-sur-Aube,30: "de garda non debet et habet cartam"; Payns,752: a widow reported that her husband owed guard but "nec eam fecit maritus suus per XL annos"; Ervy,437: "Debet gardam per XL dies, ut credit."
86. The number of families who held only from ecclesiastical institutions and nothing from the count cannot be determined. If abbeys granted out much of their

newly acquired property as fiefs in the thirteenth century, then the number of private fief holders could have increased; but there was little point to that in the thirteenth century when the count of Champagne guaranteed the peace.

VI. French Feudal Societies

1. Henri Sée, *Les classes rurales et le régime domanial en France au moyen âge,* (Paris, 1901), a masterful synthesis written after he had conducted regional studies of peasant conditions in Brittany and Champagne; and Paul Guilhiermoz, *Essai sur les origines de la noblesse en France au moyen âge* (Paris, 1902), which is especially impressive for the range of materials consulted.

2. A fine presentation of the contribution of French historians in the early part of the century is Jean Glénisson, "L'historiographie française contemporaine: tendances et réalisations," in *La recherche historique en France de 1940 à 1965,* Comité Français des Sciences Historiques (Paris, 1966), pp. ix–lxiv.

3. The comparisons here are by no means comprehensive; only some of the most important recent works and their basic conclusions are reviewed. The most convenient recent bibliography is in Robert Boutruche, *Seigneurie de féodalité,* I. *Le premier age des liens d'homme à homme* (1959; Reprint, Paris, 1968); II. *L'apogée (XIIe–XIIIe siècles)* (Paris, 1970).

4. The best summary is in Petot, "L'évolution numerique de la classe servile en France du IXe au XIVe siècle" (1959), an updated version of the original article in the same series (1937).

5. The ninth-century polyptique of Montier-en-Der confirms the small servile population: about 90 percent of its 811 manses on 22 domains were of free status; see Lalore, *Le polyptique de l'abbaye de Montier-en-Der.* A similar confirmation comes from the polyptique of Saint-Germain-des-Prés (801/20): only about 5 percent of the 9,000 tenants were qualified as *servi;* see Emily R. Coleman, "Medieval Marriage Characteristics: A Neglected Factor in the History of Medieval Serfdom," *The Journal of Interdisciplinary History* 2 (1971): 205–17.

6. The fullest presentation of Bloch's work is in his "Liberté et servitude personnelles au moyen âge, particulièrement en France: contribution à une étude des classes" (1935), printed with corrections in his *Mélanges historiques,* 2 vols. (Paris, 1963), I, pp. 286–355.

7. Several articles are in his *Mélanges;* see especially "Les transformations du servage: à propos de deux documents du XIIIe siècle relatifs à la région parisienne" (1925), in *Mélanges historiques,* I, pp. 491–502.

8. Bloch's claim ("Liberté et servitude," p. 291) that *chevage* was widespread in Champagne is not confirmed for the southern part of the county; furthermore, his example (ibid., n. 2) of the 1255 grant of the deacon of Laon, in which *chevage* replaced *mainmorte* and *formariage,* is actually an example of a commutation to a fixed-rate residence tax. There are few examples of *chevage* even in northern Champagne (see Robert Debuisson, *Etude sur la condition des personnes et des terres d'après les coutumes de Reims du XIIe au XVIe siècle* [Reims, 1930], pp. 122–23, 128).

9. Léo Verriest, *Institutions médiévales: introduction au Corpus des Records de Coutumes et des Lois de Chefs-Lieux de l'ancien comté de Hainault I* (Mons-Frameries, 1946).

10. Pierre Duparc, "La question des 'sainteurs' ou hommes des églises," *Journal des Savants,* 1972, pp. 25–48, an excellent analysis. *Chevage* occurred in some areas, but not universally. The very conditions explained by Duparc were described by Debuisson, *Etude sur la condition des personnes et des terres.*

11. Joset, *Les villes au pays de Luxembourg,* the best regional study of franchised villages.

12. Charles-Edmond Perrin, *Recherches sur la seigneurie rurale en Lorraine d'après les plus anciens censiers (IXe–XIIe siècle)* (Paris, 1935), and "Chartes de franchise et rapports de droits en Lorraine," pp. 11–42. Of the 280 charters issued by 1350, 207 were by lay lords. Of the 36 issued by abbots, 33 were in fact

"associations" and should perhaps be excluded as franchises. Michel Lebon, "Texts sur le formariage en Lorraine des origines au début du XIIIe siècle," *Annales de l'Est* 2 (1951): 53–66: permission to intermarry had been granted in the mid-eleventh century, but only to persons of other villages under the same lordship; the 1179 agreement was the first one for tenants of different lords—women went to their husbands' lords.

13. Henri Dubled, "Servitude et liberté en Alsace au moyen âge: la condition des personnes au sein de la seigneurie rurale du XIIIe au XIVe siècle," *Vierteljahrschrift für Sozial- und Wirtschaftsgeschichte* 50 (1963): 164–203, 289–324; "Taille et 'Umgeld' en Alsace au XIIIe siècle," ibid., 47 (1960): 32–47; "Administration et exploitation des terres de la seigneurie rurale en Alsace aux XIe et XIIe siècles," ibid., 47 (1960): 433–73; and "La communauté de village en Alsace au XIIIe siècle," *Revue d'histoire économique et sociale* 41 (1963): 5–33.

14. See Richard, *Les ducs de Bourgogne*, for the general situation. See also Georges Duby, *La société aux XIe et XIIe siècles dans la région mâconnaise* (Paris, 1953).

15. Marcel David, *Le patrimoine foncier de l'Eglise de Lyon de 984 à 1267: contribution à l'étude de la féodalité dans la Lyonnais* (Lyon, 1942); Etienne Fournial, *Les villes et l'économie d'échange en Forez aux XIIIe et XIVe siècles* (Paris, 1967); and especially the revealing experiment in methodology: Georges Duby, "Géographie ou chronologie du servage? Note sur les *servi* en Forez et en Mâconnais du Xe au XIIe siècle," in *Hommage à Lucien Febvre*, 2 vols. (Paris, 1953), I, pp. 147–53.

16. The importance of the Lorris customs on a regional scale was realized by Maurice Prou, but no recent study has continued his work; see his "Les coutumes de Lorris." The great efforts spent by Bloch and others on a few franchises such as that of Orly (1250) have obscured the general significance of those grants in other areas. The Orly grant clearly freed all *hospites* from *taille, mainmorte,* and *formariage;* thirty three other persons received the same exemptions and, in addition, freedom from *servitium;* see Guy Fourquin, *Les campagnes de la région parisienne à la fin du moyen âge* (Paris, 1964), pp. 161–64, who only sets the thirteenth century as a background for later developments. F. Olivier-Martin, *Histoire de la coutume de la prévôté et vicomté de Paris*, 2 vols. (Paris: vol. 1, 1922; vol. 2, 1930), contains some perceptive remarks on the status of persons and the significance of the twelfth-century franchises (vol. 1, b. 1, chap. 1), but it would be misleading to read his comments on the later custom of Paris into the twelfth century.

17. Françoise Lehoux, *Le Bourg Saint-Germain-des-Prés depuis ses origines jusqu'à la fin de la guerre de cent ans* (Paris, 1951), esp. pp. 7–15, 31–40.

18. Robert Fossier, *La terre et les hommes en Picardie jusqu'à la fin du XIIIe siècle*, 2 vols. (Paris, 1968), pp. 556 ff. An excellent review of these points is E. A. Verhulst, "A propos de 'la terre et les hommes en Picardie,' " *Cahiers de civilisation médiévale* 14 (1970): 257–64. Fossier ignored the impact of the franchises, in spite of his unpublished *thèse complémentaire*, "Chartes de coutumes de Picardie, XIe–XIIIe siècles," reviewed by R. Delort in *Revue historique* 241 (1969): 273–79.

19. Bryce Lyon, "Encore le problème de la chronologie des corvées," *Le Moyen Age* 69 (1963): 615–30, and "Medieval Real Estate Development and Freedom," *American Historical Review* 63 (1957): 47–61. The latter thesis rests on a few fragmentary references from the twelfth century. The main argument on the *hospites* depends on the evidence from Bourbourg, which is more closely analyzed by Michel Mollat, "Les hôtes de l'abbaye de Bourbourg," in *Mélanges d'histoire du moyen âge dédiés à la mémoire de Louis Halphen* (Paris, 1951), pp. 513–21. The 1254 charter for the count's domain is interpreted differently by Léo Verriest, "Le servage en Flandre, particulièrement au pays d'Alost," *Revue historique de droit français et étranger* 28 (1950): 35–65. The variety of rural conditions is evident in E. A. Verhulst, *De Sint-Baafsabdij te Gent en haar Grondbezit (VII–XIV eeuw)* (Brussels, 1958); the twelfth-century franchises of the count are assessed in idem, "Une example de la politique économique de Philippe d'Alsace: la formation de Gravelines (1163)," *Cahiers de civilisation médiévale* 10 (1967): 15–28.

20. Léopold Genicot, *L'économie rurale namuroise au bas moyen âge (1199–1429)*, 2 vols., I. *La seigneurie foncière* (Namur, 1943), esp. pp. xiii and 11–12.

21. Marcel Garaud, *Les châtelains de Poitou et l'avènement du régime féodale, XIe et XIIe siècles* (Poitiers, 1964), pp. 153, 213 ff.; George T. Beech, *A Rural Society in Medieval France: The Gâtine of Poitou in the Eleventh and Twelfth Centuries* (Baltimore, 1964), pp. 35–36, 107, 114–15; and Roland Sanfançon, *Défrichements, peuplement, et institutions seigneuriales en Haut-Poitou, du Xe au XIIIe siècle* (Quebec, 1967), chap. 3. Garaud is aware of the importance of franchises in the second half of the twelfth century but does not investigate them; Sanfançon refers to the community grants but does not elaborate, although he does note that the "burgs" that proliferated from 1075 to 1125 were not privileged areas (see n. 23 for the same conclusion on the Norman burgs). Madelaine Dillay, *Les chartes de franchises du Poitou* (Paris, 1927), supplies a catalogue, but only of those charters with explicit references to "liberties."

22. C. van de Kieft, *Etude sur le chartrier et la seigneurie du prieuré de la Chapelle-Aude (XIe–XIIIe siècle)* (Assen, 1960).

23. Most researchers have followed Léopold Delisle, *Etudes sur la condition de la classe agricole et l'état de l'agriculture en Normandie au moyen âge*, 2d ed. (Paris, 1903), but the study which should be consulted for rural conditions in Normandy is Robert Carabie, *La propriété foncière dans le très ancien droit normand (XIe–XIIIe siècle) I. La propriété domaniale* (Caen, 1943), esp. here pp. 103, 107–11, 218–19. See also Lucien Musset, "Peuplement en bourgage et bourgs ruraux en Normandie du Xe au XIIIe siècle," *Cahiers de civilisation médiévale* 9 (1966): 177–208; and Suzanne Deck, "Formation des communes en Haut-Normandie et communes ephémères," *Annales de Normandie* 10 (1960): 207–28, 317–30. Musset and Sanfançon reached similar conclusions on the burgs of Poitou and Normandy in the eleventh and twelfth centuries; follow-up studies for the community franchises in those areas from the late twelfth century would be most interesting.

24. Noël Didier, "Les plus anciens textes sur le servage dans la région dauphinoise," in *Etudes d'histoire du droit privé offerts à Pierre Petot* (Paris, 1959) pp. 131–40; Pierre Vaillant, *Les libertés des communautés dauphinoises* (Grenoble, 1951) and "Les origines d'une libre confédération de vallées: les habitants des communautés Briançonnaises au XIIIe siècle," *Bibliothèque de l'Ecole des Chartes* 125 (1967): 301–48; and Vital Chomel, "Un censier dauphinois inédit. Méthode et portée de l'édition du *Probus*," *Bulletin philologique et historique du Comité des Travaux Historiques et Scientifiques*, 1964, pp. 319–407.

25. Edouard Baratier, *Enquêtes sur les droits et revenus de Charles Ier d'Anjou en Provence (1252 et 1278)* (Paris, 1969) and *La démographie provençale*.

26. Jacques Monfrin, "A propos du vocabulaire des structures sociales du haut moyen âge," *Annales du Midi* 80 (1968): 611–20; and Paul Ourliac, "Le servage dans la région toulousaine," *X. International Congress of Historical Sciences. Communications VII* (Florence, 1955), pp. 191–93, and "Les villages de la région toulousaine au XIIe siècle," *Annales, Economies. Sociétés. Civilisations* 4 (1949): 268–77. But see Jean Ramière de Fortanier, *Chartes de franchises du Lauragais* (Toulouse, 1939), for the area south of Toulouse; for just north of the city see Charles Higounet, "L'occupation du sol entre Tarn et Garonne au moyen âge," *Annales du Midi* 65 (1953): 301–30. The evidence for Aquitaine is not clear, mainly because of few references before the thirteenth century—see Robert Boutruche, *Une société provinciale en lutte contre le régime féodal. L'alleu en Bordelais et en Bazadais du XIe au XIIIe siècle* (Rodez, 1947) and Charles Higounet, *Le Comté de Comminges*, 2 vols. (Paris-Toulouse, 1949): *homines de corpore* existed in both areas in the thirteenth century, but their relative status has not been determined.

27. The significance of rural migration in medieval England has been revealed especially by J. A. Raftis, *Tenure and Mobility: Studies in the Social History of the Medieval English Village* (Toronto, 1964), and that in Italy by Johan Plesner,

L'émigration de la campagne a la ville libre de Florence au XIIIe siècle (Copenhagen, 1934).

28. The three-part questionnaire was posed by Georges Duby, "Une enquête à poursuivre: la noblesse dans la France médiévale," *Revue historique* 226 (1961): 1–22, and retained by Léopold Genicot, "La noblesse au moyen âge dans l'ancienne 'Francie.' Continuité, rupture ou évolution?," *Comparative Studies in Society and History* 5 (1962): 52–59, and Robert Boutruche, "Histoire de France au moyen âge," *Revue historique* 233 (1965): 199–203. For the original program of questions posed in the 1930s see the Count of Neufbourg, "Projet d'une enquête sur la noblesse française," *Annales d'histoire économique et sociale* 8 (1936): 243–55, and Marc Bloch, "Sur le passé de la noblesse française: quelques jalons de recherche," ibid., pp. 366–78.

29. Guilhiermoz, *Essai sur les origines de la noblesse*, esp. pp. 349–70, 477–90.

30. Bloch, *Feudal Society*, trans. L. A. Manyon (Chicago, 1962), pp. 282–344.

31. Duby, *La société aux XIe et XIIe siècles dans la région mâconnaise*. The continuity of the Carolingian aristocracy has emerged as a central theme. See also: Werner, "Untersuchungen zur Frühzeit des französischen Fürstentums (9.–10. Jahrhundert)," *Die Welt als Geschichte* 18 (1958): 256–89, 19 (1959): 146–93, 20 (1960): 87–119; J. Wollasch, "Königtum, Adel und Kloster im Berry während des 10. Jahrhunderts," in *Neue Forschungen über Cluny und die Cluniacenser*, ed. G. Tellenbach (Freiburg, 1959); and Jacques Boussard, "L'origine des familles seigneuriales dans la région de la Loire moyenne," *Cahiers de civilisation médiévale* 5 (1962): 303–22.

32. Léopold Genicot first suggested the thesis in "Sur les origines de la noblesse dans le Namurois," *Tijdschrift voor Rechtsgeschiedenis* 20 (1952): 143–56, but for historiographical purposes his full study marked the date of arrival of the "Belgian thesis": *L'économie rurale namuroise au bas moyen âge (1199–1429)*, 2 vols., II. *Les hommes. La noblesse* (Louvain, 1960).

33. Warlop, *De Vlaamse adel voor 1300*.

34. The best synthesis of recent work is by Genicot, "La noblesse au moyen âge dans l'ancienne 'Francie.'" See also Paul Bonenfant and Georges Despy, "La noblesse en Brabant aux XIIe et XIIIe siècles," *Le Moyen Age* 64 (1958): 27–66, which is unfortunately too vague and based on poor quantitative procedures; Léo Verriest, *Noblesse, chevalerie, lignages* (Brussels, 1959), esp. sec. 4 and 9; Noël Didier, *Le droit des fiefs dans la coutume de Hainault au moyen âge* (Paris, 1945), which stresses the many small fiefs, close to peasant tenures, and the systematization of fief tenures only from the last decades of the twelfth century; and J. M. van Winter, "The Ministerial and Knightly Classes in Guelders and Zutphen," *Acta Historiae Neelandica* 1 (1966): 171–86, which is confused by an attempt to inject modern sociological theory and to distinguish "social" from "legal" classes; van Winter's position is better presented in "Note à propos l'article de M. L. Genicot 'noblesse, ministerialité et chevalerie en Gueldre et Zutphen,'" *Le Moyen Age* 72 (1966): 279–89.

35. Richard, *Les ducs de Bourgogne*; "Sur les alliances familiales des ducs de Bourgogne aux XIIe et XIIIe siècles," *Annales de Bourgogne* 30 (1958): 37–46; and "Châteaux, châtelains, et vassaux en Bourgogne aux XIe et XIIe siècles," *Cahiers de civilisation médiévale* 3 (1960): 433–447. Also Michel Belotte, "Les possessions des évêques de Langres dans la région de Mussy-sur-Seine et de Châtillon-sur-Seine du milieu du XIIe au milieu du XIVe siècle," *Annales de Bourgogne* 37 (1965): 161–97; and David, *Le patrimonie foncier de l'église de Lyon*, p. 256.

36. Duby, *La société aux XIe et XIIe siècles dans la région mâconnaise*. The figures on the origins of the knights (pp. 411–18) are faulty. Duby's own information shows (p. 463) that the six great local families were closed to all others; it was Duby's own emphasis on the common *genre de vie* that convinced him of an eleventh-century fusion of lords and knights.

37. Marcel Garaud, *Les châtelains de Poitou*, esp. pp. 3 ff., 96–99, 220–27 (his interpretation of the knights, however, is ambivalent); for the lords of Parthenay:

George T. Beech, *A Rural Society in Medieval France.* Beech notes the confusion of *miles* and *dominus* from the end of the twelfth century (pp. 91–97), and Garaud comments briefly on the thirteenth-century development (p. 227), but neither study covers the thirteenth century proper.

38. Joseph R. Strayer, "The Two Levels of Feudalism," in *Life and Thought in the Early Middle Ages,* ed. R. S. Hoyt (Minneapolis, 1967); and Boussard, "L'enquête de 1172 sur les services de chevalier en Normandie." The position of the knights by ca. 1200 is seen in E. J. Tardif, ed., *Le très ancien Coutumier de Normandie* (Paris, 1881), esp. articles II, VIII, XV, XXVI, and LVI; and S. E. Gleason, *An Ecclesiastical Barony in the Middle Ages: The Bishopric of Bayeux, 1066–1204* (Cambridge, Mass., 1936), chaps. 2 and 3. Maurice Powicke, *The Loss of Normandy, 1189–1204,* 2d ed. (Manchester, 1961), called for a systematic investigation of the Norman aristocracy in the thirteenth century, a study yet to be undertaken.

39. Fourquin, *Les campagnes de la région parisienne,* gives an excellent picture of thirteenth-century agrarian conditions but presents a diffuse image of the aristocracy. The best contemporary description of early-thirteenth-century conditions is in the Statute of Pamiers (1212), which was based on the Paris customs; the text is in Pierre Timbal, *Un conflit d'annexion au moyen âge: l'application de la coutume de Paris au pays d'albigeois* (Toulouse-Paris, 1949).

40. Barthélemy A. Pocquet du Haut-Jussé, "De la vassalité à la noblesse dans le duché de Bretagne," *Bulletin philologique et historique du Comité des Travaux Historiques et Scientifiques,* 1963, pp. 785–800.

41. A general view of the earlier period is Archibald R. Lewis, *The Development of Southern French and Catalan Society, 718–1050* (Austin, 1965). See also Elisabeth Magnou-Nortier, "Fidélité et féodalité méridionales d'après les serments de fidélité (X^e–début XIIe siècle)," *Annales du Midi* 80 (1968): 457–84; Monique Gramain, "La composition de la cour vicomtale de Narbonne aux XIIe et XIIIe siècles," ibid., 81 (1969): 121–40; Paul Ourliac, "Le pays de La Selve à la fin du XIIe siècle," ibid., 80 (1968): 581–602; and Félix Bernard, *Les origines féodales en Savoie et en Dauphiné* (Grenoble, 1949): the genealogies are far more important than the commentary, which is marred by methodological imprecision.

42. Count of Neufbourg, "Puissance relative du comte et des seigneurs en Forez au XIIIe siècle," *Le Moyen Age* 61 (1955): 405–32; and Edouard Perroy, "Social Mobility Among the French *Noblesse* in the Later Middle Ages," *Past and Present* 21 (1962): 25–38.

43. Analysis of the charters for incomes is difficult at best: the charters do not show current incomes and cannot be adjusted to a single date.

44. Fossier, *La terre et les hommes en Picardie.* These figures are from pp. 662–65. Different figures appear on pp. 511–12, but since the categories are not identical, it is impossible to resolve the discrepancies. Fossier is also ambivalent about the relationship between the knights and the old aristocracy: although recognizing the social distance between them, especially in the twelfth century, he stresses their social solidarity against the rest of society. The evolution of the titles and histories of several baronial families and the family connection between the secular and ecclesiastical aristocracy is clearly revealed in William M. Newman, *Les seigneurs de Nesle en Picardie (XIIe–XIIIe siècle),* 2 vols. (Philadelphia-Paris, 1971).

45. Henri Dubled, "Noblesse et féodalité en Alsace du XIe au XIIIe siècle," *Tijdschrift voor Rechtsgeschiedenis* 28 (1960): 129–80, attempted to demonstrate the equivalence of vassalage, nobility, and knighthood in the eleventh through thirteenth centuries, that is, to prove that the knights who held fiefs were by definition the aristocracy. The study was reviewed by J. Baerten, "L'origine de la noblesse alsacienne. A propos d'un article récent," ibid., 32 (1964): 78–82, followed by Dubled's response (pp. 83–84), which does not meet the criticisms. Baerten's point is that the aristocracy cannot be defined simply by the assumption that *miles* was equivalent to *nobilis*; he also notes that other evidence was misread.

46. Duby, "Une enquête à poursuivre." Duby extended the concept in "The

Diffusion of Cultural Patterns in Feudal Society," *Past and Present* 39 (1968): 3–10.

47. Bloch, *Feudal Society*, p. 446.

48. See especially J. F. Lemarignier, *Le gouvernement royal aux premiers temps capétiens (987–1108)* (Paris, 1965), and the review by F. L. Ganshof, "L'entourage des premiers Capétiens," *Revue historique de droit français et étranger* 46 (1968): 263–74. Ganshof accepts Lemarignier's thesis but not the suggestion that royal administration was responsible for creating a hierarchical organization.

49. An historiographical review of the concept of feudalism, which comes to quite similar conclusions, is Elizabeth A. R. Brown, "The Tyranny of a Construct: Feudalism and Historians of Medieval Europe," *The American Historical Review* 79 (1974): 1063–88.

BIBLIOGRAPHY

Primary Sources

MANUSCRIPT

Bibliothèque Nationale (Paris)
Cartulaire de Blanche, lat. 5993
Cartulaire de Larrivour (Ripatorio), n.a.lat. 1228
Cartulaire de Saint-Etienne, lat. 17098
Cartulaire de Thou, lat. 5992
Cartulaire de Vauluisant, lat. 9901
Liber pontificum (or "Cartulaire de Champagne"), lat. 5993A
Liber principum, n.a.lat. 2454
Bibliothèque de Troyes
Cartulaire de Sellières, ms. 2290

Archives du département de l'Aube (Troyes)
Only cartularies and organized collections are listed here. Individual items in series
G (secular clergy) and H (regular clergy) are indicated in the notes only, as
Arch.Aube.
Cartulaire de l'Hôtel-Dieu-le-Comte, 40 H 126
Cartulaire de Notre-Dame-des-Prés, 23 H 5
Cartulaire d'Oyes (Saint-Gond), 5 G 123
Chartes de la prieuré de Foissy, 27 H 3

PRINTED

Arbois de Jubainville, Henri d'. "Etudes sur les documents antérieur à l'année
1285, conservés dans les archives des quatre petits hôpitaux de la ville de Troyes."
Mémoires de la Société Académique de l'Aube 21 (1857): 49–116.
———. *Histoire des ducs et des comtes de Champagne.* 7 vols. Paris, 1859–69.
———. "Les premiers seigneurs de Ramerupt." *Bibliothèque de l'Ecole des Chartes*
22 (1861): 440–55.
Aubri of Trois-Fontaines. *Chronica.* In *Monumenta Germaniae Historica, Scriptores,*
XXIII, edited by Paul Scheffer-Boichorst. Hannover, 1874.
Bouquet, Martin et al. *Recueil des historiens des Gaules et de la France,* 24 vols.
Paris, 1737–1904. Vol. XVI.
Catel, Albert, and Lecomte, Maurice, eds. *Chartes et documents de l'abbaye
cistercienne de Preuilly.* Montereau, 1927.
Chapin, Elizabeth. *Les villes de foires de Champagne.* Paris, 1937.
Courtant, Lucien. *Histoire de la ville et de l'ancien comté de Bar-sur-Seine.* Bar-sur-
Seine, 1855.
Defer, E. "Histoire de l'abbaye de Saint-Martin-ès-Aires." *Mémoires de la Société
Académique de l'Aube* 39 (1875): 5–287.
Delaborde, H. F., ed. *Recueil des actes de Philippe Auguste.* Vol. 1. Paris, 1916.
Harmand, A. "Notice historique sur la Léproserie de la ville de Troyes." *Mémoires
de la Société Académique de l'Aube* 14 (1847–48): 429–669.
Lalore, Charles, ed. "Chartes de l'abbaye de Mores." *Mémoires de la Société
Académique de l'Aube* 37 (1873): 5–107.
———. *Collection des principaux cartulaires du diocèse de Troyes.* 7 vols. Paris-
Troyes, 1875–90.
———. "Documents pour servir à la généalogie des anciens seigneurs de Traînel."
Mémoires de la Société Académique de l'Aube 34 (1870): 177–271.

_____. "Documents sur l'abbaye de Notre-Dame-aux-Nonnains de Troyes." *Mémoires de la Société Academique de l'Aube* 38 (1874): 5–236.

_____. *Le polyptique de l'abbaye de Montier-en-Der.* Paris, 1878.

_____. *Les sires et les barons de Chacenay.* Troyes, 1885.

Laurent, Jacques, ed. *Cartulaires de l'abbaye de Molesme.* 2 vols. Paris, 1907–11.

Leclert, Louis. *Etude historique sur Romilly-sur-Seine.* Troyes, 1898.

Longnon, Auguste, ed. *Documents relatifs au comté de Champagne et de Brie (1172–1361).* 3 vols. Paris, 1901–14. Vols. I, *Les fiefs* (1901), and II, *Le domain comtal* (1904).

_____. *Rôles des fiefs du comté de Champagne sous le règne de Thibaut le Chansonnier (1249–52).* Paris, 1877.

Longnon, Jean. *Recherches sur la vie de Geoffroy de Villehardouin.* Paris, 1939.

Ordonnances des rois de France de la troisième race. 22 vols. Paris, 1723–1849. Vol. VI.

Petel, Auguste. *Essoyes. Histoire et statistique avec pièces justicatives inédites.* Troyes, 1893.

_____. *Les seigneurs de Ville-sur-Arce.* Troyes, 1898.

Portejoie, P., ed. *L'ancien coutumier de Champagne (XIIIe siècle).* Poitiers, 1956.

Roserot, Alphonse. *Dictionnaire historique de la Champagne méridionale (Aube) des origines à 1790.* 3 vols. Langres, 1942–48.

Socard, Emile, ed. "Chartes inédites extraites des cartulaires de Molême, intéressant un grand nombre de localités du département de l'Aube (1080–1250)." *Mémoires de la Société Academique de l'Aube* 28 (1864): 163–364.

Teulet, A., et al., eds. *Layettes du Trésor des Chartes,* 5 vols. Paris, 1863–1909.

Vallet de Viriville. *Les archives historiques du département de l'Aube.* Troyes, 1841.

Secondary Works

THE *BAILLIAGE* OF TROYES

Only works directly concerning the *bailliage* and not already included among the printed sources are listed here.

Benton, John F. "The Court of Champagne as a Literary Center." *Speculum* 36 (1961): 551–91.

_____. "The Court of Champagne under Henry the Liberal and Countess Marie." Ph.D. dissertation, Princeton, 1959.

_____. "Philip the Fair and the Jours of Troyes." *Studies in Medieval and Renaissance History* 6 (1969): 281–302.

Bibolet, Françoise. "Le rôle de la guerre de cent ans dans le développement des libertés municipales à Troyes." *Mémoires de la Société Academique de l'Aube* 99 (1939–42): 295–320.

Bourgeois, René. *Du mouvement communal dans le comté de Champagne aux XIIe et XIIIe siècles.* Paris, 1904.

Boutiot, Théophile. *Des institutions communales dans la Champagne méridionale au XIIe et au XIIIe siècle.* Troyes, 1865.

Bur, Michel. "Remarques sur les plus anciens documents concernant les foires de Champagne." In *Les Villes.* Publications de l'Université de Reims, Faculté des Lettres et Sciences Humaines no. 3. Reims, 1972.

Bur, Michel, et al. *Vestiges d'habitat seigneurial fortifié du Bas-Pays Argonnais.* Cahiers des Lettres et Sciences Humaines de l'Université de Reims. Reims, 1972.

Chaume, Maurice. "Notes sur quelques familles comtales champenois, X^e–XIe siècle." In his *Recherches d'histoire chrétienne et médiévale.* Dijon, 1947.

Crozet, René. *Histoire de Champagne.* 2d ed. Paris, 1933.

Duhem, Georges, "Les comtes de Troyes au début du Xe siècle." *Annuaire de l'Aube,* 1932, pp. 17–24.

Evergates, Theodore. "The Aristocracy of Champagne in the Mid-Thirteenth Century: A Quantitative Description." *The Journal of Interdisciplinary History* 5 (1974): 1–18.

Fossier, Robert. "Le plateau de Langres et la fondation de Clairvaux," and "L'installation et les premières années de Clairvaux." In *Bernard de Clairvaux*, Commission d'histoire de l'ordre de Cîteaux, vol. III, pp. 67–93. Paris, 1953.

Gallet, Léon. *Les traites de pariage dans la France féodale.* Paris, 1936.

Lemarignier, Jean. *Recherches sur l'hommage en marche et les frontières féodales.* Lille, 1945.

Longnon, Jean. "La Champagne." In *Histoire des institutions françaises au moyen âge.* I. *Institutions seigneuriales*, edited by F. Lot and R. Fawtier. Paris, 1957.

Painter, Sidney. *The Scourge of the Clergy: Peter of Dreux, Duke of Brittany.* Baltimore, 1937.

Petot, Pierre, "La preuve de servage en Champagne." *Revue historique de droit français et étranger* 13 (1934): 464–98.

Richard, Jean. "Le milieu familial," In *Bernard de Clairvaux*, Commission d'histoire de l'ordre de Citeaux, vol. III, pp. 3–15. Paris, 1953.

———. *Les ducs de Bourgogne et la formation du duché du XIe au XIVe siècle.* Paris, 1954.

Roserot de Melin, Joseph. *La diocèse de Troyes des origines à nos jours (IIIe siècle–1955).* Troyes, 1957.

Rubner, Heinrich. *Untersuchungen zur Forstverfassung des Mittelalterlichen Frankreich.* Wiesbaden, 1965.

Sée, Henri. "Etude sur les classes serviles en Champagne du XIe au XIVe siècle." *Revue historique* 56 (1894): 225–52; 57 (1895): 1–21.

Werner, Karl F. "Untersuchungen zur Frühzeit des französischen Fürstentums (9.–10. Jahrhundert)." *Die Welt als Geschichte* 18 (1958): 256–89; 19 (1959): 146–93; 20 (1960): 87–119.

OTHER REGIONS

Baerten, J. "L'origine de la noblesse alsacienne. A propos d'un article récent." *Tijdschrift voor Rechtsgeschiedenis* 32 (1964): 78–82.

Baratier, Edouard. *Enquêtes sur les droits et revenus de Charles Ier d'Anjou en Provence (1252 et 1278).* Paris, 1969.

———. *La démographie provençale du XIIIe au XVIe siècle.* Paris, 1961.

Beech, George T. *A Rural Society in Medieval France: The Gâtine of Poitou in the Eleventh and Twelfth Centuries.* Baltimore, 1964.

Belotte, Michel. "Les possessions des évêques de Langres dans la région de Mussy-sur-Seine et de Châtillon-sur-Seine du milieu du XIIe au milieu du XIVe siècle." *Annales de Bourgogne* 37 (1965): 161–97.

Bernard, Félix. *Les origines féodales en Savoie et en Dauphiné.* Grenoble, 1949.

Bloch, Marc. *Feudal Society.* Translated by L. A. Manyon. Chicago, 1962.

———. "Le procès des serfs de Rosnay-sous-Bois." In his *Mélanges historiques.* 2 vols. Vol. I, pp. 452–61. Paris, 1963.

———. "Les transformations du servage: à propos de deux documents du XIIIe siècle relatifs à la région parisienne." In *Mélanges historiques.* 2 vols. Vol. I, pp. 491–502. Paris, 1963.

———. "Liberté et servitude personnelles au moyen âge, particulièrement en France: contribution à une étude des classes." In *Mélanges historiques.* 2 vols. Vol. I, pp. 286–355. Paris, 1963.

———. "Sur le passé de la noblesse française: quelques jalons de recherche." *Annales d'histoire économique et social* 8 (1936): 366–78.

———. "Un problème d'histoire comparée: la ministerialité en France et en Allemagne." In *Mélanges historiques.* 2 vols. Vol. I, pp. 522–24. Paris, 1963.

Bonenfant, Paul, and Despy, Georges. "La noblesse en Brabant aux XIIe et XIIIe siècles." *Le Moyen Age* 64 (1958): 27–66.

Boussard, Jacques. "L'enquête de 1172 sur les services de chevalier en Normandie." In *Recueil de travaux offert à M. Clovis Brunel.* 2 vols. Vol. I, pp. 193–208. Paris, 1955.

_____. "L'origine des familles seigneuriales dans la région de la Loire moyenne." *Cahiers de civilisation médiévale* 5 (1962): 303–22.

Boutruche, Robert. "Histoire de France au moyen âge." *Revue historique* 233 (1965): 199–203.

_____. *La crise d'une société. Seigneurs et paysans du Bordelais pendant la guerre de cent ans.* Paris, 1947.

_____. *Seigneurie et féodalité*, I. *Le premier age des liens d'homme à homme.* 1959. Reprint. Paris, 1968. II. *L'apogée (XIe–XIIIe siècles).* Paris, 1970.

_____. *Une société provinciale en lutte contre le régime féodal. L'alleu en Bordelais et en Bazadais du XIe au XIIIe siècle.* Rodez, 1947.

_____. "Une livre de combat. Noblesse, chevalerie, lignages, par Léo Verriest." *Revue historique* 225 (1961): 73–80.

Brown, Elizabeth A. R. "The Tyranny of a Construct: Feudalism and Historians of Medieval Europe." *The American Historical Review* 79 (1974): 1063–88.

Carabie, Robert. *La propriété foncière dans le très ancien droit normand (XIe– XIIIe siècles). I. La propriété domaniale.* Caen, 1943.

Chomel, Vital. "Un censier dauphinois inédit. Méthode et portée de l'édition du Probus." *Bulletin philologique et historique du Comité des Travaux Historiques et Scientifiques*, 1964, pp. 319–407.

Coleman, Emily R.. "Medieval Marriage Characteristics: A Neglected Factor in the History of Medieval Serfdom." *The Journal of Interdisciplinary History* 2 (1971): 205–17.

David, Marcel. *Le patrimoine foncier de l'Eglise de Lyon de 984 à 1267: contribution à l'étude de la féodalité dans la Lyonnais.* Lyon, 1942.

Debuisson, Robert. *Etude sur la condition des personnes et des terres d'après les coutumes de Reims du XIIe au XVIe siècle.* Reims, 1930.

Deck, Suzanne. "Formation des communes en Haut-Normandie et communes ephémères." *Annales de Normandie* 10 (1960): 207–28, 317–30.

Delisle, Léopold. *Etudes sur la condition de la classe agricole et l'état de l'agriculture en Normandie au moyen âge.* 1st ed. 1851. 2d ed. Paris, 1903.

Despy, Georges. "Sur la noblesse dans les principautés belges au moyen âge." *Revue belge de philologie et d'histoire* 41 (1963): 471–86.

Didier, Noël. *Le droit des fiefs dans la coutume de Hainault au moyen âge.* Paris, 1945.

_____. "Les plus anciens textes sur le servage dans la région dauphinoise." In *Etudes d'histoire du droit privé offerts à Pierre Petot.* Pp. 131–40. Paris, 1959.

Dillay, Madelaine. *Les chartes de franchises du Poitou.* Paris, 1927.

Dollinger, Philippe. *L'évolution des classes rurales en Bavière.* Paris, 1949.

Dubled, Henri. "Administration et exploitation des terres de la seigneurie rurale en Alsace aux XIe et XIIe siècles." *Vierteljahrschrift für Sozial- und Wirtschaftsgeschichte* 47 (1960): 433–73.

_____. "La communauté de village en Alsace au XIIIe siècle." *Revue d'histoire économique et sociale* 41 (1963): 5–33.

_____. "Noblesse et féodalité en Alsace du XIe au XIIIe siècle." *Tijdschrift voor Rechtsgeschiedenis* 28 (1960): 129–80.

_____. "Quelques observations sur le sens du mot *villa.*" *Le Moyen Age* 59 (1953): 1–11.

_____. "Servitude et liberté en Alsace au moyen âge: la condition des personnes au sein de la seigneurie rurale du XIIIe au XIVe siècle." *Vierteljahrschrift für Sozial- und Wirtschaftsgeschichte* 50 (1963): 164–203, 289–324.

_____. "Taille et 'Umgeld' en Alsace au XIIIe siècle." *Vierteljahrschrift für Sozial- und Wirtschaftsgeschichte* 47 (1960): 32–47.

Duby, Georges. "Géographie ou chronologie du servage? Note sur les *servi* en Forez et en Mâconnais du Xe au XIIe siècle." In *Hommage à Lucien Febvre.* vol. I, pp. 147–53. Paris, 1953.

_____. *La société aux XIe et XIIe siècles dans la région mâconnaise.* Paris, 1953.

———. *L'économie rurale et la vie des campagnes dans l'occident médiéval.* 2 vols. Paris, 1962.

———. "Structures de parenté de noblesse. France du Nord. XIᵉ–XIIᵉ siècles." In *Miscellanea mediaevalia in memoriam Jan Frederik Niermeyer,* pp. 149–65. Groningen, 1967.

———. "The Diffusion of Cultural Patterns in Feudal Society." *Past and Present* 39 (1968): 3–10.

———. "Une enquête à poursuivre: la noblesse dans la France médiévale." *Revue historique* 226 (1961): 1–22.

Duparc, Pierre. "La question des 'sainteurs' ou hommes des églises." *Journal des Savants,* 1972, pp. 25–48.

Eck, Alexandre. "La notion du servage à la lumière de la méthode comparative." In *Recueils de la Société Jean Bodin, Le Servage,* pp. 339–42. 2d ed. Brussels, 1959.

Fossier, Robert. "Chartes de coutumes de Picardie, XIᵉ–XIIIᵉ siècles." *Thèse complémentaire.* Reviewed by R. Delort, *Revue historique* 241 (1969): 273–79.

———. *La terre et les hommes en Picardie jusqu'à la fin du XIIIᵉ siècle.* 2 vols. Paris, 1968.

Fournial, Etienne. *Les villes et l'économie d'échange en Forez aux XIIIᵉ et XIVᵉ siècles.* Paris, 1967.

Fournier, Gabriel. "La seigneurie en Basse-Auvergne aux XIᵉ et XIIᵉ siècles, d'après les censiers du cartulaires de Sauxillanges." In *Mélanges Louis Halphen,* pp. 238–45. Paris, 1951.

———. *Le peuplement rural en Basse Auvergne.* Paris, 1962.

Fourquin, Guy. *Les campagnes de la région parisienne à la fin du moyen âge.* Paris, 1964.

Ganshof, F. L. "L'entourage des premiers Capétiens." *Revue historique de droit français et étranger* 46 (1968): 263–74.

Garaud, Marcel. *Les châtelains de Poitou et l'avènement du régime féodale, XIᵉ et XIIᵉ siècles.* Poitiers, 1964.

Genicot, Lépold. "La noblesse au moyen âge dans l'ancienne 'Francie.' Continuité, rupture, ou évolution?" *Comparative Studies in Society and History* 5 (1962): 52–59.

———. *L'économie rurale namuroise au bas moyen âge (1199–1429). I. La seigneurie foncière.* Namur, 1943. *II. Les hommes. La noblesse.* Louvain, 1960.

———. "Sur les origines de la noblesse dans le Namurois." *Tijdschrift voor Rechtsgeschiedenis* 20 (1952): 143–56.

Gleason, S. E. *An Ecclesiastical Barony in the Middle Ages: The Bishopric of Bayeux, 1066–1204.* Cambridge, Mass., 1936.

Glénisson, Jean. "L'historiographie française contemporaire: tendances et réalisations." In *La recherche historique en France de 1940 à 1965,* Comité Français des Sciences Historiques. Paris, 1966.

Gramain, Monique. "La composition de la cour vicomtale de Narbonne aux XIIᵉ et XIIIᵉ siècles." *Annales du Midi* 81 (1969): 121–40.

Guilhiermoz, Paul. *Essai sur les origines de la noblesse en France au moyen âge.* Paris, 1902.

Héliot, Pierre. "Les demeures seigneuriales dans la région Picarde au moyen âge: châteaux ou manoirs?" *Recueil de travaux offert à M. Clovis Brunel.* 2 vols. Vol. II, pp. 574–83. Paris, 1955.

Higounet, Charles. *Le Comté de Commminges.* 2 vols. Paris-Toulouse, 1949.

———. "Le groupe aristocratique en Aquitaine et en Gascogne (fin Xᵉ–début XIIᵉ siècle)." *Annales du Midi* 80 (1968): 563–71.

———. L'occupation du sol entre Tarn et Garonne au moyen âge." *Annales du Midi* 65 (1953): 301–30.

———. "Mouvements de population dans le Midi de la France du XIᵉ au XVᵉ siècle, d'après les noms de personne et de lieu." *Annales. Economies. Sociétés. Civilisations* 8 (1953): 1–24.

_____. "Observations sur la seigneurie rurale et l'habitat en Rouergue du IX au XIVe siècle." *Annales du Midi* 62 (1950): 121–34.

Joset, Camille J. *Les villes au pays de Luxembourg (1196–1383)*. Brussels, 1940.

Kieft, C. van de. *Etude sur le chartrier et la seigneurie du prieuré de la Chapelle-Aude (XI–XIIIe siècle)*. Assen, 1960.

Lebon, Michel. "Textes sur le formariage en Lorraine des origines au début du XIIIe siècle." *Annales de l'Est* 2 (1951): 53–66.

Lehoux, Françoise. *Le Bourg Saint-Germain-des-Prés depuis ses origines jusqu'à la fin de la guerre de cent ans*. Paris, 1951.

Lemarignier, J. F. *Le gouvernement royal aux premiers temps capétiens (987–1108)*. Paris, 1965.

Lewis, Archibald R. *The Development of Southern French and Catalan Society, 718–1050*. Austin, 1965.

Lyon, Bryce. "Encore le problème de la chronologie des corvées." *Le Moyen Age* 69 (1963): 615–30.

_____. "Medieval Real Estate Development and Freedom." *American Historical Review* 63 (1957): 47–61.

Magnou-Nortier, Elisabeth. "Fidélité et féodalité méridionales d'après les serments de fidélité (X^e–début XIIe siècle)." *Annales du Midi* 80 (1968): 457–84.

Middleton, John, and Tait, David, eds. *Tribes Without Rulers: Studies in African Segmentary Systems*. London, 1958.

Mollat, Michel. "Les hôtes de l'abbaye de Bourbourg." In *Mélanges Louis Halphen*, pp. 513–21. Paris, 1951.

Monfrin, J. "A propos du vocabulaire des structures sociales du haut moyen âge." *Annales du Midi* 80 (1968): 611–20.

Morlet, Marie-Thérèse. "L'origine des habitants de Provins aux XIIIe et XIVe siècles, d'apres les noms de personne." *Bulletin Philologique et historique du Comité des Travaux Historiques et Scientifiques*, 1961, pp. 95–114.

Musset, Lucien, "Peuplement en bourgage et bourgs ruraux en Normandie du Xe au XIIIe siècle." *Cahiers de civilisation médiévale* 9 (1966): 177–208.

Neufbourg, Count of, "Projet d'une enquête sur la noblesse française." *Annales d'histoire économique et sociale* 8 (1936): 243–55.

_____. "Puissance relative du comte et des seigneurs en Forez au XIIIe siècle." *Le Moyen Age* 61 (1955): 405–32.

Newman, William M. *Les seigneurs de Nesle en Picardie (XIIe–XIIIe siècle)*. 2 vols. Philadelphia-Paris, 1971.

Olivier-Martin, F. *Histoire de la coutume de la prévôté et vicomté de Paris*. 2 vols. Paris, 1922–30.

Ourliac, Paul. "Le pays de La Selve à la fin du XIIe siècle." *Annales du Midi* 80 (1968): 581–602.

_____. "Le servage dans la région toulousaine." In *X. International Congress of Historical Sciences, Communications*, vol. VII, pp. 191–93. Florence, 1955.

_____. "Les villages de la région toulousaine au XIIe siècle." *Annales, Economies. Sociétés. Civilisations*. 4 (1949): 268–77.

Perrin, Charles-Edmond. "Chartes de franchise et rapports de droits en Lorraine." *Le Moyen Age* 52 (1946): 11–42.

_____. "Le servage en France et en Allemagne au moyen âge." In *X. International Congress of Historical Sciences*, vol. III, pp. 213–46. Florence, 1955.

_____. *Recherches sur la seigneurie rurale en Lorraine d'après les plus anciens censiers (IXe–XIIe siècle)*. Paris, 1935.

Perroy, Edouard. "Social Mobility Among the French *Noblesse* in the Later Middle Ages." *Past and Present* 21 (1962): 25–38.

Petot, Pierre. "L'évolution numerique de la classe servile en France du IXe au XIVe siècle." In *Recueils de la Société Jean Bodin*, II. *Le Servage*. 2d ed. Pp. 159–68. Brussels, 1959.

Plesner, Johan. *L'émigration de la campagne à la ville libre de Florence au XIIIe siècle*. Copenhagen, 1934.

Poquet du Haut-Jussé, Barthélemy A. "De la vassalité à la noblesse dans le duché de Bretagne." *Bulletin philologique et historique du Comité des Travaux Historiques et Scientifiques,* 1963, pp. 785–800.

Powicke, Maurice. *The Loss of Normandy, 1189–1204.* 2d ed. Manchester, 1961.

Prou, Maurice. "Les coutumes de Lorris et leur propagation aux XIIe et XIIIe siècles." *Revue historique de droit français et étranger* 18 (1884): 139–209, 267–320, 441–57, 523–56.

Raftis, J. A. *Tenure and Mobility: Studies in the Social History of the Medieval English Village.* Toronto, 1964.

Ramière de Fortanier, Jean. *Chartes de franchises du Lauragais.* Toulouse, 1939.

Richard, Jean. "Châteaux, châtelains, et vassaux en Bourgogne aux XIe et XIIe siècles." *Cahiers de civilisation médiévale* 3 (1960): 433–47.

———. "Sur les alliances familiales des ducs de Bourgogne aux XIIe et XIIIe siècles." *Annales de Bourgogne* 30 (1958): 37–46.

Russell, J. C. *Medieval Regions and Their Cities.* Bloomington, Ind., 1972.

Sanfançon, Roland. *Défrichements, peuplement, et institutions seigneuriales en Haut-Poitou, du Xe au XIIIe siècle.* Quebec, 1967.

Sée, Henri. *Les classes rurales et le régime domanial en France au moyen âge.* Paris, 1901.

Strayer, Joseph R. "The Two Levels of Feudalism." In *Life and Thought in the Early Middle Ages,* edited by R. S. Hoyt. Minneapolis, 1967.

Tardif, E. J., ed. *Le très ancien Coutumier de Normandie* and *La summa de legibus Normannie.* 2 vols. Paris, 1881–1903.

Timbal, Pierre. *Un conflit d'annexion au moyen âge: l'application de la coutume de Paris au pays d'albigeois.* Toulouse-Paris, 1949.

Vaillant, Pierre. *Les libertés des communautés dauphinoises.* Grenoble, 1951.

———. "Les origines d'une libre confédération de vallées: les habitants des communautés Briançonnaises au XIIIe siècle." *Bibliothèque de l'Ecole des Chartes* 125 (1967): 301–48.

Verhulst, E. A. "A propos de 'la terre et les hommes en Picardie.'" *Cahiers de civilisation médiévale* 14 (1970): 257–64.

———. *De Sint-Baafsabdij te Gent en haar Grondbezit (VII–XIV eeuw).* Brussels, 1958.

———. "Une example de la politique économique de Philippe d'Alsace: la formation de Gravelines (1163)." *Cahiers de civilisation médiévale* 10 (1967): 15–28.

Verriest, Léo. *Institutions médiévales: introduction au Corpus des Records de Coutumes et des Lois de Chefs-Lieux de l'ancien comté de Hainault, I.* Mons-Frameries, 1946.

———. "Le servage en Flandre, particulièrement au pays d'Alost." *Revue historique de droit français et étranger* 28 (1950): 35–65.

———. *Noblesse, chevalerie, lignages.* Brussels, 1959.

Warlop, Ernest. *De Vlaamse adel voor 1300.* 3 vols. Handzame, 1968.

Winter, J. M. van. "The Ministerial and Knightly Classes in Guelders and Zutphen." *Acta Historiae Neelandica* 1 (1966): 171–86.

———. "Note à propos l'article de M. L. Genicot 'noblesse, ministerialité et chevalerie en Gueldre et Zutphen.'" *Le Moyen Age* 72 (1966): 279–89.

Wollasch, J. "Königtum, Adel und Kloster im Berry während des 10. Jahrhunderts." In *Neue Forschungen über Cluny und die Cluniacenser,* edited by G. Tellenbach. Freiburg, 1959.

INDEX

Main entries for persons are by Christian names; family and place names are cross-indexed. Names in parentheses are nicknames or names of originating families.

Fortified houses, 75, 82, 84–85, 90, 100, 115–19, 126–27, 131–33, 166, 171, 175, 181, 193, 195, 201, 205, 209
Fouchères, 220 n.64
France. *See* Philip (Augustus) II; Philip IV
Franchises: communal, 4, 9, 11, 22, 30, 47–55, 57–59, 129, 135, 138–39; community, 9, 11–13, 15, 24, 26–27, 41–47, 52, 57–59, 144; individual, 28–30, 38, 40, 58, 121, 125, 183, 228 n.149; in other regions, 137–39
Fravaux, 216 n.20, 217 n.33
Fresnay. *See* Thibaut of Fresnay
Fromond I of Minay, 188
Fromond II of Minay, 188
Fromond III of Minay, 121–22, 188, 236 n.27
Fuligny, 171

Garin I of Barbet, 126, 159
Garin II of Barbet, 159
Garnier of Faiel, 220 n.62
Garnier (Choars) of Laubressel, 244 n.55
Garnier II (of Traînel) of Marigny, seneschal of Nevers, 105, 186, 241 n.29
Garnier III of Marigny-le-Châtel, 163, 186, 193
Garnier IV of Marigny-le-Châtel, 186
Garnier V of Marigny-le-Châtel, 105, 206, 228 n.144
Garnier of Pont-sur-Seine (and Traînel), 193
Gastablé. *See* Henri Gastablé
Gautier of Bar-sur-Seine, 160
Gautier I, count of Brienne, 164, 169
Gautier II, count of Brienne-Ramerupt, 104, 164
Gautier III, count of Brienne, 164
Gautier IV, count of Brienne, 102, 164
Gautier V, count of Brienne, 164
Gautier of Brosse, 165
Gautier of Chappes, chancellor of Champagne, 168
Gautier I of Chappes, 169
Gautier II of Chappes, 168
Gautier IV of Châtillon-sur-Seine, 177
Gautier of Courcelles-sur-Voire, 159
Gautier (Melitarius) of Isle-Aumont, 126, 183
Gautier of Joigny, 35, 198
Gautier I of Moëlan, 177
Gautier of Pougy, bishop of Nevers, 194

Gautier II of Ramerupt, 196–98
Gautier II of Ruvigny, 124–25, 203
Gautier (of Foissy) of Traînel, 206
Geoffroy of Basson, 161
Geoffroy of Chapelle-Geoffroy, 167
Geoffroy of Cirey, 179
Geoffroy Furnerius (? of Méry-sur-Seine), 216 n.22
Geoffroy I of Macey, 185
Geoffroy II of Macey, 185
Geoffroy of Méry-sur-Seine, 187
Geoffroy of Montfey, 189
Geoffroy Regis, 235 n.8
Geoffroy of Survanne, 187
Geoffroy I of Vendeuvre-sur-Barse, 207
Geoffroy II of Vendeuvre-sur-Barse, 207
Geoffroy of Villehardouin, 10, 47, 242 n.32
Gérard of Clérey, 173–75
Gérard of Chervey, 173
Gérard (Jarron) of Clérey, 175
Gérard I of Durnay, 178
Gérard III of Durnay-Vendeuvre, 108, 178, 209
Gérard (Melitarius) of Isle-Aumont, 183
Gérard I of Isle-Aumont, 183
Gérard of Montfey, 189
Gérard of Nogent-sur-Seine, 189–90
Gérard III (of Saint-Benoît) of Isle-Aumont, 70, 185
Gérard of Savoy, 223 n.96
Gérard of les Varennes, *serviens*, 29, 120,
Gérault, 171–72
Giffaumont, 219 n.51, 227 n.141
Gila of Chappes, 169
Gila of Payns, 190
Gilo of Bouy-Luxembourg, 161–62
Gilo of Plancy, 191
Gilo of Sergines, 200
Godin I of Rigny-le-Ferron, 199
Godin II of Rigny-le-Ferron, 199
Goriard. *See* Ville-sur-Arce
Grandes-Chapelles (les), 217 n.33
Grandpré. *See* Henry VI, count of Grandpré
Granges, 119, 183, 196. *See also* Herbert; Raoul (both of Granges)
Gronay. *See* Durnay.
Guibert of Courbeton, 196
Guillaume of Arcis-sur-Aube, 159
Guillaume of Bar-sur-Seine, grand master of the Templars, 160
Guillaume of Basson, 161
Guillaume I of Bouy-sur-Orvin, 163
Guillaume II of Bouy-sur-Orvin, 163
Guillaume of Clefmont, 209

THE JOHNS HOPKINS UNIVERSITY PRESS
This book was composed in Baskerville text and Americana Bold display type by The Composing Room from a design by Susan Bishop. It was printed on 50-lb. Warren 1854 regular paper and bound in Columbia Bayside vellum cloth by Universal Lithographers, Inc.

Library of Congress Cataloging in Publication Data

Evergates, Theodore
    Feudal society in the bailliage of Troyes
under the counts of Champagne, 1152–1284.

    Bibliography: pp. 252–58
    Includes index.
    1. Feudalism—Champagne. I. Title.
HD649.C5E9   301.44'43'09443   75-11346

ISBN 0-8018-1663-7